U0121988

英语词汇速记大全
语境记忆法
4

⊙ 俞敏洪／编著

音频

世界图书出版公司
北京·广州·上海·西安

　　1991 年到 1999 年的八年，是我生活中最快乐的八年，因为我每天都和学生们在一起。不管创办新东方的过程中受过多少挫折，不管个人生活遇到多少痛苦和不幸，只要一走进课堂，我就能看到学生灿烂的笑容，感受到学生为了前途而日夜奋斗的精神。学生的笑容让我兴奋，学生的精神让我感动。这些笑容和精神支撑着我枯燥的日常生活，使我渡过了很多难关。我也不断地把学生们感人的故事和我自己奋斗的故事讲给大家听。我们一起分享着学习、工作、生活的痛苦和快乐。我和学生们融为一体，尽管我叫不出大多数学生的名字，但他们成了我生活中真正的朋友和精神支柱。

　　1999 年以后，新东方越来越大，如果我每天继续走进教室教书，新东方就会在缺乏管理和秩序的混乱中崩溃。为了让新东方有序地存在并发展，为了让新东方成为优秀人才的聚集地，我忍痛割爱地放弃了每天站在讲台上的痛快，进入了枯燥而琐碎的日常管理之中。转眼新东方已经走过了 20 个年头，在这 20 年中，新东方得到了长足的发展，新东方的优秀教师越来越多，有很多教师在英语教学尤其是英语词汇教学中已经远远超过了我的水平。我感到欣慰，因为我的放弃，新东方越来越强大；我也感到遗憾，因为这么多年没有走上讲台，我自己的教学水平和词汇水平越来越低。我最大的愿望是有一天，当新东方的日常管理不需要我再操心时，我能够重新踏踏实实地研究我所爱好的英语词汇词源学，踏踏实实地写出一些有关词汇记忆和英语学习的书籍，并且踏踏实实地走进课堂，面对一张张可爱的笑脸，向他们讲述词汇的故事、学习的故事、生活的故事。那时候，我也许已经白发苍苍，但面对无数向往未来的面孔，我一定会回忆起我自己的无数青春往事，并再次点燃我自己的青春激情和火焰。

　　《英语词汇速记大全 1——词根 + 词缀记忆法》是我 1999 年的一部作品。当时我想写三到四部有关英语词汇记忆的书籍，其中第二本书《从熟悉的单词记生词》在 2000 年时我已经在电脑中完成了，但不幸的是，有一次我的手提电脑掉到了地上，结果电脑和电脑中的文字全部被摧毁，同时被摧毁的还有我重新写书的勇气。后来我懂得了机器的不可靠，学会了随时把电脑中的文字拷贝到另一个硬盘上，但书还是没有写出来。我为自己的懒惰找了很多的理由，比如太忙啦，比如有更重要的事情啦，比如要陪很多人喝酒应酬啦，但最后发现永远丢失的不仅仅是作品，还有自己的成就感，最后把自己也给丢了，唯一留下的是反复出现在心头的遗憾。

也许这样的遗憾还要出现很多次，因为新东方还有很多事情没有做完，因为我个人生活中还有很多事情要用心去完善。但我知道时间不会等我，我也知道自己不能落在地球旋转速度的后面。因此，我会在未来的岁月里，挤出时间来继续我的研究工作。书籍是唯一能够表明我曾经努力的物证，书籍也是唯一能够化解我对自己期待的良药。一切都需要重新开始，我唯一需要的就是重新开始的勇气。

《英语词汇速记大全1——词根＋词缀记忆法》是一个很好的开始。单词记忆是英语学习者的必经之路，为了帮助大家把背单词这条路铺得更加平坦和科学一点，我开始了补路和修路的工作。很多同学针对前一版提出了很多宝贵的意见，有了这些意见，我们就能更好地去修订，而这套书也能更好地服务大家。这本《语境记忆法》是我们在原有基础上新增的一本。在当今这个社会，获取信息变得十分便利，我们每天的阅读量也在逐渐加大，而通过阅读各种有趣的英文文章来学习单词，也不失为一种好方法。归根结底，我希望这本书能真正帮到大家，这样这本书也就真正实现它的意义了。

在这里，感谢新东方大愚文化传播有限公司的全体人员，正是他们的努力，使新东方一本本优秀书籍的出版成为可能。一个人的力量成不了大事，只有有着共同的志向和目标的一群人在一起努力，才能取得成功。新东方的今天就是证明。

俞敏洪

新东方教育科技集团董事长

序

众所周知，单词是学习英语的基础。俞敏洪老师曾经说过："单词记忆是英语学习者的必经之路。"单词量的大小以及对单词掌握的熟练程度在一定程度上决定了一个人能否学好英语，也是顺利通过各种考试的基本要求。可对很多人来说，记忆单词是十分枯燥乏味的学习过程，容易陷入背过就忘的记忆怪圈。如何才能高效地记忆单词，成为了很多英语学习者的难题。

记忆单词有方法！

我们的任务就是把这条记忆单词之路为广大英语学习者铺得更加平坦和科学一些。现在，大家手里拿的这本就是"英语词汇速记大全系列"的第四本——《语境记忆法》，也是一本全新的词汇书。

语境记忆，顾名思义就是通过语境学习法记忆单词。著名语言学家库克（Cook）曾经指出："人们对事物记忆的好坏主要取决于大脑对信息处理的深度。对孤立的词的重复是一种低层处理，记忆效果差；将词与所处的语法结构结合起来，则是一种较深层的处理，记忆效果最好。"所以，语境记忆是记忆单词最有效的方法之一。

我们精选了64篇内容丰富有趣的文章，旨在使读者在文章中学习单词，摆脱枯燥记忆的困境，让记忆单词变得更加有趣、高效。相信本书一定可以为苦于背单词的读者带来学习的动力。

本书特色：

一、五大篇章，64篇精彩好文，通过文章学单词。

本书共分为"美好生活""社会热点""新奇事物""温馨情感"以及"励志人生"五大篇章，精心挑选了64篇精彩文章，帮助读者通过阅读新鲜有趣的文章来学习常用单词。

二、64个主题拓展词汇，通过词族记单词。

在每篇文章后，除了对文章中出现的单词进行解释说明外，还结合文章的内容，给出相关的主题词汇，"语境＋同类"记忆，双管齐下，使单词记忆更加高效。

三、单词释义精准，用法、例句全面丰富。

针对文章中出现的单词释义，我们给出具体标注，有助于读者更加明晰单词的用法；同时也给出了单词的其他常用释义。此外，针对部分单词，我们提供其常用搭配和例句，便于加深理解，增强记忆。

编 者

Contents
目录

Chapter ①

美好生活

Passage 1

音频

Make Time Management a Lifestyle

Most of us would like to accomplish more than what we are able to in a day. How many times have you felt that it would be so much easier if you only had a few more extra hours in a day to complete the various tasks that you have on your plate? And how many times have you wished that you could do with a lesser amount of stress and strain that your workload is causing you?

The thing you need to know to overcome this feeling of being overladen with work all the time is to be able to manage your time better. And the most important thing to understand is that time management is not something that you can do as and when you feel that work is getting difficult to handle. It is a lifestyle that you need to adopt and practice each and every day of your life! It is a habit that will lead you to a life where you have peace of mind, better and more efficient work churn out and more time on your hands to do the things you enjoy.

The other thing to appreciate when you start off on your journey to be able to manage your time better is to be prepared that this change that you are going to adopt in your lifestyle will take some time to internalize. It is not something that you can switch on at will. But also be aware of the fact that once this change has been made, life will be much smoother.

There are many techniques that you can adopt to help you in managing your time better and get a kick-start in this process. And the best technique to start with is to learn how to focus on the job at hand. This can be done once you have prepared a list and prioritized the tasks that you have on hand. But once you have decided to take up a particular job, don't let yourself get distracted on the way. Don't allow thoughts on other projects to mingle and disturb your thought process. Ensure that you are determined to complete the job at hand before you allow your mind to take detours into other arenas awaiting attention. Avoid taking any kind of breaks while you are at that task and ensure that you complete it before you consider a cup of coffee or a call that you need to make.

Learning the **tricks** of **determination**, **concentration** and **discipline** shall ensure that after a while you will get so used to focusing on the task that you are doing that you will not need to **consciously** drive out **errant** thoughts from entering. At this level, you can safely assume that you have learnt one of the tricks of time management that will ensure that your work gets finished on time and is far better in quality than it used to be earlier.

让时间管理成为一种生活方式

大多数人都想要在一天之内完成超出自己所能的事情。有多少次你会觉得，如果一天再多出几个小时，你就能更轻松地完成案头的各种工作任务？有多少次你希望工作量带来的压力和负担能够少一些，自己能够更加轻松地工作？

为了克服这种总是被工作压得喘不过气的感觉，你需要知道的就是如何更好地管理自己的时间。而最重要的是，你要知道时间管理不是当你感到工作很难处理时才要做的。它是一种生活方式；你要接受这种方式，并且在生活中的每一天践行它！它是一种习惯，将会使你拥有平静的心态和更好、更高效的工作产出，并且能够有更多的时间来做自己喜欢的事情。

当你开始踏上能够更好地管理时间的旅程时，你需要知道的另外一点是这种生活方式的转变需要一段时间才能完成，你要作好心理准备。这不是你想转变就能转变的。但同时你也要意识到，一旦作出了改变，生活会比以前顺畅很多。

你可以采用很多技巧来帮助自己更好地管理时间，并敦促自己立即行动。最好的技巧是学习如何专注于手头的工作。当你列好了要做的工作清单，并按照轻重缓急排序之后，就可以采用这个技巧了。而一旦你决定开始某项特定的工作，就不要让自己中途分神。不要让关于其他项目的想法扰乱你的思路。确保自己先下定决心完成手头的工作，然后再将思路转到其他需要关注的活动上。工作时，要避免任何形式的中断，确保在你想喝杯咖啡或者需要打个电话之前先完成工作。

学习坚定、专注和自制的诀窍，这样能确保在一段时间之后你将习惯于关注正在做的工作，而不必有意识地驱除那些飘忽不定的思绪。到了这一阶段，你就可以很确定地认为自己已经学会了一种时间管理的诀窍。它将使你的工作不仅能够按时完成，而且质量也会比之前有很大提升。

accomplish [əˈkʌmplɪʃ]
释 v. 完成(任务)；达到(目的)；实现(诺言等)
例 It'll require indomitable will to *accomplish* the task. 完成这项工作需要百折不挠的毅力。

task [tɑːsk]
释 n. 任务；作业

amount [əˈmaʊnt]
释 n. 数量；总额 v. 合计
用 amount to 总计

strain [streɪn]
释 n. 拉紧，拉力；压力，负担 v. 扭伤；拉紧；尽力

workload [ˈwɜːkləʊd]
释 n. 工作量

overladen [ˌəʊvəˈleɪdn]
释 a. 超载的；负担过重的

manage [ˈmænɪdʒ]
释 v. 管理，控制；应付

lifestyle [ˈlaɪfstaɪl]
释 n. 生活方式

adopt [əˈdɒpt]
释 v. 采取；收养；正式通过
例 The courts were asked to *adopt* a more flexible approach to young offenders. 法院被要求采取更为灵活的手段来对待少年犯。

habit [ˈhæbɪt]
释 n. 习惯

lead [liːd]
释 v. 引导；领导；过(某种生活)

efficient [ɪˈfɪʃnt]
释 a. 有效率的；有能力的

internalize [ɪnˈtɜːnəlaɪz]
释 v. 使内在化

switch [swɪtʃ]
释 n. 开关；转变；鞭子 v. 转换，改变
用 switch off 关(灯、收音机等)；switch on 开(灯、收音机等)
例 Susan worked as a librarian before *switching* to journalism. 苏珊在转行从事新闻业前是一名图书管理员。

smooth [smuːð]
释 a. 顺利的；光滑的 v. 使光滑

kick-start [ˈkɪkˌstɑːt]
释 v. 脚踏启动；重振 n. 迅速开始(采取行动)

prioritize [praɪˈɒrətaɪz]
释 v. 使优先化

particular [pəˈtɪkjələ(r)]
释 a. 特定的；特别的；挑剔的 n. 详情，细节
用 in particular 特别，尤其

distracted [dɪˈstræktɪd]
释 a. 心烦意乱的；精神不集中的

mingle [ˈmɪŋgl]
释 v. (使)混合；相交往

disturb [dɪˈstɜːb]
释 v. 弄乱；打扰

ensure [ɪnˈʃʊə(r); ɪnˈʃɔː(r)]
释 v. 保证，确保

detour [ˈdiːtʊə(r)]
释 n. 绕行 v. 使…绕道而行

arena [əˈriːnə]
释 n. 圆形剧场；活动场所

consider [kənˈsɪdə(r)]
释 v. 考虑；认为；体谅

trick [trɪk]

释 n. 诡计；窍门；诀窍；把戏 v. 欺骗，哄骗

determination [dɪˌtɜːmɪ'neɪʃn]

释 n. 决心；坚定；测定

concentration [ˌkɒnsn'treɪʃn]

释 n. 专注；集中；浓度

discipline ['dɪsəplɪn]

释 v. 训练；管教 n. 纪律；学科；自制力

例 Different cultures have different ways of *disciplining* their children. 在不同国家的文化中，管教孩子有着不同的方式。

consciously ['kɒnʃəsli]

释 ad. 感觉到地，有意识地；自觉地；蓄意地

errant ['erənt]

释 a. 犯错误的；行为不当的；不定的

🔆 单词家族

工作表现

accurate ['ækjərət] a. 正确无误的；精确的

annex [ə'neks] v. 强占

assume [ə'sjuːm] v. 假定；假设；承担

conventionally [kən'venʃənəli] ad. 照惯例，照常套

dispense [dɪ'spens] v. 分配；分发

empirical [ɪm'pɪrɪkl] a. 以经验(或观察)为依据的；经验主义的

entitled [ɪn'taɪtld] a. 有资格的

exert [ɪg'zɜːt] v. 努力，尽力；运用；施加

expertise [ˌeksp3ː'tiːz] n. 专门知识(或技能等)；专长

facilitate [fə'sɪlɪteɪt] v. 促进；使便利

feat [fiːt] n. 功绩；技艺

gimmick ['gɪmɪk] n. 花招，噱头

impediment [ɪm'pedɪmənt] n. 妨碍；阻碍

impractical [ɪm'præktɪkl] a. 不切实际的

improve [ɪm'pruːv] v. 改善，改进

jargon ['dʒɑːgən] n. 行话

jobbing ['dʒɒbɪŋ] a. 打零工的；做散工的

postdate [ˌpəʊst'deɪt] v. 写上未来日期

proficient [prə'fɪʃnt] a. 熟练的；精通的

qualified ['kwɒlɪfaɪd] a. 有资格的

reliant [rɪ'laɪənt] a. 依赖性的；依靠的

schedule ['ʃedjuːl] n. 时刻表，日程安排表；课程表 v. 安排；计划

semi-skilled [ˌsemi'skɪld] a. 半熟练的

typify ['tɪpɪfaɪ] v. 代表；是…的典型

Passage 2

Recycled Sneakers Fit for Sharing

Greg Woodburn, a sophomore at the University of Southern California, spends a lot of time cleaning sneakers. Some of them once belonged to him; some belonged to his friends. But soon the shoes will have new owners: underprivileged children in the United States and 20 other countries, thanks to Woodburn's Share Our Soles (S.O.S.) charity.

A high school track star in the beach town of Ventura, California, frustrated Woodburn was sidelined for months with knee and hip injuries.

"I started thinking about all the things I got from running—the health benefits, the friendships, the confidence," he says. "And I realized there are children who don't even have shoes."

Greg Woodburn's sneakers are fit for sharing.

Woodburn gathered up his own stash of slightly worn sneakers, and then put out a call to teammates and the town. His goal was to have 100 pairs. When the count climbed to more than 500 pairs, he decided to turn the shoe drive into a year-round endeavor.

Back then, the sneakers came from donation boxes at the YMCA and the local sporting goods store and from door-to-door pickups. Woodburn has now set up collection boxes at two high schools, USC's gym and recreation center, and area races, and he has started accepting adult sizes and sandals. To date, S.O.S. has collected and donated more than 3,000 pairs.

And Woodburn has cleaned almost all of them (his parents and teammates help at exam time). "People think of it as dirty work," he says. "But I like doing it. It's inspiring. It's not work I want to pass off to somebody else." After sorting the shoes by size, Woodburn selects the sturdiest pairs for the washing machine and the threadbare ones for recycling. The rest he piles up by the kitchen sink at his family home in Ventura, and using a scrub brush and dishwashing liquid, he "gets in the zone," he says. "As I work, I imagine who will get each pair." It takes three to five minutes to clean one pair, he estimates, and he'll do up to 100 pairs at a time. "I try to set aside a good amount of time."

To ship the footwear, Woodburn teamed with Sports Gift, a nonprofit organization that provides soccer and baseball equipment to children around the world. Keven Baxter, founder and president, says, "We'd send kids shin guards, balls, and shoes, and I'd hear that for many of these kids, the **cleats** were the only pair of shoes they had. They'd wear them to school and to do their **chores**. So Greg's running shoes were a nice addition for us."

In just under three years, Woodburn has started three chapters of Share Our Soles: the original in Ventura, another at USC, and one at the College of the Holy Cross in Massachusetts last January, when a student there wrote asking to get involved. The organization's website, shareoursoles.org, keeps a tally of sneakers that have been cleaned and **distributed** and sells **wristbands** and socks (the **proceeds** go toward new shoes and socks for children).

For many **recipients**, the shoes represent opportunity. Two young boys in Southern California attended school on **alternate** days because they shared a pair of shoes, held together with duct tape. They were too big for one boy and too small for the other. Thanks to S.O.S., each brother received his own pair of shoes. The boys now attend school daily and look forward to **recess** with their friends. When they graduate, they say, they will help strangers, just as Woodburn helped them.

译文

捐出你的旧运动鞋

格雷格·伍德伯恩是南加利福尼亚大学的一名大二学生,他花费大量的时间清洗运动鞋。这些鞋有些是他自己穿过的,有些是他朋友的。但是,这些运动鞋很快就会有新主人了:他们是来自美国和其他20个国家的贫困孩子们。这要归功于伍德伯恩创办的"分享爱心鞋"(S.O.S.)慈善团体。

伍德伯恩是加州海滨城市文图拉市一所中学的田径明星,因膝盖和臀部受伤而缺席比赛几个月,为此他曾非常沮丧。

"那时我开始思考跑步带给我的所有东西——健康、友谊以及自信,"他说道,"我意识到,有些孩子甚至连鞋都没有。"

伍德伯恩的那些鞋子是用来分享的。

伍德伯恩把自己穿过的那些稍旧的运动鞋收集起来,然后号召队友和当地居民一起行动起来。他当时的目标是收集到100双运动鞋,但是当鞋子的数量达到500多双时,他决定将募集运动鞋作为常年的计划。

回顾起来,这些运动鞋主要捐自基督教青年会和当地的体育用品商店,还有一些是挨家挨户募集来的。现在,伍德伯恩已在两所中学、南加州大学的体育馆和娱乐中心,以及比赛场地设立了鞋子募捐箱。他也开始收集成人鞋码的运动鞋和拖鞋。到目前为止,他的慈善团体已经收集并捐赠了3000多双鞋。

其中绝大部分的鞋子都是伍德伯恩自己清洗的（考试期间，他的父母和队友也会帮忙）。"人们觉得这个活很脏，"他说，"但是我喜欢做。这件事让我受到鼓舞。我不想把这个工作推给别人去做。"伍德伯恩按照鞋码将鞋子分类，然后挑出最结实的鞋子放进洗衣机里清洗，再把那些非常破旧的鞋子送去回收。剩下的鞋子他会堆放在文图拉市家中的厨房水池旁，然后用硬毛刷和洗涤剂刷洗，这样他就"进入状态了"，他这样说。"清洗的时候，我会想象每双鞋子会被送到谁的手中。"他估计清洗一双鞋子大概需要3到5分钟，他每次要清理100双。"我试着腾出一整块的时间来做这个工作。"

伍德伯恩与"体育礼品"组织合作来邮寄这些运动鞋。"体育礼品"是一个非营利性组织，它为世界各地的儿童提供足球和棒球运动设备。凯文·巴克斯特是该组织的创始人兼负责人，他说："我们为孩子们提供护胫、球类和鞋子。我听说在这些孩子当中，有不少孩子仅有的鞋子就是两块'防滑板'。他们穿着这样的鞋子上学、做家务。因此格雷格的跑鞋对我们的义捐来说，是一个很好的补充。"

在仅仅不到三年的时间里，伍德伯恩建立了三处S.O.S.：总部在文图拉市，一处在南加州大学，另一处在马萨诸塞州的圣十字学院——它是因为该校的一名学生写信要求加入而于去年1月份成立的。S.O.S.的网站shareoursoles.org对被清洗干净并寄出的运动鞋做了记录，同时网站也出售腕带和袜子（这些收入将用于给孩子们购买新的鞋袜）。

对于许多受助者来说，鞋子就意味着机会。南加州的两名小男孩只有一双共用的用胶带黏合的鞋，因此只能轮流去上学。而这双鞋对其中一个男孩来说太大，对另一个男孩来说又太小了。在S.O.S.的帮助下，他们俩每人都得到了一双鞋子。两个孩子现在每天都可以去上学，并期待课后和朋友们一起玩耍。他们说，等他们毕业之后也会像伍德伯恩那样，去帮助那些素不相识的人。

💡 单词记事本

sophomore ['sɒfəmɔ:(r)]
释 *n.* 大学二年级学生

sneaker ['sni:kə(r)]
释 *n.* 运动鞋；鬼鬼祟祟的人；卑鄙者

belong [bɪ'lɒŋ]
释 *v.* 属于；适用

搭 belong with 应该在某处，通常在某处；适应某种环境

underprivileged [ˌʌndə'prɪvəlɪdʒd]
释 *a.* 贫困的

charity ['tʃærəti]
释 *n.* 慈善；施舍；慈善团体

track [træk]
释 *n.* 轨道；足迹；径赛

sideline ['saɪdlaɪn]
释 *n.* 副业，兼职 *v.* 使退出

gather ['gæðə(r)]

释 *v.* 收集；聚集；采集

用 gather up 收集，收拢；gather around 聚集，召集

stash [stæʃ]

释 *v.* 藏匿，隐藏；贮藏 *n.* 隐(贮)藏物；隐(贮)藏处

例 *Stash* your cash safely. 请安全存放您的现金。

teammate ['tiːmmeɪt]

释 *n.* 队友

endeavor [ɪn'devə(r)]

释 *v./n.* 努力，尽力

例 They *endeavored* to make the old man happy but in vain. 他们尽力使这位老人快乐，却徒劳无功。

donation [dəʊ'neɪʃn]

释 *n.* 捐赠；捐赠物，捐款

pickup ['pɪkʌp]

释 *n.* 收集；整理

collection [kə'lekʃn]

释 *n.* 收藏品；收集；征收；募捐

recreation [ˌrekri'eɪʃn]

释 *n.* 娱乐活动；消遣

例 My father's *recreations* are drinking beer and watching football. 我爸爸平时的消遣就是喝啤酒、看足球。

sandal ['sændl]

释 *n.* 凉鞋

inspiring [ɪn'spaɪərɪŋ]

释 *a.* 使人振奋的；鼓舞人心的

sort [sɔːt]

释 *n.* 种类；方式 *v.* 分类，整理

用 sort out 挑出；整理；sort through 查看并加以分类整理

sturdy ['stɜːdi]

释 *a.* 坚定的；强健的；坚固的，结实的

threadbare ['θredbeə(r)]

释 *a.* 磨破的；陈腐的

recycling [ˌriː'saɪklɪŋ]

释 *n.* 回收利用

pile [paɪl]

释 *n.* 一堆，一叠 *v.* 堆积

例 There's a mounting *pile* of studies associating increased intake of vitamin D with a lower risk of cancer. 堆积如山的研究表明，更多地摄取维生素D能减少患癌风险。

scrub [skrʌb]

释 *v.* 用力擦洗 *a.* 矮小的；卑劣的；硬毛的

footwear ['fʊtweə(r)]

释 *n.* 鞋类

nonprofit [nɒn'prɒfɪt]

释 *a.* 非营利的

shin [ʃɪn]

释 *n.* 胫；胫部 *v.* (手脚并用沿某物)向上(下)爬

cleat [kliːt]

释 *n.* 防滑鞋

chore [tʃɔː(r)]

释 *n.* 琐事；[*pl.*] 家庭杂务

distribute [dɪ'strɪbjuːt; 'dɪstrɪbjuːt]

释 *v.* 分发，分配；散布

例 The main policy difference between the two is how to *distribute* the rewards of growth. 二者之间主要的政策区别就在于如何分配经济增长的成果。

wristband ['rɪstbænd]

释 *n.* (衬衫等的)袖口；腕套

proceeds ['prəʊsiːdz]

释 *n.* 收入，收益

例 They gave a concert and donated the *proceeds* to the charity. 他们举办了一场音乐会，并将收入捐给了慈善组织。

recipient [rɪ'sɪpiənt]

圀 *n.* 接受者，收受者

alternate

圀 [ɔːl'tɜːnət] *a.* 交替的，轮流的；间隔的
['ɔːltəneɪt] *v.* (使)轮流，(使)交替

recess

圀 [rɪ'ses; 'riːses] *n.* (工作等)暂停，休息；
课间休息
[rɪ'ses] *v.* 把(某物)放在墙壁的凹处；
暂停；休息
圀 in recess 休息

💡 单词家族

体育运动

aerobics [eə'rəʊbɪks] *n.* 有氧运动
法；健美操

ascent [ə'sent] *n.* 上升；攀登

athlete ['æθliːt] *n.* 运动员；体育家

athletics [æθ'letɪks] *n.* 运动；体育

backhanded [ˌbæk'hændɪd] *a.* 间接
的；反手击球的

baseball ['beɪsbɔːl] *n.* 棒球

batter ['bætə(r)] *n.* 击球手

championship ['tʃæmpiənʃɪp] *n.* 冠军
地位；[常*pl.*] 锦标赛

coach [kəʊtʃ] *n.* 教练

competition [ˌkɒmpə'tɪʃn] *n.* 竞争；
比赛

court [kɔːt] *n.* 法院；球场

default [dɪ'fɔːlt; 'diːfɔːlt] *n.* 缺席；弃权

elongate ['iːlɒŋgeɪt] *v.* 延长；伸长

event [ɪ'vent] *n.* 事件；比赛项目

fighter ['faɪtə(r)] *n.* (职业)拳击手；斗
争者；战斗机

gallop ['gæləp] *v.* 奔驰，飞跑

golf [gɒlf] *n.* 高尔夫球

gym [dʒɪm] *n.* 体育馆，健身房

gymnasium [dʒɪm'neɪziəm] *n.* 健身
房；体育馆

handicap ['hændikæp] *n.* 障碍；障碍赛

hike [haɪk] *n.* 徒步旅行；(数量、价格
等的)增加或上升

hockey ['hɒki] *n.* 曲棍球；冰球

jogging ['dʒɒgɪŋ] *n.* 慢跑

limber ['lɪmbə(r)] *a.* 易弯曲的，敏捷的

marathon ['mærəθən] *n.* 马拉松赛跑

matador ['mætədɔː(r)] *n.* 斗牛士

match [mætʃ] *n.* 比赛；对手

membership ['membəʃɪp] *n.* 会员身
份；全体会员

muscle ['mʌsl] *n.* 肌肉；体力

promptness ['prɒmptnəs] *n.* 敏捷，迅速

pulsation [pʌl'seɪʃn] *n.* 脉动；跳动

racket ['rækɪt] *n.* (网球等的)球拍

raft [rɑːft] *n.* 救生艇

referee [ˌrefə'riː] *n.* 仲裁人；裁判员

relay ['riːleɪ] *n.* 接力赛；中继设备

rival ['raɪvl] *n.* 竞争对手；可与匹敌的
人(或物)

rivalry ['raɪvlri] *n.* 竞争；对抗

sportsman ['spɔːtsmən] *n.* 运动员

squash [skwɒʃ] *n.* 软式墙网球；壁球

stadium ['steɪdiəm] *n.* 露天大型运动场

sweater ['swetə(r)] *n.* 厚运动衫；毛线衫

swiftness ['swɪftnəs] *n.* 迅速

timeout ['taɪmaʊt] *n.* (球类比赛进行
中的)暂停；(工作等活动中的)暂停
时间

tournament ['tʊənəmənt; 'tɜːnəmənt;
'tɔːnəmənt] *n.* 锦标赛，比赛

trainer ['treɪnə(r)] *n.* 训练者；驯服者

tramp [træmp] *n.* 徒步旅行

trot [trɒt] *v.* 快步走；小步跑

wheeze [wiːz] *v.* 喘息，发出呼哧呼哧
的声音

wrestle ['resl] *n.* 摔跤，扭斗

Passage 3

Live Your Life without an Eraser

I think my business colleague was a bit nervous when he first got into my Eagle Talon sports car. I was driving us to a few appointments that day. About halfway into our day on the road together, he said that he was pleasantly surprised about my driving. For some reason, he thought that since I drove a black sports car, I would be driving like a wild man. But much to his surprise, he noticed that I never sped or drove very aggressively. This is when I told him about my story about an accident many years ago that changed my driving habits forever.

Negative Experiences That Change You for the Better

I was a young man in my mid twenties just starting my career. I decided to reward myself with a new car. It was a black Toyota Supra, the first car I ever bought on my own. After seeing the black Ferrari on *Miami Vice*, I wanted a black sports car as well. I seem to have a thing for black sports cars as I'm currently on my fourth one now and the next one will likely be a black Mustang.

I was driving in the fast lane westbound on the QEW (Queen Elizabeth Way), which is the highway that runs around Lake Ontario from Toronto to Niagara Falls. It was a Canadian winter day but the weather was clear and so were the roads, or so I thought.

Like many other vehicles on the highway, I was doing about 120 kilometers per hour in a 100 kilometers speed limit. Everything was smooth sailing on the highway until my car started to somehow lose grip on the road. I spun around 180 degrees and actually saw the other cars coming toward me as I went across all three lanes. Fortunately, my Supra ended up off the highway on the far side shoulder.

It was a miracle that I didn't get hit by any of the other vehicles as I went across the lanes but the side of my car did hit a post which resulted in my side window smashing apart. I was not hurt though so I came out extremely lucky.

What must have happened was that I hit some "black ice" on the highway. This is a term we use here in Canada that describes ice on the roads that drivers can't see. In my case, I was driving too fast in black ice conditions I was not aware of.

This single negative experience on the road changed my driving habits forever. Although it didn't change my personal taste for black sports cars, I no longer speed especially on the highways during winter months. Quite often in **questionable** winter days, I'm actually well under the speed limit and don't mind almost every other vehicle on the road passing me, even if they are driven by little old ladies. I would rather make it to my **destinations** in one piece.

Life Without an Eraser

My real **estate agent** sends me regular **newsletters** and in one issue, I saw the following **quote** by John Gardner.

"Life is the art of drawing without an eraser."

This quote pretty well sums up how to **realistically** live our lives. We all make mistakes and have some negative experiences in life. We don't have giant erasers to erase the bad **circumstances** we all go through. However, if we learn from these negative experiences, we can live our lives better in the future much like how the developing artist learns to draw better each day.

In my Toyota Supra black ice accident, which I can't erase, I quickly learned to change my driving habits. As a result, I have been accident free for the last twenty five years as a driver ever since (except for one small **incident** when another driver hit my car in a shopping mall parking lot).

Each day is a learning opportunity for us and having some bad experiences from time to time is just reality. We can't erase these bad experiences whether they are accidents, failures or mistakes, but we can certainly learn from them.

译文

生命中没有橡皮擦

我想我的同事初次坐上我的Eagle Talon跑车时一定有些紧张。那天我开车载着他一起去参加了几个预约好的会面。大概过了当天一半的路程后,他说我的驾驶技术让他有些意外。可能因为我开的是黑色的跑车,他就想当然地以为我是飙车族,结果令他大为吃惊的是,他发现我从来没有超速行驶或者横冲直撞。就在那时,我跟他说起了多年前我亲身经历的一场车祸,正是它彻底改变了我的驾驶习惯。

吃一堑,长一智

那时我才25岁左右,事业刚刚起步。我决定奖励自己一辆新车。那是一辆黑色的丰田Supra跑车,也是我自己买的第一辆车。看过电影《迈阿密风云》中那辆黑色的法拉利后,我就也想要一辆黑色跑车。我似乎很青睐黑色的跑车，现在这辆已经是我拥有的第四辆了，接下来我还可能买一辆黑色的Mustang跑车。

当时我正开车在伊丽莎白女王大道的快车道上向西行驶。这是一条从多伦多到尼亚加拉瀑布、绕安大略湖而行的公路。那时正是加拿大的冬天，但是天气晴朗，路面也毫无障碍，至少我当时是这么认为的。

像公路上行驶的许多其他车辆一样，我以每小时约120公里的速度在限速100公里的公路上疾驰。一切都很顺利，直到我的车开始失去控制。在180度的急转弯后，我看到其他车辆向我迎面开来，这时候我已经横着穿过了三条车道。幸运的是，我的车最后冲出了公路，停在了最外侧的路肩上。

横穿过几条车道却没有被任何车辆撞上，这真是个奇迹。车的一侧撞到了柱子上，侧窗被撞碎，而我却安然无恙，可见我是多么幸运。

这起事故的起因肯定是我遇到了公路上的所谓"黑冰"。这是加拿大的常用术语，用来形容司机无法看到的路面上所结的冰。对于我而言，这起车祸则是因为我在容易形成黑冰的天气条件下开得太快，而我没有意识到这一点。

这仅有的一次负面的驾驶经历让我彻底改变了驾驶习惯。尽管这没有改变我对黑色跑车的钟爱，但我再也不敢超速驾驶了，尤其是在冬天的公路上。在事故频发的冬天，我常常以远远低于限速的速度行驶，完全不介意几乎所有的车都超我而去，即使开车的是个子小的老太太。我只愿自己可以安然无恙地到达目的地。

生命没有橡皮擦

我的房地产经纪人定期给我发送新闻简报，有一期引用了约翰·加德纳的这样一句话：

"生命是一门无法擦拭的绘画艺术。"

这句话很到位地概括了我们应该如何现实地经营生活。在生活中，我们都会犯错，也会有一些不好的经历。我们没有巨大的橡皮擦，去擦除经历过的所有不好的境遇。然而，如果我们能从这些不好的经历中学习，就可以让将来的生活变得更好，就像画家从不满意的作品中吸取教训，使绘画水平每天都得到提高一样。

正是无法擦除的"丰田Supra跑车黑冰事故"，让我得以很快地学着改变驾驶习惯。结果是，在之后的25年里，我一直保持着零事故驾驶（只有一次小的事故，那是在一个商场的停车场里，我的车被其他司机撞了一下）。

对于我们来说，每天都是一次学习的机会，时不时地经历一些挫折也正是现实所在。我们不能擦除这些糟糕的经历，不管是事故、失败还是错误，但我们一定可以从中受益。

nervous ['nɜːvəs]
释 *a.* 神经紧张的；神经系统的；神经性的

appointment [ə'pɔɪntmənt]
释 *n.* 约会，预约；任命，委派；委任的职位

aggressively [ə'ɡresɪvli]
释 *ad.* 侵略地；攻击性地；强劲地；迅速地

currently ['kʌrəntli]
释 *ad.* 现在，当前；普遍地；通常地

grip [ɡrɪp]
释 *n.* 紧握；掌握 *v.* 握紧；吸引住…的注意力(或想象力等)
用 come/get to grips (认真)对付(或处理)
例 There's nothing here to show that the economy and the market are pulling out of the *grip* of recession. 目前并没有迹象表明我们的经济和市场会走出困境。

spin [spɪn]
释 *v.* (使)旋转；纺(纱)；甩干 *n.* 旋转；自转

miracle ['mɪrəkl]
释 *n.* 令人惊奇的人(或事)；奇迹

smash [smæʃ]
释 *v.* 粉碎；崩溃 *n.* 破碎

extremely [ɪk'striːmli]
释 *ad.* 极端地；非常地

term [tɜːm]
释 *n.* 术语；学期；条款

aware [ə'weə(r)]
释 *a.* 知道的，意识到的

negative ['neɡətɪv]
释 *a.* 否定的；消极的；负面的 *n.* 底片；负数
例 Pollution has a *negative* effect on the health of everyone, not to mention the damage to the environment. 污染对每个人的健康都有不好的影响，更不用说对环境的破坏了。

questionable ['kwestʃənəbl]
释 *a.* 有问题的；可疑的；不可靠的

destination [ˌdestɪ'neɪʃn]
释 *n.* 目的地

estate [ɪ'steɪt]
释 *n.* 地产；个人财产
用 real estate 房地产

agent ['eɪdʒənt]
释 *n.* 代理人，经纪人；施动者，动因

newsletter ['njuːzletə(r)]
释 *n.* 时事通讯；简讯

quote [kwəʊt]
释 *n.* 引文，引语；估价，报价 *v.* 引用，引述
例 There may be a variation of plus or minus 5% in the prices that are *quoted*. 报价可能有上下5%的浮动。

realistically [ˌriːə'lɪstɪkli, ˌrɪə'lɪstɪkli]
释 *ad.* 现实主义地；实事求是地

circumstance ['sɜːkəmstəns; 'sɜːkəmstɑːns]
释 *n.* 环境；情况；[*pl.*] 经济情况
用 under no circumstances 无论如何都不，决不；in/under the circumstances 在这种情况下，(情况)既然如此

例 No matter what the *circumstances* are, street violence should never be justified. 不论在什么情况下，街头暴力事件都是不正当的。

incident ['ɪnsɪdənt]

释 n. 发生的事；事件，事变

例 The FBI has launched its own investigation of the *incident*. 美国联邦调查局针对此事展开了独立调查。

单词家族

地面交通

aberration [ˌæbəˈreɪʃn] n. 脱离常轨；失常

access [ˈækses] n. 接近，进入；接近(或进入)的方法；入口，通道

airsick [ˈeəsɪk] a. 晕机的

apace [əˈpeɪs] ad. 快速地，急速地

avenue [ˈævənjuː] n. 林荫道，大街；途径，手段

balky [ˈbɔːlki; ˈbɔːki] a. 停止不前的；倔强的

barge [bɑːdʒ] n. 驳船；游艇 v. 用船运输

barricade [ˌbærɪˈkeɪd] v. 设路障 n. 路障

belated [bɪˈleɪtɪd] a. 迟来的

berth [bɜːθ] n. 停泊处；卧铺 v. 使停泊

buggy [ˈbʌgi] n. 童车

bunk [bʌŋk] n. (轮船、火车等的)铺位

bypass [ˈbaɪpɑːs] n. (绕过市镇的)旁道，迂回道；分流术，旁通管 v. 在(市镇等)外围辟一条旁道；走旁道以绕过或避开(某物)

cab [kæb] n. 出租车；轻便马车；司机室，驾驶室

canoe [kəˈnuː] n. 独木舟

carriage [ˈkærɪdʒ] n. (四轮)马车；(火车)客车厢

collide [kəˈlaɪd] v. 碰撞，互撞；冲突，抵触

commute [kəˈmjuːt] v. 通勤

compartment [kəmˈpɑːtmənt] n. 卧车包房，隔间

congested [kənˈdʒestɪd] a. 拥挤的；堵塞的

cycle [ˈsaɪkl] n. 自行车；摩托车；循环 v. 骑自行车；骑摩托车；循环

depot [ˈdepəʊ] n. 仓库；栈房；火车站；公共汽车站

diversion [daɪˈvɜːʃn] n. 转移，转向(道路禁止通行时的)临时绕行路；消遣，娱乐

divert [daɪˈvɜːt] v. 使转向；使改道(或绕道)；转移；使娱乐，使消遣

embark [ɪmˈbɑːk] v. (使)上船或飞机；(使)从事

engine [ˈendʒɪn] n. 发动机，引擎；机车；火车头

excursion [ɪkˈskɜːʃn] n. 远足；短途旅行

flyover [ˈflaɪəʊvə(r)] n. 天桥；立交桥

gearshift [ˈgɪə(r)ˌʃɪft] n. 变速杆；换挡杆

glide [glaɪd] n./v. 滑行，滑翔

hangar [ˈhæŋə(r); ˈhæŋgə(r)] n. 飞机库

hatchback [ˈhætʃbæk] n. 舱盖式汽车

haven [ˈheɪvn] n. 港口；避难所

hovercraft [ˈhɒvəkrɑːft] n. 气垫船

itinerary [aɪˈtɪnərəri] n. 旅程；路线

jam [dʒæm] *n.* 果酱；阻塞；轧住 *v.* (使)阻塞；(使)轧住不动

landmark ['lændmɑːk] *n.* 路标，地标

lane [leɪn] *n.* 小巷；车道

locomotive [ˌləʊkə'məʊtɪv] *a.* 火车头的；运动的，移动的

lorry ['lɒri] *n.* 卡车；运货汽车

metro ['metrəʊ] *n.* 地铁

minibus ['mɪnibʌs] *n.* 小型公共汽车

obstruct [əb'strʌkt] *v.* 阻塞；阻碍

odometer [əʊ'dɒmɪtə(r)] *n.* 里程表

overpass ['əʊvəpɑːs] *n.* 天桥；立交桥

passport ['pɑːspɔːt] *n.* 护照；通行证

patrol [pə'trəʊl] *v./n.* 巡逻，巡查

pavement ['peɪvmənt] *n.* 人行道

pedestrian [pə'destriən] *a.* 徒步的 *n.* 行人

queue [kjuː] *n.* 行列；长队 *v.* 排队，排队等待

rein [reɪn] *n.* 缰绳 *v.* 勒缰使(马)停步

roundabout ['raʊndəbaʊt] *a.* 迂回的，拐弯抹角的 *n.* 环状交叉路

route [ruːt] *n.* 路线，路程

rumble ['rʌmbl] *v.* 发出低沉的隆隆声

shipwreck ['ʃɪprek] *n.* 船只失事；海难

stagecoach ['steɪdʒkəʊtʃ] *n.* 公共马车

steer [stɪə(r)] *v.* 控制；引导；驾驶

steward ['stjuːəd] *n.* 乘务员

subway ['sʌbweɪ] *n.* 地下通道；地铁

swerve [swɜːv] *v.* 突然转向 *n.* 突然的转向

taxicab ['tæksikæb] *n.* 出租车

terminal ['tɜːmɪnl] *n.* 终点站；终端，接线端；终端机

terminus ['tɜːmɪnəs] *n.* (火车、汽车的)终点站；界标

terrestrial [tə'restriəl] *a.* 陆地的；陆生的；陆栖的

tractor ['træktə(r)] *n.* 拖拉机；牵引车

tram [træm] *n.* 有轨电车

transport [træn'spɔːt] *v.* 运输，运送 ['trænspɔːt] *n.* 运输；运输系统；运输工具

turnpike ['tɜːnpaɪk] *n.* 收费高速公路

twist [twɪst] *v.* 使缠绕；曲折前进 *n.* 弯曲；旋转

van [væn] *n.* 大篷车，货车；有篷货运车厢

vehicle ['viːəkl] *n.* 交通工具，车辆；传播媒介；工具，手段

waggon ['wægən] *n.* 货车；四轮马车

Self-exploring is great, as during this process you can foster your confidence.
——Bill Gates

自我的探索是非常伟大的，因为在这个过程中你可以培养起自信。

——比尔·盖茨

音频

Passage 4

When Marriage Gets Tough

Have you ever been at a place in your marriage where you wondered if you would make it? Or where you felt **trapped** because **divorce** was simply not an option but it seemed so hard to consider the future in relation to your present?

I have.

I should say we have, because I know Sean has felt these same things.

Marriage is hard work, and "they" tell you that all the time before you get married—your **pastor** and **mentors** and friends and books…they all tell you. But when you're in love and have a dreamy-eyed view of marriage, it just doesn't sink in what "hard" means. Sure, he'll leave his socks on the floor, and I'll just pick them up and put them in the basket. Sure, we fight sometimes, but it'll be easier when we're married. Sure, we both have **baggage** from our past, but we love each other, and that's all that matters.

If you're married, I know you're shaking your head right along with me. It doesn't take very long for the truth to become **apparent**.

Our Story

I still remember our first fight after we were married. I don't remember what it was about, just that it was on the second day of our **honeymoon**. Two days as a married couple, we already didn't want to be in the same room.

Things were good for a while. We took a cross-country **adventure**, moving to Utah for two years, and we started a family. But we also had a **miscarriage**, dealt with **layoffs** and some really tough financial times and faced the inevitable loneliness that happens when you move to a state where you **literally** know no one.

We added a second baby, built a house and moved when I was eight months **pregnant** with our third daughter.

And that's when things started to go downhill.

I was **incredibly** hormonal. The littlest thing set me off, and the angrier I got, the more Sean pulled away. But who could blame him, really?

Divorce was not an option for us, but I think we both wished it was at one time or another.

Hanging on

Somehow, though, while raising three little ones under three years old, we hung on. Barely, by the skin of our teeth, but the important part of the story is we hung on.

The turning point for us, looking back, was our decision to attend a marriage conference at church. If you know my husband, conferences are not his thing. At all. But he went, and for that I am incredibly thankful.

I don't remember most of what was said at that conference, but as we stood in the doorway to the sanctuary with our six-month-old, the female speaker told the story of her hormonal outbursts following the birth of their second child. She was weepy, angry, short-tempered and more (sound familiar?). She said that her doctor told her that following the birth of each child, it takes your hormones an additional year to get back into balance. So your first child, one year. Second child, two years. Third child, three years. And so on.

I don't know if that's really true or not, but it resonated with me.

She was put on a low dose of antidepressants and slowly things improved and they were able to work on the issues in their marriage without her hormones interfering.

After the session, we were sent out to walk around outside and just talk and reflect as a couple on the things we had heard throughout the day.

We made the decision then and there to call the doctor and schedule an appointment. Antidepressants weren't something I really wanted to consider while still nursing, but something had to change.

Healing

As it turns out, I never made the appointment. For me, acknowledging the cause of our issues—and having my husband understand that it was really, truly a biological, hormonal issue—was enough for us to start the healing process.

But if it hadn't changed? I would have gone, and I would have accepted the prescription slip. This may not be a popular thing to say, but I would have even weaned the baby in order to save my marriage, if that's what it had taken.

Thankfully, it didn't take that, and slowly we started to heal.

And Now

Today, three and a half years later, I am incredibly, head-over-heels in love with my husband. He is an amazingly supportive guy, a wonderful dad and my best friend. He walks into a room and my heart skips a beat. And my girls roll their eyes several times a week when I tell them how much I love their daddy.

It didn't happen overnight, but I am so thankful that we not only "stuck it out" but actually made a decision to seek help.

I say this, not to gloat, but to encourage you. If things are tough in your marriage right now, there is hope.

There's hope.

当婚姻陷入困境

在婚姻中，你是否曾怀疑过自己能否坚持下去？或者，你是否曾经感到陷入困境，看不到将来，但又不能简单地用离婚来收场？

我有过这样的经历。

我应该说我们有过，因为我知道肖恩和我有相同的感受。

婚姻是不容易的，结婚前总是会听"他们"——你的牧师、师长、朋友以及书上这样说。但当你坠入爱河、渴望婚姻时，是无法理解"不容易"的含义的。当然，丈夫会把袜子乱扔在地板上，但我会捡起来放在篮子里。当然，我们有时也会争吵，但结婚后就会好多了。当然，我们都有着自己的过去，但我们彼此相爱，这是最重要的。

如果你是已婚人士，我知道此刻的你正和我一样，对以上那些想法摇头否定。因为用不了多久，婚姻的真相就会渐渐浮现。

我们的故事

我仍然记得婚后的第一次争吵。内容已经记不得了，只记得那是我们蜜月的第二天。才做了短短两天的夫妻，我们就已经不想再处于同一屋檐下了。

之后我们的关系又好了一段时间。我们尝试了一次越野冒险，搬到犹他州住了两年，开始了家庭生活。但同时我们也遭遇了孩子流产、几次被解雇以及经济非常拮据的时期，也感受了在陌生的城市中孤立无援的寂寞。

然后我们有了第二个孩子，盖了座房子，并在我怀第三个女儿八个月时又搬了一次家。

此后，我们的婚姻状况开始急转直下。

当时我深受荷尔蒙的影响，一点小事都能让我恼火。而我的火气越大，肖恩就躲得越远。其实这又怎能怪他？

对我们来说，离婚不是解决问题的办法，但我知道我们有时都想干脆离婚算了。

坚持

然而，不知为何，虽然抚养着三个不到三岁的孩子，我们的婚姻却维持了下来。尽管十分侥幸，但重要的是，我们都坚持了下来。

回头想想，我们的婚姻之所以出现转机是因为我们两人决定去参加一场在教堂举办的婚姻研讨会。了解我丈夫的人都知道，他是一点儿都不喜欢参加这种活动的。但那天他去了，为此我非常感激。

我已经不记得那天研讨会上所讲的大部分内容，只记得当我们带着六个月大的孩子站在通往圣堂的门口时，一位妇女正在讲述自己生育第二个孩子后荷尔蒙失调的经历。她变得爱哭、易怒、脾气暴躁等等（听起来很熟悉吧？）。她说医生告诉她，每多生一个孩子，荷尔蒙就需要多一年的时间恢复平衡。也就是说生完第一个孩子，需要一年来恢复；第二个孩子，需要两年；第三个孩子，需要三年。以此类推。

我不知道这个说法是否正确，但我对此产生了共鸣。

她服用了小剂量的抗抑郁药剂，情况开始慢慢好转。没有了荷尔蒙的干扰，她可以和丈夫共同解决婚姻中的问题了。

研讨会之后，主办方让我们去外面散步，并以夫妻的姿态谈论、反思在会上听到的内容。

正是在那时，我和我丈夫决定联系医生并预约诊治。我当时正处于哺乳期，不太愿意服用抗抑郁药物，但我们的确需要一些改变。

治疗

最终我没有预约诊治。对我来说，知道我们之间问题的原因——并让丈夫理解这真的是一种生理上的、与荷尔蒙有关的问题——已足以让我们开始治疗了。

但如果情况仍没有改变呢？那我就会去预约诊治，接受吃药。我的这种想法可能不太常见，但如果真的需要这样去做，我会为了挽救自己的婚姻而给孩子断奶。

谢天谢地，这种情况并没有发生，我们慢慢地开始自行治疗。

现在

三年半后的今天，我完全深爱着我的丈夫。他是一个支持我的好男人、一个好爸爸，也是我最亲密的朋友。看到他走进房间我就会心跳加速。每周我都会对女儿们说好几次自己有多爱她们的父亲，每次她们都会睁大眼睛，惊讶不已。

这样的改变不是一夜之间就完成的，但是我非常感恩，因为我们不仅仅"坚持了下来"，而且作出了寻求帮助的决定。

我说这些不是为了炫耀自己，而是为了鼓励你。如果你的婚姻现在已陷入危机，要相信还有希望。

凡事都有希望。

trapped [træpt]

释 a. 陷入困境的

divorce [dɪ'vɔːs]

释 n. 离婚；分离 v. 与…离婚；分离

pastor ['pɑːstə(r)]

释 n. 牧师；牧人

mentor ['mentɔː(r)]

释 n. 顾问；导师

baggage ['bægɪdʒ]

释 n. 行李；(感情或思想上的)包袱

apparent [ə'pærənt]

释 a. 明显的；表面上的；貌似(真实)的

例 Have you ever had the experience that your credit card interest rate rose out of the blue for no *apparent* reason? 你有过信用卡的利率突然被莫名其妙地提高的经历吗？

honeymoon ['hʌnimuːn]

释 n. 蜜月；初期和谐的新关系

adventure [əd'ventʃə(r)]

释 n. 冒险；奇遇

miscarriage ['mɪskærɪdʒ; ˌmɪs'kærɪdʒ]

释 n. 流产；(货物的)误送，误投；失败

layoff ['leɪɒf]

释 n. (临时)解雇；失业期

literally ['lɪtərəli]

释 ad. 照原文地，照字面地；真正地，确实地；简直

例 We've got to get the economy under control or it will *literally* eat us up. 我们必须控制住经济，否则它真的会把我们击垮。

pregnant ['pregnənt]

释 a. 怀孕的；充满的

incredibly [ɪn'kredəbli]

释 ad. 非常地，极端地；难以置信地

barely ['beəli]

释 ad. 仅仅，只不过；几乎没有

例 The professor's speech seemed endless and many students were *barely* able to stay awake. 教授的演讲似乎没完没了，很多学生已克制不住开始昏昏欲睡了。

sanctuary ['sæŋktʃuəri]

释 n. 圣堂；避难所；动物保护区

outburst ['aʊtbɜːst]

释 n. 爆发；爆炸

用 an outburst of anger 突然大怒

weepy ['wiːpi]

释 a. 催人泪下的；爱哭的

hormone ['hɔːməʊn]

释 n. 激素；荷尔蒙

resonate ['rezəneɪt]

释 v. 共鸣；共振

dose [dəʊs]

释 n. 一剂，一服；剂量

antidepressant [ˌæntidɪ'presnt]

释 a. 抗抑郁的 n. 抗抑郁剂

interfere [ˌɪntə'fɪə(r)]

释 v. 干扰；干涉

session ['seʃn]

释 n. 会议，讲习会；学年，学期

例 After two late night *sessions*, the Security Council still failed to reach agreement. 开过两次深夜会议之后，安理会仍未能达成协议。

biological [ˌbaɪə'lɒdʒɪkl]

释 a. 生物的；生理的；生物学的

prescription [prɪˈskrɪpʃn]
释 n. 处方，药方

wean [wiːn]
释 v. 使(孩子)断奶；戒掉

gloat [gləʊt]
释 v. 沾沾自喜，得意洋洋

💡 单词家族

婚姻生活

affinity [əˈfɪnəti] n. 吸引力；姻亲关系

avuncular [əˈvʌŋkjələ(r)] a. 叔伯的

bastard [ˈbɑːstəd; ˈbæstəd] n. 私生子

beatific [ˌbiːəˈtɪfɪk] a. 快乐而安详的；幸福的

behoove [bɪˈhuːv] v. 理应；有义务

bicker [ˈbɪkə(r)] n. 争吵，口角

brat [bræt] n. 孩子；顽童

brattish [ˈbrætɪʃ] a. (指小孩)被惯坏的，不礼貌的

brawl [brɔːl] n. 争吵；打架

confide [kənˈfaɪd] v. 倾诉；信赖

conjugal [ˈkɒndʒəgl] a. 婚姻的；夫妻之间的

connubial [kəˈnjuːbiəl] a. 婚姻的；夫妻的

discrepancy [dɪsˈkrepənsi] n. 不同；矛盾

divergence [daɪˈvɜːdʒəns] n. 分歧

doting [ˈdəʊtɪŋ] a. 溺爱的

ejaculate [iˈdʒækjuleɪt] v. (从体内)射出或迅速排出液体；(尤指)射精；突然而简短地说

elysian [ɪˈlɪziən] a. 幸福的

eugenic [juːˈdʒenɪk] a. 优生(学)的

filial [ˈfɪliəl] a. 子女的

fondle [ˈfɒndl] v. 抚弄，抚摸

hassle [ˈhæsl] n. 激烈的辩论；困难，麻烦

homely [ˈhəʊmli] a. 家庭的；平凡的

household [ˈhaʊshəʊld] n. 一家人；家庭

illegitimate [ˌɪləˈdʒɪtəmət] a. 私生的；不合法的

lamentable [ˈlæməntəbl; ləˈmentəbl] a. 令人惋惜的；悔恨的

launder [ˈlɔːndə(r)] v. 洗涤；清洗

lineal [ˈlɪniəl] a. 直系的；嫡系的

matrimony [ˈmætrɪməni] n. 婚姻生活；婚姻

mollycoddle [ˈmɒlikɒdl] v. 娇宠；溺爱；纵容

monogamy [məˈnɒgəmi] n. 一夫一妻(制)

nestle [ˈnesl] v. 舒适地安顿；依偎

nubile [ˈnjuːbaɪl] a. 迷人的

paunchy [ˈpɔːntʃi] a. 大腹便便的

procreate [ˈprəʊkrieɪt] v. 生育；生殖

prolixity [prəʊˈlɪksəti] n. 啰唆

puny [ˈpjuːni] a. 弱小的；发育不良的

querulous [ˈkwerələs; ˈkwerjələs] a. 暴躁的；爱发牢骚的

scion [ˈsaɪən] n. 子孙；后裔

tenement [ˈtenəmənt] n. 房屋；住户

tiff [tɪf] n. 吵嘴；怄气

trifling [ˈtraɪflɪŋ] a. 琐碎的，微不足道的

unrequited [ˌʌnrɪˈkwaɪtɪd] a. (尤指爱情)无回应的

woo [wuː] v. 向(女子)求婚；求爱；争取…的支持

wrangle [ˈræŋgl] v. 争吵；吵架

Passage 5

音频

Seven Steps to a More Fulfilling Job

Many people today find themselves in unfulfilling work situations. Their career path may be **financially rewarding**, but it doesn't meet their emotional, social or **creative** needs. They're **stuck**, unhappy, and have no idea what to do about it, except move to another job.

Mary Lyn Miller, **veteran** career consultant and founder of the Life and Career Clinic, says that when most people are unhappy about their work, their first thought is to get a different job. Instead, Miller suggests looking at the possibility of a different life. Through her book, *8 Myths of Making a Living*, as well as workshops, seminars and **personal** coaching and consulting, she has helped thousands of dissatisfied workers **reassess** life and work.

Miller developed a 7-step process to help **potential** job seekers assess their current situation and beliefs, identify their real passion, and start on a journey that allows them to **pursue** their passion through work.

Step 1: **Willingness** to do something different.

Breaking the cycle of doing what you have always done is one of the most difficult tasks for job seekers. Many find it difficult to steer away from a career path or make a change, even if it doesn't feel right.

Step 2: **Commitment** to being who you are, not who or what someone wants you to be.

Look at the gifts and **talents** you have and make a commitment to pursue those things that you love most. If you love the social aspects of your job, but are stuck inside an office or "chained to your desk" most of the time, **vow** to follow your **instinct** and **investigate** alternative careers and work that allow you more time to interact with others.

Step 3: Self-definition.

Miller suggests that once job seekers know who they are, they need to know how to sell themselves. "In the job market, you are a product. And just like a product, you must know the features and **benefits** that you have to offer a potential **client**, or employer." Examine the skills and knowledge that you have and **identify** how they can apply to your desired occupation. Your qualities will exhibit to employers why they should hire you over other **candidates**.

Step 4: Attain a level of self-honoring.

Self-honoring or self-love may seem like an odd step for job hunters, but being to accept yourself, without judgment, helps eliminate insecurities and will make you more self-assured. By accepting who you are—all your emotions, hopes and dreams, your personality, and your unique way of being—you'll project more confidence when networking and talking with potential employers. The power of self-honoring can help to break all the falsehoods you were programmed to believe—those that made you feel that you were not good enough, or strong enough, or intelligent enough to do what you truly desire.

Step 5: Vision.

Miller suggests that job seekers develop a vision that embraces the answer to "What do I really want to do?" One should create a solid statement in a dozen or so sentences that describe in detail how they see their life related to work.

Step 6: Appropriate risk.

Some philosophers believe that the way to enlightenment comes through facing obstacles and difficulties. Once people discover their passion, many are too scared to do anything about it. Instead, they do nothing. With this step, job seekers should assess what they are willing to give up, or risk, in pursuit of their dream. You'll move one step closer to your ideal work life if you identify how much risk you are willing to take and the sacrifices you are willing to make.

Step 7: Action.

Some teachers of philosophy describe it in this way: "If one wants to get to the top of a mountain, just sitting at the foot thinking about it will not bring one there. It is by making the effort of climbing up the mountain, step by step, that eventually the summit is reached." All too often, it is the lack of action that ultimately holds people back from attaining their ideals. Creating a plan and taking it one step at a time can lead to new and different job opportunities. Job-hunting tasks gain added meaning as you sense their importance in your quest for a more meaningful work life. The plan can include researching industries and occupations, talking to people who are in your desired area of work, taking classes, or accepting volunteer work in your targeted field.

Each of these steps will lead you on a journey to a happier and more rewarding work life. After all, it is the journey, not the destination, that is most important.

七步找到更加满意的工作

如今，许多人发现自己对工作不满意。他们的工作也许报酬不错，却不能满足他们的情感需求、社会需求或创新需求。他们被禁锢在那里，不开心，也不知道该怎么做，只能换一份工作。

玛丽·琳恩·米勒是生活与职业诊所的资深职业顾问，也是该诊所的创办者。她说，大多数人在对工作感到不满的时候，首先想到的就是换份工作。但是，米勒建议先看看有没有选择不同生活的可能性。通过她的书《八个谋生神话》和她的讲习班、研讨会以及个人辅导与咨询，她已经帮了数千名对工作不满的人重新衡量生活和工作。

米勒制定了一个七步方案来帮助潜在的求职者评估他们目前的处境和信念，找到他们真正喜欢的事物，然后开始一段能够让他们在工作中追求自己爱好的旅程。

步骤一：愿意尝试不同的事物。

对求职者来说，最困难的事情之一便是打破原来做事所固有的套路。许多人发现转换职业或者作出改变很难，即使自己所做的工作并不合适。

步骤二：坚定地做自己，而不是别人期望你成为的样子。

看看你所拥有的天赋和特长，坚定地追寻那些你最喜欢的事情。如果你喜欢工作中与人打交道的方面，但是大多数时间都被困在办公室里或者被束缚在办公桌前，那么你一定要顺从自己的本性，去发现其他能够给你更多时间来与人接触的工作和职业。

步骤三：自我定义。

米勒建议，求职者在了解了自己后，就需要知道如何推销自己。"在就业市场中，你就是一件商品。所以就像商品一样，你必须知道你能向潜在的客户或雇主提供哪些卖点和利益。"审视你所拥有的技术和知识，然后确定如何将它们应用到你渴望从事的工作中去。你的素质将向雇主证明为什么他们应该雇用你而非其他求职者。

步骤四：获得一定程度的自尊。

对求职者来说，自尊或者自爱可能像是一个很奇怪的步骤，但是不加评判地接受自我能帮助你消除不安全感，并让你更加自信。一旦接受了自己，包括自己的全部情绪、希望、梦想、个性及独特的存在方式，你在与潜在的雇主沟通、谈话时就会表现出更多的自信。自尊的力量能帮助你消除你被灌输的所有错误的信念——那些让你觉得自己不够好、不够强大、不够智慧，以至于不能去做你真正想做之事的错觉。

步骤五：视野。

米勒建议求职者开阔视野，去发现自己真正想做的事情。求职者应该用十几句话充分而详尽地描述他们是如何看待自己的生活与工作的关系的。

步骤六：适当的冒险。

一些哲学家认为人能通过面对障碍和困难受到启发。在发现了他们所热爱的事物之后，很多人会因过于害怕而什么事都不敢去做。结果什么也没做。在这一步骤中，求职者应判断出为了追逐梦想，自己愿意放弃什么或冒什么风险。如果你认清了自己愿意承受多大的风险、作出多大的牺牲，你就离你理想的职业人生更近了一步。

步骤七：行动。

有些哲学老师这样描述行动："如果一个人想爬上山顶，只是坐在山脚空想是不可能到达的。只有一步一步努力地向上攀登，他才能最终抵达。"缺少行动往往就是阻碍人们实现理想的根本原因。制订一个计划，一次一步地实施它，这样才会使你拥有新的、不同的工作机会。当你在追求一种更有意义的职业生涯时能够认识到这些实际行动的重要性，那为找工作所作的准备工作也就有了更多的含义。你所制订的计划可能包括研究行业和职业，与在你期望的工作领域工作的人交流，参加与你的目标领域相关的课程或志愿者活动。

每一个步骤都将把你带到一个更满意、更有意义的职业道路上。毕竟，最重要的是过程，而不是终点。

💡 单词记事本

financially [faɪ'nænʃəli; fə'nænʃəli]
释 *ad.* 财政上；金融上；经济上

rewarding [rɪ'wɔːdɪŋ]
释 *a.* 有报酬的，报答的；有益的；值得的

creative [kri'eɪtɪv]
释 *a.* 创造性的；创作的；有创造力的
例 *Creative* thinking is the key to winning the competition. 创造性思维是赢得比赛的关键。

stuck [stʌk]
释 *a.* 不能动的；遇到困难(干不下去)的

veteran ['vetərən]
释 *n.* 经验丰富的人；老兵；老手

personal ['pɜːsənl]
释 *a.* 个人的；亲自的；针对个人的

reassess [,riːə'ses]
释 *v.* 重新评价，再评价；重新估价

potential [pə'tenʃl]
释 *a.* 潜在的；可能的 *n.* 潜能；可能性；电势；电压
例 Don't let your *potential* customer wander off. 别让你的潜在客户离你而去。

pursue [pə'sjuː]
释 *v.* 追求；追赶；继续进行；从事

willingness ['wɪlɪŋnəs]
释 *n.* 乐意；自动自发

26

commitment [kə'mɪtmənt]

释 n. 承诺；承担；致力，献身

talent ['tælənt]

释 n. 天资，才能；人才

vow [vaʊ]

释 n. 誓约，誓言 v. 发誓；郑重宣告

instinct ['ɪnstɪŋkt]

释 n. 本能，直觉；生性，天性

investigate [ɪn'vestɪɡeɪt]

释 v. 调查；审查；详细研究

benefit ['benɪfɪt]

释 n. 利益，益处；恩惠；救济金 v. 有益于；得益

用 benefit from 得益于；mutual benefit 互惠互利

例 The manager did his best for the company's benefit, but failed. 经理为了公司的利益竭尽全力，但最终失败了。

client ['klaɪənt]

释 n. 委托人，当事人；顾客，主顾

identify [aɪ'dentɪfaɪ]

释 v. 确定；认出，识别；把…等同于

candidate ['kændɪdət; 'kændɪdeɪt]

释 n. 申请人，候选人；投考者

attain [ə'teɪn]

释 v. 获得；达到，实现

例 If you have an aim, just work hard and attain it. 如果你有一个目标，那就努力奋斗去实现它。

hunter ['hʌntə(r)]

释 n. 猎人；猎狗；搜寻者

judgment ['dʒʌdʒmənt]

释 n. 看法，判断；审判

emotion [ɪ'məʊʃn]

释 n. 感情；情绪

personality [ˌpɜːsə'næləti]

释 n. 个性；名人

project

释 ['prɒdʒekt] n. 计划；项目；课题 [prə'dʒekt] v. 拟定(计划等)；投射；发射；向他人表现出

用 advanced project 尖端的研究计划，已提出的计划；project oneself 突出自己，表现自己

confidence ['kɒnfɪdəns]

释 n. 信任；信心

例 With confidence, Lily promises to make it on time. 莉莉满怀信心，承诺准时完成。

intelligent [ɪn'telɪdʒənt]

释 a. 聪明的，有才智的；理解力强的

solid ['sɒlɪd]

释 n. 固体 a. 固体的；结实的；可靠的，理由充分的

statement ['steɪtmənt]

释 n. 陈述，声明；结算单，报表

detail ['diːteɪl]

释 n. 细节，详情；枝节，琐事 v. 详述
用 in detail 详细地

enlightenment [ɪn'laɪtnmənt]

释 n. 启迪，启发

obstacle ['ɒbstəkl]

释 n. 障碍；干扰

assess [ə'ses]

释 v. 评定；估价

用 How to assess the workers' performance is a tough question. 如何评估工人的工作表现是个棘手的问题。

pursuit [pə'sjuːt]

释 n. 追求，寻求；[常pl.]花时间、精力等做的事；职业

用 in pursuit of 追求

sacrifice ['sækrɪfaɪs]

释 *n.* 牺牲；献祭；祭品 *v.* 牺牲；献出；献祭

用 at the sacrifice of 以牺牲⋯为代价

summit ['sʌmɪt]

释 *n.* 最高点，顶峰；最高级会议

ultimately ['ʌltɪmətli]

释 *ad.* 最终；终于；根本

quest [kwest]

释 *n.* 寻找，追求；审问，调查 *v.* 寻找，追求

用 in quest of 试图找到，寻求

volunteer [ˌvɒlən'tɪə(r)]

释 *n.* 志愿者；志愿兵 *v.* 自愿(做)

用 volunteer services 义工服务

例 He *volunteered* for military service. 他志愿去服兵役。

💡 单词家族

工作求职

accelerate [ək'seləreɪt] *v.* 加速；促进

accomplish [ə'kʌmplɪʃ] *v.* 完成(任务)；实现

achievement [ə'tʃiːvmənt] *n.* 工作业绩；成就

administer [əd'mɪnɪstə(r)] *v.* 管理；执行

dismissal [dɪs'mɪsl] *n.* 解雇；免职

foreman ['fɔːmən] *n.* 领班；陪审团主席

function ['fʌŋkʃn] *n.* 功能；作用；职责

image ['ɪmɪdʒ] *n.* 形象；印象；图像

internship ['ɪntɜːnʃɪp] *n.* 实习

payroll ['peɪrəʊl] *n.* 工资单

premium ['priːmiəm] *n.* 奖金；保险费

probation [prə'beɪʃn] *n.* 试用；缓刑

promote [prə'məʊt] *v.* 提升；促进

shift [ʃɪft] *n.* 轮班

update [ˌʌp'deɪt] *v.* 使现代化；修正；更新

upgrade [ˌʌp'greɪd] *v.* 提高级别或等级

vacancy ['veɪkənsi] *n.* 空缺；空位；空白

workshop ['wɜːkʃɒp] *n.* 车间；研讨会

Passage 6

音频

Seven Ways to Save the World

Forget the old idea that conserving energy is a form of self-denial—riding bicycles, dimming the lights, and taking fewer showers. These days conservation is all about efficiency: getting the same—or better—results from just a fraction of the energy. When a slump in business travel forced Ulrich Rõmer to cut costs at his family-owned hotel in Germany, he replaced hundreds of the hotel's wasteful light bulbs, getting the same light for 80 percent less power. He bought a new water boiler with a digitally controlled pump, and wrapped insulation around the pipes. Spending about €100,000 on these and other improvements, he slashed his €90,000 fuel and power bill by €60,000. As a bonus, the hotel's lower energy needs have reduced its annual carbon emissions by more than 200 metric tons. "For us, saving energy has been very, very profitable," he says. "And most importantly, we're not giving up a single comfort for our guests."

Efficiency is also a great way to lower carbon emissions and help slow global warming. But the best argument for efficiency is its cost—or, more precisely, its profitability. That's because quickly growing energy demand requires immense investment in new supply, not to mention the drain of rising energy prices.

No wonder efficiency has moved to the top of the political agenda. On Jan. 10, the European Union unveiled a plan to cut energy use across the continent by 20 percent by 2020. Last March, China imposed a 20 percent increase in energy efficiency by 2020.

The good news is that the world is full of proven, cheap ways to save energy. Here are the seven that could have the biggest impact:

Insulate

Space heating and cooling eats up 36 percent of all the world's energy. There's virtually no limit to how much of that can be saved, as prototype "zero-energy homes" in Switzerland and Germany have shown. There's been a surge in new ways of keeping heat in and cold out (or vice versa). The most advanced insulation follows the law of increasing returns: if you add enough, you can scale down or even eliminate heating and air-conditioning equipment, lowering costs even before you start saving on utility bills. Studies have shown that green workplaces (ones that don't constantly need to have the heat or air-conditioner running) have higher worker productivity and lower sick rates.

29

Change Bulbs

Lighting eats up 20 percent of the world's electricity, or the equivalent of roughly 600,000 tons of coal a day. Forty percent of that powers old-fashioned incandescent light bulbs—a 19th-century technology that wastes most of the power it consumes on unwanted heat.

Comfort Zone

Water boilers, space heaters and air conditioners have been notoriously inefficient. The heat pump has altered that equation. It removes heat from the air outside or the ground below and uses it to supply heat to a building or its water supply. In summer, the system can be reversed to cool buildings as well.

Remake Factories

From steel mills to paper factories, industry eats up about a third of the world's energy. The opportunities to save are vast. In Ludwigshafen, German chemicals giant BASF runs an interconnected complex of more than 200 chemical factories, where heat produced by one chemical process is used to power the next.

Green Driving

A quarter of the world's energy—including two thirds of the annual production of oil—is used for transportation. Some savings come free of charge: you can boost fuel efficiency by 6 percent simply by keeping your car's tires properly inflated.

A Better Fridge

More than half of all residential power goes into running household appliances, producing a fifth of the world's carbon emissions. And that's true even though manufacturers have already hiked the efficiency of refrigerators and other white goods by as much as 70 percent since the 1980s. According to an International Energy Agency study, if consumers chose those models that would save them the most money over the life of the appliance, they'd cut global residential power consumption (and their utility bills) by 43 percent.

Flexible Payment

Who says you have to pay for all your conservation investments? "Energy service contractors" will pay for retrofitting in return for a share of the client's annual utility-bill savings. If saving energy is so easy and profitable, why isn't everyone doing it? It has to do with psychology and a lack of information. Most of us tend to look at today's price tag more than tomorrow's potential savings. That holds double for the landlord or developer, who won't actually see a penny of the savings his investment in better insulation or a better heating system might generate. In many people's minds, conservation is still associated with self-denial. Many environmentalists still push that view.

The most powerful **incentives**, of course, will come from the market itself. Over the past year, sky-high fuel prices have focused minds on efficiency like never before. Ever-increasing pressure to cut costs has finally forced more companies to do some math on their energy use.

拯救世界的七种办法

骑自行车、调暗灯光和少洗澡以节约水资源的节能方式在老观念中被看作是一种克己行为，现在应该摒弃这种旧思想。如今提倡的节能都与提高能源效率有关：从一小部分能源里得到相同的或者更好的产出。商务旅游的衰退迫使乌尔里希·勒默尔削减他在德国的家族酒店的开支。他更换了酒店里几百个费电的灯泡，少用了80%的电，同时得到了同样的照明效果。他买了一个带有数控水泵的新锅炉，并在水管周围裹了一层绝缘材料。在这些设备及其他改进措施上花了大约10万欧元后，他将公司原来高达9万欧元的燃料费和电费削减了6万欧元。另一个意外的收获是，较低的能源需求将该酒店的二氧化碳年排放量降低了200多吨。"对于我们来说，节能可以产生非常大的利润。"他说，"最重要的是，我们丝毫没有降低为每位客人服务的质量。"

提高能源效率也是降低二氧化碳排放量和缓解全球变暖的好办法。而提高能源效率的最佳理由就是其成本——或者，更确切地说，是它的营利能力。这是因为快速增长的能源需求需要投入大量的资金开发新能源，更不用说因能源价格上涨所消耗的资金。

难怪提高能源效率成为了政治议程的重中之重。1月10日，欧盟公布了一项降低能源消耗的计划，计划表示到2020年整个欧洲大陆将降低20%的能源消耗。上一年3月，中国提出到2020年将能源利用率提高20%。

可喜的是世界各地到处是行之有效且成本低廉的节能方法。以下是七种最有效的方法：

绝缘

采暖和降温消耗着全世界36%的能源。像瑞士和德国提出的"零能源住宅"模型显示的那样，可节省的能源量几乎是无限的。现在涌现出很多保持热进冷出（或冷进热出）的新方法。最先进的绝缘材料遵循收益递增的规律：如果你添加的绝缘材料足够多，你就可以减少使用或者甚至不使用取暖和空调设备，甚至在你准备节省物业费之前就已经降低了成本。研究表明，在绿色工作场所，即那些不需要经常使用供暖或空调设备的地方，工人的生产效率较高，且患病率较低。

换灯泡

照明消耗着全世界20%的电能，或者相当于每天消耗约60万吨煤。其中的40%都被老式白炽灯泡所消耗，而这种白炽灯使用的19世纪的技术使其消耗的电能中的大部分都被发热浪费掉了。

舒适区

热水器、暖气和空调已成为众所周知的低效能电器。热泵已经改变了它们的工作方式。它从建筑物外部的空气中或地下汲取热量，并将这些热量提供给建筑物或其供水系统。在夏天，该系统反过来也可用于给建筑物降温。

改造工厂

从钢铁厂到造纸厂，工业消耗着全世界约三分之一的能源。节能的可能性非常大。在路德维希港，德国的化工巨头巴斯夫公司经营了一个连通200多家化工厂的综合大工厂。在这里，一个化学过程产生的热量可以为下一个化学过程提供能源。

绿色驾驶

全世界四分之一的能源——包括三分之二的年石油产量——都被用于运输。有些节能方法是免费的：只要保持你的汽车轮胎气量充足，你就可以将燃料利用率提高6%。

一台好冰箱

家电的使用消耗着一半以上的居民用电，并排放着占全世界五分之一的二氧化碳量。即使自20世纪80年代以来，制造商已经将冰箱和其他的白色家电的用电效率提高了70%，这仍然是个事实。根据一家国际能源协会的研究，如果消费者选择能替他们省下最多钱的家电型号而非使用寿命最长的型号，将会使全球的住宅用电量（和居民水电费）减少43%。

灵活的付款方式

谁说你必须为所有的节能投资买单？"能源服务承包商"将支付翻新改造的费用，并收取客户每年节约下来的水电费中的一部分作为收益。如果节能这么简单并有利可图，为什么不是人人都这么做呢？这与人的心理和信息匮乏有关。大多数人往往关注的是今天的价格，而不是明天可能节约多少。业主或是开发商更是如此，他们根本看不到对更好的绝缘材料或供热系统的投资所能省下来的钱。在许多人看来，节能仍然和克己联系在一起。许多环保主义者也仍然大力推崇这种观点。

当然，最有效的刺激因素来源于市场本身。在过去的一年里，居高不下的燃油价格都令人们前所未有地着眼于能源效率。最终，在降低成本方面不断增长的压力迫使更多的企业开始对他们的能源使用精打细算。

conserve [kən'sɜːv]
释 v. 保全；节约；保存

efficiency [ɪ'fɪʃnsi]
释 n. 效率；性能
用 high efficiency 高效率；production efficiency 生产效率
例 You lose your *efficiency* for some reason. 因为某种原因，你办事不再有效率了。

fraction ['frækʃn]
释 n. (某物的)小部分；一点儿；分数，小数

slump [slʌmp]
释 v. 大幅度下降；猛然落下 n. 经济衰退；低潮状态

replace [rɪ'pleɪs]
释 v. 代替；更换；把…放回原处
例 The only way is to *replace* it with a new part. 唯一的办法就是用一个新零件来替换它。

digitally ['dɪdʒɪtəli]
释 ad. 数字地

pipe [paɪp]
释 n. 管子；烟斗 v. 用管道输送

improvement [ɪm'pruːvmənt]
释 n. 改进；改进措施

slash [slæʃ]
释 v. (用刀、剑等)乱砍；在(衣服上)开长缝；严厉地批评；大幅削减或降低
用 slash one's way through/past sth. 挥刀、剑等开路
例 The country will proceed with the plan to *slash* the number of troops. 这个国家将继续推进削减军队数量的计划。

bonus ['bəʊnəs]
释 n. 奖金，红利；意外的好处

emission [i'mɪʃn]
释 n. (光、热等的)散发；散发物

profitable ['prɒfɪtəbl]
释 a. 有利可图的；有益的

single ['sɪŋgl]
释 a. 单一的，单个的；单身的；单人的；单程的 n. 单个；单程票 v. 选出

lower ['ləʊə(r)]
释 a. 较低的；下面的 v. 降低；减少

argument ['ɑːgjumənt]
释 n. 争论；论据，理由；概要；主题

immense [ɪ'mens]
释 a. 巨大的；广大的

investment [ɪn'vestmənt]
释 n. 投资(额)；(时间、精力等的)投入
例 More measures should be taken to attract foreign *investment*. 应该采取更多的措施来吸引外资。

drain [dreɪn]
释 v. 喝光；耗尽；排水；(使)流出；(使)枯竭 n. 排水；下水道；(精力、时间、金钱等的)消耗
用 drain away 逐渐消失，渐渐枯竭；go down the drain (情况)越来越糟，(人)每况愈下；落空，破产
例 The passion was slowly *draining* from him. 他的热情逐渐消失了。

agenda [ə'dʒendə]
释 n. 议程，议程表

unveil [ˌʌn'veɪl]
释 v. 揭去面纱；揭幕；公开，揭露

virtually ['vɜːtʃuəli]
释 ad. 实际上，事实上；几乎

prototype ['prəʊtətaɪp]
释 n. 原型，蓝本

utility [juːˈtɪləti]
释 *n.* 功用，效用；公用事业

workplace [ˈwɜːkpleɪs]
释 工作场所，车间

productivity [ˌprɒdʌkˈtɪvəti]
释 *n.* 生产力；生产效率

rate [reɪt]
释 *n.* 比率，率；速度；费用，价格；等级 *v.* 对…估价，评估；责骂

roughly [ˈrʌfli]
释 *ad.* 大概，大约；粗略地；粗暴地

consume [kənˈsjuːm]
释 *v.* 消耗，花费；毁掉；吃或喝
用 consume away 消耗掉；枯萎，凋谢；be consumed with 因…而变得憔悴
例 The hotel was quickly *consumed* by fire. 那座旅馆很快被大火吞噬。

notoriously [nəʊˈtɔːriəsli]
释 *ad.* 众所周知地；臭名昭彰地

alter [ˈɔːltə(r)]
释 *v.* 改变；修改

reverse [rɪˈvɜːs]
释 *v.* (使)变得相反；撤销；反转 *n.* 相反的情况；反面；逆转，灾难 *a.* 反向的，相反的

chemical [ˈkemɪkl]
释 *a.* 化学的 *n.* 化学制品；化学物

complex [ˈkɒmpleks]
释 *a.* 合成的；复杂的 *n.* 综合体；情结

transportation [ˌtrænspɔːˈteɪʃn]
释 *n.* 运输；运输工具；交通业

charge [tʃɑːdʒ]
释 *n.* 费用；管理；控告；电荷 *v.* 索(价)；控告；使充电

用 in charge of 负责；free of charge 免费；charge sb. with 控告某人

boost [buːst]
释 *v.* 提高，增加，促进；支援；宣传 *n.* 推动；帮助；宣传
例 The unexpected good news *boosted* the team's morale. 这个意外的好消息鼓舞了整个团队的士气。

simply [ˈsɪmpli]
释 *ad.* 简单地；完全；仅仅，只不过；朴素地

properly [ˈprɒpəli]
释 *ad.* 适当地，正确地；完全，非常；彻底地

share [ʃeə(r)]
释 *v.* 分享；分担；分配 *n.* 一份，份额；股票，股份
例 *Sharing* your information with others, you'll get more in return. 与他人分享你所知的信息，作为回报你将得到更多。

landlord [ˈlændlɔːd]
释 *n.* 地主；房主；(旅店等的)店主，主人

developer [dɪˈveləpə(r)]
释 *n.* 显影剂；开发商

generate [ˈdʒenəreɪt]
释 *v.* 生成；产生(光、热、电等)；引起，导致
例 Wind is employed to *generate* electricity across the world. 全世界都在利用风来发电。

incentive [ɪnˈsentɪv]
释 *n.* 刺激某人做某事的事物；刺激；动机 *a.* 刺激性的；鼓励性的
用 economic incentive 经济刺激；fiscal incentive 财政刺激

环境保护

climatologist [ˌklaɪmə'tɒlədʒist] n. 气候学家

coal-mining ['kəʊlˌmaɪnɪŋ] a. 煤矿业的

confluence ['kɒnfluəns] n. (两河)汇合处

contaminant [kən'tæmɪnənt] n. 污染物

cooperative [kəʊ'ɒpərətɪv] a. 合作的，协力的

dearth [dɜːθ] n. 缺乏

deficiency [dɪ'fɪʃnsi] n. 缺乏，不足

deplete [dɪ'pliːt] v. (使)枯竭；消耗

desolate ['desələt] a. 荒凉的，无人烟的

deteriorate [dɪ'tɪəriəreɪt] v. 恶化，变坏

devastation [ˌdevə'steɪʃn] n. 毁坏；荒废

dung [dʌŋ] n. (牛、马等的)粪，肥料

erosion [ɪ'rəʊʒn] n. 腐蚀，侵蚀

havoc ['hævək] n. 破坏，浩劫

hurricane ['hʌrɪkən] n. 飓风

industrialization [ɪnˌdʌstriəlaɪ'zeɪʃn] n. 工业化

inundate ['ɪnʌndeɪt] v. 泛滥；淹没

landfill ['lændfɪl] n. 垃圾堆；废渣埋填地

landslide ['lændslaɪd] n. 山崩，滑坡

nontoxic [nɒn'tɒksɪk] a. 无毒的

pollutant [pə'luːtənt] n. 污染物质

pristine ['prɪstiːn] a. 原始的；未被破坏的

solar ['səʊlə(r)] a. 太阳的；(利用)太阳能的

sublimate ['sʌblɪmeɪt] v. (使)升华；(使)净化

symbiosis [ˌsɪmbaɪ'əʊsɪs] n. 共生(关系)，共栖

tainted ['teɪntɪd] a. 受污染的

terrain [tə'reɪn] n. 地形；地势

untapped [ˌʌn'tæpt] a. 未开发的

viability [ˌvaɪə'bɪləti] n. 生存能力

The world won't care about your self-esteem. The world will expect you to accomplish something before you feel good about yourself.

—Bill Gates

这世界并不会在意你的自尊。这世界指望你在自我感觉良好之前先要有所成就。

——比尔·盖茨

Passage 7

Supersize Surprise

Ask anyone why there is an **obesity epidemic** and they will tell you that it's all down to eating too much and burning too few calories. That explanation **appeals** to common sense and has dominated efforts to get to the root of the obesity epidemic and reverse it. Yet obesity researchers are increasingly dissatisfied with it. Many now believe that something else must have changed in our environment to **precipitate** such **dramatic** rises in obesity over the past 40 years or so. Nobody is saying that the "big two"—reduced **physical** activity and increased **availability** of food—are not important **contributors** to the epidemic, but they cannot explain it all.

Earlier this year a review paper by 20 obesity experts set out the 7 most plausible **alternative** explanations for the epidemic. Here they are.

1. Not Enough Sleep

It is widely believed that sleep is for the brain, not the body. Could a shortage of shut-eye also be helping to make us fat?

Several large-scale studies suggest there may be a link. The US Nurses' Health Study, which tracked 68,000 women for 16 years, found that those who slept an average of 5 hours a night gained more weight during the study period than women who slept 6 hours, who in turn gained more than those who slept 7.

It's well known that obesity **impairs** sleep, so perhaps people get fat first and sleep less **afterwards**. But the nurses' study suggests that it can work in the other direction too: sleep loss may precipitate weight gain.

2. Climate Control

We humans, like all warm-blooded animals, can keep our core body temperatures pretty much constant **regardless** of what's going on in the world around us. We do this by **altering** our **metabolic** rate, **shivering** or **sweating**. Keeping warm and staying cool take energy unless we are in the "thermo-neutral zone", which is increasingly where we choose to live and work.

Could air conditioning in summer and heating in winter really make a difference to our weight? Sadly, there is some evidence that it does—at least with regard to heating. Studies show that in comfortable temperatures we use less energy.

3. Less Smoking

Bad news: smokers really do tend to be thinner than the rest of us, and quitting really does pack on the pounds, though no one is sure why. It probably has something to do with the fact that nicotine is an appetite suppressant and appears to up your metabolic rate.

4. Genetic Effects

Your chances of becoming fat may be set, at least in part, before you were even born. Children of obese mothers are much more likely to become obese themselves later in life. Offspring of mice fed a high-fat diet during pregnancy are much more likely to become fat than the offspring of identical mice fed a normal diet. Intriguingly, the effect persists for two or three generations. Grand-children of mice fed a high-fat diet grow up fat even if their own mother is fed normally—so your fate may have been sealed even before you were conceived.

5. A Little Older…

Some groups of people just happen to be fatter than others. Surveys carried out by the US National Center for Health Statistics found that adults aged 40 to 79 were around three times as likely to be obese as younger people. Non-white females also tend to fall at the fatter end of the spectrum: Mexican-American women are 30% more likely than white women to be obese, and black women have twice the risk.

6. Mature Mums

Results from the US National Heart, Lung and Blood Institute's study found that the odds of a child being obese increase about 14% for every five extra years of their mother's age, though why this should be so is not entirely clear.

Michael Symonds at the University of Nottingham, UK, found that first-born children have more fat than younger ones. As family size decreases, firstborns account for a greater share of the population. In 1964, British women gave birth to an average of 2.95 children; by 2005 that figure had fallen to 1.79. In the US in 1976, 9.6% of women in their 40s had only one child; in 2004 it was 17.4%. This combination of older mothers and more single children could be contributing to the obesity epidemic.

7. Like Marrying Like

Just as people pair off according to looks, so they do for size. Lean people are more likely to marry lean and fat more likely to marry fat. On its own, "like marrying like" cannot account for any increase in obesity. But combined with others—particularly the fact that obesity is partly genetic, and that heavier people have more children—it amplifies the increase from other causes.

肥胖的原因

随便问一个人为什么肥胖症这么普遍，他们都会告诉你，那全是由于平时吃得太多而消耗的热量太少造成的。这种解释与常识一致，易于接受，也是人们试图破解肥胖症流行的根源并扭转这一形势的主要努力方向。然而，肥胖症研究人员却对此日益不满。现在他们中的很多人都认为我们生存环境中的其他事物一定发生了改变，从而促使过去40多年以来肥胖人数的激增。无人否认"两大因素"——减少运动和增加食物摄入量——是造成肥胖症流行的主要原因，但是它们不能完全解释这一现象。

早在前段时间，一份由20位肥胖专家撰写的综述论文列出了7个最可能的因素来解释肥胖流行的原因。分别是：

1. 睡眠不足

人们普遍认为睡眠与大脑有关，与身体无关。难道缺乏睡眠也会使人变胖吗？

几项大型的研究表明睡眠与肥胖是有关联的。美国护士健康研究耗时16年，跟踪调查了6.8万名妇女，发现在该项调查研究期间，每晚睡眠时间平均为5个小时的女性的体重要重于每晚睡眠时间为6个小时的女性；相应地，睡眠时间为6个小时的女性又比7个小时的女性要胖。

众所周知，肥胖会削弱睡眠质量，所以人们或许是先变胖而后才睡得少的。但是该项护士研究向我们表明这一规律也可反其道而行之：睡得少也可能造成体重增加。

2. 气候控制

我们人类像其他温血动物一样，无论周遭环境如何变化，都能使核心体温基本保持恒定。我们通过改变新陈代谢、哆嗦或出汗来保持体温不变。除非我们处于温度适宜的环境里，否则保持恒温状态就要消耗我们的能量。现在我们之中越来越多的人选择在温度适宜的环境中生活和工作。

夏季使用空调、冬季使用暖气真的会影响我们的体重吗？可悲的是，有证据表明，空调和暖气确实对人的体重有影响——至少暖气是这样。研究表明，在适宜的温度下，人的能量消耗会减少。

3. 抽烟少

坏消息是吸烟者确实往往比其他人瘦，而戒烟的确能使他们长胖，虽然没有人知道是什么原因。这可能与尼古丁能抑制你的食欲、加快你的新陈代谢率有关。

4. 遗传效应

在出生之前，你变胖的几率，至少在某种程度上，可能就已经被确定下来了。胖妈妈的孩子长大后更容易变胖。怀孕期间食用高脂饲料的老鼠的后代，相比食用正常饲料的老鼠的后代，更容易变胖。非常有趣的是，这种影响能持续到第二代或第三代。用高脂饲料喂养的老鼠的第三代长大后也会变胖，即使它们自己的妈妈是用正常饲料喂养的——因此，甚至在你尚在妈妈腹中之时，你是否会变胖的命运就已成定局。

5. 年龄变大

某些人群恰巧比其他人群胖。美国国家卫生统计中心所作的多项调查研究发现，年龄在40岁至79岁之间的人群变胖的几率是较年轻人群的3倍左右。有色人种的女性也容易触及此年龄段肥胖谱的肥胖端：墨西哥裔美国女性比白人女性变胖的几率高出30%，而黑人女性则高出一倍。

6. 育龄较晚

美国国家心肺血液研究所的调查结果发现，孕妇年龄每增加5岁，她们的孩子变胖的几率就会上升14%，但是尚不完全清楚为什么会这样。

来自英国诺丁汉大学的迈克尔·西蒙兹发现，头胎孩子比之后生的孩子的脂肪要多。随着家庭人口的减少，头胎子女在人口中的比率也越来越大。1964年，英国妇女平均生育2.95个孩子，而到了2005年这一数字已经下降至1.79。1976年，美国40多岁的女性中只有9.6%的人仅有一个孩子，而到了2004年，这一数字已上升至17.4%。高龄孕妇和独生子女的增多可能共同导致了肥胖症的流行。

7. 相似的人跟相似的人结婚

就像人们会根据相貌选择配偶一样，人们也会根据身材来选择。瘦人更倾向于和瘦人结婚，胖人则更可能与胖人结婚。就其本身而言，相似的人跟相似的人结婚并不能导致肥胖者数量的增加。但是，如果再结合其他因素，特别是肥胖的部分原因是遗传效应以及肥胖者拥有更多孩子这样的事实，它就能扩大其他因素的影响。

obesity [əʊ'biːsəti]

释 n. 过度肥胖；肥胖症

epidemic [ˌepɪ'demɪk]

释 n. 流行；流行病 a. 流行性的；传染性的

用 epidemic disease 流行病

appeal [ə'piːl]

释 n. 呼吁，恳求；吸引力；上诉 v. 呼吁；有吸引力；上诉；迎合

用 appeal court 上诉法院；appeal for 恳求；要求

例 People in danger *appealed* to us for help. 处于危险中的人们向我们求救。

precipitate [prɪ'sɪpɪteɪt]

释 v. (使突如其来地)发生；促成；(使)沉淀；降水 n. 沉淀物 a. 突如其来的

dramatic [drə'mætɪk]

释 a. 显著的；戏剧性的；激动人心的

physical ['fɪzɪkl]

释 a. 身体的，肉体的；物理的；物质的 n. 体格检查

用 physical checkup 健康检查

availability [əˌveɪlə'bɪləti]

释 n. 可利用性；可利用的人或物

contributor [kən'trɪbjətə(r)]

释 n. 贡献者；捐助者；投稿者；促成因素，原因之一

alternative [ɔːl'tɜːnətɪv]

释 n. 替换物；选择的自由，选择的余地 a. 二选一的；另类的

impair [ɪm'peə(r)]

释 v. 削弱，损害

例 Excessive caffeine can *impair* your ability to relax, and it can interfere with your usual sleep patterns, too. 摄入过多的咖啡因会削弱你放松的能力，而且还会干扰你的日常睡眠状况。

afterwards ['ɑːftəwədz]

释 ad. 后来

regardless [rɪ'ɡɑːdləs]

释 ad. 不顾；不理会

用 regardless of 不管，不顾

alter ['ɔːltə(r)]

释 v. 改变；改动

例 I'll try to persuade her to *alter* her mind. 我会尽力劝她改变主意。

metabolic [ˌmetə'bɒlɪk]

释 a. 新陈代谢的；变化的

shiver ['ʃɪvə(r)]

释 v./n. 战栗，发抖

sweat [swet]

释 n. 汗，汗水 v. (使)出汗；流汗

例 Passing the entrance exam involves much *sweat*. 要想通过入学考试，需要付出很多的汗水。

tend [tend]

释 v. 倾向；朝某方向；照管

pound [paʊnd]

释 n. 磅；英镑 v. 强烈打击；(指心脏)剧烈地跳动

nicotine ['nɪkətiːn]

释 n. 尼古丁

appetite ['æpɪtaɪt]

释 n. 胃口，食欲；欲望

例 In order to satisfy his *appetite* for challenge, he climbs mountains every weekend. 为了满足自己的挑战欲望，他每周末都去爬山。

suppressant [sə'presnt]

释 n. 抑制药 a. 抑制性的

chance [tʃɑːns]

释 n. 可能性；机会 v. 碰巧；冒…的险

offspring ['ɒfsprɪŋ]

释 n. (动物的)崽；子孙，后代

pregnancy ['preɡnənsi]

释 n. 怀孕(期)

identical [aɪ'dentɪkl]
释 a. 相同的；同一的

persist [pə'sɪst]
释 v. 坚持不懈；持续，继续存在

generation [ˌdʒenə'reɪʃn]
释 n. 一代人；产生，发生

seal [siːl]
释 v. 盖章；粘住；封印；注定，确定 n. 海豹；密封；封印

conceive [kən'siːv]
释 v. 怀孕；构思
用 conceive of 想象

statistics [stə'tɪstɪks]
释 n. 统计；统计资料；统计学

mature [mə'tʃʊə(r); mə'tjʊə(r)]
释 a. 成熟的；到期的；深思熟虑的 v. (使)成熟

institute ['ɪnstɪtjuːt]
释 n. 学会，研究所；学院 v. 设立，制定

entirely [ɪn'taɪəli]
释 a. 全部地，完全地

lean [liːn]
释 a. 瘦的；贫瘠的；少量的 v. 倚靠；(使)倾斜；屈身

单词家族

养生瘦身

abstinent ['æbstɪnənt] a. 饮食有度的，节制的

aerobic [eə'rəʊbɪk] a. 需氧的；有氧健身法的

appetizing ['æpɪtaɪzɪŋ] a. 促进食欲的

aromatherapy [əˌrəʊmə'θerəpi] n. 芳香疗法

cater ['keɪtə(r)] v. 迎合；提供饮食及服务

cellulose ['seljuləʊs] n. 纤维素

chaff [tʃɑːf] n. 谷物的皮壳，米糠

cloying ['klɔɪɪŋ] a. 倒胃口的

condiment ['kɒndɪmənt] n. 调味品

cornstarch ['kɔːnstɑːtʃ] n. 玉米淀粉

culinary ['kʌlɪnəri] a. 厨房的；烹调用的

edible ['edəbl] a. 可以吃的，可食用的

fatigue [fə'tiːg] n. 疲劳

gluttonous ['glʌtənəs] a. 贪吃的，贪嘴的

gobble ['gɒbl] v. 贪食

gourmet ['gʊəmeɪ] n. 美食家

gracile ['græsaɪl] a. 纤细优美的

grease [griːs] n. 动物油脂

guzzle ['gʌzl] v. 大吃大喝

haggard ['hægəd] a. 憔悴的；消瘦的

imbibe [ɪm'baɪb] v. 饮(尤指酒类)；吸收

pallid ['pælɪd] a. 苍白的，没血色的

pant [pænt] n. 喘气

plump [plʌmp] a. 丰满的，胖乎乎的

rationing ['ræʃənɪŋ] n. (食物等的)定量配给

ravenous ['rævənəs] a. 极饿的

refresh [rɪ'freʃ] v. 给…新的力量或活力

rubicund ['ruːbɪkənd] a. (脸色)红润的

starchy ['stɑːtʃi] a. 含淀粉的

stew [stjuː] n. 炖(煨或焖)的食物

willowy ['wɪləʊi] a. 苗条的

yummy ['jʌmi] a. 美味的，可口的

音频

Passage 8

Language and Gender

The use of **deferential** language is **symbolic** of the Confucian ideal of the woman, which **dominates conservative** gender **norms** in Japan. This ideal presents a woman who **withdraws quietly** to the background, subordinating her life and needs to those of her family and its male head. She is a **dutiful** daughter, wife, and mother, and a **master** of the **domestic** arts. The **typical** refined Japanese woman **excels** in **modesty** and **delicacy**; she "**treads** softly in the world", **elevating** feminine beauty and grace to an art form.

Nowadays, it is commonly observed that young women are not **conforming** to the **feminine** linguistic ideal. They are using fewer of the very deferential "women's" forms, and even using the few strong forms that are known as "men's". This, of course, attracts **considerable** attention and has led to an outcry in the Japanese media against the defeminization of women's language. Indeed, we didn't hear about "men's language" until people began to **respond** to girls' appropriation of forms normally reserved for boys and men. There is considerable **sentiment** about the "**corruption**" of women's language—which of course is viewed as part of the loss of feminine ideals and **morality**—and this sentiment is **crystallized** by **nationwide** opinion **polls** that are regularly carried out by the media.

Yoshiko Matsumoto has argued that young women probably never used as many of the highly deferential forms as older women. This highly polite style is no doubt something that young women have been expected to "grow into"—after all, it is a sign not simply of femininity, but of **maturity** and **refinement**, and its use could be taken to indicate a change in the nature of one's social relations as well. One might well imagine little girls using **exceedingly** polite forms when playing house or **imitating** older women—in a **fashion analogous** to little girls' use of a high-pitched voice to do "teacher talk" or "mother talk" in role play.

The fact that young Japanese women are using less deferential language is a sure **sign** of change—of social change and of linguistic change. But it is most certainly not a sign of the "masculinization" of girls. In some **instances**, it may be a sign that girls are making the same **claim** to authority as boys and men, but that is very different from saying that they are trying to be "masculine". Katsue Reynolds has argued that girls nowadays are using more **assertive** language **strategies** in order to be able to **compete** with boys in schools and out. Social change also brings not simply different **positions** for women and girls, but different relations to life stages, and **adolescent** girls are **participating** in new subcultural forms. Thus, what may, to an older speaker, seem like a "masculine" speech may seem to an adolescent like a "**liberated**" or "hip" speech.

译文

语言与性别

使用敬语是儒家思想中妇女的象征，它主宰着日本的传统性别标准。这种观念展现了一个默默退到幕后的女人，一个将自己的生活和需要从属于家庭和男主人的女人的形象。她是听话的女儿、尽职的妻子和称职的母亲，也是干家务活的能手。典型的、有教养的日本妇女非常谦逊、谨慎；她们"事事谨言慎行"，将女性的美丽和优雅提升到了艺术高度。

如今，人们普遍认为年轻的女子并没有遵循这种女性用语的观念。她们较少使用很恭敬的"女性的"表达方式，而且甚至会用到个别带有强烈的"男性色彩的"用语。毫无疑问，这引起了极大的关注。日本媒体一片哗然，强烈抗议女性用语的失女性化。事实上，在人们开始抗议女性挪用通常专为男性使用的语言形式之前，我们从来没有听说过"男性用语"这种说法。社会对女性语言的"腐化"有相当大的情绪（毫无疑问，这被看作是女性思想和道德的部分沦丧），从媒体定期进行的全国民意调查来看，这一情绪被明确地表达了出来。

松本良子认为，年轻女性可能不再像老一辈的妇女一样使用很多非常恭敬的用语。但毫无疑问社会期望这种高度礼貌的用语风格能够为年轻女性所拥有，因为毕竟这不单是女性化的标志，也是成熟和优雅的象征，而且它的使用也被看作是一个人的社会关系发生质的改变的标志。可以想象一下小女孩们在玩过家家或者模仿大人时使用极度礼貌的用语的场景，那种方式跟小女孩们用一种音调很高的声音扮演"老师说"或者"妈妈说"中的角色类似。

年轻的日本女子较少使用女性用语这一事实，明显是社会变化和语言变化的一种标志。但它肯定不是女孩子"男性化"的标志。在某些情况下，它可能是女性呼吁要与男性权力平等的标志，但这与认为女孩子试图变得"男性化"是完全不同的概念。胜家·雷诺兹认为，如今的女孩子们使用显得更加自信的语言策略是为了在学校或者社会上与男孩子竞争。社会变化带给女孩子或妇女们的不仅仅是地位的不同，而且是人生阶段的不同关系。未成年少女开始参与到新的亚文化形态里。因此，对那些老一辈人来说可能属于"男性化"的语言，对年轻人来说就是"无拘无束的"或者"时髦的"语言。

deferential [defə'renʃl]
释 a. 表示敬意的，恭敬的

symbolic [sɪm'bɒlɪk]
释 a. 象征的；符号的

dominate ['dɒmɪneɪt]
释 v. 支配，统治；控制；在…中占首要地位
用 dominate the market 占据绝对份额；欺行霸市
例 No children likes to be completely *dominated* by the family. 没有孩子喜欢完全受控于家庭。

conservative [kən'sɜːvətɪv]
释 a. 保守的；传统的 n. 保守党

norm [nɔːm]
释 n. 规范，准则；模范，典型

withdraw [wɪð'drɔː; wɪθ'drɔː]
释 v. 撤退；收回；离开；取钱
用 withdraw from 退出；withdraw money 取钱
例 Because of the sudden attack, the army has to *withdraw*. 由于遭到突袭，军队不得不撤退。

quietly ['kwaɪətli]
释 ad. 平静地；静静地

dutiful ['djuːtɪfl]
释 a. 恭敬顺从的，尽职的

master ['mɑːstə(r)]
释 n. 主人；能手；大师；硕士 v. 精通；控制
用 master of 精通…的人

domestic [də'mestɪk]
释 a. 本国的，国内的；家(庭)的；驯养的
例 As a matter of fact, *domestic* trivialities are almost driving her crazy. 事实上，家庭琐事快把她逼疯了。

typical ['tɪpɪkl]
释 a. 典型的，有代表性的；特有的，独特的

excel [ɪk'sel]
释 v. 擅长；胜过
用 excel in/at 擅长；excel oneself 胜过过去
例 She is good at playing the piano, but this time she's *excelled* herself. 她一直很擅长弹钢琴，但这次比以前弹得都好。

modesty ['mɒdəsti]
释 n. 谦虚；谨慎；端庄
例 *Modesty* is a must for making progress. 谦虚使人进步。

delicacy ['delɪkəsi]
释 n. 精致，优雅；谨慎；敏感；细嫩；微妙

tread [tred]
释 v. 踩，踏，行走 n. 轮胎面；脚步声
用 tread on air 欢天喜地；tread on sb.'s corns/toes 冒犯或得罪某人；tread on sb.'s heels 紧跟某人
例 He *trod* lightly so as not to wake the sleeping baby. 他脚步很轻，以免吵醒熟睡的孩子。

elevate ['elɪveɪt]
释 v. 举起；使上升，提升；使情绪高昂
例 The father hoped to *elevate* the mind of his young child by reading him stories. 这位父亲希望通过给自己的孩子读故事来提高他的修养。

conform [kən'fɔːm]
释 v. 遵守；适应，顺从；一致，符合
用 conform to 遵守
例 This building does not *conform* to safety regulations. 这栋建筑不符合安全条例。

feminine ['femənɪn]

释 *a.* 女性的；女人般的

considerable [kən'sɪdərəbl]

释 *a.* 相当大(或多)的；值得考虑的

例 *Considerable* time is consumed by travails. 大量的时间都花在了艰苦劳动上。

respond [rɪ'spɒnd]

释 *v.* 回答，答复；作出反应，响应

sentiment ['sentɪmənt]

释 *n.* 思想感情；情绪；意见，观点

corruption [kə'rʌpʃn]

释 *n.* 腐化，堕落；腐烂；腐败

用 combat corruption 反腐；crime of corruption 贪污罪；腐化罪

例 The official *corruption* was exposed by the local newspaper. 当地报纸曝光了官员的腐败行为。

morality [mə'ræləti]

释 *n.* 道德，伦理；道德原则

crystallize ['krɪstəlaɪz]

释 *v.* 明确，(使)具体化；(使)结晶

例 His speech helped me *crystallize* some activities in my mind. 他的话语帮助我明确了头脑中的某些想法。

nationwide [,neɪʃn'waɪd]

释 *ad./a.* 遍及全国(的)，全国性(的)

poll [pəʊl]

释 *n.* 民意调查；投票；票数 *v.* 对…进行民意调查；获得(一定数量的选票)

maturity [mə'tʃʊərəti; mə'tjʊərəti]

释 *n.* 成熟；完备；有经验

refinement [rɪ'faɪnmənt]

释 *n.* 精(提)炼，提纯；改良；优雅

exceedingly [ɪk'siːdɪŋli]

释 *ad.* 极端地

imitate ['ɪmɪteɪt]

释 *v.* 模仿；仿制，仿造

例 The little girl is *imitating* her older sister's language and behavior. 小女孩正在模仿她姐姐的言行。

fashion ['fæʃn]

释 *n.* 方式；时尚；流行款式，时装

analogous [ə'næləgəs]

释 *a.* 类似的

sign [saɪn]

释 *n.* 标记，符号；招牌；征兆；标志 *v.* 签(名)

instance ['ɪnstəns]

释 *n.* 例子

claim [kleɪm]

释 *v.* 声称，断言；对…提出要求 *n.* 要求；认领；索赔；声称，断言

assertive [ə'sɜːtɪv]

释 *a.* 坚定而自信的；断言的

strategy ['strætədʒi]

释 *n.* 谋略，策略；战略；政策

compete [kəm'piːt]

释 *v.* 竞争；对抗；比赛

用 compete in 参加比赛；compete against 与…竞争

例 Your only enemy is yourself, so try to *compete* with yourself. 你唯一的敌人就是你自己，所以努力和自己比吧。

position [pə'zɪʃn]

释 *n.* 地位；位置；职位；姿势；见解 *v.* 安放，安置

用 in position 在适当的位置，适得其所；out of position 在不适当的位置；put oneself in sb.'s position 设身处地；take up the position that 主张，认为

adolescent [,ædə'lesnt]

释 *n.* 青少年 *a.* 青春期的，青少年的

participate [pɑː'tɪsɪpeɪt]

释 *v.* 参与，参加

用 participate in 参加

liberated ['lɪbəreɪtɪd]

释 *a.* 解放的，不受传统思想束缚的

45

性格态度

antipathy [æn'tɪpəθi] n. 反感；厌恶

ceremonious [ˌserə'məʊniəs] a. 讲究礼节的

chaff [tʃɑːf] v. 玩笑，戏弄

circuitous [sə'kjuːɪtəs] a. 迂回的

cranky ['kræŋki] a. 怪僻的

deride [dɪ'raɪd] v. 嘲弄；嘲笑

detestable [dɪ'testəbl] a. 可憎的

entreaty [ɪn'triːti] n. 恳求

frivolous ['frɪvələs] a. 轻率的

hospitality [ˌhɒspɪ'tæləti] n. 好客，款待

inhospitable [ˌɪnhɒ'spɪtəbl] a. 不好客的，不友好的

lavish ['lævɪʃ] a. 慷慨的

mawkish ['mɔːkɪʃ] a. 多愁善感的

persnickety [pə'snɪkəti] a. 吹毛求疵的

punctual ['pʌŋktʃuəl] a. 准时的，守时的

reverent ['revərənt] a. 恭敬的；虔诚的

snob [snɒb] n. 势利小人

stilted ['stɪltɪd] a. 矫揉造作的

supplicate ['sʌplɪkeɪt] v. 恳求；乞求

thoroughness ['θʌrənəs] n. 周到；完全

timid ['tɪmɪd] a. 胆怯的

venerate ['venəreɪt] v. 崇敬

yell [jel] v. 叫喊；大声抗议

No pain, no palm; no thorns, no throne; no gall, no glory; no cross, no crown.
　　　　　　　　　　　　　　　　　　—William Penn

没有播种，何来收获；没有辛劳，何来成功；没有磨难，何来荣耀；没有挫折，何来辉煌。　　　　　　——威廉·佩恩

音频

Passage 9

原 文

A Grassroots Remedy

Most of us spend our lives seeking the natural world. To this end, we walk the dog, play golf, go fishing, sit in the garden, drink outside rather than inside the pub, have a picnic, live in the suburbs, go to the seaside, and buy a weekend place in the country. The most popular leisure activity in Britain is going for a walk. And when joggers jog, they don't run the streets. Every one of them instinctively heads to the park or the river. It is my profound belief that not only do we all need nature, but we all seek nature, whether we know we are doing so or not.

But despite this, our children are growing up nature deprived. I spent my boyhood climbing trees on Streatham Common, South London. These days, children are robbed of these ancient freedoms, due to problems like crime, traffic, the loss of the open spaces and odd new perceptions about what is best for children, that is to say, things that can be bought rather than things that can be found.

The truth is to be found elsewhere. A study in the US: families had moved to better housing and the children were assessed for ADHD—attention deficit hyperactivity disorder. Those whose accommodation had more natural views showed an improvement of 19%; those who had the same improvement in material surroundings but no nice view improved just 4%.

But children are frequently discouraged from involvement with natural spaces, for health and safety reasons, for fear that they might get dirty or that they might cause damage. So, instead, the damage is done to the children themselves: not to their bodies but to their souls.

One of the great problems of modern childhood is ADHD, now increasingly and expensively treated with drugs. Yet one study after another indicates that contact with nature gives huge benefits to ADHD children. However, we spend money on drugs rather than on green places.

The life of old people is measurably better when they have access to nature. The increasing emphasis for the growing population of old people is in quality rather than quantity of years. And study after study finds that a garden is the single most important thing in finding that quality.

In wider and more difficult areas of life, there is evidence to indicate that natural surroundings improve all kinds of things. Even problems with crime and aggressive behaviour are reduced when there is contact with the natural world.

Human beings are a species of mammals. For seven million years they lived on the planet as part of nature. Our **ancestral** selves miss the natural world and long for contact with non-human life. Anyone who has patted a dog, stroked a cat, sat under a tree with a pint of beer, given or received a bunch of flowers or chosen to walk through the park on a nice day understands that.

We need the wild world. It is essential to our well-being, our health, our happiness. Without the wild world we are not more but less **civilized**. Without other living things around us we are less than human.

Five ways to find **harmony** with the natural world:

Walk: Break the **rhythm** of **permanently** being under a **roof**. Get off a stop earlier, make a **circuit** of the park at lunchtime, walk the child to and from school, get a dog, feel yourself moving in moving air, look, listen, **absorb**.

Sit: Take a moment, every now and then, to be still in an open space. In the garden, anywhere that's not in the office, anywhere out of house, away from the routine. Sit under a tree, look at water, and feel **refreshed**, ever so slightly **renewed**.

Drink: The best way to enjoy the natural world is by yourself; the second best way is in company. Take a drink outside with a good person, a good **gathering**; talk with the sun and the wind with birdsong for background.

Learn: Expand your **boundaries**. Learn five **species** of birds, five butterflies, five trees, five **birdsongs**. That way, you see and hear more; and your mind responds **gratefully** to the greater amount of wildness in your life.

Travel: The places you always wanted to visit; by the seaside, in the country, in the hills. Take a weekend break, a day-trip, get out there and do it: for the **scenery**, for the way through the woods, for the birds, for the bees. Go somewhere special and bring specialness home. It lasts forever, after all.

译文

大自然疗法

我们中的大多数人一生都在追寻自然世界。为此，我们遛狗、打高尔夫球、钓鱼、在花园小坐、在露天酒吧小酌、去野餐、在郊区居住、去海边游玩，以及在乡下购置供周末休息的住所。在英国，最流行的休闲方式是散步。慢跑者跑步时，不会选择街道，而是本能地朝着公园或者河边跑去。我深信，我们所有人不仅需要自然，而且都在寻找自然，不管我们是否意识到我们正在这么做。

但是尽管如此，我们的孩子却在一个缺乏自然的环境里成长。我的少年时代是在伦敦南部的斯特里塔姆公园爬树度过的。而如今的孩子已经丧失了这些从前的自由，这是由于犯罪、车祸、露天场所的缺失以及关于什么对孩子最好的新奇观念造成的。这些观念认为，能买到的东西而非能被发现的东西对于儿童是最好的。

这一点在别处也能得到证明。美国进行了这样一份研究：对搬进了物质条件更好的住房的家庭中的孩子进行多动症测评。那些居住的地方能看到更多的自然风景的儿童，其多动症的治愈率为19%，而那些居住的地方看不见自然景色的儿童，即使住所的物质条件与前者相同，其多动症的治愈率也仅有4%。

然而，出于健康和安全考虑，现在的大人们往往并不鼓励孩子们去野外活动，担心他们把自己弄脏或者受到伤害。结果孩子反而受到了伤害，在心灵上而非身体上。

多动症是现代儿童的重大问题之一，越来越多的孩子在接受昂贵的药物治疗。然而，一项又一项的研究表明，亲近自然对治疗儿童的多动症大有裨益。但是，我们宁可花钱买药，也不愿带孩子亲近自然。

老人们在接近自然时，生活状况明显要好很多。对于老龄人口的增加，人们越来越关注的是他们的生活质量而非生活年限。多项研究表明，花园是提高老年人生活质量的最重要的一种事物。

在更广阔、更艰难的生活领域，有证据显示自然环境能改善各种事情。甚至只要与自然界接触，犯罪行为和攻击行为都能得到减少。

人类属于哺乳动物，早在七百万年前就已经作为自然界的一部分生存在地球上。我们像我们的祖先一样，想念自然世界，渴望与非人类的生命接触。那些轻拍过小狗、抚摸过小猫、坐在树下喝过啤酒、送过或收到过鲜花，或者在风和日丽的日子里在公园散过步的人最能体会这种情怀。

我们需要自然界，它对我们整个人类的安乐、健康和幸福来说都至关重要。没有了大自然，我们的文明程度不会更高，只会更低；没有了其他生物围绕着我们，我们也难以以人类自居。

五种与自然世界和谐相处的方式：

步行：打破在室内一成不变的生活规律。提早一站下车，午饭时间绕着公园走一圈，步行接送孩子上下学，养只狗，感觉自己在流动的空气里慢慢行走，浏览、倾听、吸纳。

静坐：经常抽出一点时间，到户外静坐。抛开日常工作，在花园里或者除了办公室和家以外的其他地方静坐。坐在树下，望着水面，感觉神清气爽，有一点重获新生的感觉。

畅饮：享受自然的最佳方式是独自一人去感受，其次是与他人一起分享。找个合适的人，或三五成群，一起到户外喝喝小酒，以小鸟的歌声为背景音乐，同阳光交谈，与柔风私语。

学习：扩大自己的知识面。了解五种鸟类、五种蝴蝶、五种树木以及五种鸟叫声。通过这种方法，你将会看到、听到更多；你将以一颗感恩的心去回应生命中更多美妙的自然风景。

旅行：去那些你一直想去的地方——海边、郊外，或者山林。利用周末的时间，哪怕一天也好，动身前往自己想去的地方吧：为了那些美丽的风景，为了林间的小路，为了小鸟，为了蜜蜂。去个特别的地方，把欢乐带回家吧。不管怎样，这都会是一段永久的回忆。

💡 单词记事本

instinctively [ɪnˈstɪŋktɪvli]
释 *ad.* 本能地；凭直觉地

profound [prəˈfaʊnd]
释 *a.* 深切的；见解深刻的；深奥的
例 *Profound* implications are between the lines of his writings. 他的作品字里行间都充满深刻的含义。

deprived [dɪˈpraɪvd]
释 *a.* 贫苦的，穷苦的；缺乏教育的；匮乏的

rob [rɒb]
释 *v.* 抢劫，盗窃；(非法)剥夺，使丧失

perception [pəˈsepʃn]
释 *n.* 感觉；洞察力；看法

deficit [ˈdefɪsɪt]
释 *n.* 不足，缺陷；赤字，亏损
用 budget deficit 预算赤字

disorder [dɪsˈɔːdə(r)]
释 *n.* 混乱；骚乱；(身心、机能的)失调，疾病 *v.* 扰乱；使失调

accommodation [əˌkɒməˈdeɪʃn]
释 *n.* 住处；适应，调节；[*pl.*]膳宿

discourage [dɪsˈkʌrɪdʒ]
释 *v.* 使泄气，使灰心；阻止，劝阻
例 *Discouraged* in her marriage, she decided to leave him. 她对自己的婚姻很灰心，决定离开他。

involvement [ɪnˈvɒlvmənt]
释 *n.* 包含；需要；参与，卷入

soul [səʊl]
释 *n.* 灵魂，精神；人
用 soulmate 精神伴侣
例 Although they prepared for the project with heart and *soul*, they failed. 尽管他们全心全意地为项目做准备，但还是失败了。

treat [triːt]
释 *v.* 对待；治疗；款待 *n.* 款待

emphasis [ˈemfəsɪs]
释 *n.* 强调，重点

quality [ˈkwɒləti]
释 *n.* 质量；优点；性质 *a.* 上等品质的

quantity [ˈkwɒntəti]
释 *n.* 数量

indicate [ˈɪndɪkeɪt]
释 *v.* 显示；象征，表明

surrounding [səˈraʊndɪŋ]
释 *n.* [常*pl.*]周围的事物；环境 *a.* 周围的

aggressive [əˈgresɪv]
释 *a.* 侵略的；攻击的；有进取心的
用 aggressive behavior 攻击行为
例 What we need is an *aggressive* and active applicant. 我们需要的是一位积极主动的申请者。

ancestral [æn'sestrəl]
释 a. 祖先的；祖传的

civilized ['sɪvəlaɪzd]
释 a. 文明的；有礼的

harmony ['hɑːməni]
释 n. 相符，一致；和谐，融洽
用 in harmony with 与…协调

rhythm ['rɪðəm]
释 n. 节奏，韵律

permanently ['pɜːmənəntli]
释 adv. 永久地，长期不变地

roof [ruːf]
释 n. 屋顶；顶部

circuit ['sɜːkɪt]
释 n. 电路，线路；环行，圈；巡回审判（地区）

absorb [əb'sɔːb; əb'zɔːb]
释 v. 吸收；减轻作用或影响；完全吸引住兴趣或注意力
用 be absorbed in 全神贯注于

refreshed [rɪ'freʃt]
释 a. 精神振作的
例 It is said that a cup of coffee in the morning will keep you *refreshed*. 据说每天早晨喝一杯咖啡能使你神清气爽。

renewed [rɪ'njuːd]
释 a. 体力恢复的，重新振作的

gathering ['gæðərɪŋ]
释 n. 聚集，集会；捐赠

boundary ['baʊndri]
释 n. 分界线，边界；眼界；范围
例 The *boundary* between the two countries remains a hot topic. 两国之间的边界线仍然是个热门话题。

species ['spiːʃiːz]
释 n. 种类，类群

gratefully ['greɪtfəli]
释 ad. 感激地，感谢地

scenery ['siːnəri]
释 n. 风景，景色；舞台布景

💡 单词家族

休闲娱乐

auditorium [ˌɔːdɪ'tɔːriəm] n. 听众席；观众席

bassoon [bə'suːn] n. 低音管

boisterous ['bɔɪstərəs] a. 喧闹的；兴高采烈的

cast [kɑːst] n. 角色分配；全体演员

cineaste ['sɪniæst] n. 影迷；电影制作人

cinematograph [ˌsɪnɪ'mætəgrɑːf] n. 电影放映机

coda ['kəʊdə] n. (乐曲的)尾声

dulcet ['dʌlsɪt] a. 美妙的；动听的

euphonious [juː'fəʊniəs] a. 悦耳的

gamut ['gæmət] n. 全音阶

histrionic [ˌhɪstri'ɒnɪk] a. 夸张的；戏剧化的

jockey ['dʒɒki] n. 骑师；职业赛马骑师

libretto [lɪ'bretəʊ] n. (歌剧等的)歌词；剧本

marionette [ˌmæriə'net] n. 木偶

melody ['melədi] n. 曲调，旋律

moderato [ˌmɒdə'rɑːtəʊ] a. 中速的

overexposure [ˌəʊvərɪk'spəʊʒə(r)] n. 曝光过度

pirouette [ˌpɪru'et] n. (芭蕾舞者的)单足旋转

repertoire ['repətwɑː(r)] n. 保留剧目

versatile ['vɜːsətaɪl] a. 多才多艺的

virtuoso [ˌvɜːtʃu'əʊsəʊ; ˌvɜːtʃu'əʊzəʊ] n. 艺术大师；演奏家

vocalist ['vəʊkəlɪst] n. 声乐家；歌唱者

Passage 10

音频

Is Alcohol Good for Me?

Alcohol can be a disease-fighter in moderation, but drinking too much poses a long list of health threats. If you're a woman and you enjoy alcoholic beverages, one per day is the max, while men should have no more than two (one drink is 12 ounces of beer, 5 ounces of wine, or 1.5 ounces of liquor). Drinking within these limits may lower your risk for several diseases, including the following.

What Alcohol Can Help

• **Heart disease**. Moderate drinking cuts the risk for heart attacks by 30 to 50 percent.

Alcohol raises HDL cholesterol—the good kind—by about 12 percent, makes blood less likely to clot, and has other heart-friendly qualities. Any type of alcohol helps, but some research suggests that wine protects the heart better than beer and liquor. That may be because wine, particularly red varieties, contains a potent antioxidant called resveratrol.

• **Strokes**. Researchers have also found that up to two drinks per day may slash in half the risk for ischemic strokes, the most common type, which occur when arteries that feed blood to the brain become blocked.

• **Diabetes**. People who drink small amounts of alcohol are more likely to maintain healthy blood sugar levels, research suggests. A Harvard study found that men who had one or two drinks per day cut their risk for type 2 diabetes by 36 percent.

• **Dementia**. Compared with abstainers, people who drink alcohol are 34 percent less likely to develop Alzheimer's disease and nearly 50 percent less likely to be diagnosed with other forms of dementia, such as those caused by diseased blood vessels. It's not clear why drinking guards against dementia, though it may be alcohol's capacity to maintain healthy blood flow to the brain.

What Alcohol Can Cause

• **Liver disease**. Between 10 and 20 percent of heavy drinkers develop cirrhosis, a serious condition caused as healthy liver tissue is replaced by scar tissue.

• **Cancer**. Drinking alcohol has been linked to many forms of this disease, including cancers of the mouth, throat, liver, **colon**, **rectum**, and, in women, breast. As for the latter, a study determined that alcohol **abuse** may be responsible for up to 11 percent of all breast cancer cases.

• **Obesity**. Wonder where beer **bellies** come from? Each can of ale or lager contains about 150 calories. A glass of Cabernet will set you back 127 calories.

• **High blood pressure**. If you have high blood pressure, cutting back on **booze** could produce a small but **significant** drop of 2 to 4 mm Hg **systolic** (the top number) and 1 to 2 mm Hg **diastolic** (the bottom number).

译文

饮酒对我有益吗？

适量饮酒可以防治疾病，但过量饮酒会对健康造成一系列的威胁。喜欢饮酒的女士每天最多只能饮一杯酒，而男士一天不应饮酒超过两杯（一杯的量指的是啤酒12盎司、红酒5盎司或者烈性酒1.5盎司）。将饮酒量控制在这个范围内，可以降低患以下几种疾病的风险。

饮酒有助于预防的疾病

• **心脏病**。适量饮酒可以使心脏病发作的风险降低30%至50%。

酒可以将血液中对人体有益的高密度脂蛋白胆固醇的含量提高12%左右，使得血液不易凝固，同时酒还具备对心脏有益的其他特质。任何酒都对心脏有益，但是某些研究显示，红酒对心脏的保护功效要比啤酒和烈性酒强。这可能与红酒，尤其是红葡萄酒中含有的一种名为"白藜芦醇"的强抗氧化剂有关。

• **中风**。研究人员还发现，每天饮酒不超过两杯可以使缺血性中风的发病风险降低一半。缺血性中风是最常见的一种中风类型，会在给大脑供血的动脉出现阻塞时发病。

• **糖尿病**。研究显示，少量饮酒的人更有可能保持正常的血糖水平。哈佛大学的一项研究发现，每天喝一到两杯酒的男性会将自身患II型糖尿病的风险降低36%。

• **痴呆**。与不饮酒的人相比，饮酒的人患老年痴呆症的可能性要低34%，患上其他类型的痴呆症，如血管疾病引发的痴呆症的几率要低将近50%。这可能是由于酒精具有保持大脑血液正常流动的特性，但饮酒能够预防痴呆的真正原因尚不清楚。

饮酒可能引发的疾病

·**肝病**。过量饮酒的人当中，有10%—20%的人患有肝硬化，产生这一危险状况的原因是健康的肝脏组织被瘢痕组织所取代。

·**癌症**。饮酒与多种癌症有关，包括口腔癌、咽喉癌、肝癌、结肠癌、直肠癌以及女性的乳腺癌。一项研究证实，所有的乳腺癌病例中，有高达11%的患者可能是由于过量饮酒而患病。

·**肥胖**。想知道啤酒肚是怎么产生的吗？每罐麦芽酒或窖藏啤酒中含有大约150卡路里的热量，而一杯"解百纳"红葡萄酒只含有127卡的热量。

·**高血压**。如果你患有高血压，那么减少饮酒会使你的心脏收缩压（高压数值）下降2至4毫米汞柱，心脏舒张压（低压数值）下降1至2毫米汞柱。下降的数值虽然不大，但对于患者病情的改善有着重大的意义。

💡 单词记事本

moderation [ˌmɒdəˈreɪʃn]
释 n. 温和；适度
用 in moderation (指吸烟、饮酒等)适度地，不过分

beverage [ˈbevərɪdʒ]
释 n. 酒水，饮料

cholesterol [kəˈlestərɒl]
释 n. 胆固醇

clot [klɒt]
释 n. 凝块；笨蛋 v. (使)凝结成块

particularly [pəˈtɪkjələli]
释 ad. 特别，尤其

potent [ˈpəʊtnt]
释 a. 强有力的，有说服力的；威力大的；(药等)效力大的
用 a potent argument 有力的论据

antioxidant [ˌænti'ɒksɪdənt]
释 n. 抗氧化剂

resveratrol [rɪzˈvɪrəˌtrɒl]
释 n. 白藜芦醇

stroke [strəʊk]
释 n. 中风；击，打击；击球；一次划水；一次努力；轻抚 v. 击球；抚摸
用 at a/one stroke 一下子，一举；stroke sb. down 平息某人的怒气

slash [slæʃ]
释 v. 砍；猛打；严厉地批评；大幅度削减 n. 砍，抽；削减；斜线
例 Upscale merchants *slash* prices and offer cheaper goods, making mainstream stores lose customers to discounters. 高档商家大幅度降价来为顾客提供更廉价的商品，这使得主流商店的很多客户都流失了。

ischemic [ɪˈskemɪk]
释 a. 缺血性的

artery [ˈɑːtəri]
释 n. 动脉；干线，要道

diabetes [ˌdaɪəˈbiːtiːz]
释 n. 糖尿病

dementia [dɪˈmenʃə]
释 n. 痴呆

abstainer　　　　　　　　[əbˈsteɪnə(r)]
释 n. 戒酒者；(投票)弃权者

vessel　　　　　　　　　[ˈvesl]
释 n. 船只(总称)；容器，器皿；血管，脉管

capacity　　　　　　　　[kəˈpæsəti]
释 n. 能力；容量；资格，地位；生产力
例 The expert said that shipping *capacity* would exceed the needs of the market by between 50% and 70% in the near future. 专家说，在不远的将来，船舶货运能力将超过市场需求的50%到70%之多。

cirrhosis　　　　　　　[səˈrəʊsɪs]
释 n. 肝硬化

tissue　　　　　　　[ˈtɪʃuː; ˈtɪsjuː]
释 n. (动植物的)组织；薄纱，织物；卫生纸；连篇谎言
用 facial tissues 面巾纸

colon　　　　　　　　[ˈkəʊlən]
释 n. 冒号；结肠

rectum　　　　　　　[ˈrektəm]
释 n. 直肠

abuse　　　　　　　　[əˈbjuːs]
释 n./v. 滥用；虐待；辱骂
用 abuse one's authority 滥用职权
例 32% of the adults sampled admitted having had problems with alcohol *abuse*. 参加抽样调查的成年人中有32%的人承认自己有酗酒的问题。

belly　　　　　　　　[ˈbeli]
释 n. 肚子

booze　　　　　　　　[buːz]
释 n. 烈性酒；酒宴 v. 痛饮

significant　　　　　　[sɪɡˈnɪfɪkənt]
释 a. 相当数量的；显著的；意义重大的
例 It suggests that obese people would have to exercise at least an hour at a time to see any *significant* difference in their weight. 这说明，肥胖人群要想看到体重出现显著的变化，每次的运动时间至少要一个小时。

systolic　　　　　　　[ˌsɪsˈtɒlɪk]
释 a. 心脏收缩的

diastolic　　　　　　[ˌdaɪəˈstɒlɪk]
释 a. 心脏舒张的

单词家族

各种疾病

albino [ælˈbiːnəʊ] n. 白化病者；白化现象

asphyxiate [əsˈfɪksieɪt] v. (使)无法呼吸；(使)窒息

asthmatic [æsˈmætɪk] a. 气喘的，患气喘病的 n. 气喘患者

astigmatic [ˌæstɪɡˈmætɪk] a. 散光的，乱视的

haemophilia [ˌhiːməˈfɪliə] n. 血友病；出血不止

irremediable [ˌɪrɪˈmiːdiəbl] a. 无法治愈的；不能挽回的

mumps [mʌmps] n. 腮腺炎

oafishness [ˈəʊfɪʃnəs] n. 痴呆

phobia [ˈfəʊbiə] n. 恐惧症；恐怖，憎恶

piteous [ˈpɪtiəs] a. 值得同情的，可怜的

pullulate [ˈpʌljʊleɪt] v. 繁殖；成长；发芽

septic [ˈseptɪk] a. 脓毒性的；败血病的

55

Passage 11

The Difficulty of Losing
Weight Is Captured in a New Model

The answer to obesity is obvious: eat less and exercise more. However, years of exhortation have failed to persuade most of those affected actually to do this. In particular, it is much harder to shift surplus lard once it has accumulated than it is to avoid putting it on in the first place. Oddly, though, a convenient mathematical model describing this fact has yet to be widely adopted. But a paper in this week's *Lancet*, by Kevin Hall of America's National Institutes of Health (NIH) and his colleagues, aims to change that.

The conventional rule for slimming, espoused by both the NIH and Britain's National Health Service, has the benefit of simplicity: cut 500 calories each day and lose half a kilo (about a pound) a week. Most experts, though, acknowledge that this rule is too blunt as it fails to account for shifts in the body's metabolism as the kilos pile on. Dr. Hall's model tries to do this. It also accounts for baseline characteristics that differ from person to person. Fat and muscle, for example, respond differently to shifts in diet, so the same intake will have one effect on a podgy person and another on a brawny one. The result is a more realistic assessment of what someone needs to do to get slim.

According to the old version, for example, abstaining from a daily 250-calorie bottle of cola would lead to the loss of 35kg over three years. Dr. Hall's model predicts an average loss of just 11kg. Furthermore, it also acknowledges that a dieter's weight will eventually reach a plateau—far more realistic than the old advice, which implied, incorrectly, that weight loss will continue steadily.

Gaining weight is easy. A surprisingly small imbalance, just ten extra calories a day, has driven the 9kg jump in the average American's weight over the past 30 years. The reason reversing such gains is hard is that servicing this extra flesh means a person's maintenance diet (the food required to keep his body ticking over) creeps up with his weight—and so does his appetite. That 9kg increase implies a daily maintenance diet that has 220 more calories in it than three decades ago. Returning to the average of the past means reversing every one of those 220 calories. Half-measures will result in a new equilibrium, but one that is still too heavy.

For example, a 23-year-old man who is 170cm tall should weigh 70kg, and be eating 2,294 calories a day. If he actually weighs 110kg he will be eating 3,080 calories to maintain his extra flesh and he thus needs to make a **permanent** cut of 786 calories from his daily diet if he is to get back to the 70kg **desideratum**. If he cuts less than this he will lose some weight, but eventually his intake will match the maintenance level for what he now weighs, and without further cuts his weight will **stabilize**. Someone who weighs 90kg, by contrast, need cut only 435 calories a day to get to his target—a far more **manageable** proposition.

In **principle**, the heavier person could make the necessary cuts in stages—reducing his daily intake again and again as he loses weight. In practice, that would take a will of iron, and the few people who have such **willpower** rarely get fat in the first place. The lesson, then, is to stay, rather than become, slim. Not easy, in a world whose economic **imperative** is to satisfy every appetite, but perhaps a little more **urgent** now Dr. Hall has put numbers on it.

译 文

新模式解读减肥难题

要想减肥很简单：少吃多动。然而，这样的老生常谈并没能成功劝服大多数肥胖之人去付诸行动。尤其是减掉身上堆积的多余脂肪要比刚开始就避免长出多余脂肪困难得多。奇怪的是，尽管如此，人们并没有广泛接受阐述这一事实的简单数学模型。但是就职于美国国立卫生研究院的凯文·哈尔及他的同事在这周的《柳叶刀》杂志上发表了一篇论文，旨在改变这一现状。

美国国立卫生研究院和英国国家卫生署所推崇的传统的瘦身法具有简单易行的好处：每天减少500卡路里的热量摄入，一星期就能减掉半公斤（约一磅）的重量。然而，多数专家认为这个标准太过死板，因为它没有考虑到当体重增加时，体内的新陈代谢也会发生变化。哈尔博士的模型则试图解决这一问题，同时它还会考虑到每个人不同的基本身体特征。比如，改变饮食后，脂肪和肌肉的相应反应就有所不同。因此，同样的摄入量对矮胖的人和健壮的人的影响也是不一样的。最后它会针对一个人需要怎样做才能成功减肥作出更加实际的评估。

比如，根据传统的方法，每天少喝一瓶热量为250卡路里的可乐，三年内就可以减掉35公斤。而根据哈尔博士的模型，平均减少的体重只有11公斤。不仅如此，该模式认为减肥者的体重最终会达到一个稳定阶段——这比以往的建议更加符合事实。以往的建议都错误地认为减肥者的体重将会一直平稳地降下去。

增肥很容易。在过去30年中，每天多摄入10卡路里这种微不足道的饮食失衡，已使美国人的平均体重暴增了9公斤。这些增加的体重很难减掉。这是由于体重的增加会带动一个人日常饮食量（维持身体正常运转需要的食物）的增加，胃口也会随之变大。这增加的9公斤意味着人们每天的正常饮食摄入量要比30年前增加220卡路里。要恢复到原来的平均体重，就表示每个人每天都应该减少220卡路里的热量摄入。折中的办法就是形成一个新的平衡，但这样，人们的体重将仍然超重。

举例来说，一位23岁、身高170厘米的男士的标准体重应该是70公斤，每天的摄入量为2294卡路里。但如果他的实际体重是110公斤，他就要摄入3080卡路里的热量以维持超出的体重。因此，如果他想减回70公斤的理想体重，他就需要每天坚持少摄入786卡路里的热量。如果他减少的摄入量小于这个数字，他的体重会下降一些，但是，最终摄入量会与体重水平匹配；如果摄入量不再减少，他的体重将会保持不变。相比而言，一个体重90公斤的人每天只需要减少435卡路里的热量摄入就能达到目标体重——这个目标明显更容易实现。

理论上，体重偏重的人可以分阶段地减少必需的饮食摄入——在减肥的过程中逐渐减少日常摄入量。事实上，这需要钢铁般的意志。很少有人有这样的意志力，而有这种意志力的人基本上不会变胖。因此，我们得到的教训就是：与其减肥，不如不要长胖。在当今这个世界，经济发展的使命就是要满足每个人的各种欲望，因此要不长胖确实不容易。但是，经过哈尔博士用具体数字说明之后，减肥这件事似乎变得比以前迫切了一些。

💡 单词记事本

obesity [əʊ'biːsəti]
释 n. 过度肥胖；肥胖症

obvious ['ɒbvɪəs]
释 a. 显然的，明显的

exhortation [ˌegzɔː'teɪʃn]
释 n. 讲道词，训词；劝告

surplus ['sɜːpləs]
释 a. 过剩的，多余的 n. 过剩，剩余；盈余，顺差
用 surplus value 剩余价值
例 We have a trade *surplus* of 600 million yuan. 我们有6亿元的贸易顺差。

accumulate [ə'kjuːmjəleɪt]
释 v. 积累，堆积；增加
例 It is worthwhile to invest savings when they *accumulate* to a certain sum. 当储蓄款积攒到一定数量的时候，拿来投资是值得的。

espouse [ɪ'spaʊz]
释 v. 支持，拥护

simplicity [sɪm'plɪsəti]
释 n. 简单，简易；直率，天真；朴素；无知，愚蠢

blunt [blʌnt]

释 *a.* 钝的；坦率的，不客气的 *v.* 使变钝

metabolism [mə'tæbəlɪzəm]

释 *n.* 新陈代谢

baseline ['beɪslaɪn]

释 *n.* 基线；底线 *a.* 基本的；原始的

characteristic [ˌkærəktə'rɪstɪk]

释 *a.* 特有的；典型的 *n.* 特性，特征

例 Windmills are a *characteristic* feature of the landscape of the Netherlands. 风车是荷兰风光的一个典型的特色。

intake ['ɪnteɪk]

释 *n.* 吸入，纳入；进气口，流入口；(一定时期内)进入或纳入的人数；摄取量

podgy ['pɒdʒi]

释 *a.* 矮胖的

brawny ['brɔːni]

释 *a.* (人)强壮的

assessment [ə'sesmənt]

释 *n.* 评估；核定的付款额；估价

例 Countries like the UK, France, and Germany always measure up in *assessments* of European science, whether by funding or citations. 在欧洲科学评估中，英国、法国和德国等国家无论是在资金还是引证方面都符合要求。

abstain [əb'steɪn]

释 *v.* 戒掉；弃权

predict [prɪ'dɪkt]

释 *v.* 预言，预测

dieter ['daɪətə(r)]

释 *n.* 节食者

plateau ['plætəʊ]

释 *n.* 高原；(上升后的)稳定时期(或状态)

maintenance ['meɪntənəns]

释 *n.* 保持，维持；维护，维修；抚养费

tick [tɪk]

释 *n.* 记号；滴答声 *v.* 给…标记号；滴答地记录；正常运转

用 tick away/by (时间一分一秒地)过去

equilibrium [ˌiːkwɪ'lɪbriəm; ˌekwɪ'lɪbriəm]

释 *n.* 平衡；平静

permanent ['pɜːmənənt]

释 *a.* 长期的；永久的，永恒的

例 The *permanent* achievements of her reign were not surpassed by any other ruler of the age. 她统治时期所取得的持久性的功绩是同时代的其他统治者所不能超越的。

desideratum [dɪˌzɪdə'raːtəm; dɪˌzɪdə'reɪtəm]

释 *n.* 必需品；所愿之物

stabilize ['steɪbəlaɪz]

释 *v.* 稳定，稳固

manageable ['mænɪdʒəbl]

释 *a.* 易管理的；易控制的，能处理的

principle ['prɪnsəpl]

释 *n.* 原则，原理；[*pl.*]道德准则，基本信念；道义，操守；工作原理，操作方法

willpower ['wɪlpaʊə(r)]

释 *n.* 毅力，意志力

imperative [ɪm'perətɪv]

释 *a.* 必要的，极重要的；必须服从的，强制的 *n.* 必要的事，必须履行的责任

例 Once a patient hits his target weight, she says, it's *imperative* that he stick with his exercise and diet regimen to maintain his new weight. 她说，一旦患者达到了目标体重，他必须要做的就是坚持锻炼和控制饮食，以继续保持新的体重。

urgent ['ɜːdʒənt]

释 *a.* 迫切的，紧急的

健康生活

abstinent ['æbstɪnənt] *a.* 饮食有度的；有节制的

badminton ['bædmɪntən] *n.* 羽毛球运动

bowling ['bəʊlɪŋ] *n.* 保龄球运动

cater ['keɪtə(r)] *v.* 迎合，满足需要；提供饮食及服务

cellulose ['seljuləʊs] *n.* 纤维素

cider ['saɪdə(r)] *n.* 苹果酒

cricket ['krɪkɪt] *n.* 板球

culinary ['kʌlɪnəri] *a.* 厨房的，烹调用的

dine [daɪn] *v.* 吃饭，进餐

fig [fɪg] *n.* 无花果；一点儿

healthful ['helθfl] *a.* 有益健康的

maize [meɪz] *n.* 玉米；玉蜀黍；玉米色 *a.* 玉米色的

potable ['pəʊtəbl] *a.* 适于饮用的

recipe ['resəpi] *n.* 烹饪法，食谱；秘诀，诀窍；处方，照处方配成的药

refresh [rɪ'freʃ] *v.* (使)精神振作，(使)精力恢复；(使)更新，(使)得到补充

winnow ['wɪnəʊ] *v.* 把(谷物的)杂质吹掉，筛掉(米糠等)

We learn more from failure than from success.

—Samuel Smiles

我们从失败中学到的东西要比从成功中学到的多得多。

——塞缪尔·斯迈尔斯

Passage 12

Why We Pay More Attention to Beautiful People

They say that physical beauty is only skin deep. But is there more to it? Research has shown that individuals tend to find attractive people more intelligent, friendly and competent than others. But do we pay more attention to attractive people?

A University of British Columbia study has found that people identify the personality traits of people who are physically attractive more accurately than others during short encounters.

The study, published in *Psychological Science*, suggests people pay closer attention to people they find attractive, and is the latest scientific evidence of the advantages of perceived beauty. The goal of the study was to determine whether a person's attractiveness impacts others' ability to discern their personality traits, says Prof. Jeremy Biesanz, UBC Dept. of Psychology, who co-authored the study with PhD. student Lauren Human and undergraduate student Genevieve Lorenzo.

For the study, researchers placed more than 75 male and female participants into groups of 5 to 11 people for three-minute, one-on-one conversations. After each interaction, study participants rated partners on physical attractiveness and five major personality traits: openness, conscientiousness, extraversion, agreeableness and neuroticism. Each person also rated their own personality.

Researchers were able to determine the accuracy of people's perceptions by comparing participants' ratings of others' personality traits with how individuals rated their own traits, says Biesanz, adding that steps were taken to control for the positive bias that can occur in self-reporting.

Despite an overall positive bias towards people they found attractive (as expected from previous research), study participants identified the "relative ordering" of personality traits of attractive participants more accurately than others, researchers found.

"If people think Jane is beautiful, and she is very organized and somewhat generous, people will see her as more organized and generous than she actually is," says Biesanz. "Despite this bias, our study shows that people will also correctly discern the relative ordering of Jane's personality traits—that she is more organized than generous—better than others they find less attractive."

The researchers say this is because people are motivated to pay closer attention to beautiful people for many reasons, including curiosity, romantic interest or a desire for friendship or social status. "Not only do we judge books by their covers, we read the ones with beautiful covers much closer than others," says Biesanz, noting the study focused on first impressions of personality in social situations, like cocktail parties.

Although participants largely agreed on group members' attractiveness, the study reaffirms that beauty is in the eye of the beholder. Participants were best at identifying the personalities of people they found attractive, regardless of whether others found them attractive.

According to Biesanz, scientists spent considerable efforts a half-century ago seeking to determine what types of people perceive personality best, to largely mixed results. With this study, the team chose to investigate this longstanding question from another direction, he says, focusing not on who judges personality best, but rather whether some people's personalities are better perceived.

译文

为什么我们更关注好看的人？

人们说外在美是肤浅的。不过，外在美是否具有更深层次的含义呢？研究显示，人们常常认为有魅力的人比其他人更聪明、友好，也更有能力。但是，我们真的会更加关注有魅力的人吗？

英属哥伦比亚大学的一项研究发现，在短暂的邂逅中，相对于其他人而言，人们能更加准确地判断出外表好看的人的个人品质。

这项发表在《心理科学》上的研究指出，人们更加注意那些他们认为有魅力的人，这也是所谓"外在美"能带来优势的最新科学依据。英属哥伦比亚大学心理学系教授杰里米·毕森兹说，这项研究的目的是确定一个人的吸引力是否会影响其他人辨别其个人品质的能力。而此项研究就是由杰里米·毕森兹教授和博士生洛朗·休曼以及本科生吉纳维芙·洛伦佐合作发表的。

为了进行此项研究，研究者将超过75名男女参与者分为5至11人的小组，并让他们进行为时三分钟的一对一交流。每组的交流结束后，参与者要对搭档的外表吸引力和五个主要的个性特征，即坦率、责任心、外向性、随和性和神经质的程度作出评价。此外，每个人也需要对自己的个性特征进行评价。

毕森兹说，通过将参与者对他人和自己的个性特征的评价进行对比，研究者们能够确定人们感知的准确度。他还补充说，一些措施还被用于控制在自我评定中可能会产生的积极偏向。

研究者们发现，尽管总体上参与者对他们认为有魅力的人存在积极偏向（根据之前的研究也可以预测到），但他给出的外表好看的参与者的个性品质"相对顺序"要比其他人的更准确。

"如果人们认为简长得好看，而简做事非常有条理，为人还有点儿慷慨，人们就会认为她比实际上更有条理，也更慷慨。"毕森兹说，"尽管有此倾向，我们的研究仍然表明，相对于他们认为不够有吸引力的人，他们能更好地察觉出简的人格特征的相对顺序——她虽慷慨，但她更有条理。"

研究者们认为，这是由于人们受到多种因素的驱使，故而更加关注好看的人。这些因素包括好奇心、男女之间的吸引力或者对友情和社会地位的渴望。毕森兹说："我们不只会以貌取人，还会对外貌漂亮的人更加关注。"他指出，这项研究主要以在社交场合中，比如在鸡尾酒会上，人们的个人品质给人留下的第一印象为研究对象。

尽管参与者在组内成员是否有吸引力的问题上大体达成了一致，但这项研究还重新证实了"美在观者眼中"的观点。参与者们最擅长识别他们认为有魅力的人的个性，而不在乎其他人是否认为他们好看。

根据毕森兹所说，在半世纪之前，科学家们花费了相当大的努力，试图确定哪种类型的人最擅长辨别他人的个性，结果是各占一半。他说，通过这项研究，他们的团队从另一个角度探索了这个由来已久的问题：他们没有致力于研究谁最擅长判断他人的个性，而是研究是否有一些人的个性更容易被别人鉴别。

💡 单词记事本

intelligent [ɪnˈtelɪdʒənt]
释 a. 聪明的，有才智的

competent [ˈkɒmpɪtənt]
释 a. 有能力的，能胜任的；不错的

identify [aɪˈdentɪfaɪ]
释 v. 识别，鉴定；把…等同于；认为与…有关系
用 identify oneself with 支持；参与；与…密切结合；和…打成一片

trait [treɪt]
释 n. 个性特点；显著特征；一点儿，少许
用 a trait of 一点儿，少许，微量

accurately [ˈækjərətli]
释 ad. 正确地；精确地

discern [dɪˈsɜːn]
释 v. 辨别，察觉，了解；看出，认出

co-author [ˌkəʊˈɔːθə(r)]
释 v. 合著，合作

undergraduate [ˌʌndə'grædʒuət]

释 n. 大学生

用 undergraduate courses 本科课程

interaction [ˌɪntər'ækʃn]

释 n. 相互作用，互动；交流

conscientiousness [ˌkɒnʃi'enʃəsnəs]

释 n. 良心，责任心

extraversion [ˌekstrə'vɜːʃn]

释 n. 外向性

agreeableness [ə'griːəblnəs]

释 n. 适合；一致；随和性

neuroticism [njʊə'rɒtɪsɪzəm]

释 n. 神经质；神经过敏症

accuracy ['ækjərəsi]

释 n. 准确(性)，精确(性)

rating ['reɪtɪŋ]

释 n. 等级，级别；[pl.](电视节目、唱片等的)收视率，收听率，普及率；(个人在财务上的)信誉，信用程度

positive ['pɒzətɪv]

释 a. 积极的；正的；正极的；确定的，肯定的；实际的，真实的

例 I'm trying to be more *positive* in dealing with problems. 我在尝试以更加积极的心态解决问题。

bias ['baɪəs]

释 n. 偏见，偏心；偏斜 v. 对…有偏见

例 New research suggests that you may have been subjected to a cognitive distortion called "restraint *bias*". 新的研究认为，你可能遭受了一种被称为"克制偏见"的认知扭曲。

generous ['dʒenərəs]

释 a. 慷慨的，大方的；宽宏大量的

motivate ['məʊtɪveɪt]

释 v. 使有动机，驱使；刺激，激励

例 It's really critical to ensure that your people are *motivated*. 确保你的员工受到了激励是至关重要的。

cocktail ['kɒkteɪl]

释 n. 鸡尾酒；混合物

reaffirm [ˌriːə'fɜːm]

释 v. 重申，再确认

beholder [bɪ'həʊldə(r)]

释 n. 旁观者，观看者

investigate [ɪn'vestɪgeɪt]

释 v. 调查，研究

longstanding [ˌlɒŋ'stændɪŋ]

释 a. 长期存在的；长时间的

💡 单词家族

穿衣打扮

attire [ə'taɪə(r)] *n.* 服装，衣服

beautician [bjuː'tɪʃn] *n.* 美容师

bonnet ['bɒnɪt] *n.* (婴儿和旧时女子戴的)在颏下系带的帽子

boutique [buː'tiːk] *n.* 精品店；专卖流行衣服的小商店

cosmetic [kɒz'metɪk] *n.* 化妆品

customize ['kʌstəmaɪz] *v.* 定制

dandy ['dændi] *n.* 过分注意衣着和外表的男人；花花公子

epaulet ['epəlet] *n.* 肩章，肩饰

faddish ['fædɪʃ] *a.* 流行一时的；时尚的

frock [frɒk] *n.* 连衣裙

garment ['gɑːmənt] *n.* 衣服；外表

henna ['henə] n. 指甲花；散沫花；棕红色

luxurious [lʌɡ'ʒʊəriəs] a. 奢侈的，豪华的；极舒适的

magenta [mə'dʒentə] n. 洋红色；洋红染料 a. 洋红色的

obsolescent [ˌɒbsə'lesnt] a. 逐渐被废弃的；即将过时的

panache [pə'næʃ] n. 神气十足；派头

plush [plʌʃ] n. 长毛绒 a. 豪华的

poncho ['pɒntʃəʊ] n. 斗篷；雨衣

primp [prɪmp] v. 精心打扮

recherche [rə'ʃeəʃeɪ] a. 精选的

ribbon ['rɪbən] n. 缎带，丝带

ringlet ['rɪŋlət] n. 下垂的长卷发

ritzy ['rɪtsi] a. 时髦的；豪华的；文雅的

sash [sæʃ] n. 腰带；肩带

sleek [sliːk] a. (毛发等)光滑而有光泽的；时髦的

toiletry ['tɔɪlətrɪ] n. 化妆品；化妆用具

vogue [vəʊɡ] n. 时尚；流行；流行物

No great people complain that they are short of opportunity.

—Ralph Waldo Emerson

没有一个伟人抱怨自己缺乏机会。

——R. W. 爱默生

Passage 13

 原 文

Life's Too Short for So Much E-mail

Just thinking about my e-mail in-box makes me sad.

This month alone, I received more than 6,000 e-mails. That doesn't include spam, **notifications** or daily deals, either. With all those messages, I have no desire to respond to even a **fraction** of them. I can just picture my **tombstone**: "Here lies Nick Bilton, who responded to thousands of e-mails a month. May he rest in peace."

It's not that I'm so popular.

Royal Pingdom, which monitors Internet usage, said that in 2010, 107 **trillion** e-mails were sent. A report this year from the Radicati Group, a market research firm, found that in 2011, there were 3.1 billion active e-mail accounts in the world. The report noted that, on average, **corporate** employees sent and received 105 e-mails a day.

Sure, some of those e-mails are important. But 105 a day?

All of this has led me to believe that something is **terribly** wrong with e-mail. What's more, I don't believe it can be fixed.

I've tried everything. **Priority** mail, **filters**, more filters, filters within filters, away messages, third-party e-mail tools. None of these supposed solutions work.

Last year, I decided to try to reach In-box Zero, the Zen-like state of a **consistently** empty in-box. I spent **countless** hours one evening replying to **neglected** messages. I woke up the next morning to find that most of my replies had received replies, and so, once again, my in-box was brimming. It all felt like one big practical joke.

Meanwhile, all of this e-mail could be increasing our stress.

A research report issued this year by the University of California, Irvine, found that people who did not look at e-mail regularly at work were less stressed and more **productive** than others.

Gloria Mark, an **informatics** professor who studies the effects of e-mail and **multitasking** in the workplace and is a co-author of the study, said, "One person in our e-mail study told us after: I let the sound of the bell and **pop-ups** rule my life."

Ms. Mark says one of the main problems with e-mail is that there isn't an off switch.

"E-mail is an **asynchronous** technology, so you don't need to be on it to receive a message," she said. "**Synchronous** technologies, like **instant** messenger, depend on people being present."Although some people allow their instant messenger services to save **offline** messages, most cannot receive messages if they are not logged on. With e-mail, it is different. If you go away, e-mails pile up waiting for your return.

Avoiding new messages is as impossible as trying to play a game of hide-and-seek in an empty New York City studio apartment. There is nowhere to hide.

I recently sent an e-mail to a teenage cousin who responded with a text message. I responded again through e-mail, and this time she answered with Facebook Messenger. She was obviously seeing the e-mails but kept choosing a more **concise** way to reply. Our conversation moved to Twitter's direct messages, where it was ended quickly by the 140-character limit.

Later, we talked about the exchanges, and she explained that she saw e-mail as something for "old people." It's too slow for her, and the messages are too long. Sometimes, she said, as with a Facebook status update, you don't even need to respond at all.

Since technology hasn't solved the problem it has created with e-mail, it looks as if some younger people might come up with their own answer—not to use e-mail at all.

So I'm taking a **cue** from them.

I'll look at my e-mail as it comes in. Maybe I'll respond with a text, Google Chat, Twitter or Facebook message. But chances are, as with many messages sent via Facebook or Twitter, I won't need to respond at all.

译文

生命太短，邮件太长

只要一想到我收件箱里的邮件我就感到难受。

仅仅在这个月内，我就收到了超过6000封邮件。这还不包括垃圾邮件、消息通知和每日团购邮件。面对这么多邮件，我一封也不想回复。我能想象我的墓碑上刻着这样一句话："这里躺着的是尼克·比尔顿，他每个月要回数千封邮件，愿他安息。"

这也并不是因为我受欢迎。

网络使用监控公司皇家平多姆提到，在2010年共有107万亿封邮件被发送。今年市场调查公司瑞迪卡迪集团的一份报告则称，在2011年，全世界有31亿个活跃的电子邮箱。报告指出，公司员工平均每天要收发105封邮件。

诚然，其中有些邮件的确是重要的。不过每天105封邮件也太多了吧？

所有这些让我觉得电子邮件有什么地方不对劲了。而且，我认为它已经病入膏肓了。

我尝试了各种方法：优先级邮件、过滤器、更多的过滤器、过滤过滤器的过滤器、离线消息自动回复以及第三方电邮工具，结果没有一种方法管用。

去年，我决定试着做到"收件箱为零"，也就是将收件箱一直保持在零封新邮件的状态。我耗费了一个晚上的很多时间去回复被忽略的邮件，然而第二天醒来发现我回复的大部分邮件又有了新的回复。如此循环往复，我的收件箱又塞满了。这简直就像是个大恶作剧！

而同时，所有这些邮件还会不断地增加我们的压力。

今年加州大学欧文分校的一份研究报告发现，工作时不去定时检查邮件的人比其他人压力小且效率高。

格洛丽亚·马克是一名信息学教授，她研究电子邮件的效用和工作场所的多任务化，也是上述研究报告的合著者。她说："这项邮件课题研究的一位参与者后来告诉我们：'邮件声音提醒和弹出窗口主宰了我的生活。'"

马克女士称目前电邮的主要问题之一就是缺少一个关闭开关。

"电子邮件采用的是一种非同步的技术，所以你不用在线也能收到消息。"她说，"而同步技术，像即时通信软件，需要使用者一直在线。"虽然有些人允许他们的即时通信软件保存离线消息，但只要不登录，大部分人就收不到消息。电子邮件就不一样了。你不在的时候，电子邮件堆在那里等你回来。

避开新的邮件就像要在纽约市的一间空荡荡的公寓里玩捉迷藏一样不可能，因为根本无处可藏。

我最近给小表妹发了封电子邮件，她用手机短信回复了我。我又给她回了一封邮件，这回她用脸谱网的短消息回复了我。显然她看到了邮件，但之后她选择了一种更简洁的方式回复我。我们的谈话之后转移到了推特的私信上，因为它有140个字的限制，所以非常快捷。

后来，我们聊到了交流平台的转变，她说她认为电邮是那些"跟不上时代的人"才用的。电邮对她来说太慢，也太冗长了。她说，有时候你把脸谱网的状态更新了之后，甚至都不用回复。

在技术不能解决电邮所产生的问题的情况下，或许一些年轻人已经有了他们的解决方法，那就是干脆不用电子邮件了。

于是我打算照他们的方法来做。

以后收到邮件我会先看看，然后我可能会用短信、谷歌聊天软件、推特或者脸谱网的短消息功能等回复。但很可能的是，通过脸谱网或者推特发布了很多信息之后，我根本都不用回复了。

notification [ˌnəʊtɪfɪˈkeɪʃn]
释 *n.* 通知，通告

fraction [ˈfrækʃn]
释 *n.* (某物的)小部分，少许；分数；小数
用 decimal fraction 小数
例 I got the shoes at a *fraction* of the original price. 我以远远低于原价的价格买到了这双鞋。

tombstone [ˈtuːmstəʊn]
释 *n.* 墓碑

trillion [ˈtrɪljən]
释 *num.* 万亿(个)

corporate [ˈkɔːpərət]
释 *a.* 团体的，共同的；公司的

terribly [ˈterəbli]
释 *ad.* 可怕地；很，非常

priority [praɪˈɒrəti]
释 *n.* 在先，居前；优先权，优先考虑的事
例 There has been a measurable change in society's commitment to literacy. Reading has become a higher *priority*. 社会对读写能力的认识发生了巨大改变。读书变得更加重要。

filter [ˈfɪltə(r)]
释 *n.* 过滤器 *v.* 过滤；(消息等)走漏
用 filter tip 香烟的过滤嘴
例 The news of the defeat *filtered* through from London last night. 昨晚，从伦敦传来了战败的消息。

consistently [kənˈsɪstəntli]
释 *ad.* 一贯地，始终如一地

countless [ˈkaʊntləs]
释 *a.* 无数的，多得数不清的

neglected [nɪˈglektɪd]
释 *a.* 被忽视的

productive [prəˈdʌktɪv]
释 *a.* 生产(性)的，有生产能力的；多产的，富有成效的
用 a productive meeting 富有成效的会议

informatics [ˌɪnfəˈmætɪks]
释 *n.* 信息学

multitasking [ˌmʌltiˈtɑːskɪŋ]
释 *n.* 多重任务处理

pop-up [ˈpɒpʌp]
释 *a.* 弹起的；有自动起跳装置的 *n.* 弹出窗口

asynchronous [eɪˈsɪŋkrənəs]
释 *a.* 异步的，不同时的

synchronous [ˈsɪŋkrənəs]
释 *a.* 同时发生的，同步的

instant [ˈɪnstənt]
释 *a.* 立即的，即刻的；紧急的；(食品)速溶的 *n.* 瞬间；立即；片刻
用 for an instant 片刻，一瞬间；on the instant 立即，马上；in an instant 立即；from instant to instant 时时刻刻；the instant... 一…（就…）；instant coffee 速溶咖啡

offline [ˌɒfˈlaɪn]
释 *a.* 下线的，离线的

avoid [əˈvɔɪd]
释 *v.* 避开，躲开；避免；撤销
例 Participants could earn a prize only if they *avoided* smoking for the entire 95-minute film. 参与者只要在接下来看电影的95分钟里面没有吸烟，就能获得奖金。

concise [kən'saɪs]

释 *a.* 简洁的；简明的

cue [kjuː]

释 *n.* 提示，暗示，线索；榜样；球杆

v. 提示，暗示，给…提供线索

用 (right) on cue 恰好在这时候；take one's cue from 学…的样

💡 单词家族

生活琐事

aeration [eə'reɪʃn] *n.* 通风

affinity [ə'fɪnəti] *n.* 密切关系；吸引

ajar [ə'dʒɑː(r)] *a.* (门、窗等)微开的

bicker ['bɪkə(r)] *v.* 争吵，发生口角

brawl [brɔːl] *v.* 争吵，怒骂

chafe [tʃeɪf] *v.* 恼怒，不耐烦；擦破

circumspect ['sɜːkəmspekt] *a.* 慎重的；周到的

confide [kən'faɪd] *v.* 向某人吐露，倾诉；充分信赖

consecutive [kən'sekjətɪv] *a.* 连续不断的

digression [daɪ'greʃn] *n.* 离题；偏离特定路线；脱轨

discrepancy [dɪs'krepənsi] *n.* 不同，矛盾

dissenter [dɪ'sentə(r)] *n.* 反对者

dissenting [dɪ'sentɪŋ] *a.* 不同意的

divergence [daɪ'vɜːdʒəns] *n.* 分歧

drainage ['dreɪnɪdʒ] *n.* 排水(系统)

entail [ɪn'teɪl] *v.* 牵涉；需要；使承担；使(某事物)成为必要

entanglement [ɪn'tæŋglmənt] *n.* 纠缠

fray [freɪ] *v.* 打斗，争吵，争辩

hassle ['hæsl] *n.* 激烈的辩论，争吵；困难；斗争

launder ['lɔːndə(r)] *v.* 洗熨(衣物等)

leaky ['liːki] *a.* 漏的

nuisance ['njuːsns] *n.* 令人讨厌的人(或东西)；麻烦事

perplexing [pə'pleksɪŋ] *a.* 复杂的；令人费解的

purported [pə'pɔːtɪd] *a.* 谣传的；声张的

querulous ['kwerələs; 'kwerjələs] *a.* 抱怨的，爱发牢骚的；易怒的，暴躁的

redundant [rɪ'dʌndənt] *a.* 多余的；过量的

sanitation [ˌsænɪ'teɪʃn] *n.* 环境卫生；卫生设施

sewer ['suːə(r); 'sjuːə(r)] *n.* 下水道，排水管

shutter ['ʃʌtə(r)] *n.* 百叶窗；(照相机的)快门

subsidise ['sʌbsɪdaɪz] *v.* 津贴，资助

trifling ['traɪflɪŋ] *a.* 微小的，不重要的

Chapter ②

社会热点

Passage 14

音频

原 文

More UK Universities
Should Be Profiting from Ideas

A recurring criticism of the UK's university sector is its perceived weakness in translating new knowledge into new products and services.

Recently, the UK National Stem Cell Network warned the UK could lose its place among the world leaders in stem cell research unless adequate funding and legislation could be assured. We should take this concern seriously as universities are key in the national innovation system.

However, we do have to challenge the unthinking complaint that the sector does not do enough in taking ideas to market. The most recent comparative data on the performance of universities and research institutions in Australia, Canada, USA and UK shows that, from a relatively weak starting position, the UK now leads on many indicators of commercialization activity.

When viewed at the national level, the policy interventions of the past decade have helped transform the performance of UK universities. Evidence suggests the UK's position is much stronger than in the recent past and is still showing improvement. But national data masks the very large variation in the performance of individual universities. The evidence shows that a large number of universities have fallen off the back of the pack, a few perform strongly and the rest chase the leaders.

This type of uneven distribution is not peculiar to the UK and is mirrored across other economies. In the UK, research is concentrated: less than 25% of universities receive 75% of the research funding. These same universities are also the institutions producing the greatest share of PhD graduates, science citations, patents and licence income. The effect of policies generating long-term resource concentration has also created a distinctive set of universities which are research-led and commercially active. It seems clear that the concentration of research and commercialization work creates differences between universities.

The core objective for universities which are research-led must be to maximize the impact of their research efforts. These universities should be generating the widest range of social, economic and environmental benefits. In return for the scale of investment, they should share their expertise in order to build greater confidence in the sector.

Part of the economic recovery of the UK will be driven by the next generation of research commercialization **spilling** out of our universities. There are three dozen universities in the UK which are actively **engaged** in **advanced** research training and commercialization work.

If there were a greater **coordination** of technology **transfer** offices within regions and a **simultaneous** investment in the scale and functions of our graduate schools, universities could, and should, play a key role in positioning the UK for the next growth cycle.

译文

应有更多英国大学正在从创意中获益

针对英国的大学反复出现的一项批评就是它在将新知识转化成新产品和服务方面存在明显的缺陷。

最近，英国国家干细胞网络发出警告：如果没有充足的资金和立法保障，英国可能会失去其在干细胞研究领域的世界领先地位。我们应当认真考虑这一警告，因为大学是国家创新体系的关键所在。

然而，仅仅不经思考地抱怨大学在将想法投放到市场时做得不够是不行的，我们必须对此提出质疑。最近对澳大利亚、加拿大、美国和英国的大学和研究机构的业绩所作的比较数据显示：虽然起点相对较低，但英国如今在许多商业化活动的指标方面都处于领先地位。

从国家层面来看，在过去十年中采取的政策干预措施已经帮助英国大学的业绩发生了转变。证据表明英国大学的地位比过去几年更加稳固，而且仍在取得进步。但是国家数据掩盖了各个大学的表现之间所存在的巨大差异。该证据表明许多大学已经远远落后，少数大学进展飞速，而剩余大学则在追赶着这些领先者。

这种分布不均衡的状态并非英国独有，其他经济体也都出现了这一现象。在英国，研究比较集中：不到25%的大学获得了75%的研究资金。这些大学在培养博士毕业生、发表科学文献、发明专利和获得许可证收入方面同样也是最多的。导致长期资源集中的政策所产生的影响还造就了一批出色的大学，它们在研究方面处于领先地位，在商业方面也表现活跃。似乎很明显，研究和商业化运作的集中使各所大学之间产生了差异。

以研究为主导的大学的核心目标必须是使其研究成果产生最大化的效果。这些大学应当产生最大范围内的社会、经济和环境效益。为了换取投资规模，他们应当分享其专业技术，以使社会对大学产生更大的信心。

英国的经济复苏一定程度上要靠我们大学中涌现出来的下一代商业化研究成果来驱动。英国目前有36所大学正在积极进行先进的研究培训和商业化运作。

如果各地区的技术转化部门之间能有更好的协作，同时对我们的研究生院在规模和功能方面进行投资，那么大学就能够而且应当在英国下一轮的经济增长中发挥至关重要的作用。

🔆 单词记事本

recurring [rɪˈkɜː(r)ɪŋ]
释 *a.* 反复的；再发生的
例 Some of my *recurring* resolutions came year in, year out. 年复一年，我下着同样的决心。

weakness [ˈwiːknəs]
释 *n.* 软弱；弱点；薄弱；癖好
例 You should have a clear knowledge of your *weakness.* 你应该清楚自己的弱点所在。

translate [trænsˈleɪt; trænzˈleɪt]
释 *v.* 翻译；转化；调动；解释，说明

adequate [ˈædɪkwət]
释 *a.* 足够的；适当的
用 be adequate for 胜任
例 There was not *adequate* preparation for the war. 战争没有经过充分的准备。

legislation [ˌledʒɪsˈleɪʃn]
释 *n.* 法律；立法

innovation [ˌɪnəˈveɪʃn]
释 *n.* 新事物；创新；改革，革新

unthinking [ʌnˈθɪŋkɪŋ]
释 *a.* 未经思考的；考虑不周的

comparative [kəmˈpærətɪv]
释 *a.* 比较的，相比的；相对的

institution [ˌɪnstɪˈtjuːʃn]
释 *n.* 公共机构；制度；习俗；设立

transform [trænsˈfɔːm]
释 *v.* 转变，改变；转换；改造
例 It was an accident that *transformed* my life. 一场意外改变了我的生活。

mask [maːsk]
释 *v.* 掩饰；遮盖 *n.* 面具，面罩；伪装

variation [ˌveəriˈeɪʃn]
释 *n.* 变化，变动；变异，变种；变奏

uneven [ʌnˈiːvn]
释 *a.* 不平坦的；不均匀的；不一致的

distribution [ˌdɪstrɪˈbjuːʃn]
释 *n.* 分发；配给物；分布

peculiar [pɪˈkjuːliə(r)]
释 *a.* 奇怪的；独特的；私有的

patent [ˈpeɪtnt]
释 *n.* 专利证书，许可证；专利权 *a.* 有专利的；受专利保护的；明显的

distinctive [dɪˈstɪŋktɪv]
释 *a.* 出众的；有特色的
例 Clothes with *distinctive* style are popular. 有特色的衣服受欢迎。

maximize [ˈmæksɪmaɪz]
释 *v.* 使增至最大限度

range [reɪndʒ]
释 *n.* 一系列；幅度；范围 *v.* (在某范围内)变动
用 in the range of 在…范围之内

例 It is difficult to find a car in our price *range*. 很难找到一辆我们能买得起的车。

expertise [ˌekspɜː'tiːz]
释 *n.* 专门知识或技能，专长

spill [spɪl]
释 *v.* 溢，溅；涌出；摔下 *n.* 溢出；摔下；泄露；木片
用 oil spill 漏油；spill over 溢出

engage [ɪn'ɡeɪdʒ]
释 *v.* 从事，忙于；雇用；占用

advanced [əd'vɑːnst]
释 *a.* 先进的；前进的；超前的；高级的

coordination [kəʊˌɔːdɪ'neɪʃn]
释 *n.* 协调；协作

transfer
释 ['trænsfɜː(r)] *n.* 转移；换乘
['trænsˈfɜː(r)] *v.* 转移；调动；转让；换乘
用 data transfer 数据传送
例 Please *transfer* at the next station. 请在下一站换乘。

simultaneous [ˌsɪml'teɪniəs]
释 *a.* 同时的；同步的

💡 单词家族

科学研究

configuration [kənˌfɪɡə'reɪʃn] *n.* 结构；组合
construe [kən'struː] *v.* 分析；翻译
dilute [daɪ'luːt; daɪ'ljuːt] *v.* 稀释
fusion ['fjuːʒn] *n.* 熔化；核聚变
infrared [ˌɪnfrə'red] *a.* 红外线的
originator [ə'rɪdʒɪneɪtə(r)] *n.* 发起者；起因
postulate ['pɒstjuleɪt] *v.* 假定；假设

precursor [priː'kɜːsə(r)] *n.* 先驱；先兆
quest [kwest] *n./v.* 搜寻；探索
refinement [rɪ'faɪnmənt] *n.* 精炼；改进的地方
substantiate [səb'stænʃieɪt] *v.* 使具体化；证实
unsubstantiated [ˌʌnsəb'stænʃieɪtɪd] *a.* 未经证实的

Passage 15

Caught in the Web

A few months ago, it wasn't unusual for 47-year-old Carla Toebe to spend 15 hours per day online. She'd wake up early, turn on her laptop and chat on Internet dating sites and instant-messaging programs—leaving her bed for only brief intervals. Her household bills piled up, along with the dishes and dirty laundry, but it took near-constant complaints from her four daughters before she realized she had a problem.

"I was starting to feel like my whole world was falling apart—kind of slipping into a depression," said Carla. "I knew that if I didn't get off the dating sites, I'd just keep going," detaching herself further from the outside world.

Toebe's conclusion: She felt like she was "addicted" to the Internet. She's not alone.

Concern about excessive Internet use isn't new. As far back as 1995, articles in medical journals and the establishment of a Pennsylvania treatment center for overusers generated interest in the subject. There's still no consensus on how much time online constitutes too much or whether addiction is possible.

But as reliance on the Web grows, there are signs that the question is getting more serious attention: Last month, a study published in *CNS Spectrums* claimed to be the first large-scale look at excessive Internet use. The new *CNS Spectrums* study was based on results of a nationwide telephone survey of more than 2,500 adults. Like the 2005 survey, this one was conducted by Stanford University researchers. About 6% of respondents reported that "their relationships suffered because of excessive Internet use". About 9% attempted to conceal "nonessential Internet use", and nearly 4% reported feeling "preoccupied by the Internet when offline". About 8% said they used the Internet as a way to escape problems, and almost 14% reported they "found it hard to stay away from the Internet for several days at a time".

Excessive Internet use should be defined not by the number of hours spent online but "in terms of losses", said Maressa Orzack, a Harvard University professor. "If it's a loss [where] you're not getting to work, and family relationships are breaking down as a result, then it's too much."

Since the early 1990s, several clinics have been established in the U.S. to treat heavy Internet users. They include the Center for Internet Addiction Recovery and the Center for Internet Behavior.

The website for Orzack's center lists the following among the **psychological symptoms** of computer addiction:

- Having a sense of well-being or excitement while at the computer.
- Longing for more and more time at the computer.
- Neglect of family and friends.
- Feeling empty, **depressed** or irritable when not at the computer.
- Lying to employers and family about activities.
- Inability to stop the activity.
- Problems with school or job.

Physical symptoms listed include dry eyes, **backaches**, skipping meals, poor personal **hygiene** and sleep disturbances.

译文

上网成瘾

几个月前，47岁的卡拉·特贝每天花15个小时上网，这对她来说是极为平常的。她很早就会起床，然后打开笔记本电脑，在交友网站和即时消息程序上聊天，离开床的时间很短。她的家用账单积成一摞，碟子和脏衣服也堆了一堆，然而，在她的四个女儿不断地抱怨之后，她才意识到自己有问题。

卡拉说："我开始感觉好像我的整个世界正在走向崩溃，慢慢滑入低谷。我知道如果不摆脱那些交友网站，我还会继续沉迷下去。"这会使她更加脱离外面的世界。

卡拉的结论是：她觉得她好像对网络"上瘾"了。有这种问题的人并不止她一个。

人们并不是刚刚才开始关注过度上网。早在1995年的时候，医学期刊上发表的一些文章和宾夕法尼亚过度上网者治疗中心的建立就已经让人们对这一问题产生了兴趣。目前，就上网多长时间属于过度上网和是否可能上网成瘾这两个问题，人们还未达成共识。

但是，有迹象表明，随着人们对网络的依赖程度越来越高，这些问题也越来越严重：上个月，在《中枢神经系统谱系》上发表的一项研究宣称首次对过度上网进行了大规模的研究。《中枢神经系统谱系》发表的这项新研究以对全国2500多位成年人进行的一项电话调查结果为依据。与2005年的调查一样，这个调查也是由斯坦福大学的研究人员进行的。约有6%的受访者表示"他们的人际关系由于过度上网而受到影响"。约有9%的人试着隐瞒"不必要的网上冲浪"，还有接近4%的人感觉"即使下线心里也想着网络"。大约8%的人表示他们将上网视为逃避问题的方法，而将近14%的人称他们"发现自己远离网络几天很困难"。

过度上网不应该根据上网的时间来定义，而要"根据它所造成的损失来定义"，哈佛大学教授马里萨·奥扎克说道。"如果上网导致的损失是你不去上班或你的家庭关系破裂，那么你就上网过度了。"

自20世纪90年代初以来，美国成立了一些专门治疗严重上网成瘾的机构。它们包括网络成瘾恢复中心和网络行为中心。

奥扎克中心的网站将下列现象列为电脑成瘾的心理症状：

- 使用电脑时感到幸福或兴奋。
- 渴望花越来越多的时间在电脑上。
- 忽略家人和朋友。
- 不用电脑时，感到空虚、沮丧或易怒。
- 由于上网而对老板和家人说谎。
- 无法停止上网。
- 学业或工作上存在问题。

列出的生理症状包括眼睛干涩、背疼、不吃正餐、不注意个人卫生以及睡眠障碍。

单词记事本

laptop [ˈlæptɒp]
释 *n.* 便携式电脑

brief [briːf]
释 *a.* 短暂的；简洁的；(衣服)短的 *v.* 作…的提要 *n.* 摘要
用 brief introduction 简介；brief sb. on sth. 向某人简要介绍某事；in brief 简言之
例 Being *brief* and elegant, the composition attracted a lot of people. 文章简洁而优美，吸引了很多人。

interval [ˈɪntəvl]
释 *n.* 间隔时间；间隔空间；幕间(或工间)休息；停顿，中断

用 at intervals 时时，不时；time interval 时间间隔

laundry [ˈlɔːndri]
释 *n.* 洗衣店；洗好的衣服；待洗的衣服

depression [dɪˈpreʃn]
释 *n.* 忧愁，消沉；低压；萧条(期)
用 economic depression 经济萧条
例 He suffered great *depression* after losing his child. 他失去孩子后心情非常消沉。

detach [dɪˈtætʃ]
释 *v.* 分开，分离；分遣

addicted [ə'dɪktɪd]

释 *a.* 沉溺的；上瘾的

excessive [ɪk'sesɪv]

释 *a.* 过度的；额外的；极端的

用 excessive competition 过度竞争

例 The elder complained about the *excessive* noise coming from upstairs. 这位老人抱怨楼上的噪声太大。

journal ['dʒɜːnl]

释 *n.* 定期刊物，报纸；日记

establishment [ɪ'stæblɪʃmənt]

释 *n.* 建立；机构

例 The speaker announced the *establishment* of diplomatic relations between the two countries. 发言人宣布两国建立外交关系。

overuser [ˌəʊvə'juːzə(r)]

释 *n.* 过度使用者

generate ['dʒenəreɪt]

释 *v.* 使产生，发生

例 His actions *generated* a great deal of suspicion. 他的行为招来大量的猜疑。

consensus [kən'sensəs]

释 *n.* 共识，(意见)一致

用 reach a consensus 达成共识

例 There seems to be a *consensus* that the project should be carried out. 人们似乎已经达成共识，认为应该执行这个项目。

constitute ['kɒnstɪtjuːt]

释 *v.* 是；组成，构成；建立

例 The failure *constitutes* a major setback for our decision. 这次失败是我们决策上的重大挫折。

addiction [ə'dɪkʃn]

释 *n.* 上瘾；沉溺

用 addiction to smoking 烟瘾

reliance [rɪ'laɪəns]

释 *n.* 信任；依靠

用 reliance on 依靠

例 This new learning method doesn't encourage too much *reliance* upon the teacher. 这种新的学习方法不鼓励学生太依赖老师。

suffer ['sʌfə(r)]

释 *v.* 遭受；容忍；受苦；患病；变坏，变差

用 suffer from 遭受

例 Many companies are *suffering* from a shortage of experienced manager. 许多公司都缺乏有经验的管理人员。

conceal [kən'siːl]

释 *v.* 隐藏，隐瞒；掩盖

用 conceal from 对…隐瞒

例 He tried to *conceal* his heavy drinking from his girlfriend. 他极力对他的女朋友隐瞒自己酗酒的事。

psychological [ˌsaɪkə'lɒdʒɪkl]

释 *a.* 心理的；精神上的；心理学的

symptom ['sɪmptəm]

释 *n.* 症状；征兆

depressed [dɪ'prest]

释 *a.* 抑郁的，消沉的；萧条的

用 depressed mood 情绪低落

backache ['bækeɪk]

释 *n.* 背痛，腰痛

hygiene ['haɪdʒiːn]

释 *n.* 卫生(学)

多彩生活

amateur ['æmətə(r); 'æmətʃə(r)] n. 业余爱好者

amenity [ə'miːnəti] n. [常pl.]娱乐场所；福利设施

angler ['æŋglə(r)] n. 钓鱼者

bibliophile ['bɪbliəfaɪl] n. 爱书者；藏书家

camper ['kæmpə(r)] n. 露营者

caption ['kæpʃn] n. 说明文字；字幕

carnival ['kɑːnɪvl] n. 狂欢节

carousel [ˌkærə'sel] n. 旋转木马

chord [kɔːd] n. 和弦；弦

choreography [ˌkɒri'ɒɡrəfi] n. 舞步；舞蹈编排

commentary ['kɒməntri] n. 现场解说

delectation [ˌdiːlek'teɪʃn] n. 享受；愉快

expedition [ˌekspə'dɪʃn] n. 远征(队)；探险(队)

fanatical [fə'nætɪkl] a. 狂热的；入迷的

numismatist [njuː'mɪzmətɪst] n. 钱币学家；钱币收藏家

odyssey ['ɒdəsi] n. 长期的冒险旅行

pantomime ['pæntəmaɪm] n. 童话剧；哑剧

philately [fɪ'lætəli] n. 集邮

philharmonic [ˌfɪlɑː'mɒnɪk] n. 交响乐团；爱好音乐者

piazza [pi'ætsə] n. 广场；露天市场

poker ['pəʊkə(r)] n. 纸牌；扑克牌游戏

preview ['priːvjuː] n. 预览；试映

projectionist [prə'dʒekʃənɪst] n. 电影放映员

promenade [ˌprɒmə'nɑːd] n. 散步；开车兜风

quaff [kwɒf] v. 痛饮，畅饮

ramble ['ræmbl] v./n. 漫步

reverie ['revəri] n. 幻想；梦幻曲

sally ['sæli] v. 远足；漫游

saunter ['sɔːntə(r)] v. 闲逛，漫步

sled [sled] n. 滑雪橇 v. 用雪橇运

troll [trɒl; trəʊl] v. 钓鱼

trumpeter ['trʌmpɪtə(r)] n. 喇叭手；号兵

venturesome ['ventʃəsəm] a. 冒险的

versant ['vɜːsənt] a. 熟悉的；精通的

wizardry ['wɪzədri] n. 魔术；魔力

音频

Passage 16

 原 文

Women Really Do Find
the Silent, Brooding Type Sexier

Women find happy men significantly less sexually attractive than those who swagger or brood, researchers said today.

They are least attracted to smiling men, instead preferring those who looked proud and powerful, or moody and ashamed, according to a study.

In contrast, men are most sexually attracted to women who look happy, and least attracted to those who appear proud and confident.

The University of British Columbia study, which is the first to report a significant gender difference in the attractiveness of smiles, helps explain the enduring allure of "bad boys" and other iconic gender stereotypes.

It is also the first study to investigate the attractiveness of displays of pride and shame.

Lead researcher Professor Jessica Tracy said "While showing a happy face is considered essential to friendly social interactions, including those involving sexual attraction—few studies have actually examined whether a smile is, in fact, attractive.

"This study finds that men and women respond very differently to displays of emotion, including smiles."

More than 1,000 adult participants rated the sexual attractiveness of hundreds of images of the opposite sex.

These photos included universal displays of happiness (broad smiles), pride (raised heads, puffed-up chests) and shame (lowered heads, averted eyes).

The researchers found that women were least attracted to smiling, happy men—in contrast to men, who were most attracted to women who looked happy.

Overall, the researchers said, men rank women more attractive than women rank men.

Study co-author Alec Beall said "It is important to remember that this study explored first-impressions of sexual attraction to images of the opposite sex.

"We were not asking participants if they thought these targets would make a good boyfriend or wife—we wanted their gut reactions on carnal, sexual attraction."

He said previous studies have found positive emotional **traits** and a nice personality to be highly desirable in a relationship between partners.

For example, **evolutionary** theories suggest females are attracted to male displays of pride because they **imply status**, **competence** and an ability to provide for a partner and offspring.

According to Mr. Beall, the pride expression **accentuates** typically **masculine** physical features, such as upper body size and **muscularity**.

"Previous research has shown that these features are among the most attractive male physical characteristics, as judged by women," he said.

The researchers said more work is needed to understand the differing responses to happiness, but suggested the **phenomenon** can also be understood according to **principles** of evolutionary psychology, as well as socio-cultural gender norms.

For example, past research has associated smiling with a lack of **dominance**, which is **consistent** with traditional gender norms of the "**submissive** and **vulnerable**" woman, but **inconsistent** with the "strong, silent" man.

Professor Tracy said, "Generally, the results appear to reflect some very traditional gender norms and cultural values that have emerged, developed and been reinforced through history, at least in Western cultures.

"These include norms and values that many would consider old-fashioned and perhaps hope that we've moved beyond."

译 文

女性认为沉默忧郁的男人更性感

研究者今天表示，女性认为快乐的男性远没有趾高气扬或忧伤阴郁的男性有吸引力。

根据一项研究可知，女人们不喜欢爱笑的男人，而容易被那些看上去骄傲、强势或者忧郁、害羞的男人所吸引。

相比之下，男人却更喜欢那些看起来开开心心的女人，而不太喜欢那些看上去傲慢与自信的女人。

英属哥伦比亚大学是首个报道微笑吸引力在两性之间的差别表现的机构，其研究解释了"坏男孩"具有长久吸引力的原因以及其他一些象征性的性别角色定型。

这个研究也首次探究了骄傲和害羞两种表情的吸引力。

研究负责人杰西卡·特蕾西教授说："在社交中，尽管展现一种快乐的表情是进行友好交往的基本要素，这其中包括两性之间的吸引，但很少有研究证明微笑是否真的吸引人。

"这项研究还发现男人和女人对别人所流露出的感情的反应完全不同，这包括对微笑的反应。"

超过1000名成年人参与了该研究，他们按照吸引力等级，对看到的数百张异性的照片进行划分。

这些照片包括了常见的几种表情，如：高兴（开怀大笑）、骄傲（昂首挺胸）以及害羞（低头、眼神飘忽）。

研究者发现，女性对爱笑的、开心的男性最不感兴趣，而男性则恰恰相反，他们更喜欢看起来快乐的女性。

总之，研究人员称，两性之间，男性更易被女性所吸引。

合作研究者亚历克·比尔称："该研究探索了第一眼看到异性时所感受到的吸引力，注意到这一点很重要。"

"我们并没有询问参与者他们是否认为照片中的人会成为好的交往对象或伴侣，我们只是想知道他们身体的本能反应，即是否感觉被吸引。"

他称之前的研究发现，积极的情感特征以及良好的个性在两性关系中尤为重要。

例如，进化论认为女性会被看起来骄傲的男性吸引，因为这种特质预示着地位、竞争力和供养伴侣和后代的能力。

根据比尔先生的理论，骄傲的表情突出了男性的典型生理特征，例如宽肩阔背和发达的肌肉。

他说："之前的研究表明，女性认为这些特征是最具有吸引力的男性身体特征。"

研究者称，要理解男性和女性对待快乐的不同反应，还需要进行更多的研究，但这一现象还可根据进化心理学的原则及社会文化性别规范来理解。

例如，过去的研究认为笑与缺乏支配力有关系，这与传统性别规范中认为女性"顺从且脆弱"的观念是相符的，而与认为男性"强壮而沉默"的观念不符。

特蕾西教授说："通常，研究结果会反映出某些十分传统的性别规范和文化价值观，这种规范和价值观在历史发展的过程中出现、发展并得到巩固，至少在西方文化中是这样。

"其中也包括那些被许多人认为是过时的，或许还希望将其摒弃的规范和价值观。"

sexually ['sekʃəli]
释 ad. 两性之间地

swagger ['swægə(r)]
释 v. 趾高气扬地行走或行事 n. 趾高气扬

brood [bruːd]
释 v. 忧闷地沉思；孵雏 n. (一窝孵出的)幼鸟；(一次产出的)动物

moody ['muːdi]
释 a. 喜怒无常的；郁郁寡欢的

gender ['dʒendə(r)]
释 n. 性，性别；(语法中的)性

attractiveness [ə'træktɪvnəs]
释 n. 吸引力；引起兴趣的事物

enduring [ɪn'djʊərɪŋ]
释 a. 持久的，持续的

allure [ə'lʊə(r)]
释 n. 诱惑力；吸引力 v. 诱惑；吸引

iconic [aɪ'kɒnɪk]
释 a. 图标的；标志性的

stereotype ['steriətaɪp]
释 n. 陈规；固定形式 v. 成固定形象

essential [ɪ'senʃl]
释 a. 本质的；非常重要的 n. 要素；实质
例 Historical memory is *essential* to a free people. 铭记历史对于一个解放的民族来说是非常重要的。

averted [ə'vɜːtɪd]
释 a. 转移的，移开的

gut [gʌt]
释 a. 本能的，直觉的 n. 内脏；重要部分；[pl.]勇气 v. 毁坏(建筑物等的)内部
用 hate sb.'s guts 对某人恨之入骨

carnal ['kɑːnl]
释 a. 肉体的；感官的

trait [treɪt]
释 n. 特征，特点

evolutionary [ˌiːvə'luːʃənri; ˌevə'luːʃənri]
释 a. 进化的；发展的

imply [ɪm'plaɪ]
释 v. 意味；暗示，暗指

status ['steɪtəs]
释 n. 身份，地位；情形，状况

competence ['kɒmpɪtəns]
释 n. 胜任；能力

accentuate [ək'sentʃueɪt]
释 v. 突出；强调
例 Other projects will *accentuate* the difference between the highest-paid and lowest-paid employees in an organization. 其他项目会突出同一系统内最高收入员工与最低收入员工间的差异。

masculine ['mæskjəlɪn]
释 a. 男性的；男子气概的

muscularity [ˌmʌskju'lærətɪ]
释 n. 肌肉发达；强壮

phenomenon [fə'nɒmɪnən]
释 n. 现象；非凡的人
用 the phenomena (phenomenon的复数形式) of nature 自然现象
例 The *phenomenon* has even been the subject of scholarly research. 这个现象甚至曾经是学术研究的课题。

principle ['prɪnsəpl]
释 n. 原则，原理；道德准则

dominance ['dɒmɪnəns]
释 n. 支配，统治；优势

consistent [kən'sɪstənt]
释 a. 一致的；坚持的

submissive [səb'mɪsɪv]

释 *a.* 顺从的；服从的

vulnerable ['vʌlnərəbl]

释 *a.* 脆弱的；易受攻击的

例 What's more, the parts of the world where populations are growing fastest are also those most *vulnerable* to climate change. 更重要的是，世界上人口增长最快的地区也是最难以抵御气候变化的地区。

inconsistent [ˌɪnkən'sɪstənt]

释 *a.* 不一致的；矛盾的

 单词家族

不良品质

aloof [ə'luːf] *a.* 远离的；冷淡的
bohemian [bəʊ'hiːmiən] *a.* 放荡不羁的
boring ['bɔːrɪŋ] *a.* 令人厌烦的
brassy ['brɑːsi] *a.* 厚脸皮的；无礼的
clumsy ['klʌmzi] *a.* 笨拙的
exceptionable [ɪk'sepʃənəbl] *a.* 引起反感的
frightful ['fraɪtfl] *a.* 可怕的；讨厌的
hideous ['hɪdiəs] *a.* 讨厌的；丑恶的
ignoble [ɪg'nəʊbl] *a.* 卑鄙的
peremptory [pə'remptəri] *a.* 专横的，霸道的

pontifical [pɒn'tɪfɪkl] *a.* 独断专行的；固执武断的
provincial [prə'vɪnʃl] *a.* 偏狭的；守旧的
rebarbative [rɪ'bɑːbətɪv] *a.* 令人讨厌的；冒犯人的
silly ['sɪli] *a.* 愚蠢的；糊涂的；傻的
snobbish ['snɒbɪʃ] *a.* 势利的；谄上欺下的
tedious ['tiːdiəs] *a.* 令人厌倦的；烦人的
unregenerate [ˌʌnrɪ'dʒenərət] *a.* 不知悔改的；顽固不化的

The greatest test of courage on earth is to bear defeat without losing heart.
　　　　　　　　　　　　　　—Robert Ingersoll
世间对勇气的最大考验乃是容忍失败、决不丧志。
　　　　　　　　　　　　　　——罗伯特·英格索

Passage 17

原文

US Government: There Are No Mermaids

The United States government has assured its citizens that, much like zombies, mermaids probably do not exist, saying in an official post, "No evidence of aquatic humanoids has ever been found."

"Mermaids—those half-human, half-fish sirens of the sea—are legendary sea creatures," read the online statement from the National Ocean Service (NOS).

The agency, charged with responding to natural hazards, received letters inquiring about the existence of the sea maidens after the Discovery Channel's Animal Planet network broadcast *Mermaids: The Body Found* in May.

The show "paints a wildly convincing picture of the existence of mermaids, what they may look like, and why they've stayed hidden...until now," a Discovery Channel press release says.

Conversely, the US government declaration offered no conclusive proof to deny the existence of mermaids.

The statement comes after another government agency, this time the US Centers for Disease Control and Prevention (CDC), declared there was no conclusive evidence for the existence of zombies.

The CDC had published instructional materials on how to survive a "zombie apocalypse," in what the agency now calls "a tongue in cheek campaign to engage new audiences with messages of preparedness."

The campaign was followed by a series of cannibalistic attacks in North America.

In one such attack on May 26, a 31-year-old Miami man stripped naked and chewed off most of a homeless man's face.

The Twittersphere was suddenly alive with people talking about the real and present danger of a zombie apocalypse.

The CDC was quick to respond to allegations of corpses rising from the dead to eat the living.

"CDC does not know of a virus or condition that would reanimate the dead," a government spokesperson wrote in an email to *The Huffington Post*.

While zombies would be a big problem, popular folklore holds that mermaids are relatively benign creatures.

But the NOS statement associated the finned friends with more threatening **mythological** beasts.

"Half-human creatures, called **chimeras**, also abound in mythology—in **addition** to mermaids, there were wise **centaurs**, wild **satyrs**, and frightful **minotaurs**, to name but a few," it said.

译文

美国政府称不存在美人鱼

美国政府向民众保证，如僵尸一样，美人鱼很可能并不存在，并在一项官方声明中称："没有任何证据表明曾发现水中类人生物。"

美国国家海洋局的网上声明中说："美人鱼——这种半身为人、半身为鱼的海妖——只是一种传说中的海洋生物。"

五月份，探索频道的"动物星球"栏目播出了《真实美人鱼：科学的假设》之后，负责应对自然灾害的国家海洋局收到了多封询问美人鱼是否存在的来信。

探索频道的一篇新闻稿指出，该节目"在美人鱼是否存在，它们的外形如何，以及为什么至今仍隐于世等方面，展示了一幅极具说服力的画面"。

相对地，美国政府的声明并没有提供任何确凿的证据来证明美人鱼并不存在。

在这份声明发布之前，另一个政府机构——美国疾病控制和预防中心宣称没有令人信服的证据证明僵尸存在。

美国疾病控制和预防中心曾出版了一些指导性的资料，告诉人们如何在"僵尸末日"生存下来。而该机构现在称"这场宣传活动不必当真，它只是用来吸引那些准备预防僵尸来袭的新观众的"。

但在这场宣传活动之后，北美发生了一连串食人袭击案。

在5月26日的一次类似的袭击中，一名31岁的迈阿密人浑身赤裸，啃掉了一名流浪汉的多半张脸。

推特圈顿时一片哗然，人们纷纷谈论起"僵尸末日"的真实性以及目前所面临的危险。

疾病控制和预防中心迅速对"僵尸复活啃噬活人"的谣言作出了回应。

一位政府发言人在写给《赫芬顿邮报》的一封邮件中称："疾病控制和预防中心并没有发现可使死人复活的病毒或条件。"

虽然僵尸可能会成为一个大问题，但广为流传的说法认为美人鱼是一种对人相对友善的生物。

然而，国家海洋局的声明却将这些长着鱼鳍的朋友与神话中的那些更具危险性的怪兽联系了起来。

声明称："半人半兽的生物被称为虚构的怪物，它们在神话中大量出现。除了美人鱼之外，神话故事中还有睿智的半人半马怪、狂野的半羊人和可怕的人身牛头怪物等，数量很多。"

💡 单词记事本

assure [ə'ʃʊə(r); ə'ʃɔ:(r)]
释 v. 使确信，向…保证；担保

mermaid ['mɜ:meɪd]
释 n. 美人鱼

aquatic [ə'kwætɪk]
释 a. 水生的，水中的

humanoid ['hju:mənɔɪd]
释 a. 像人的

siren ['saɪrən]
释 n. 警报声；迷人的女人；妖妇

legendary ['ledʒəndri]
释 a. 传说的；有名的

creature ['kri:tʃə(r)]
释 n. 生物；人；创造物

hazard ['hæzəd]
释 n. 危险，有危险的事物；障碍物 v. 尝试着做（或提出）；冒…风险
例 That pile of rubbish is a fire *hazard*. 那堆垃圾存在失火的隐患。

inquire [ɪn'kwaɪə(r)]
释 v. 打听，询问；调查

existence [ɪg'zɪstəns]
释 n. 存在；生活，生活（方式）
例 I was unaware of his *existence* until today. 直到今天我才知道有他这么个人。

maiden ['meɪdn]
释 n. 少女；未婚女子 a. 首次的，初次的

convincing [kən'vɪnsɪŋ]
释 a. 令人信服的；有力的

declaration [ˌdeklə'reɪʃn]
释 n. 宣布；声明（书）；申报

conclusive [kən'klu:sɪv]
释 a. 最后的；确凿的；决定性的

proof [pru:f]
释 n. 证据；验证 a. 耐…的
例 This room is *proof* against sounds. 这个房间隔音。

declare [dɪ'kleə(r)]
释 v. 正式宣布；断言，宣称；申报

instructional [ɪn'strʌkʃənl]
释 a. 指导的；教学的；有教育内容的

apocalypse [ə'pɒkəlɪps]
释 n. 世界末日

preparedness [prɪ'peərɪdnəs]
释 n. 有所准备

campaign [kæm'peɪn]
释 n. （政治或商业性）活动，运动；战役 v. 参加活动；作战

cannibalistic [ˌkænɪbə'lɪstɪk]
释 a. 同类相食的，自相残杀的

naked ['neɪkɪd]
释 a. 赤裸的；直率的

allegation [ˌælə'geɪʃn]
释 n. 宣称，声称；指控

例 The President has denied the *allegations*, which he said were fabricated by his political opponents. 总统否认了指控，称那是他的政敌编造出来的。

corpse [kɔːps]
释 n. 尸体

reanimate [riːˈænɪmeɪt]
释 v. 使复活；鼓舞

folklore [ˈfəʊklɔː(r)]
释 n. 民间传说；民俗学

benign [bɪˈnaɪn]
释 a. 无危险的；慈祥的；(肿瘤等)良性的
用 benign tumour 良性肿瘤；a benign old lady 和蔼的老妇人

mythological [ˌmɪθəˈlɒdʒɪkl]
释 a. 神话学的；虚构的

chimera [kaɪˈmɪərə]
释 n. 虚构的怪物；梦幻

addition [əˈdɪʃn]
释 n. 加，加法；增加的人(或物)

centaur [ˈsentɔː(r)]
释 n. 半人半马怪

satyr [ˈsætə(r)]
释 n. (希腊及罗马神话中半人半羊的)森林之神

minotaur [ˈmaɪnətɔː(r); ˈmɪnətɔː(r)]
释 n. 人身牛头怪物

单词家族

文化历史

archaeology [ˌɑːkiˈɒlədʒi] n. 考古学

aristocratic [ˌærɪstəˈkrætɪk] a. 贵族的；贵族统治的

biography [baɪˈɒɡrəfi] n. 传记

classic [ˈklæsɪk] a. 经典的；典型的 n. 经典作品；[pl.] 古典文学

colony [ˈkɒləni] n. 殖民地；(生物)群体

conserve [kənˈsɜːv] v. 保存；保藏

contemporary [kənˈtemprəri] a. 当代的 n. 同时代的人

context [ˈkɒntekst] n. 上下文；背景；环境

convention [kənˈvenʃn] n. 习俗，惯例；公约；(正式)会议

critic [ˈkrɪtɪk] n. 评论家，批评家

cuneiform [ˈkjuːnɪfɔːm] a. 楔形的，用楔形文字写的

diction [ˈdɪkʃn] n. 语言风格；措辞，用语

distinguished [dɪˈstɪŋɡwɪʃt] a. 卓越的，杰出的

doctrine [ˈdɒktrɪn] n. 教条，教义；学说

fable [ˈfeɪbl] n. 寓言；神话

factual [ˈfæktʃuəl] a. 根据事实的，真实的

herald [ˈherəld] n. (旧时) 传令官，使者，信使

ironic [aɪˈrɒnɪk] a. 用反语的；讽刺的

naturalist [ˈnætʃrəlɪst] n. 自然主义者；博物学家

pictograph [ˈpɪktəˌɡræf] n. 象形文字

prehistoric [ˌpriːhɪˈstɒrɪk] a. 史前的；陈旧的

primitive [ˈprɪmətɪv] a. 原始的，远古的

relic [ˈrelɪk] n. 遗迹

rhetoric [ˈretərɪk] n. 修辞；修辞学

romantic [rəʊˈmæntɪk] a. (指音乐、文学等)浪漫主义的

snippet [ˈsnɪpɪt] n. 片段；摘录

stanza [ˈstænzə] n. (诗)节，段

undistorted [ˌʌndɪsˈtɔːtɪd] a. 未失真的；逼真的

Passage 18

Media Selection for Advertisements

After determining the target audience for a product or service, advertising agencies must select the appropriate media for the advertisement. We discuss here the major types of media used in advertising. We focus our attention on seven types of advertising: television, newspapers, radio, magazines, out-of-home, Internet, and direct mail.

Television

Television is an attractive medium for advertising because it delivers mass audiences to advertisers. When advertisers create a brand, for example, they want to impress consumers with the brand and its image. Television provides an ideal vehicle for this type of communication. But television is an expensive medium, and not all advertisers can afford to use it.

Television's influence on advertising is fourfold. First, narrowcasting means that television channels are seen by an increasingly narrow segment of the audience. Thus, audiences are smaller and more homogeneous than they have been in the past. Second, there is an increase in the number of television channels available to viewers, and thus, advertisers. This has also resulted in an increase in the sheer number of advertisements to which audiences are exposed. Third, digital recording devices allow audience members more control over which commercials they watch. Fourth, control over programming is being passed from the networks to local cable operators and satellite programmers.

Newspapers

After television, the medium attracting the next largest annual ad revenue is newspapers. Locally, newspapers are the largest advertising medium.

Newspapers are a less expensive advertising medium than television and provide a way for advertisers to communicate a longer, more detailed message to their audience than they can through television. Given new production techniques, advertisements can be printed in newspapers in about 48 hours, meaning newspapers are also a quick way of getting the message out. Newspapers are often the most important form of news for a local community, and they develop a high degree of loyalty from local readers.

Radio

Advertising on radio continues to grow. Radio is often used in conjunction with outdoor billboards and the Internet to reach even more customers than television. Advertisers are likely to use radio because it is a less expensive medium than television, which means advertisers can afford to repeat their ads often. Internet companies are also turning to radio advertising. Radio provides a way for advertisers to communicate with audience members all times of the day. Consumers listen to radio on their way to school or work, at work, on the way home, and in the evening hours.

Magazines

Magazines are popular with advertisers because of the narrow market that they deliver. A broadcast medium such as network television attracts all types of audience members, but magazine audiences are more homogeneous. Advertisers using the print media—magazines and newspapers—will need to adapt to two main changes. First, the Internet will bring larger audiences to local newspapers. These audiences will be more diverse and geographically dispersed than in the past. Second, advertisers will have to understand how to use an increasing number of magazines for their target audiences. Although some magazines will maintain national audiences, a large number of magazines will entertain narrower audiences.

Out-of-home Advertising

Out-of-home advertising, also called place-based advertising, has become an increasingly effective way of reaching consumers, who are more active than ever before. Many consumers today do not sit at home and watch television. Using billboards, newsstands, and bus shelters for advertising is an effective way of reaching those on-the-go consumers. Technology has changed the nature of the billboard business, making it a more effective medium than in the past. Using digital printing, billboard companies can print a billboard in 2 hours, compared with 6 days previously. This allows advertisers more variety in the types of messages they create because they can change their messages more quickly.

Internet

As consumers become more comfortable with online shopping, advertisers will seek to reach this market. As consumers get more of their news and information from the Internet, the ability of television and radio to get the word out to consumers will decrease. The challenge to Internet advertisers is to create ads that audience members will remember.

Internet advertising will play a more prominent role in organizations' advertising in the near future. Internet audiences tend to be quite homogeneous, but small. Advertisers will have to adjust their methods to reach these audiences and will have to adapt their persuasive strategies to the online medium as well.

Direct Mail

A final advertising medium is direct mail, which uses mailings to consumers to communicate a client's message. Direct mail includes newsletters, postcards, and special promotions. Direct mail is an effective way to build relationships with consumers. For many businesses, direct mail is the most effective form of advertising.

广告媒介的选择

在确定了一种产品或服务的目标受众之后，广告公司就必须选择一种恰当的媒介来投放广告。我们在这儿要谈论的是投放广告的几种主要媒介。我们关注的媒介主要有七种：电视、报纸、广播、杂志、户外广告、互联网和直投广告。

电视

电视是一种引人注目的广告媒介，因为它为广告商带来了大量的观众。比如，当广告商新推出一个品牌时，他们想让这个品牌及其品牌形象给观众留下深刻的印象。电视是达到这种传播效果的理想方式。但电视这种媒介很昂贵，不是所有的广告商都能承担得起这笔费用。

电视对广告有四重影响。首先，窄带播放意味着不同的电视频道的观众都是越来越细分的群体。因此，与从前相比，现在的观众群体变得更小，共同点也更多。第二，观众可使用的电视频道越来越多，对广告商而言也是如此。这就使得观众看到的广告数量也大幅增长。第三，数码录像设备使得观众对于看什么样的广告更有控制权。第四，对节目安排的控制正在由网络转向地方有线运营商和卫星程序员。

报纸

仅次于电视，获得年度第二大广告收入的媒介便是报纸。在地方上，报纸是最大的广告媒介。

与电视相比，报纸是更为便宜的广告媒介，而且它还能让广告商向读者传递更长、更详尽的信息。得益于新的生产技术，报纸可以在48小时内将广告信息印刷出来，这表明报纸也是传播信息的快速途径。报纸通常也是当地社区中最重要的信息载体，在当地拥有忠诚度颇高的读者群。

广播

广播广告的数量在持续增长。广播通常与户外广告牌及互联网一起使用，因此它们的客户覆盖面甚至比电视还要广。广告商更倾向于使用广播来投放广告，因为广播广告的成本比电视广告低，这就意味着广告商能支付得起经常重播广告的费用。互联网公司也开始利用广播广告。广播为广告商提供了向观众全天播放广告的途径。消费者在上学或上班途中、工作时、回家路上以及晚上都会收听广播。

杂志

由于投放市场的细分，杂志很受广告商青睐。像网络电视这样的广播媒介吸引着各个层面的观众，而杂志的读者群则更为单一。使用杂志和报纸这类纸质媒介的广告商需适应两大主要的变化。第一，互联网会为当地报纸带来更多的受众。比起过去，这些受众群将更加多样化，散布地区也将更广。第二，广告商需要懂得如何利用日益增多的杂志种类来赢得目标受众。虽然一些杂志能够吸引全国的读者，但仍有很大一部分杂志的受众面比较窄。

户外广告

户外广告也叫实体广告。因为消费者变得比以前更加活跃，所以户外广告已经成为一种接触消费者越来越有效的广告方式。如今很多消费者都不会待在家里看电视。使用广告牌、报摊和公共汽车候车亭做广告已成为接触这些忙碌的消费者的一种有效的方式。科技改变了广告牌业务的性质，使它成为了一种比以前更为有效的广告媒介。通过数字印刷，广告牌制作公司两小时内就可以完成一个广告牌的印刷，而原来这需要六天。由于广告商可以更快地更改广告信息，这使得他们在信息的种类上有了更多的变化。

互联网

因为消费者越来越习惯网上购物，所以广告商们也在试图开拓这个市场。随着消费者从互联网上获得的新闻和信息越来越多，电视和广播的信息传播能力将会下降。这给互联网广告商带来的挑战就是要制作出能让观众记住的广告。

在不远的将来，互联网会在团体广告方面发挥更加突出的作用。互联网受众群往往十分相似，但人数较少。广告商必须调整方式以接触到这些受众，同时，他们还必须调整其诱导策略来适应这种在线媒介。

直投

最后一种广告媒介是直投，它利用信件将广告客户的信息传达给消费者。直投包括简报、明信片和特价促销广告。直投是同消费者建立关系的有效方式。对很多企业来说，直投是最有效的广告形式。

determine [dɪ'tɜːmɪn]
释 v. 确定；决定；测定
例 Present devotion to your work will *determine* your future. 你现在对工作的投入将决定你的未来。

agency ['eɪdʒənsi]
释 n. 代理；代理处，公司；政府的特种机构
用 travel agency 旅行社

select [sɪ'lekt]
释 v. 选择，挑选 a. 精选的；优等的

medium ['miːdiəm]
释 n. [常pl.] 媒介；手段 a. 中等的；平均的

advertiser ['ædvətaɪzə(r)]
释 n. 刊登广告者，广告客户

create [kri'eɪt]
释 v. 创造；引起，产生；任命

brand [brænd]
释 n. 商标，牌子；烙印 v. 铭刻；打烙印于；侮辱

consumer [kən'sjuːmə(r)]
释 n. 消费者；用户

vehicle ['viːəkl]
释 n. 交通工具；工具，手段

fourfold ['fɔːfəʊld]
释 a. 四倍的；四重的 ad. 四倍；四重

narrowcasting ['nærəʊkɑːstɪŋ]
释 n. 窄播

channel ['tʃænl]
释 n. 频道；渠道；海峡；航道

narrow ['nærəʊ]
释 a. 狭窄的；受限制的；勉强的；精确的 v. (使)变窄
用 narrow down 缩小；限制

例 It takes a lot of courage to pass the *narrow* path. 需要很大的勇气才能通过这条狭窄的小路。

segment ['segmənt]
释 n. 部分；线段；弦；瓣

homogeneous [ˌhɒmə'dʒiːniəs]
释 a. 同类的；均匀的

available [ə'veɪləbl]
释 a. 可用的；空闲的；可得到的

sheer [ʃɪə(r)]
释 a. 完全的，纯粹的；陡峭的 ad. 陡峭地 v. 急转向

digital ['dɪdʒɪtl]
释 a. 数字的，数码的；手指的

operator ['ɒpəreɪtə(r)]
释 n. 操作者；经营者；话务员

annual ['ænjuəl]
释 a. 每年的，年度的 n. 年报，年刊；一年生植物
用 annual meeting 年会；annual report 年报

locally ['ləʊkəli]
释 ad. 局部地；在地方上，在本地

communicate [kə'mjuːnɪkeɪt]
释 v. 沟通；传播，传送；使知晓
用 communicate with 与…交流
例 In order to *communicate* globally we must learn foreign languages. 为了进行全球性的交流，我们必须学习外语。

community [kə'mjuːnəti]
释 n. 社区；团体；(动植物的)群落

conjunction [kən'dʒʌŋkʃn]
释 n. 联合，结合；同时发生；连词

billboard ['bɪlbɔːd]
释 n. 告示牌，广告牌

dispersed [dɪ'spɜːst]
罐 *a.* 散布的，分散的；细分的

maintain [meɪn'teɪn]
罐 *v.* 维持；维修；坚持；抚养
用 maintain contact with 与…保持联系
例 It is our common goal to *maintain* the world peace. 维护世界和平是我们共同的目标。

entertain [ˌentə'teɪn]
罐 *v.* 招待，款待；使娱乐；使感兴趣；抱有；容纳，接受

newsstand ['njuːzstænd]
罐 *n.* 报摊，杂志摊

shelter ['ʃeltə(r)]
罐 *n.* 遮蔽，庇护；遮蔽处；收容所 *v.* 掩蔽；躲避

previously ['priːviəsli]
罐 *ad.* 以前，先前

prominent ['prɒmɪnənt]
罐 *a.* 杰出的；突出的

organization [ˌɔːgənaɪ'zeɪʃn]
罐 *n.* 团体，机构，组织；组织的活动

adjust [ə'dʒʌst]
罐 *v.* 校正，校准；整理，安排；调整；改变…以适应
用 adjust to 适应

persuasive [pə'sweɪsɪv]
罐 *a.* 有说服力的

promotion [prə'məʊʃn]
罐 *n.* 促进；提升；广告宣传，推销活动

💡 单词家族

传播媒介

bookstall ['bʊkstɔːl] *n.* 书报摊
brochure ['brəʊʃə(r)] *n.* 小册子；说明书
dissemination [dɪˌsemɪ'neɪʃn] *n.* 散布，传播
editorial [ˌedɪ'tɔːriəl] *n.* 社论
excerpt ['eksɜːpt] *n.* (书、电影等的)节录
exclusive [ɪk'skluːsɪv] *n.* 独家新闻
factsheet ['fæktʃiːt] *n.* (电视节目中插入的)字幕新闻

handout ['hændaʊt] *n.* 传单；救济品
multimedia [ˌmʌlti'miːdiə] *n.* 多媒体 *a.* 多媒体的
newsreel ['njuːzriːl] *n.* 新闻短片
originality [əˌrɪdʒə'næləti] *n.* 创造性；原创
photocopy ['fəʊtəʊkɒpi] *v.* 影印；复印
projector [prə'dʒektə(r)] *n.* 放映机；投影仪
telex ['teleks] *n.* 电报；电传收发机

Passage 19

原 文

That's Enough, Kids

It was a lovely day at the park and Stella Bianchi was enjoying the sunshine with her two children when a young boy, aged about four, approached her two-year-old son and pushed him to the ground.

"I'd watched him for a little while and my son was the fourth or fifth child he'd shoved," she says. "I went over to them, picked up my son, turned to the boy and said, firmly, 'No, we don't push.'" What happened next was unexpected.

"The boy's mother ran toward me from across the park," Stella says. "I thought she was coming over to apologize, but instead she started shouting at me for 'disciplining her child'. All I did was let him know his behaviour was unacceptable. Was I supposed to sit back while her kid did whatever he wanted, hurting other children in the process?"

Getting your own children to play nice is difficult enough. Dealing with other people's children has become a minefield.

In my house, jumping on the sofa is not allowed. In my sister's house it's encouraged. For her it's about kids being kids: "If you can't do it at three, when can you do it?"

Each of these philosophies is valid and, it has to be said, my son loves visiting his aunt's house. But I find myself saying "no" a lot when her kids are over at mine. That's OK between sisters but becomes dangerous territory when you're talking to the children of friends or acquaintances.

"Kids aren't all raised the same," agrees Professor Naomi White of Monash University. "But there's still an idea that they're the property of the parents. We see our children as an extension of ourselves, so if you're saying that my child is behaving inappropriately, then that's somehow a criticism of me."

In those circumstances, it's difficult to know whether to approach the child directly or the parent first. There are two schools of thought.

"I'd go to the child first," says Andrew Fuller, author of *Tricky Kids*. "Usually a quiet reminder that 'we don't do that here' is enough. Kids have finely tuned antennae for how to behave in different settings."

He points out that bringing it up with the parent first may make them feel neglectful, which could cause problems. Of course, approaching the child first can bring its own headaches, too.

This is why White recommends that you approach the parents first. "**Raise** your concerns with the parents if they're there and ask them to deal with it," she says.

Asked how to approach a parent in this situation, psychologist Meredith Fuller answers, "Explain your needs as well as stressing the importance of the friendship. **Preface** your remarks with something like: 'I know you will think I'm silly but in my house I don't want...'"

When it comes to situations where you're caring for another child, White is straightforward: "Common sense must **prevail**. If things don't go well then have a chat."

Men might feel **uneasy** about dealing with other people's children. "Men feel nervous," White says. "A new set of **considerations** has come to the fore as part of the debate about how we **handle** children."

"Children have to learn to negotiate the world on their own, within reasonable boundaries," White says. White believes our notions of a more child-centered society should be challenged.

Back at the park, Bianchi's **intervention** on her son's **behalf** ended in an **undignified exchange** of **insulting** words with the other boy's mother.

As Bianchi approached the park bench where she'd been sitting, other mums came up to her and congratulated her on taking a stand. "**Apparently** the boy had a longstanding **reputation** for bad behaviour and his mum for even worse behaviour if he was challenged."

Andrew Fuller doesn't believe that we should be afraid of dealing with other people's kids. "Look at kids that aren't your own as a potential minefield," he says. He recommends that we don't stay silent over inappropriate behaviour, particularly with regular visitors.

译文

够了，孩子们

那天天气很好，斯特拉·比安基和她的两个孩子正在公园里享受阳光。这时，一个四岁左右的小男孩走到她两岁的儿子的身边，把他推倒在地。

"我已经观察他一会儿了。我儿子是他推倒的第四或第五个孩子。"她说，"我走到他们身边，扶起我儿子，转身对那个男孩坚决地说：'我们不能推别人。'"接下来发生的事情出乎意料。

"那个男孩的妈妈从公园的另一边跑过来。"斯特拉说，"我原以为她是来道歉的，但是她却开始对我大喊大叫，说我'教训了她的孩子'。我所做的只是让他知道他的行为是不被接受的。难道在她的孩子为所欲为、伤害其他孩子时，我应该袖手旁观吗？"

让自己的孩子好好表现已经很不容易了，应对别人的孩子更是难上加难。

在我家是不允许孩子在沙发上跳的，而我妹妹家却鼓励这么做。对她来说，孩子就是孩子："如果你三岁时都不能这么做，那什么时候可以呢？"

每一条理论都是有依据的，而且不得不说的是，我儿子喜欢去他姑（或姨）家。但是我发现她的孩子在我家时，我说"不"的时候很多。这在姐妹间还好，但是当你对朋友或熟人的孩子这么说时，你就踏入了危险地带。

"并非所有的孩子都是以同样的方式抚养大的。"莫纳什大学的娜奥米·怀特教授认同这个说法，"但是还有一个观点认为孩子是父母的财产。我们把孩子看作是自己的外延，这样的话如果你说我的孩子表现不好，那么在某种程度上也是对我的批评。"

在这种情况下，是应该直接去找孩子还是先去找父母就很难决断了。在这方面有以下两种观点。

"我会先去找孩子。"《狡猾的孩子》的作者安德鲁·富勒说，"通常一句小声的提醒'在这儿我们不能那么做'就够了。孩子们对在不同场合该有怎样的表现有很敏锐的直觉。"

他指出，如果先跟父母提起这件事会让孩子感觉被忽视，这可能会带来麻烦。当然，先跟孩子接触也会带来令人头疼的问题。

这就是为什么怀特建议先跟父母接触的原因。她说："如果父母在场，就把你的问题告诉他们并要求他们来处理。"

当被问到在这种情况下怎样同孩子的父母接触时，心理学家梅雷迪思·富勒回答说："在强调友谊的重要性的同时，解释你的需求。开场白要像这样：'我知道你会觉得我很可笑，但在我家我不希望……'"

当谈到你同时还要照顾另一个孩子的情况时，怀特很直接地说："常识最重要。如果事情进展得不顺利就有必要谈谈了。"

同别人家的孩子打交道时，人们会感到不自在。"人们会感觉紧张。"怀特说，"一些新的顾虑已经摆在面前，也成了我们该如何对待孩子的争论的一部分。"

"在合理的范围内，孩子们必须学会自己来应对这个世界。"怀特说。她相信，社会应该更加以孩子为中心的观念应该受到质疑。

回到公园事件上，比安基为了她儿子进行的干预最终以另一个男孩的母亲的不雅斥责告终。

当比安基回到她之前坐的长椅上时，其他妈妈们都走过来，称赞了她表明自己立场的做法。"很显然，这个男孩因其恶劣行为早已臭名远扬了，而她妈妈也因为在儿子受到批评后所表现出的更糟的行为而遭人唾弃。"

安德鲁·富勒认为我们不应该害怕跟别人的孩子打交道。他说："要把别人的孩子看作是一片潜在的雷区。"他建议，对于不当行为我们不能噤声，特别是面对常有此种行为的人时。

💡 单词记事本

approach [ə'prəʊtʃ]
释 v. 接近，靠近；探讨，分析 n. 方法，手段
用 at the approach of 在…快到的时候
例 We *approached* the crossroad when an accident took place. 事故发生的时候，我们刚到十字路口附近。

shove [ʃʌv]
释 v. 乱推，挤，撞；随意将某物放在某处

firmly ['fɜːmli]
释 ad. 坚决地；坚定地；坚固地

unexpected [ˌʌnɪk'spektɪd]
释 a. 未料到的，意外的
用 unexpected news 意外的消息

discipline ['dɪsəplɪn]
释 v. 教训，训导；训练；惩戒 n. 学科；纪律；惩戒

unacceptable [ˌʌnək'septəbl]
释 a. 不能接受的；无法原谅的

process ['prəʊses]
释 n. 过程；工序；程序 v. 加工，处理
用 in the process of 在…的过程中
例 Could you describe the complicated *process* in detail? 你能详细描述一下那个复杂的程序吗？

minefield ['maɪnfiːld]
释 n. 雷区，危险区域；危险形势，充满问题的情况

valid ['vælɪd]
释 a. 有根据的，有理的；有效的

territory ['terətri]
释 n. 领土，版图；领域；范围；地区

acquaintance [ə'kweɪntəns]
释 n. 认识，了解；熟人
用 make the acquaintance of 结识某人；have no acquaintance with 不熟悉，不了解；have a nodding/bowing acquaintance with 与某人有点头之交；(对某学科)略知一二

property ['prɒpəti]
释 n. 财产，所有物；性质；房产

extension [ɪk'stenʃn]
释 n. 伸展，延伸；提供，给予；延期；电话分机

inappropriately [ˌɪnə'prəʊpriətli]
释 ad. 不合适地；不相称地

criticism ['krɪtɪsɪzəm]
释 n. 批评；评判；评论

tuned [tjuːnd]
释 a. 经调谐的；调好台的

antennae [æn'teniː]
释 n. 动物的触角，触须；直觉

raise [reɪz]
释 v. 举起；增加；筹集；唤起；提出；养育 n. 上升；加薪
用 raise money 筹款
例 In order to get a *raise*, you have to work harder. 要想加薪，你必须工作得更加努力。

preface ['prefəs]

释 n. 序言，前言；开场白 v. 给某书作序；开始(讲话等)

prevail [prɪ'veɪl]

释 v. 战胜，压倒，占优势；盛行，流行

例 Jack's songs still *prevail* among the young generation. 杰克的歌仍然在年轻一代中流行着。

uneasy [ʌn'iːzi]

释 a. 不自在的；不安的，焦虑的

consideration [kən,sɪdə'reɪʃn]

释 n. 考虑；要考虑的事

handle ['hændl]

释 v. 处理，应付；操作；对待 n. 柄；把柄

例 Frankly speaking, it's not the proper way to *handle* the matter. 坦率来讲，这不是处理这件事情的适当方法。

intervention [,ɪntə'venʃn]

释 n. 干涉，介入

behalf [bɪ'hɑːf]

释 n. 利益；方面；维护

用 on behalf of 代表

undignified [ʌn'dɪɡnɪfaɪd]

释 a. 不庄重的，不像样子的

exchange [ɪks'tʃeɪndʒ]

释 n. 交换；交流；交易所；兑换 v. 交换；交易

用 exchange rate 汇率；the Stock Exchange 证券交易所

例 I'd like to do anything in *exchange* for your love. 我愿意做任何事来换取你的爱。

insulting [ɪn'sʌltɪŋ]

释 a. 侮辱的，有冒犯性的，无礼的

apparently [ə'pærəntli]

释 ad. 显然地；似乎

reputation [,repju'teɪʃn]

释 n. 名声；名誉；声望

用 have a reputation for 因…而著名

例 The writer enjoys a high *reputation* across the globe. 这位作家享誉全球。

💡 单词家族

家庭生活

album ['ælbəm] n. 照相簿；集邮本

aquarium [ə'kweəriəm] n. 养鱼缸；水族箱

breadwinner ['bredwɪnə(r)] n. 养家糊口的人

chore [tʃɔː(r)] n. 家务杂事

dehumidifier [,diːhjuː'mɪdɪfaɪə(r)] n. 除湿器

detergent [dɪ'tɜːdʒənt] n. 清洁剂

dispose [dɪ'spəʊz] v. 布置，陈列

domicile ['dɒmɪsaɪl] n. 住处，住所

fixture ['fɪkstʃə(r)] n. [常pl.] (房屋等的)固定装置

frugality [fru'gæləti] n. 节约，节俭

furnace ['fɜːnɪs] n. 暖气炉

lounge [laʊndʒ] n. 起居室；休息室

renovate ['renəveɪt] v. 修复，翻新

Passage 20

How Do You See Diversity?

As a manager, Tiffany is responsible for interviewing applicants for some of the positions with her company. During one interview, she noticed that the candidate never made direct eye contact. She was puzzled and somewhat disappointed because she liked the individual otherwise.

He had a perfect résumé and gave good responses to her questions, but the fact that he never looked her in the eye said "untrustworthy", so she decided to offer the job to her second choice.

"It wasn't until I attended a diversity workshop that I realized the person we passed over was the perfect person," Tiffany confesses. What she hadn't known at the time of the interview was that the candidate's "different" behavior was simply a cultural misunderstanding. He was an Asian-American raised in a household where respect for those in authority was shown by averting their eyes.

"I was just thrown off by the lack of eye contact; not realizing it was cultural," Tiffany says, "I missed out, but will not miss that opportunity again."

Many of us have had similar encounters with behaviors we perceive as different. As the world becomes smaller and our workplaces more diverse, it is becoming essential to expand our understanding of others and to reexamine some of our false assumptions.

Hire Advantage

At a time when hiring qualified people is becoming more difficult, employers who can eliminate invalid biases from the process have a distinct advantage. "During my Mindsets coaching session, I was taught how to recruit a diversified workforce. I recruited people from different cultures and skill sets. The agents were able to utilize their full potential and experiences to build up the company. When the real estate market began to change, it was because we had a diverse agent pool that we were able to stay in the real estate market much longer than others in the same profession."

Blinded by Gender

"I had a management position open in my department; and the two finalists were a man and a woman. Had I not attended this workshop, I would have automatically assumed the man was the best candidate because the position required quite a bit of extensive travel. My reasoning would have been that even though both candidates were great and could have been successful in the position, I assumed the woman would have wanted to be home with her children and not travel." Dale's assumptions are another example of the well-intentioned but incorrect thinking that limits an organization's ability to tap into the full potential of a diverse workforce.

"I learned from the class that instead of imposing my gender biases into the situation, I needed to present the full range of duties, responsibilities and expectations to all candidates and allow them to make an informed decision." Dale credits the workshop, "Because it helped me make decisions based on fairness."

Year of the Know-It-All

"Attending the diversity workshop helped me realize how much I could learn by simply asking questions and creating dialogues with my employees, rather than making assumptions and trying to be a know-it-all," Doug admits. "The biggest thing I took away from the workshop is learning how to be more 'inclusive' to differences."

A Better Bottom Line

An open mind about diversity not only improves organizations internally, it is profitable as well. These comments from a customer service representative show how an inclusive attitude can improve sales. "Most of my customers speak English as a second language. One of the best things my company has done is to contract with a language service that offers translations over the phone. It wasn't until my boss received Mindsets' training that she was able to understand how important inclusiveness was to customer service. As a result, our customer base has increased."

Once we start to see people as individuals, and discard the stereotypes, we can move positively toward inclusiveness for everyone. Diversity is about coming together and taking advantage of our differences and similarities. It is about building better communities and organizations that enhance us as individuals and reinforce our shared humanity.

When we begin to question our assumptions and challenge what we think we have learned from our past, from the media, peers, family, friends, etc., we begin to realize that some of our conclusions are flawed or contrary to our fundamental values. We need to train ourselves to think differently, shift our mindsets and realize that diversity opens doors for all of us, creating opportunities in organizations and communities that benefit everyone.

你如何看待多元化？

作为经理，蒂法妮负责与同事一起为公司的某些职位面试新员工。在一场面试中，她发现那位应聘者从未与她有过目光接触。这让她感到困惑，同时又有些失望，因为除此之外，她还挺欣赏这位应聘者的。

这位应聘者有堪称完美的简历，对她提出的问题也能对答如流，唯一不足的是他不肯正视蒂法妮的眼睛。这让她感觉这个人"不可靠"。因此，她决定把这份工作给她的第二人选。

蒂法妮坦言道："直到参加了一个关于多元化的专题研讨会，我才意识到我们错失了一个完美人选。"她在面试时并不知道那位应聘者的"异样"行为只不过是文化误解而已。那位应聘者是亚裔美国人，在他成长的家庭中，对权威者的尊重就是通过避免直视对方来表达的。

"我对他没有与我进行眼神交流感到困惑，却没有意识到那是文化差异。"蒂法妮说，"我错过了那次机会，但我以后不会再错过同样的机会了。"

在看待我们所认为的异样行为上，我们当中的不少人都有过类似的遭遇。随着世界变得越来越小，我们的工作环境变得越来越多元化，拓展我们对他人的了解以及重新审视我们的一些错误的假设也变得越来越重要。

招聘优势

在越来越难聘用到合格员工的时期，雇主若能在招聘过程中消除毫无根据的偏见，就会具有明显的优势。"在关于思维模式培训的研讨会中，我学到了怎样招聘到多样化的员工。我招到了具有不同文化和技术背景的员工。公司代理人能充分发挥他们的潜力和经验来促进公司的发展。当房地产市场开始变化时，正是因为拥有多元化的代理人团队，我们才能比同行业的其他公司做得更为长久。"

性别盲区

"我们部门有一个管理岗位空缺，最后的人选是一男一女两名候选人。如果没有参加过这次研讨会，我会很自然地认定那位男士是最佳候选人，因为这个职位需要经常出差。我的理由是：尽管这两位都很优秀，且都能胜任这份工作，但我猜想那位女士一定希望能够在家里同孩子待在一起，而不是出差。"戴尔的个人假设是另外一个出于好意但想法错误的例子。这种错误的假设会限制一个组织对多元化团队中的潜力进行充分挖掘的能力。

"从这个课程中，我学到了不要在工作中存在性别偏见，我需要向所有的候选人说明所应聘职位的职责、他们肩负的责任以及公司对他们的期望，并让他们自行决定。"戴尔认为这是研讨会的功劳，"因为它帮助我在公平的基础上作出了决定。"

无所不知的时代

　　"参加这次关于文化多元化的研讨会，帮助我意识到仅仅通过对员工进行提问和与员工对话，就能学到很多东西，而不是自己作出假设并试图做到无所不知。"道格坦言，"从研讨会中，我学到的最重要的东西就是如何做到更加包容别人的不同。"

更好的底线

　　对多元化持开放包容的态度不仅可以从内部促进企业的发展，还能带来经济效益。下面是来自一位客服代表的评论，显示出了包容的态度是如何提升销售业绩的。"我的大部分顾客都以英语为第二语言。我们公司做得最好的一件事就是与一家语言服务机构订立了协议，让他们通过电话提供翻译服务。直到参加了思维模式的培训，我的老板才意识到这种包容的态度对于客户服务是多么重要。因此，我们的客户群增加了很多。"

　　当我们开始把大众按不同的个人来对待，并摒除固有的思维模式时，我们就可以更加积极地包容每个人。多元化就是各种不同的文化汇聚在一起，并很好地利用各自的不同和相似之处。它指的是建立更加优秀的团体和组织，以改善我们作为个体的个性，并增强我们作为人类的共性。

　　当我们开始质疑自己的假设，并向我们从过去、媒体、同辈、家庭或朋友等处学到的知识发起挑战时，我们就会意识到我们的一些结论存在缺陷或违背了我们的基本价值观。我们需要训练自己从不同的角度进行思考的能力，改变我们的思维模式，同时领会到多元化向我们所有人敞开着大门，从而在组织和团队中创造出一些让所有的人都受益的机会。

💡 单词记事本

responsible　[rɪ'spɒnsəbl]
释 *a.* 需负责任的；有责任感的
用 be responsible for 对…负责

applicant　['æplɪkənt]
释 *n.* 申请人

disappointed　[ˌdɪsə'pɔɪntɪd]
释 *a.* 失望的；失意的；受挫的
例 Don't be *disappointed* with life, for there is always hope. 不要对生活失望，因为希望永远存在。

individual [ˌɪndɪ'vɪdʒuəl]
释 *n.* 个人；个体 *a.* 个别的；独特的

response [rɪ'spɒns]
释 *n.* 回答；答复；反应，响应
用 in response to 回应；响应
例 Every time the boss asks something, he needs a positive *response*. 每当老板问问题的时候，他需要的都是一个肯定的回答。

untrustworthy [ʌn'trʌstwɜ:ði]
释 *a.* 不值得信赖的，不可靠的

attend [ə'tend]
释 *v.* 出席，参加；照料；专心
用 attend a meeting 参加会议
例 I'm afraid that you don't *attend* school on time every day. 恐怕你并没有每天都准时上学。

workshop ['wɜ:kʃɒp]
释 *n.* 车间；研讨会，讲习班

confess [kən'fes]
释 *v.* 承认；供认；坦白；忏悔；告解

household ['haʊshəʊld]
释 *n.* 家庭；一家人 *a.* 家庭的；家常的

respect [rɪ'spekt]
释 *v.* 尊敬；尊重；关心 *n.* 尊敬；尊重；方面；尊敬之情
用 respect for 尊敬；in respect of 关于，涉及
例 I can't totally agree with you in some *respects*. 在某些方面，我不能完全同意你的意见。

avert [ə'vɜ:t]
释 *v.* 防止，避免；转移(目光、注意力等)
例 Discovering the danger, he broke hard and *averted* an accident. 他发现了危险，猛踩刹车避免了事故的发生。

encounter [ɪn'kaʊntə(r)]
释 *v.* 偶然碰到；邂逅；遭遇 *n.* 遭遇；意外相见
用 encounter with 突然相遇，意外遭遇

perceive [pə'si:v]
释 *v.* 感知，察觉；认识到，理解
用 perceive sth. as 理解；视为

expand [ɪk'spænd]
释 *v.* 扩大，增加；伸展；展开

reexamine [ˌri:ɪg'zæmɪn]
释 *v.* 重考；再检查，回顾

qualified ['kwɒlɪfaɪd]
释 *a.* 有资格的；合格的，胜任的；有限制的
用 be qualified for 有担任…的资格；适于担任

invalid
释 [ɪn'vælɪd] *a.* 无可靠根据的；(指法律上)无效的；伤残的
['ɪnvəlɪd; 'ɪnvəli:d] *n.* 病弱者，残疾者

mindset ['maɪndset]
释 *n.* 思想倾向；精神状态

recruit [rɪ'kru:t]
释 *n.* 新兵；新成员 *v.* 招募(新兵)；吸收(新成员)

diversified [daɪ'vɜ:sɪfaɪd]
释 *a.* 多样化的

utilize ['ju:təlaɪz]
释 *v.* 利用；应用

diverse [daɪ'vɜ:s]
释 *a.* 多样的；不同的

pool [pu:l]
释 *n.* 水池；水塘；集中使用的资金、物资等；(人员等的)储备

profession [prə'feʃn]
释 *n.* 职业；声明；表白；[the ~] 同行，(某)职业界

finalist ['faɪnəlɪst]
圝 n. 参加决赛的选手；最后的竞争者

tap [tæp]
圝 n. 龙头；轻拍；熄灯号 v. 轻拍；放出液体；窃听；自…引出或获取

impose [ɪm'pəʊz]
圝 v. 强加；征税；以…欺骗
用 impose on/upon 强加于；利用，欺骗

informed [ɪn'fɔːmd]
圝 a. 见多识广的；消息灵通的；知情的；(猜测或决策)明智的

inclusive [ɪn'kluːsɪv]
圝 a. 包括的，包容的；包含的；内容丰富的

internally [ɪn'tɜːnəli]
圝 ad. 在内部；在国内；内在地

profitable ['prɒfɪtəbl]
圝 a. 可获利润或好处的；有益的

representative [ˌreprɪ'zentətɪv]
圝 n. 代表；代理人；有代表性的人或物 a. 有代表性的；典型的

contract
圝 ['kɒntrækt] n. 合同，契约
[kən'trækt] v. 订合同；收缩；感染
例 A *contract* was signed after several negotiations between the two sides. 双方经过几轮谈判之后才签订了合同。

discard [dɪs'kaːd]
圝 v. 扔掉，丢弃；不再使用，不再穿戴；出牌

enhance [ɪn'haːns]
圝 v. 增强，提高；夸张；宣扬

reinforce [ˌriːɪn'fɔːs]
圝 v. 加强；加固；增援；补充

humanity [hjuː'mænəti]
圝 n. 人类；人性；人道

flawed [flɔːd]
圝 a. 有缺陷的

fundamental [ˌfʌndə'mentl]
圝 a. 根本的；基础的；十分重要的 n. 基本原则

💡 单词家族

多样文化

bacchanal ['bækənl] n. 狂饮；酒神节
chapel ['tʃæpl] n. 小教堂；祈祷室
choreographic [ˌkɒriə'ɡræfɪk] a. 舞蹈术的；舞台舞蹈的
civilian [sə'vɪliən] n. 平民；百姓 a. 民间的；民用的
congruent ['kɒŋɡruənt] a. 适合的；一致的，和谐的
conjure ['kʌndʒə(r)] v. 变魔术
construction [kən'strʌkʃn] n. 建筑物；构造

dabbler ['dæblə(r)] n. 涉猎者；爱好者
embody [ɪm'bɒdi] v. 体现；使具体化
identical [aɪ'dentɪkl] a. 相同的；同一的
juggle ['dʒʌɡl] v. 玩杂耍
masquerade [ˌmæskə'reɪd] n. 化装舞会；假装，伪装
ornamental [ˌɔːnə'mentl] a. 装饰的
pundit ['pʌndɪt] n. 权威人士；博学者

Passage 21

音频

Google's Plan for World's Biggest Online Library

In recent years, teams of workers dispatched by Google have been working hard to make digital copies of books. So far, Google has scanned more than 10 million titles from libraries in America and Europe—including half a million volumes held by the Bodleian in Oxford. The exact method it uses is unclear; the company does not allow outsiders to observe the process.

Why is Google undertaking such a venture? Why is it even interested in all those out-of-print library books, most of which have been gathering dust on forgotten shelves for decades? The company claims its motives are essentially public-spirited. Its overall mission, after all, is to "organize the world's information", so it would be odd if that information did not include books.

The company likes to present itself as having lofty aspirations. "This really isn't about making money. We are doing this for the good of society." As Santiago de la Mora, head of Google Books for Europe, puts it: "By making it possible to search the millions of books that exist today, we hope to expand the frontiers of human knowledge."

Dan Clancy, the chief architect of Google Books, does seem genuine in his conviction that this is primarily a philanthropic exercise. "Google's core business is search and find, so obviously what helps improve Google's search engine is good for Google," he says. "But we have never built a spreadsheet outlining the financial benefits of this, and I have never had to justify the amount I am spending to the company's founders."

It is easy, talking to Clancy and his colleagues, to be swept along by their missionary passion. But Google's book-scanning project is proving controversial. Several opponents have recently emerged, ranging from rival tech giants such as Microsoft and Amazon to small bodies representing authors and publishers across the world. In broad terms, these opponents have levelled two sets of criticisms at Google.

First, they have questioned whether the primary responsibility for digitally archiving the world's books should be allowed to fall to a commercial company. The second related criticism is that Google's scanning of books is actually illegal.

This **allegation** has led to Google becoming mired in a legal battle whose **scope** and complexity makes the Jarndyce and Jarndyce case in Charles Dickens' *Bleak House* look **straightforward**.

At its center, however, is one simple issue: that of copyright. The inconvenient fact about most books, to which Google has arguably paid **insufficient** attention, is that they are protected by copyright. Copyright laws differ from country to country, but in general protection extends for the **duration** of an author's life and for a substantial period afterwards, thus allowing the author's heirs to benefit.

Outside the US, Google has made sure only to scan books that are out of copyright and thus in the "public **domain**" (works such as the Bodleian's first **edition** of *Middlemarch*, which anyone can read for free on Google Books Search).

But, within the US, the company has scanned both in-copyright and out-of-copyright works. In its defence, Google points out that it **displays** only small segments of books that are in copyright—arguing that such displays are "fair use". But critics **allege** that by making electronic copies of these books without first seeking the **permission** of copyright **holders**, Google has **committed** piracy.

Critics point out that, by giving Google the right to commercially exploit its database, the settlement paves the way for a **subtle** shift in the company's role from provider of information to seller.

No one knows the **precise** use Google will make of the **intellectual** property it has gained by scanning the world's library books, and the truth, as Gleick, an American science writer and member of the Authors Guild, points out, is that the company probably doesn't even know itself. But what is certain is that, in some way or other, Google's **entrance** into digital bookselling will have a significant impact on the book world in the years to come.

译文

谷歌欲建世界最大的在线图书馆

近年来，谷歌公司分派的工作团队一直在辛苦地制作数字图书。到目前为止，谷歌已经从美国和欧洲的图书馆扫描了逾1000万册图书——其中包括取自牛津大学波德林图书馆的50万册。谷歌采用的具体方法尚不清楚；它不允许外部人员参观这一过程。

谷歌公司为什么要承担这样一种挑战？它为什么会对所有那些馆藏绝版书籍感兴趣？何况这类书籍中的大部分早在几十年前就被人们束之高阁，布满了灰尘。该公司声称其动机本质上是服务于公众。毕竟，它的总体目标是"整合全球的信息资源"，因此将书籍列入其中也是自然而然的事。

谷歌公司喜欢向公众展示自己具有崇高愿景的形象。"这确实不是为了赚钱。我们这样做是为了社会的利益。"谷歌图书欧洲分部的负责人圣地亚哥·德拉莫拉说，"通过实现对现存的数以百万计的书籍的搜索，我们希望能拓展人类的知识范畴。"

负责谷歌图书项目的总工程师丹·克兰西似乎完全确信谷歌的这一举动从根本上讲是一项慈善活动。"谷歌的核心业务是搜索和查找信息，所以很显然，有助于改善谷歌的搜索引擎的功能就会为谷歌公司带来好处。"他说，"但是我们从未做过什么电子数据表来罗列此种做法能够带来的经济收益，而且我也从不需要向公司创始人交代所支出金额的合理性。"

与克兰西和他的同事谈话，很容易就被他们言语中的热情所感染。但是谷歌的图书扫描计划也引起了人们的争议。最近出现了一些反对者，包括从其竞争对手微软和亚马逊这样的科技巨头到全球各地代表作者和出版商利益的小型组织。总的来说，这些反对者主要从两方面对谷歌提出了批评。

第一，他们质疑对全球藏书进行数字归档的职责是否应该落在一家商业公司头上。第二，他们指责谷歌的书籍扫描行为其实是违法的。这项指控导致谷歌陷入了一场官司，这场官司的范围和复杂性使得查尔斯·狄更斯的《荒凉山庄》中的"贾戴斯控贾戴斯案"都显得小儿科。

但其本质上只是一个简单的问题：版权。关于大部分书籍的一个难以忽视的真相就是它们都是受版权保护的，但有充分的证据证明谷歌对此没有给予充分的重视。版权法因国家而异，但总体上版权的保护期限都包含作者的一生乃至作者过世之后相当长的一段时期，这样可以使作者的继承人受益。

在美国之外，谷歌能够确保只扫描已经不受版权保护而进入"公共领域"的书籍（类似于波德林所收藏的《米德尔马契》的第一版，任何人都可以在谷歌图书搜索中免费阅读）。

但在美国境内，谷歌扫描的书籍既有不受版权保护的，也有仍受保护的。对于受版权保护的书籍，谷歌辩称，它只会显示书籍的一小部分——并辩解说这种显示属于"合理使用"。但批评人士称，谷歌未经版权所有者的允许而擅自制作电子版图书，已经构成剽窃行为。

批评者指出，赋予谷歌将数据库用作商业用途的权利，将为谷歌从信息提供者到销售者的微妙转变铺平道路。

没有人知道谷歌通过扫描全世界的图书馆藏书得到的知识产权的确切用处，但真相正如美国科普作家、作家协会会员格莱克所说，谷歌自身可能还不清楚。但可以肯定的是，从某种意义上讲，谷歌介入数字图书销售市场将在未来几年对图书领域产生深远的影响。

dispatch [dɪ'spætʃ]
释 *n./v.* 分派；派遣

scan [skæn]
释 *n./v.* 扫描；细看；浏览

volume ['vɒljuːm]
释 *n.* 本，册，卷；容量；音量；数量；许多

undertake [ˌʌndə'teɪk]
释 *v.* 承担(某事物)；同意，答应
例 The new employee will *undertake* the responsibility for the work next week. 这名新员工将从下周开始承担工作责任。

venture ['ventʃə(r)]
释 *n.* 冒险，冒险的事业；投资 *v.* 敢于；冒…风险；拿…投机

motive ['məʊtɪv]
释 *n.* 动机；原因 *a.* 发动的；产生运动的
例 That his *motive* of crime is money is evident. 很明显，他的犯罪动机是为了金钱。

lofty ['lɒfti]
释 *a.* 崇高的；高傲的；高耸的

aspiration [ˌæspə'reɪʃn]
释 *n.* 志向；抱负

frontier ['frʌntɪə(r)]
释 *n.* 国界；边境；边疆；[the ~s] (尤指有关某事物的知识)界限

chief [tʃiːf]
释 *n.* 首领；族长；首长 *a.* 主要的；重要的；首席的；最高级别的
用 chief editor 总编；in chief 主要地
例 The company has thus lost most of its *chief* advocates. 这家公司因此失去了大部分重要的支持者。

genuine ['dʒenjuɪn]
释 *a.* 真正的；真诚的

primarily [praɪ'merəli; 'praɪmərəli]
释 *ad.* 主要地；根本上；首先，最初

philanthropic [ˌfɪlən'θrɒpɪk]
释 *a.* 慈善的；慈善事业的

core [kɔː(r)]
释 *n.* 果心；核心 *v.* 去掉某物的中心部分

justify ['dʒʌstɪfaɪ]
释 *v.* 表明或证明…是正当(或有理)的；为…辩护

project
释 ['prɒdʒekt] *n.* 计划；项目；工程 [prə'dʒekt] *v.* 投射；规划；发出

controversial [ˌkɒntrə'vɜːʃl]
释 *a.* 引起或可能引起争论的

rival ['raɪvl]
释 *n.* 竞争者 *a.* 竞争的 *v.* 与…竞争
例 The number of its *rival* firms is on the decrease. 其竞争公司的数量在减少。

represent [ˌreprɪ'zent]
释 *v.* 作为…的代表(或代理)；表现；描绘，塑造；陈述

opponent [ə'pəʊnənt]
释 *n.* 对手；反对者 *a.* 对立的；对抗的

level ['levl]
释 *a.* 水平的；等高的；平稳的 *n.* 水平线；水平；级别 *v.* 使平坦；夷平，摧毁；瞄准；提出责难或控告

commercial [kə'mɜːʃl]
释 *a.* 商业的；商品化的 *n.* 商业广告

allegation [ˌælə'geɪʃn]
释 *n.* 陈述，宣称，指控；辩解；(无证据的)陈词

110

scope [skəʊp]

释 n. 范围；余地，机会

用 business scope 营业范围；within the scope of 在…范围内

straightforward [ˌstreɪt'fɔːwəd]

释 a. 直截了当的；坦率的，老实的；简单的 ad. 坦率地

insufficient [ˌɪnsə'fɪʃnt]

释 a. 不足的，不够的；不充分的

用 insufficient memory 内存空间不足

例 Insufficient financial resources have caused a growing number of firms' bankruptcy. 资金来源不足导致越来越多的公司破产。

duration [djʊ'reɪʃn]

释 n. 持续的时间，期间

domain [də'meɪn; dəʊ'meɪn]

释 n. 领土；领域

edition [ɪ'dɪʃn]

释 n. 版本；(书报等)一次发行的总数

display [dɪ'spleɪ]

释 v./n. 陈列，展览，显示；表现

用 on display 展示

allege [ə'ledʒ]

释 v. 断言，宣称；辩解

例 It has been alleged that the bank has been robbed. 据称有人抢劫了银行。

permission [pə'mɪʃn]

释 n. 许可，允许

holder ['həʊldə(r)]

释 n. 持有者，所有者；(支票等的)持有人；支托物

commit [kə'mɪt]

释 v. 犯(错误、罪等)；托付；承诺；使承担任务

用 commit suicide 自杀；commit a crime 犯罪

例 People who commit violent crimes have some psychological problems. 暴力犯罪的人有某些心理问题。

subtle ['sʌtl]

释 a. 微妙的；细微的；精巧的

precise [prɪ'saɪs]

释 a. 准确的；严谨的

intellectual [ˌɪntə'lektʃuəl]

释 a. 智力的 n. 知识分子

例 The master's degree is a starting point for her as an intellectual. 硕士学位是她成为知识分子的起点。

entrance ['entrəns]

释 n. 入口；进入

单词家族

网络通信

amplifier ['æmplɪfaɪə(r)] n. 放大器；扩音器

analogue ['ænəlɒg] a. 模拟计算机的

cyberspace ['saɪbəspeɪs] n. 网络空间

decimal ['desɪml] a. 小数的，十进制的

decode [ˌdiː'kəʊd] v. 解码，译码

delete [dɪ'liːt] v. 删除

device [dɪ'vaɪs] n. 器械，装置；手段

format ['fɔːmæt] n. 格式 v. 使格式化

formulation [ˌfɔːmju'leɪʃn] n. 公式化，格式化；确切的表达

hub [hʌb] n. 中心；网络集线器

input ['ɪnpʊt] n. 输入；输入的数据 v. 把…输入计算机

parameter [pə'ræmɪtə(r)] n. 参数

Passage 22

Prestige Panic

In the college-admissions wars, we parents are the true **fighters**. We're pushing our kids to get good **grades**, take SAT preparatory courses and build résumés so they can get into the college of our first choice. I've twice been to the wars, and as I survey the battlefield, something different is happening. We see our kids' college background as a **prize demonstrating** how well we've raised them. But we can't **acknowledge** that our **obsession** is more about us than them. So we've **contrived** various **justifications** that turn out to be half-truths, prejudices or **myths**. It actually doesn't matter much whether Aaron and Nicole go to Stanford.

We have a full-blown **prestige** panic; we worry that there won't be enough prizes to go around. **Fearful** parents urge their children to apply to more schools than ever. **Underlying** the hysteria is the **belief** that **scarce elite** degrees must be highly valuable and their graduates must enjoy more success because they get a better education and develop better contacts. All that is **plausible**—and mostly wrong. We haven't found any **convincing** evidence that selectivity or prestige matters. Selective schools don't **systematically** employ better instructional approaches than less selective schools. On two **measures**—professors' **feedback** and the number of essay exams—selective schools do **slightly** worse.

By some studies, selective schools do **enhance** their graduates' lifetime earnings. The gain is **reckoned** at 2%–4% for every 100-point increase in a school's average SAT scores. But even this advantage is probably a **statistical fluke**. A well-known study examined students who got into highly selective schools and then went elsewhere. They earned just as much as graduates from higher-status schools.

Kids count more than their colleges. Getting into Yale may **signify** intelligence, talent and ambition. But it's not the only **indicator** and, **paradoxically**, its significance is declining. The reason: so many similar people go elsewhere. Getting into college isn't life's only competition. Old-boy networks are breaking down. Princeton economist Alan Krueger studied **admissions** to one top Ph.D. program. High scores on the GRE helped explain who got in; degrees of prestigious universities didn't.

So, parents, **lighten** up. The stakes have been **vastly exaggerated**. Up to a point, we can **rationalize** our pushness. America is a **competitive** society; our kids need to adjust to that. But too much pushiness can be **destructive**. The very ambition we **impose** on our children may get some into Harvard but may also set them up for disappointment. One study found that, other things being equal, graduates of highly selective schools experienced more job **dissatisfaction**. They may have been so **conditioned** to being on top that anything less disappoints.

译文

威望恐慌

在大学入学考试这场战役中，父母才是真正的战斗者。我们督促孩子取得好成绩、参加SAT预备课程，为孩子设计简历，以使其能进入我们的首选大学。我经历过两次这样的战役，但当我观察战场时，我发现一些不同的事情正在发生。我们把孩子的大学背景当成一种战利品，以显示我们把孩子教育得有多好。但是我们并不承认我们的痴迷更多的是关于自己，而不是他们。所以我们巧妙策划的种种辩解理由最终都被证明是半真半假的陈词，或是我们的偏见和幻想。事实上，亚伦和妮科尔是否进入了斯坦福大学并没有多大的意义。

我们陷入了全面的威望恐慌中；我们担心战利品不够。恐慌的父母督促孩子们申请更多的学校。在他们歇斯底里的背后，是这样一种信念："稀缺的名校学位一定有着很高的价值。这些学校的毕业生一定会获取更大的成功，因为他们受过更好的教育，有着更好的人际关系。"这一切似乎都是有道理的——但大多都是错误的。我们还没有发现任何令人信服的证据，能够表明选拔性或声望很重要。和一般学校相比，名校并没有系统地采用更好的教学方法。从教授的反馈和论文考试的数量这两个标准来衡量，名校的表现也略差。

根据一些研究，名校确实提高了其毕业生的终身收入。学校的SAT平均成绩每增加100分，学生的收入便会增加2%—4%。但是，即便是这个优势也可能是统计上的一种偶然性。有一个著名的研究对在名校学习过然后转去别的学校的学生进行了调查。这些学生的收入和更好的学校的毕业生差不多。

孩子自身的价值不仅仅体现在他的学校上。进入耶鲁大学也许意味着有智慧、有才气、有抱负，但这不是人生的唯一指标，而且相反的是，它的意义正在日渐淡化。原因是很多这样的人都去了别的学校。进入大学并不是人生的唯一竞赛。老同学关系网正在渐渐失效。普林斯顿大学的经济学家艾伦·克鲁格对一个顶尖博士项目的录取工作进行了研究，他发现在GRE考试中获得高分的学生会被录取，而名校生则不一定。

因此，父母们，放松下来吧。学校这一赌注已经被大大夸大了。在某种程度上，我们可以为我们的督促辩解，使其合理化：美国是一个竞争激烈的社会；我们的孩子需要适应这个社会。但是太多的督促会具有毁灭性。我们强加给孩子的抱负可能会让他们进入哈佛大学，但也可能会让他们失望。一项研究发现，在其他条件相同的情况下，名校毕业生对工作不满的经历更多。他们可能已完全习惯于处处拔尖，所以任何稍差一些的事物都会令其失望。

💡 单词记事本

fighter ['faɪtə(r)]
释 n. 战士；战斗机；拳击手

grade [greɪd]
释 n. 分数；等级；年级 v. 将…分等；对…进行评分

prize [praɪz]
释 n. 奖品；奖金；值得争取的有价值的事物；战利品 a. 该得奖的；出类拔萃的 v. 重视；珍视
用 Nobel Prize 诺贝尔奖；prize winner 得奖者

demonstrate ['demənstreɪt]
释 v. 证明，论证；表明，表示；示范；举行示威游行

acknowledge [ək'nɒlɪdʒ]
释 v. 承认…属实；确认；对…表示感谢

obsession [əb'seʃn]
释 n. 痴迷，执意

contrive [kən'traɪv]
释 v. 图谋；设计；发明；想尽办法做某事
例 The life, in fact, can not be *contrived*. 事实上，生活是无法被设计的。

justification [ˌdʒʌstɪfɪ'keɪʃn]
释 n. 正当理由；辩解，借口

myth [mɪθ]
释 n. 神话；想象或虚构出来的人(或事物)

prestige [pre'stiːʒ]
释 n. 威信，威望
例 It has been proved to be an effective way to earn international *prestige*. 它已被证明是一种赢得国际声誉的有效方法。

fearful ['fɪəfl]
释 a. 可怕的；不安的，忧虑的

underlie [ˌʌndə'laɪ]
释 v. 位于…之下；构成…的基础

belief [bɪ'liːf]
释 n. 相信；信仰；信念
用 firm belief 坚定的信念；beyond belief 难以置信
例 We should all maintain the optimistic *belief* even if in difficulty. 我们即使身处困境，也应保持乐观的信念。

scarce [skeəs]
释 a. 缺乏的，不足的；稀少的，难得的

elite [eɪ'liːt；ɪ'liːt]
释 n. 精英；中坚

plausible ['plɔːzəbl]
释 a. 似有道理的；能说会道的

convincing [kən'vɪnsɪŋ]
释 a. 令人信服的

systematically [ˌsɪstə'mætɪkli]
释 ad. 有系统地；有组织地

measure ['meʒə(r)]

释 *n.* 计量单位；测量；(衡量的)标准，尺度；[常*pl.*]措施 *v.* 测量；衡量

feedback ['fi:dbæk]

释 *n.* 反馈；反馈信息

用 information feedback 信息反馈

例 You'd better try to get the *feedback* as early as possible. 你最好努力尽早得到反馈。

slightly ['slaɪtli]

释 *ad.* 轻微地；苗条

enhance [ɪn'hɑ:ns]

释 *v.* 提高；增强；美化

reckon ['rekən]

释 *v.* 测算，计算；猜想；认为

statistical [stə'tɪstɪkl]

释 *a.* 统计的；统计学的

fluke [flu:k]

释 *n.* 侥幸，偶然，意外

signify ['sɪgnɪfaɪ]

释 *v.* 意味，表明，表示；有重要性

indicator ['ɪndɪkeɪtə(r)]

释 *n.* 指标；指示器；指示剂；指示牌

paradoxically [ˌpærə'dɒksɪkli]

释 *ad.* 自相矛盾地；反论地，似非而是地；反常地

admission [əd'mɪʃn]

释 *n.* 准许进入；入场券，入场费；承认，坦白

用 admission ticket 入场券；准考证；admission office 招生办；住院处

lighten ['laɪtn]

释 *v.* (使)变轻；(使)令人放心，解除忧虑；使更明亮；容光焕发

用 lighten up 放松；不要生气

vastly ['vɑ:stli]

释 *ad.* 极大地；深远地

exaggerate [ɪg'zædʒəreɪt]

释 *v.* 夸张，夸大

例 Don't be the person who is always *exaggerating*. 不要做总是夸大其词的人。

rationalize ['ræʃnəlaɪz]

释 *v.* 使有合理依据；使更合理(一致)

competitive [kəm'petətɪv]

释 *a.* 竞争的；与…不相上下的

用 competitive advantage 竞争优势；competitive spirit 竞争意识，好胜心

例 The only way to survive in the market is being highly *competitive*. 只有保持很强的竞争力，才能在市场中生存。

destructive [dɪ'strʌktɪv]

释 *a.* 破坏性的，毁灭性的

impose [ɪm'pəʊz]

释 *v.* 把…强加于；征(税等)；处以(罚款、监禁等)

用 impose on 强加于；利用；施加影响于；impose a fine 处以罚款

例 They *impose* duties on imported cigarettes according to the law. 他们根据法律对进口香烟征税。

dissatisfaction [ˌdɪsˌsætɪs'fækʃn]

释 *n.* 不满；令人不满的事物

conditioned [kən'dɪʃnd]

释 *a.* 受条件限制的，制约的；受调节的；适合…的，习惯…的

运气意外

abrupt [ə'brʌpt] *a.* 突然的；唐突的；陡峭的

accidental [ˌæksɪ'dentl] *a.* 意外的；偶然的；附属的

adventitious [ˌædven'tɪʃəs] *a.* 偶然的

aleatory ['eɪlɪətəri] *a.* 偶然的；侥幸的

bonanza [bə'nænzə] *n.* 带来好运的事

boon [buːn] *n.* 恩惠；福利

coincidence [kəʊ'ɪnsɪdəns] *n.* 巧合；一致

destiny ['destəni] *n.* 命运；定数

fate [feɪt] *n.* 命运；命中注定的事；结局

fortuitous [fɔː'tjuːɪtəs] *a.* 偶然发生的；巧合的

fortune ['fɔːtʃuːn] *n.* 运气；命运；财富

garbled ['gɑːbld] *a.* 引起误解的

illusory [ɪ'luːsəri] *a.* 虚幻的

lot [lɒt] *n.* 许多；份额；抽签；运气；命运

misfortune [ˌmɪs'fɔːtʃuːn] *n.* 不幸；灾祸，灾难

occasional [ə'keɪʒənl] *a.* 偶然的；临时的；应景的

portion ['pɔːʃn] *n.* 部分；一份；命运

preposterous [prɪ'pɒstərəs] *a.* 反常的

presumable [prɪ'zjuːməbl] *a.* 可推测的

scram [skræm] *v.* 匆忙离开

spell [spel] *v.* 招致

tribulation [ˌtrɪbju'leɪʃn] *n.* 苦难，灾难

triumphant [traɪ'ʌmfənt] *a.* 胜利的，成功的

unexpected [ˌʌnɪk'spektɪd] *a.* 意外的；未料到的

unfortunate [ʌn'fɔːtʃənət] *a.* 不幸的；不合适的；令人遗憾的

untoward [ˌʌntə'wɔːd] *a.* 不幸的

A man can succeed at almost anything for which he has unlimited enthusiasm.
　　　　　　　　　　　　—Charles Michael Schwab
一个人只要有无限的热情，几乎可以在任何事情上取得成功。
　　　　　　　　　　　——查尔斯·迈克尔·施瓦布

Passage 23

音频

原 文

Sustainable Development on Agriculture

Sustainable development is applied to just about everything from energy to clean water and economic growth, and as a result it has become difficult to question either the basic assumptions behind it or the way the concept is put to use. This is especially true in agriculture, where sustainable development is often taken as the sole measure of progress without a proper appreciation of historical and cultural perspectives.

To start with, it is important to remember that the nature of agriculture has changed markedly throughout history, and will continue to do so. Medieval agriculture in northern Europe fed, clothed and sheltered a predominantly rural society with a much lower population density than it is today. It had a minimal effect on biodiversity, and any pollution it caused was typically localized. In terms of energy use and the nutrients captured in the product, it was relatively inefficient.

Contrast this with farming since the start of the industrial revolution. Competition from overseas led farmers to specialize and increase yields. Throughout this period food became cheaper, safer and more reliable. However, these changes have also led to habitat loss and to diminishing biodiversity.

What's more, demand for animal products in developing countries is growing so fast that meeting it will require an extra 300 million tons of grain a year by 2050. Yet the growth of cities and industry is reducing the amount of water available for agriculture in many regions.

All this means that agriculture in the 21st century will have to be very different from how it was in the 20th. This will require radical thinking. For example, we need to move away from the idea that traditional practices are inevitably more sustainable than new ones. We also need to abandon the notion that agriculture can be "zero impact". The key will be to abandon the rather simple and static measures of sustainability, which center on the need to maintain production without increasing damage.

Instead we need a more dynamic interpretation, one that looks at the pros and cons of all the various ways land is used. There are many different ways to measure agricultural performance besides food yield: energy use, environmental costs, water purity, carbon footprint and biodiversity. It is clear, for example, that the carbon of transporting tomatoes from Spain to the UK is less than that of producing them in the UK with additional heating and lighting. But we do not know whether lower carbon footprints will always be better for biodiversity.

What is crucial is recognizing that **sustainable** agriculture is not just about sustainable food production.

译文

农业的可持续发展

可持续发展可应用到生活的方方面面，从能源到清洁水，再到经济增长。因此，去质疑可持续发展背后的基本假设理念或其实施方式已经变得非常困难。在农业方面尤其如此，因为可持续发展经常被当作衡量农业进步的唯一标准，而没有从历史和文化角度来作适当的评判。

首先，要牢记农业的本质在历史发展过程中已经发生了明显的改变，并且还会继续改变下去，这一点很重要。在中世纪的北欧，农业占据着农村社会的主导地位，并给人口密度远低于当今的社会提供衣食和住所。它对生物多样性的影响甚微，并且它所造成的任何污染通常都局限于某一地区。但就能源利用和农产品中所含的营养成分而言，中世纪农业的效率相对较低。

我们把它与工业革命开始以来的农业对比一下。来自海外的竞争使得农民在种植方面更加专业化并提高了产量。在此期间，食物变得比以前便宜、安全和可靠。然而这些改变也导致了动物栖息地的丧失以及生物多样性的下降。

此外，发展中国家对动物产品的需求增长得如此之快，以至于到2050年要满足此需求，每年额外需要3亿吨粮食。而在许多地区，城市和工业的发展使得农业用水正在减少。

所有这些都意味着21世纪的农业将与20世纪的农业有着极大的不同，而这需要革命性的思考方式。例如，我们要摒弃传统农业必然比现代农业更有利于可持续发展的观点。我们也要摒除农业是"零污染"的想法。最重要的是要摒弃那些过于简单而又一成不变的衡量可持续性的方式，这些方式往往在不加大破坏的前提下以维持产量为中心。

相反，我们需要一种更加动态的诠释，即能兼顾各种土地使用方式优缺点的诠释。除了粮食产量，还有许多不同的方式能衡量农业的表现，如能源利用、环境成本、水纯度、碳排放量以及生物多样性。例如，从西班牙把西红柿运至英国产生的碳排放量比在英国耗费额外的光和热种植西红柿产生的明显要少。然而，降低碳排放量是否会一直有利于生物的多样性，我们还不得而知。

关键是我们要认识到，农业的可持续发展不单单是粮食生产的可持续发展。

sustainable [sə'steɪnəbl]
释 *a.* 可以忍受的；足可支撑的；可持续的
用 sustainable development 可持续发展
例 Various measures have been taken to achieve *sustainable* economic growth. 已经采取了多种措施来实现经济的可持续发展。

apply [ə'plaɪ]
释 *v.* 申请；适用；使用；涂，敷，施
用 apply for 申请
例 The rule, I'm afraid, doesn't *apply* here. 恐怕这个规定在此并不适用。

agriculture ['ægrɪkʌltʃə(r)]
释 *n.* 农业；农学
用 organic agriculture 有机农业
例 *Agriculture*, the basic sector of national economy, plays an important role. 作为国民经济的基础部门，农业作用重大。

sole [səʊl]
释 *a.* 唯一的，独有的 *n.* 脚掌；鞋底，袜底

appreciation [ə,priːʃi'eɪʃn]
释 *n.* 欣赏；感激；鉴定；评价
例 You are eager for the *appreciation* and recognition from others. 你非常渴望他人的欣赏与认可。

perspective [pə'spektɪv]
释 *n.* (判断事物的)角度；透视法；景色

markedly ['maːkɪdli]
释 *ad.* 显著地，明显地
例 The advantages of the two methods are *markedly* different. 两种方法的优势明显不同。

density ['densəti]
释 *n.* 密度；浓度

typically ['tɪpɪkli]
释 *ad.* 典型地；有代表性地；通常，一般地

nutrient ['njuːtriənt]
释 *n.* 养分；营养物质

inefficient [,ɪnɪ'fɪʃnt]
释 *a.* 效率低的；不能胜任的
例 There are many factors leading to the *inefficient* performance. 有很多因素导致了效率低下。

specialize ['speʃəlaɪz]
释 *v.* 专门从事；专攻

yield [jiːld]
释 *v.* 生产，产出；屈服；放弃 *n.* 产量；收益

reliable [rɪ'laɪəbl]
释 *a.* 可靠的，可信赖的

habitat ['hæbɪtæt]
释 *n.* 栖息地；自然环境

region ['riːdʒən]
释 *n.* 地区；范围；行政区

traditional [trə'dɪʃənl]
释 *a.* 传统的；惯例的

inevitably [ɪn'evɪtəbli]
释 *ad.* 必然地；不可避免地

notion ['nəʊʃn]
释 *n.* 观念，想法；明白，理解
例 The *notion* that don't waste time is popular. 不要浪费时间的观念深入人心。

static ['stætɪk]
释 *a.* 静态的；固定的，不变的 *n.* 静电

dynamic [daɪ'næmɪk]
释 *a.* 动态的；动力的；有活力的 *n.* 动力；动态

interpretation [ɪn,tɜːprɪ'teɪʃn]
释 *n.* 解释；说明

performance [pə'fɔ:məns]
释 n. 演出；履行，施行；表现，成就；性能
用 performance management 绩效管理

purity ['pjʊərəti]
释 n. 纯洁，纯净；纯度

footprint ['fʊtprɪnt]
释 n. 足迹，脚印

transport ['trænspɔ:t]
释 v. 运输 n. 运输；运输系统；运输工具

单词家族

农业相关

abundance [ə'bʌndəns] n. 丰富，充裕
affluent ['æfluənt] a. 丰富的；富裕的
barn [ba:n] n. 谷仓；畜棚
barren ['bærən] a. 贫瘠的；不结果的
breed [bri:d] v. 繁殖；饲养；养育
burgeon ['bɜ:dʒən] v. 萌芽；迅速成长
cactus ['kæktəs] n. 仙人掌
cereal ['sɪərɪəl] n. 谷类植物；谷物产品
coexist [,kəʊɪg'zɪst] v. 共存
cultivate ['kʌltɪveɪt] v. 种植；培养
daisy ['deɪzi] n. 雏菊
desiccate ['desɪkeɪt] v. 使完全干涸；(使)脱水
diversify [daɪ'vɜ:sɪfaɪ] v. (使)不同；(使)多元化
evergreen ['evəgri:n] a. 常绿的
exuberant [ɪg'zju:bərənt] a. 繁茂的；充满活力的
fertile ['fɜ:taɪl] a. 肥沃的，富饶的；能繁殖的
fertilizer ['fɜ:təlaɪzə(r)] n. 肥料
flaggy ['flægi] a. 凋零的；松软无力的
floral ['flɔ:rəl] a. 花的；植物的
foliage ['fəʊliɪdʒ] n. 植物的叶子
fruition [fru'ɪʃn] n. 结果实；实现，完成
germinate ['dʒɜ:mɪneɪt] v. 发芽；发展
herbal ['hɜ:bl] a. 草本植物的

irrigation [,ɪrɪ'geɪʃn] n. 灌溉
meadow ['medəʊ] n. 草地；牧场
orchard ['ɔ:tʃəd] n. 果园
orchid ['ɔ:kɪd] n. 兰花
pasture ['pa:stʃə(r)] n. 牧草；牧场
pest [pest] n. 害虫；有害物
pesticide ['pestɪsaɪd] n. 杀虫剂；农药
pollination [,pɒlə'neɪʃn] n. 授粉
poultry ['pəʊltri] n. 家禽
prolific [prə'lɪfɪk] a. 多产的；丰富的
prune [pru:n] v. 修剪，修整；删除，削减
ramify ['ræmɪfaɪ] v. (使)分枝
reap [ri:p] v. 收割；收获
reclaim [rɪ'kleɪm] v. 开垦；回收
scatter ['skætə(r)] v. 撒，散播
shear [ʃɪə(r)] v. 剪；剥夺
shrivel ['ʃrɪvl] v. (使)枯萎
sow [səʊ] v. 播种
spade [speɪd] n. 锹；铲
sprout [spraʊt] n. 萌芽；幼苗
stall [stɔ:l] n. 畜栏，厩
sterile ['steraɪl] a. 贫瘠的；无结果的
thorn [θɔ:n] n. 刺；荆棘
tow [təʊ] v./n. 拖，拉；牵引
verdant ['vɜ:dnt] a. 青翠的，翠绿的
wither ['wɪðə(r)] v. (使)凋谢
yoke [jəʊk] n. 牛轭；束缚

120

Passage 24

Shortage of Primary Care

Crippling health care bills, long emergency-room waits and the inability to find a primary care physician just scratch the surface of the problems that patients face daily.

Primary care should be the backbone of any health care system. Countries with appropriate primary care resources score highly when it comes to health outcomes and cost. The U.S. takes the opposite approach by emphasizing the specialist rather than the primary care physician.

A recent study analyzed the providers who treat Medicare beneficiaries. The startling finding was that the average Medicare patient saw a total of seven doctors—two primary care physicians and five specialists—in a given year. Contrary to popular belief, the more physicians taking care of you doesn't guarantee better care. Actually, increasing fragmentation of care results in a corresponding rise in cost and medical errors.

How did we let primary care slip so far? The key is how doctors are paid. Most physicians are paid whenever they perform a medical service. The more a physician does, regardless of quality or outcome, the better he's reimbursed. Moreover, the amount a physician receives leans heavily toward medical or surgical procedures. A specialist who performs a procedure in a 30-minute visit can be paid three times more than a primary care physician using that same 30 minutes to discuss a patient's disease. Combine this fact with annual government threats to indiscriminately cut reimbursements, physicians are faced with no choice but to increase quantity to boost income.

Primary care physicians who refuse to compromise quality are either driven out of business or to cash-only practices, further contributing to the decline of primary care.

Medical students aren't blind to this scenario. They see how heavily the reimbursement deck is stacked against primary care. The recent numbers show that since 1997, newly graduated U.S. medical students who choose primary care as a career have declined by 50%. This trend results in emergency rooms being overwhelmed with patients without regular doctors.

How do we fix this problem?

It starts with reforming the physician reimbursement system. Remove the pressure from primary care physicians to **squeeze** in more patients per hour, and reward them for **optimally** managing their diseases and practicing evidence-based medicine. Make primary care more attractive to medical students by forgiving student **loans** for those who choose primary care as a career and **reconciling** the marked difference between specialist and primary care physician salaries.

We're at a point where primary care is needed more than ever. Within a few years, the first wave of the 76 million Baby Boomers will become **eligible** for Medicare. Patients older than 85, who need **chronic** care most, will rise by 50% this decade.

Who will be there to treat them?

译文

初级护理的缺乏

惊人的医疗账单、急救室的漫长等待和无法找到初级护理医师等问题仅仅触及了病人每天所面对的问题的表象。

初级护理应该是医疗护理体系的支柱。当考虑到医疗成效和医疗成本的问题时，那些拥有适当的初级护理资源的国家得分很高。美国却背道而驰，重视专科医生而非初级护理医师。

最近有一项研究分析了老年医保受惠人医疗服务的提供者，并得出了一个令人震惊的结果：一年内，平均每位老年医保受惠人共看过七位医生，其中有两位是初级护理医师，五位是专科医生。与普通观念相反的是，越多的医生照顾你并不能保证你就会被照顾得越好。事实上，护理越来越细化会导致成本和医疗失误相应上升。

我们是如何让初级护理衰退得如此严重的呢？关键在于医生的薪酬发放方式。大多数医生的薪酬是根据其提供的医疗服务发放的。不论其质量或效果，医生提供的医疗服务越多，得到的返还费用就越高。而且，医生收入的高低更多依赖于内科或外科治疗。专科医生完成一个30分钟的治疗所得到的薪水，比初级护理医师花费同样多的时间与病人谈论病情所得到的报酬多3倍。加上政府每年都声称要一视同仁地减少返还费用，医生别无选择，只能增加所看病人的数量来提高收入。

那些不愿降低医疗质量的初级护理医生要么被迫退出此行业，要么只好去那些只收现金的诊所，这进一步加剧了初级护理的衰退。

医学专业的学生也注意到了这种现象。他们明白返还费用的减少对初级护理有着多么严重的不利影响。最近的数据显示，自1997年以来，美国医学专业的应届毕业生中，选择初级护理作为职业的人数下降了50%。这种趋势导致了急救室内人满为患而又没有合格的医生。

我们该如何解决这个问题呢？

首先，要改革医生返还费用体制。解除初级护理医师每小时挤时间看更多病人的压力，并对最佳地治疗病患和对症用药的医师给予奖励。免除那些选择初级护理作为职业的学生的贷款债务，消除专科医生和初级护理医师在工资方面的显著差异，以使初级护理对于医学专业的学生来说更有吸引力。

我们处在一个比以往任何时候都更需要初级护理的时刻。几年之内，第一拨7600万婴儿潮时期出生的人将成为老年医保受患者。那些85岁以上的最需要长期护理的病人在10年内将增加50%。

到那时谁来对他们进行治疗呢？

💡 单词记事本

crippling [ˈkrɪplɪŋ]
释 a. 极限的；造成严重后果的

care [keə(r)]
释 v. 关心；介意；喜欢 n. 护理，照顾；小心；忧虑
用 take care of 照顾；care about 担心；care for 关心；喜欢
例 I'll continue whether you *care* it or not. 不管你是否在意，我都会继续。

inability [ˌɪnəˈbɪləti]
释 n. 无能，无力

physician [fɪˈzɪʃn]
释 n. 医生；(尤指)内科医生

backbone [ˈbækbəʊn]
释 n. 脊椎，中枢；支柱；决心，毅力

analyze [ˈænəlaɪz]
释 v. 分析；解析

treat [triːt]
释 v. 对待；款待；视为；探讨；医治 n. 款待，招待；乐事
用 treat with 谈判；交涉
例 It's my turn to *treat* this time. 这次我请客。

startling [ˈstɑːtlɪŋ]
释 a. 令人吃惊的

guarantee [ˌɡærənˈtiː]
释 v. 保证，担保；约定，许诺 n. 担保；保证书
用 quality guarantee 质量保证
例 No one can *guarantee* your safety during the journey. 在旅途中，没有人能保证你的安全。

fragmentation [ˌfræɡmenˈteɪʃn]
释 n. 细分；破裂；碎裂

corresponding [ˌkɒrəˈspɒndɪŋ]
释 a. 相应的；一致的；通信的

slip [slɪp]
释 n. 滑倒；下跌；错误；事故；纸片 v. 滑动；减退，衰退；犯错

perform [pəˈfɔːm]
释 v. 执行，完成；表演
例 *Performing* only three steps will make you succeed. 只要完成三个步骤你就能成功。

outcome ['aʊtkʌm]
释 n. 效果；结果

reimburse [ˌriːɪm'bɜːs]
释 v. 返还费用；偿还；报销

procedure [prə'siːdʒə(r)]
释 n. 程序；手续；步骤，过程；手术

scenario [sə'nɑːriəʊ]
释 n. 现象；情节；剧本

trend [trend]
释 n. 趋势；流行 v. 伸向；倾向

emergency [i'mɜːdʒənsi]
释 n. 紧急情况；紧急事件
用 emergency room 急诊室

overwhelm [ˌəʊvə'welm]
释 v. 淹没，覆盖；压倒，制服；使不知所措
例 Children are *overwhelmed* with lucky money during the Spring Festival. 孩子们在春节时会收到很多压岁钱。

squeeze [skwiːz]
释 v. 挤；压榨，剥削；缩减 n. 挤；握

optimally ['ɒptɪməli]
释 ad. 最佳地；最适宜地

loan [ləʊn]
释 n. 贷款；借出物 v. 借出；贷给

reconcile ['rekənsaɪl]
释 v. 使一致，使相协调；调停；使和解

eligible ['elɪdʒəbl]
释 a. 有资格的，合格的
用 be eligible for 有资格
例 Are there any solutions for selecting the *eligible* products? 有什么方法来筛选合格产品吗？

chronic ['krɒnɪk]
释 a. 慢性的，长期的；习惯性的；极坏的

看病就医

ailment ['eɪlmənt] n. 疾病；小病
airborne ['eəbɔːn] a. 空气传播的
bloated ['bləʊtɪd] a. 肿胀的；傲慢的
canker ['kæŋkə(r)] n. 溃疡；口疮
concussion [kən'kʌʃn] n. 脑震荡
convalesce [ˌkɒnvə'les] v. 康复；复原
delirious [dɪ'lɪriəs] a. 精神错乱的
deracinate [ˌdiː'ræsɪneɪt] v. 根除；杜绝
dyspeptic [dɪs'peptɪk] a. 消化不良的
hysteria [hɪ'stɪəriə] n. 歇斯底里症
inoculate [ɪ'nɒkjuleɪt] v. 疫苗注射
insane [ɪn'seɪn] a. 患精神病的；极愚蠢的
leukaemia [luː'kiːmiə] n. 白血病
lint [lɪnt] n. 纱布
lunatic ['luːnətɪk] n. 精神失常者
malaise [mə'leɪz] n. 微恙，不适

myopia [maɪ'əʊpiə] n. 近视
palate ['pælət] n. 上腭
palpitate ['pælpɪteɪt] v. (心脏)跳动；颤抖
paralyze ['pærəlaɪz] v. 使瘫痪
paranoid ['pærənɔɪd] a. 妄想狂的
plague [pleɪg] n. 瘟疫
purblind ['pɜːblaɪnd] a. 视力不佳的
quack [kwæk] n. 庸医
salve [sælv] n. 药膏
stricken ['strɪkən] a. 患病的；被击中的
stupor ['stjuːpə(r)] n. 昏迷
syrup ['sɪrəp] n. 糖浆
tuberculosis [tjuːˌbɜːkju'ləʊsɪs] n. 肺结核
unguent ['ʌŋgwənt] n. 药膏；软膏
vaccinate ['væksɪneɪt] v. 接种疫苗

音频

Passage 25

Protect Your Privacy
When Job-Hunting Online

Identity theft and identity fraud are terms used to refer to all types of crime in which someone wrongfully obtains and uses another person's personal data in some way that involves fraud or deception, typically for economic gain.

Unlike your fingerprints, which are unique to you and cannot be given to someone else for their use, your personal data, especially your social security number, your bank account or credit card number, your telephone calling card number, and other valuable identifying data, can be used, if they fall into the wrong hands, to personally profit at your expense. The key to a successful online job search is learning to manage the risks. Here are some tips for staying safe while conducting a job search on the Internet.

1. Check for a privacy policy.

If you are considering posting your résumé online, make sure the job search site you are considering has a privacy policy, like CareerBuilder.com. The policy should spell out how your information will be used, stored and whether or not it will be shared. You may want to think twice about posting your résumé on a site that automatically shares your information with others. You could be opening yourself up to unwanted calls from solicitors.

When reviewing the site's privacy policy, you'll be able to delete your résumé just as easily as you posted it. You won't necessarily want your résumé to remain out there on the Internet once you land a job. Remember, the longer your résumé remains posted on a job board, the more exposure, both positive and not-so-positive, it will receive.

2. Take advantages of site features.

Lawful job search sites offer levels of privacy protection. Before posting your résumé, carefully consider your job search objectives and the level of risk you are willing to assume.

The first is standard posting. This option gives job seekers who post their résumés the most visibility to the broadest employer audience possible.

The second is anonymous posting. This option allows job seekers the same visibility as those in the standard posting category without any of their contact information being displayed. Job seekers who wish to remain anonymous but want to share some other information may choose which pieces of contact information to display.

The third is private posting. This option allows a job seeker to post a résumé without having it searched by employers. Private posting allows job seekers to quickly and easily apply for jobs that appear on websites without retyping their information.

3. Safeguard your identity.

Career experts say that one of the ways job seekers can stay safe while using the Internet to search out jobs is to conceal their identities. Replace your name on your résumé with a generic identifier.

You should also consider eliminating the name and location of your current employer. Depending on your title, it may not be all that difficult to determine who you are once the name of your company is provided. If your job title is unique, consider using the generic equivalent instead of the exact title assigned by your employer.

4. Establish an email address for your search.

Another way to protect your privacy while seeking employment online is to open up an email account specifically for your online job search. This will safeguard your existing email box in the event someone you don't know gets hold of your email address and shares it with others.

Using an email address specifically for your job search also eliminates the possibility that you will receive unwelcome emails in your primary mailbox. When naming your new email address, be sure that it doesn't contain references to your name or other information that will give away your identity. The best solution is an email address that is relevant to the job you are seeking such as salesmgr2004@provider.com.

5. Protect your references.

If your résumé contains a section with the names and contact information of your references, take it out. There's no sense in safeguarding your information while sharing private contact information of your references.

6. Keep confidential information confidential.

Do not, under any circumstances, share your social security, driver's license and bank account numbers or other personal information. Honest employers do not need this information with an initial application. Don't provide this even if they say they need it in order to conduct a background check. This is one of the oldest tricks in the book—don't fall for it.

网上求职时，保护好你的隐私

"身份盗窃"和"身份诈骗"这两个术语是指所有通过欺诈等不正当手段窃取或使用他人个人信息的犯罪类型，它们通常以获得经济利益为目的。

你的指纹是独一无二的，无法被别人使用，但你的个人信息，特别是社会保险号码、银行账号、信用卡号、电话卡号以及其他有价值的身份识别数据则不同，一旦落入不法分子之手，就会被用来谋取个人利益，而这都是以你的损失为代价的。网上求职成功的关键在于学会风险管理。这里有一些在进行网上求职时保护自己隐私安全的小提示。

1. 检查隐私权政策

如果你正考虑把自己的简历上传至网上，请确认你所考虑的求职网站是否像CareerBuilder.com一样拥有隐私权政策。隐私权政策里应明确说明你的信息将如何被使用、保存及是否会被共享。在将你的简历上传到能够自动与他人共享你的信息的网站前，请三思，因为这样做可能会使你收到许多来自推销员的骚扰电话。

在再次审查网站的隐私权政策时，确保你删除简历时能跟上传简历一样容易。一旦找到了工作，你肯定不想把自己的简历继续张贴在网上了。切记，你的简历在求职板上张贴的时间越长，被暴露的风险也就越大，带来的结果也有好有坏。

2. 利用网站的特色

合法的求职网站提供多个等级的隐私保护。上传简历之前，要仔细考虑你的求职目标以及你愿意承担的风险等级。

第一个等级为标准上传。此选项可以将求职者上传的简历在最大范围内对最广泛的雇主公开。

第二个等级为匿名上传。此选项可以让求职者的简历跟标准上传的可见度一样，但联系方式不会被公开显示。希望匿名但又想公开部分信息的求职者可以选择公开哪几条联系信息。

第三个等级为私人上传。此选项可以让求职者上传简历，但这份简历雇主搜索不到。私人上传能让求职者快速、轻松地申请到网站上发布的职位，而无须重复输入个人信息。

3. 保护你的身份

求职专家表示，在网上求职时，求职者保护自己的方法之一就是隐藏身份。把简历上的名字替换成一个泛指的名称。

你还需考虑去掉你目前所在公司的名称和地址。如果你提供了公司名称，根据你的头衔判断出你是谁并不难。如果你的职位名称是独一无二的，请考虑使用泛指的对应词来代替当前雇主分配给你的确切头衔。

4. 创建一个求职专用电子邮箱

另外一种在网上求职时保护个人隐私的方法就是创建一个网上求职专用电子邮箱。这会保护你现有的电子邮箱，以防你的电子邮件地址被陌生人获知并与其他人共享。

使用求职专用电子邮箱还会使你的常用邮箱避免收到垃圾邮件。在为新的电子邮箱命名时，请确保其没有包含任何能推断出你姓名或透露你身份的信息。最好的解决方法就是使用一个与你求职目标相关的电子邮箱名称，如 salesmgr2004@provider.com。

5. 保护你的介绍人

如果简历中有一栏写有你的介绍人的姓名和联系方式，请删除。在保护自己信息的同时，你没有理由公开你的介绍人的个人联系方式。

6. 让机密的信息成为机密

无论在什么情况下都不要公开你的社会保险、驾驶执照和银行账户号码以及其他个人信息。初步申请时，真诚的雇主并不需要这类信息。即便他们说需要这些信息来进行背景调查，也不要向其提供。这是最古老的骗术之一——千万别上当。

💡 单词记事本

fraud [frɔːd]
释 n. 诈骗，欺骗；骗子

term [tɜːm]
释 n. 术语；期限；学期；[pl.]条款 v. 把…称为
用 in terms of 依据，按照；在…方面；in the long term 从长远来看；in any term 无论如何，在任何情况下；come to terms 让步，妥协

obtain [əb'teɪn]
释 v. 获得，得到；流行；通用
例 Obviously, there are many ways to *obtain* information. 显然，有很多种方式可以获得信息。

deception [dɪ'sepʃn]
释 n. 欺骗；诡计
例 It is a *deception* which no self-respecting people like to indulge in. 这是个有自尊心的人都不愿参与的骗局。

gain　　　　　　　　　　　　　　[geɪn]

释 n. 收益，利润；增加 v. 获得；增加

用 gain in 增长；改进；weight gain 体重增加

例 *Gaining* some work experience is a must for graduates. 毕业生必须获得一些工作经验。

fingerprint　　　　　　　['fɪŋɡəprɪnt]

释 n. 指纹，手印；特点

account　　　　　　　　　[ə'kaʊnt]

释 n. 账户；账目；报告，描述；原因；利益 v. 说明…的原因；认为；(在数量、比例方面)占

用 account for 说明原因；解释；take into account 考虑，重视；on account of 由于，因为

credit　　　　　　　　　　['kredɪt]

释 n. 信贷；荣誉；学分；信任 v. 信任；把…记入贷方；把…归于

expense　　　　　　　　　[ɪk'spens]

释 n. 价钱；[*pl.*]开支；代价

risk　　　　　　　　　　　[rɪsk]

释 n. 风险；危险；保险金额 v. 冒…的危险

用 at risk 处于危险中；take the risk 承担风险；high risk 高风险

例 Great return is always accompanied with great *risk*. 高回报总是伴随着高风险。

tip　　　　　　　　　　　　[tɪp]

释 n. 尖端；小费；有用的小建议 v. 使倾斜；倒(入)；给小费

consider　　　　　　　　[kən'sɪdə(r)]

释 v. 考虑，细想；把…看作；尊重；顾及

post　　　　　　　　　　　[pəʊst]

释 n. (支)柱，标杆；(速度竞赛的)起点或终点标志；职位 v. 投寄；张贴，公开贴出；(在网站上)公布，发布(资讯)，发(帖)

résumé　　　　　　　　　['rezjumeɪ]

释 n. 简历；摘要

site　　　　　　　　　　　[saɪt]

释 n. 网址；位置，地点；场所 v. 使坐落在；设置

automatically　　　　　[ˌɔːtə'mætɪkli]

释 ad. 自动地；机械地；无意识地

solicitor　　　　　　　　[sə'lɪsɪtə(r)]

释 n. 推销员；游说者；初级律师

exposure　　　　　　　　[ɪk'spəʊʒə(r)]

释 n. 暴露；曝光；揭露

advantage　　　　　　　[əd'vɑːntɪdʒ]

释 n. 优点，有利条件；利益，好处

用 take advantage of 利用；have an advantage over 胜过，优于

例 So what is the *advantage* of this so-called advanced method? 那么，这种所谓的先进方法有什么优势呢？

feature　　　　　　　　　['fiːtʃə(r)]

释 n. 特征，特色；[*pl.*]面貌；特写；专题节目 v. 以…为特色；给…以显著地位；由…主演

lawful　　　　　　　　　　['lɔːfl]

释 a. 合法的；法定的；法律承认的

assume　　　　　　　　　[ə'sjuːm]

释 v. 假设；承担；假装

option　　　　　　　　　　['ɒpʃn]

释 n. 选择；选择权；(供)选择的对象

visibility　　　　　　　　[ˌvɪzə'bɪləti]

释 n. 可见性；可见度

anonymous　　　　　　　[ə'nɒnɪməs]

释 a. 匿名的；无特色的

category ['kætəɡəri]
释 n. 类别；范畴

safeguard ['seɪfɡɑːd]
释 n. 预防措施；安全装置 v. 保护

generic [dʒə'nerɪk]
释 a. 种类的，类属的；一般的

eliminate [ɪ'lɪmɪneɪt]
释 v. 消除，清除；淘汰

current ['kʌrənt]
释 a. 当前的；最近的；流通的 n. (水、电)流；潮流

title ['taɪtl]
释 n. 标题；头衔；权益 v. 赋予头衔；加标题于

equivalent [ɪ'kwɪvələnt]
释 a. 相同的，相当的 n. 相等的事物或数量；对应物

assign [ə'saɪn]
释 v. 分配；指派；指定(时间、地点等)

event [ɪ'vent]
释 n. 事件；偶然事件，可能发生的事；比赛项目
用 in the event that 如果；在…情况下

primary ['praɪməri]
释 a. 最初的；主要的，首要的
用 primary school 小学
例 It is the *primary* question that we have to deal with. 这正是我们要处理的首要问题。

name [neɪm]
释 n. 名字；名声 v. 命名，给…取名；说出…的名字；列举；任命，提名

contain [kən'teɪn]
释 v. 包含；控制；阻止

solution [sə'luːʃn]
释 n. 溶液；解决；解决办法
例 The only possible *solution* is to hold a meeting to discuss it as soon as possible. 唯一可能的解决方案是尽快召开会议进行讨论。

reference ['refrəns]
释 n. 提到；参考；参考书目；证明(信)，介绍(信)；证明人，介绍人

section ['sekʃn]
释 n. 部分；(文章等的)段落；地区；部门；截面

confidential [ˌkɒnfɪ'denʃl]
释 a. 机密的；极受信任的；担任机密工作的

initial [ɪ'nɪʃl]
释 a. 最初的，开始的；开头的 n. (姓名、名称等的)首字母

application [ˌæplɪ'keɪʃn]
释 n. 申请；申请表；应用；施用

conduct [kən'dʌkt]
释 v. 进行；管理；传导(热、电等)；表现

💡 单词家族

法律相关

abolish [ə'bɒlɪʃ] v. 彻底废除，废止
abscond [əb'skɒnd] v. 潜逃，逃亡
accuse [ə'kjuːz] v. 指控，控告；指责

adjourn [ə'dʒɜːn] v. (使)休庭；(使)休会
amend [ə'mend] v. 修改，修订；改进
canard [kæ'nɑːd; 'kænɑːd] n. 谣言

comply [kəm'plaɪ] v. 遵从，服从

conform [kən'fɔ:m] v. 遵守；符合

constitution [ˌkɒnstɪ'tju:ʃn] n. 宪法；章程

convict [kən'vɪkt] v. 宣判…有罪；证明…有罪 n. 囚犯

debunk [ˌdi:'bʌŋk] v. 揭穿

defendant [dɪ'fendənt] n. 被告

defer [dɪ'fɜ:(r)] v. 推迟，拖延；遵从

defy [dɪ'faɪ] v. (公然)违抗；挑衅

deportation [ˌdi:pɔ:'teɪʃn] n. 驱逐出境

deprive [dɪ'praɪv] v. 剥夺，使丧失

enact [ɪ'nækt] v. 制定(法律)；颁布；扮演

enforce [ɪn'fɔ:s] v. 实施，执行；强迫

forfeit ['fɔ:fɪt] v. (因犯罪等而)丧失(所有权) n. 丧失的东西

judicial [dʒu'dɪʃl] a. 司法的；审判的；明断的

jury ['dʒʊəri] n. 陪审团；(竞赛或展览的)评判委员会

legal ['li:gl] a. 法律(上)的；合法的

legislation [ˌledʒɪs'leɪʃn] n. 法律，法规；立法

legitimate [lɪ'dʒɪtɪmət] a. 合法的 v. 使合法

liable ['laɪəbl] a. 有法律责任的；易于…的

mediate ['mi:dieɪt] v. 调解；斡旋；居间促成

penalty ['penəlti] n. 处罚，惩罚；罚金

piracy ['paɪrəsi] n. 海盗行为；剽窃；盗版

ratify ['rætɪfaɪ] v. 批准，使正式生效

restrict [rɪ'strɪkt] v. 限制；约束

scrutiny ['skru:təni] n. 细察，监督

slanderous ['sla:ndərəs] a. 诽谤的；造谣中伤的

verdict ['vɜ:dɪkt] n. (陪审团的)裁判，裁决；决定，意见

vilify ['vɪlɪfaɪ] v. 辱骂，诽谤

Natural abilities are like natural plants that need pruning by study.
——Francis Bacon
天生的才干如同天生的植物一样，需要靠学习来修剪。
——弗朗西斯·培根

音频

Passage 26

Into the Unknown

Until the early 1990s nobody much thought about whole populations getting older. The UN had the foresight to convene a "world assembly on ageing" back in 1982, but that came and went. By 1994 the World Bank had noticed that something big was happening. In a report entitled "Averting the Old Age Crisis", it argued that pension arrangements in most countries were unsustainable.

For the next ten years a succession of books, mainly by Americans, sounded the alarm.

Since then the debate has become less emotional, not least because a lot more is known about the subject.

By far the most effective method to restrain pension spending is to give people the opportunity to work longer, because it increases tax revenues and reduces spending on pensions at the same time. It may even keep them alive longer. John Rother, the AARP's head of policy and strategy, points to studies showing that other things being equal, people who remain at work have lower death rates than their retired peers.

Younger people today mostly accept that they will have to work for longer and that their pensions will be less generous. Employers still need to be persuaded that older workers are worth holding on to. That may be because they have had plenty of younger ones to choose from, partly thanks to the post-war baby boom and partly because over the past few decades many more women have entered the labour force, increasing employers' choice. But the reservoir of women able and willing to take up paid work is running low, and the baby-boomers are going grey.

To tackle the problem of ageing populations at its root, "old" countries would have to rejuvenate themselves by having more of their own children. A number of them have tried, some more successfully than others. But it is not a simple matter of offering financial incentives or providing more child care. Modern urban life in rich countries is not well adapted to large families. Women find it hard to combine family and career. They often compromise by having just one child.

And what if fertility in ageing countries does not pick up? It will not be the end of the world, at least not for quite a while yet, but the world will slowly become a different place. Older societies may be less innovative and more strongly disinclined to take risks than younger ones. By 2025 at the latest, about half the voters in America and most of those in Western European countries will be over 50—and older people turn out to vote in much greater number than younger ones. Academic studies have found no evidence so far that older voters have used their power at the ballot box to push for policies that specifically benefit them, though if in future there are many more of them they might start doing so.

Nor is there any sign of the intergenerational warfare predicted in the 1990s. After all, older people themselves mostly have families. In a recent study of parents and grown-up children in 11 European countries, Karsten Hank of Mannheim University found that 85% of them lived within 25km from each other and the majority of them were in touch at least once a week.

Even so, the shift in the center of gravity to older age groups is bound to have a profound effect on societies, not just economically and politically but in all sorts of other ways too. Richard Jackson and Neil Howe of America's CSIS, in a thoughtful book called *The Graying of the Great Powers*, argue that, among other things, the ageing of the developed countries will have a number of serious security implications.

There is little that can be done to stop population ageing, so the world will have to live with it. But some of the consequences can be alleviated. Many experts now believe that given the right policies, the effects, though grave, need not be catastrophic. Most countries have recognized the need to do something and are beginning to act.

But even then there is no guarantee that their efforts will work. What is happening now is historically unprecedented. Ronald Lee, director of the Center on the Economics and Demography of Ageing at the University of California, Berkeley, puts it briefly and clearly: "We don't really know what population ageing will be like because nobody has done it yet."

 译文

走向未知

直到20世纪90年代初,人们才开始考虑整体人口的老龄化问题。联合国富有先见之明,早在1982年就召开了第一届"世界老龄化问题大会",但是这并没有引起什么反响。到1994年,世界银行已经意识到了一些重大问题即将发生。它在一份题为《避免老龄化危机》的报告中指出,大多数国家的养老金计划都无法维持下去。

在接下来的十年里,主要由美国人撰写的一系列书籍对此敲响了警钟。

从那以后,对于老龄化问题的争论就变得没那么情绪化了,尤其是当人们对这方面的事情有了更多的了解之后。

到目前为止，控制养老金支出最有效的方法是给人们提供工作更长时间的机会，因为这样既可以增加税收，又可以减少养老金的支出。这样做甚至还有可能延长人们的寿命。美国退休者协会负责政策和战略的约翰·罗瑟指出，研究表明在其他各种因素都相同的情况下，仍然从事工作的人与已退休的同龄人相比，其死亡率更低。

　　如今的年轻人基本上已经接受了他们将不得不工作更长时间而养老金会变少的现实。但我们仍需要说服雇主：老龄雇员是值得继续留用的。之所以需要这么做，可能是因为雇主们有大量的年轻人可供选择，其中部分原因是战后出现的婴儿潮，部分原因是因为在过去的几十年里更多的女性进入了劳动力市场，这些都使雇主的选择范围扩大了。但是有能力且愿意从事有偿工作的女性正在减少，婴儿潮时期出生的人也正在变老。

　　要从根本上解决人口老龄化问题，老龄化的国家必须通过生育更多孩子来使自己年轻化。有许多国家已经尝试过了，其中一些国家比其他国家更为成功。但是这不是仅通过提供财政刺激或提供更多的育儿服务就能解决的。发达国家的现代城市生活并不太适合大家庭。女性发现很难同时兼顾家庭和工作。她们经常会只生一个孩子以在两者间取得平衡。

　　那么如果老龄化国家的人口出生率没有提高怎么办呢？那不会是世界末日，至少在很长一段时间内都不会，但是世界会慢慢地变成一个不同的世界。与年轻化社会相比，老龄化社会可能不够创新，也更不愿意冒险。最迟到2025年，美国大约有一半的选民将超过50岁，而西欧国家的大多数选民都会超过50岁，这样老年选民的人数将远远超过年轻选民的人数。学术研究发现，到目前为止，还没有证据表明老年选民利用他们在选举上的权力极力争取特别有利于他们自己的政策，但如果未来他们的人数增多，他们可能就会这么做了。

　　人们在20世纪90年代所预测的代际冲突现在也没有出现的迹象。毕竟，大部分老年人自己都有家庭。在最近的一项对欧洲11个国家的父母和成年子女的调查中，曼海姆大学的卡斯滕·汉克发现，85%的父母和子女居住的距离在25公里以内，他们中的大多数一周至少都会联系一次。

　　尽管如此，重心向老年人群体的转移必定会对社会产生深远的影响，这不仅表现在经济和政治方面，还表现在其他各个方面。在发人深省的《超级大国的老去》一书中，美国国际战略研究中心的理查德·杰克逊和尼尔·豪指出，除了其他方面外，发达国家的老龄化还会引发很多严重的安全问题。

　　没有什么可以遏制人口老龄化，所以世界将不得不与其共存，但是它所造成的一些后果是可以减轻的。现在许多专家都相信，如果实施正确的政策，它所造成的影响尽管依然很严重，但不会是灾难性的。大多数国家已经意识到需要做些什么了，并且正在开始采取行动。

但即使如此，也不能保证他们的努力就一定会起作用。目前所发生的事是在历史上前所未有的。加州大学伯克利分校的经济学与人口老龄化中心主任罗纳德·李简洁明了地说："我们确实不知道人口老龄化将会是什么样子，因为还没有人经历过。"

单词记事本

foresight ['fɔːsaɪt]
释 *n.* 远见，深谋远虑

convene [kən'viːn]
释 *v.* 召集，召开；集合

assembly [ə'sembli]
释 *n.* 集会，集合；装配，安装

entitle [ɪn'taɪtl]
释 *v.* 给…命名；使有权(做某事)
用 be entitled to 享有…权利
例 What is the brand new book *entitled*? 那本新书叫什么名字？

pension ['penʃn]
释 *n.* 养老金 *v.* 给…发养老金

unsustainable [ˌʌnsə'steɪnəbl]
释 *a.* 无法支撑的，无法维持的

succession [sək'seʃn]
释 *n.* 一系列；连续；接替

restrain [rɪ'streɪn]
释 *v.* 抑制，约束

peer [pɪə(r)]
释 *n.* 同龄人；同等地位的人 *v.* 凝视；比得上

generous ['dʒenərəs]
释 *a.* 慷慨的，大方的；丰富的；大量的
例 No one can deny the fact that Mr. Li is a *generous* man. 人人都认可李先生是个慷慨的人。

reservoir ['rezəvwɑː(r)]
释 *n.* 水库，蓄水池；(知识、人才等的)储藏，汇集

tackle ['tækl]
释 *v.* 处理；向某人提起 *n.* 滑轮(组)；用具，器械
例 How to *tackle* the problem is beyond me. 我不知道怎么处理这个问题。

rejuvenate [rɪ'dʒuːvəneɪt]
释 *v.* 使年轻，使恢复活力；使复原

financial [faɪ'nænʃl]
释 *a.* 财政的，财务的；金融的
用 financial statement 财务报表；financial market 金融市场

incentive [ɪn'sentɪv]
释 *n.* 刺激；奖励

urban ['ɜːbən]
释 *a.* 城市的，都市的
例 *Urban* life never fails to appeal to me tremendously. 城市生活一直让我非常着迷。

combine [kəm'baɪn]
释 *v.* 联合，结合；同时做，兼顾 *n.* 联合企业(或团体)

fertility [fə'tɪləti]
释 *n.* 肥沃，富饶；多产；人口出生率

innovative ['ɪnəveɪtɪv]
释 *a.* 创新的，革新的

voter ['vəʊtə(r)]
释 *n.* 投票者，选举人

academic [ˌækə'demɪk]
释 *a.* 学校的；学术的

evidence ['evɪdəns]

释 *n.* 根据；证据

用 in evidence 明显地；strong evidence 有力证据

例 All the *evidence* suggests that the data is reliable. 所有的证据都表明这些数据是可靠的。

ballot ['bælət]

释 *n.* 无记名投票；选票；投票数 *v.* (使)投票选举

specifically [spə'sɪfɪkli]

释 *ad.* 特别地；明确地

warfare ['wɔːfeə(r)]

释 *n.* 战争(状态)；冲突

predict [prɪ'dɪkt]

释 *v.* 预言，预测

majority [mə'dʒɒrəti]

释 *n.* 大多数，多半；超过对方的票数

thoughtful ['θɔːtfl]

释 *a.* 发人深思的；体贴的

security [sɪ'kjʊərəti]

释 *n.* 安全；安全措施；抵押品；[*pl.*]证券

用 security check 安检

implication [,ɪmplɪ'keɪʃn]

释 *n.* 含义；暗示；卷入，牵连；可能的结果

consequence ['kɒnsɪkwəns]

释 *n.* 后果，影响；重要性

alleviate [ə'liːvieɪt]

释 *v.* 减轻，缓解

例 People involved with the pollution are trying to *alleviate* the environmental damage. 涉及此次污染的相关人员正在努力减轻对环境的危害。

grave [greɪv]

释 *n.* 坟墓 *a.* 严峻的；严肃的

catastrophic [,kætə'strɒfɪk]

释 *a.* 灾难性的

unprecedented [ʌn'presɪdentɪd]

释 *a.* 前所未有的

💡 单词家族

老龄特征

bequeath [bɪ'kwiːð] *v.* 遗赠
blather ['blæðə(r)] *v.* 喋喋不休
bleary ['blɪəri] *a.* 视线模糊的
doddering ['dɒdərɪŋ] *n.* 蹒跚的
dyslexia [dɪs'leksiə] *n.* 阅读困难
epitaph ['epɪtɑːf] *n.* 墓志铭
garrulous ['gærələs] *a.* 唠叨的
hale [heɪl] *a.* 矍铄的
ingrained [ɪn'greɪnd] *a.* 根深蒂固的
inter [ɪn'tɜː(r)] *v.* 埋葬
intestate [ɪn'testeɪt] *a.* 未留遗嘱的
meddlesome ['medlsəm] *a.* 爱管闲事的
moribund ['mɒrɪbʌnd] *a.* 垂死的
muzzy ['mʌzi] *a.* 糊涂的

nag [næg] *v.* 唠叨；烦扰
necropolis [nə'krɒpəlɪs] *n.* 墓地；公墓
octogenarian [,ɒktədʒə'neəriən] *n.* 八旬老人
passe ['pæseɪ] *a.* 已过盛年的
patrimony ['pætrɪməni] *n.* 祖传的财物；继承物
regressive [rɪ'gresɪv] *a.* 退化的
sag [sɑːg] *v.* 松弛；下跌
shroud [ʃraʊd] *n.* 寿衣
solicitude [sə'lɪsɪtjuːd] *n.* 关怀，牵挂
tantrum ['tæntrəm] *n.* 发脾气
whine [waɪn] *v.* 抱怨，发牢骚

Chapter 3

新奇事物

Passage 27

音频

原 文

Your Battery Gauge
Is Lying to You

Climbing out of bed, about to start your day, you **unplug** your new **smartphone** from its wall **charger** and quickly check your email. You've left it plugged in overnight, and the **battery gauge** shows 100%. After a quick shower, you remember that you forgot to send your client a file last night. You pick up your phone again, but the battery gauge now reads 90%. A 10% drop in 10 minutes? The phone must be **defective**, right?

A common complaint about today's smartphones is their short battery life compared to older cell phones. Years ago, if you **accidentally** left your charger at home, your phone could still make it through a **weeklong** vacation with life to spare (I did it more than once). With the newest phones on the market, you might be lucky enough to make it through a weekend.

And why should we expect anything else? Phones used to have a very short list of features: making and receiving phone calls. Today we use them for email, web **surfing**, GPS **navigation**, photos, video, games, and a host of other tasks. They used to sport tiny displays, while we now have giant touch screens with bright and **vibrant** colors. All of these features come at a cost: large energy requirements.

Interestingly enough, improvements in battery management technology have **compounded** the average users' perception of this problem. Older phones were rather **inelegant** in their charging behavior; usually filling the battery to capacity and then switching to a **trickle** current to maintain the highest charge possible. This offered the highest usage time in the short-term, but was damaging the battery over the course of ownership. As explained at Battery University, "The time at which the battery stays at maximum charge should be as short as possible. **Prolonged** high voltage promotes **corrosion**, especially at elevated temperatures."

This is why many new phones will "lose" up to 10% within a few minutes of coming off the charger. The reality is that the battery was only at 100% capacity for a brief moment, after which the battery management system allowed it to slowly dip down to around 90%. Leaving the phone plugged in overnight does not make a difference: the phone only uses the wall current to maintain a partial charge state.

The phone manufacturers essentially have three choices:

1. Use older charging styles which actually maintain a full battery, thereby decreasing its eventual life.

2. Use new charging methods and have an accurate battery gauge.

3. Use new charging methods and have the inaccurate battery gauge.

Option one has clearly fallen out of favor as it prematurely wears devices. Option two, while being honest, would most likely be met with many complaints. After all, how many people want to see their phone draining down to 90% while it is still plugged in? Option three therefore offers an odd compromise. Maybe phone companies think that users will be less likely to worry about a quick drop off the charger than they will worry about a "defective" charger that doesn't keep their phone at 100% while plugged in.

If you absolutely need the highest capacity on a device like this, you will need to bump charge. There are currently people experimenting with "fixes" for this, but I have yet to see one that works. Be warned, however, that repeated bump charging will wear your battery faster and begin to reduce its capacity. If you are a "power user" who will buy a new battery a few months from now anyway, this presumably isn't a concern. If you are an average consumer who uses a device for a few years, I would recommend that you stay away from bump charging. The bottom line is that you don't really "need" to do it unless you are actually depleting your battery to 0% on a regular basis.

If you are someone who can top off your phone on a regular basis, do it. Plug it in when you're at home. Plug it in when you're at your desk. As explained by Battery University: Several partial discharges with frequent recharges are better for lithium-ion batteries than one deep one. Recharging a partially charged lithium-ion battery does not cause harm because there is no memory.

Beyond that, the best advice I can offer is to stop paying such close attention to your battery gauge and to just use your phone. Charge it whenever you can, and then stop obsessing over the exact numbers. If you really need more usage time, buy an extended-capacity battery and use it normally.

别被电量指示欺骗了

当你从床上爬起、准备开始新的一天时，你会先把新买的智能手机从充电器上拔下来，然后迅速地查一下邮箱里是否有新邮件。你给手机充了整整一晚上的电，电量指示显示已充满。在你快速地冲了个澡之后，你想起昨晚忘记给客户发文件了。于是你又拿起了手机，却发现电量只有90%了。10分钟电量就下降了10%？手机一定有什么毛病吧？

和旧式手机相比，如今的智能手机因为其电池不耐用而遭到了人们的普遍抱怨。想想几年前，即使偶然将手机充电器落在家，手机电量也能维持到为期一周的假期结束，而且还绰绰有余（这种事我干过不止一次）。而现今市场上出售的最新型手机能撑过周末两天的时间就已经相当不错了。

我们还有什么可期待的呢？过去，手机的功能非常简单，无非就是接听、拨打电话。而如今，我们使用手机来收发邮件、浏览网页、进行GPS导航、拍照、看视频、玩游戏以及处理其他一大堆任务。过去的手机只有一块很小的显示屏，而现在的手机却有着巨大的可触摸屏，并且显示的色彩鲜明而亮丽。所有这些功能的代价就是会消耗大量的电量。

非常有趣的是，电量管理技术的改进让普通用户加深了对这一问题的认识。旧式手机的充电方式相当粗放，通常在电池充满之后就切换为微弱的电流，从而使手机维持在最高的电量上。这样能使手机电池在短期内保持较长的使用时间，但从长远来看却会损害电池的使用寿命。正如电池百科网站解释的那样："电池保持在最高电量的时间越短越好，因为长时间的高电压会加速电池的腐蚀，尤其是在温度较高的情况下。"

这就是许多新型手机从充电器上拔下来之后会在几分钟之内"流失"高达10%的电量的原因。事实上，电池只能在很短的时间内保持满电，之后电池自身的管理程序会让电量逐渐下降到90%左右。即使将电池充上一整晚的电，也不会有什么区别：手机只是在利用固定电源来维持一种不完全充电的状态。

对于充电模式问题，手机制造商基本上有三种选择：

1. 使用过去的充电模式，这样能维持电池的满电状态，但会损害电池的寿命。

2. 使用新的充电模式，同时精确地显示电量。

3. 使用新的充电模式，同时不精确地显示电量。

显然，第一个方案不会受到大家的欢迎，因为它会让手机过早报废。第二个方案虽然是实话实说，但可能会遭到许多人的抱怨。毕竟，有多少人愿意看到自己的手机还在充着电，电量就降到了90%呢？因此，第三个方案是一种折中的方法。或许手机制造公司认为，用户可能不太关注拔下充电器后电量迅速下降的情况，而是更担心手机充电器是否有什么"缺陷"，导致他们的手机即使插在充电器上也总是充不满电。

如果你确实需要最大的电量，可以使用插拔法进行充电。现在有很多人利用"补丁程序"来试验这种方法，但我还没有看到有哪一个起了作用。然而，需要注意的是，反复插拔充电不但会减少电池的使用寿命，还会降低电池容量。如果你是一个"手机大户"，用一段时间之后就会去买一块新的电池，那么这一点可能就不是问题。如果你只是一个普通用户，几年内都不准备换手机，那么我建议你还是不要使用插拔充电法了。总之，除非你真的总是把电池电量用尽才去充电，否则这样做没什么必要。

如果你可以经常给手机充电，那么继续这样做吧。当你在家或在办公桌旁时，就给手机充上电。正如电池百科中解释的那样：对于锂电池来说，多次不完全的放电和充电，比把全部电量耗尽再充电更好。这样做不会给锂电池造成任何损害，因为锂电池没有记忆性。

除此之外，我能给你的最好的建议就是：不要太在意手机的电量指示，尽管放心地使用吧。需要充电的时候就充电，不要被精确的电量指示所困扰。如果你确实需要更长的使用时间，那就去买一块大容量的电池，然后像往常一样使用吧。

💡 单词记事本

unplug [ˌʌnˈplʌg]
释 v. 拔去(塞子、插头)；除掉…的障碍物

smartphone [ˈsmɑːtfəʊn]
释 n. 智能手机

charger [ˈtʃɑːdʒə(r)]
释 n. 充电器；军马；控诉者

battery [ˈbætri; ˈbætəri]
释 n. 电池；一系列

gauge [geɪdʒ]
释 n. 标准量度，规格；计量器 v. 测量(某物)；判断(某事物)
例 Anthropologists and archaeologists rely on stone tools and other artifacts to *gauge* the sophistication of ancient humans. 人类学家和考古学家依靠石制工具和其他史前古物来判断古人类头脑的复杂程度。

defective [dɪˈfektɪv]
释 a. 有缺点的；不完美的；有毛病的

accidentally [ˌæksɪˈdentəli]
释 ad. 意外地；偶然地

weeklong [ˈwiːklɒŋ]
释 a. 持续一星期的

surfing [ˈsɜːfɪŋ]
释 n. (互联网上的)冲浪，漫游，浏览

navigation ['nævɪ'geɪʃn]

释 n. 导航；航行，航海

vibrant ['vaɪbrənt]

释 a. 振动的；充满生气的；(尤指颜色)鲜明的，醒目的

compound

释 ['kɒmpaʊnd] n. 化合物 a. 复合的
[kəm'paʊnd] v. 化合；混合；使(坏事)更坏

例 Bisphenol A, a *compound* found in certain hard, clear plastics, has raised widespread concerns. 双酚A这一发现于某种坚硬的透明塑料中的化合物受到了广泛的关注。

inelegant [ɪn'elɪgənt]

释 a. 粗暴的；不雅的

trickle ['trɪkl]

释 n. 细流 v. 一滴滴地流

prolonged [prə'lɒŋd]

释 a. 延长的

corrosion [kə'rəʊʒn]

释 n. 腐蚀(状态)，侵蚀；衰败

partial ['pɑːʃl]

释 a. 部分的；偏心的

manufacturer [ˌmænju'fæktʃərə(r)]

释 n. 制造商；制造厂

essentially [ɪ'senʃəli]

释 ad. 基本上；本质上

例 This review was intended to serve *essentially* as a background of how science and technology could impede or promote development. 该评论旨在为科学技术如何阻碍或推进发展这一问题提供基本的背景信息。

eventual [ɪ'ventʃuəl]

释 a. 最终的；可能的

inaccurate [ɪn'ækjərət]

释 a. 不准确的；错误的

prematurely ['premətʃə(r)li]

释 ad. 过早地；早熟地；早产地

compromise ['kɒmprəmaɪz]

释 n. 折中办法；妥协 v. 妥协；危及；放弃(原则、理想等)

例 As soon as you *compromise* your principles, you lose. 只要你放弃原则，你就输了。

bump [bʌmp]

释 v. 碰撞；敲击 n. 撞击；肿块 ad. 突然地

用 bump along/down 颠簸着前进；bump into 偶然遇见

presumably [prɪ'zjuːməbli]

释 ad. 大概，可能；据推测

lithium ['lɪθiəm]

释 n. 锂

obsess [əb'ses]

释 v. 困扰；迷住

💡 单词家族

科学理论

astronomy [ə'strɒnəmi] n. 天文学
fundamental [ˌfʌndə'mentl] a. 基础的，基本的 n. [pl.]基本原理
genetics [dʒə'netɪks] n. 遗传学
geology [dʒi'ɒlədʒi] n. 地质(学)

module ['mɒdjuːl] n. 建筑部件，家具组件；模块；(航空器中的)舱
multiply ['mʌltɪplaɪ] v. 乘；繁殖；(使)倍增，增加
nucleus ['njuːkliəs] n. 核，原子核；核心

Passage 28

音频

Spectacular Invention

In ancient Greek **mythology**, Medusa's gaze turns **onlookers** to stone. Yang Shuo, a junior software **major** at Wuhan University, can crush fruit in the Fruit Ninja game simply by moving his eyes. The 21-year-old and his teammates recently developed a mask which operates a computer by eye movement.

The aim is to help physically challenged people and possibly to **pioneer** a new area in computer control technology. Their product enables users, who have weak muscles or are disabled, to operate a computer.

Their eye movement is **captured** by digital cameras fixed to the glasses, enabling the eyes to act like a computer mouse.

"We wanted to develop a technology that helps others and solves the toughest problems," said Yang, leader of the team named "Xight".

Li Jin, 21, a junior software major at the university, found a challenging problem during his visit to Chongqing Disabled Person's **Federation** in an off-campus activity last year. Li noticed that disabled people wanted to communicate via the Internet, but many were unable to because of their physical condition.

"Let's see what we can do," said Yang.

The idea of using the eyes to control a computer came up. "Because the eye is one of the most **agile** parts of the human body," said Li.

However, the team discovered that eyes can be too quick to be captured by camera for an accurate **positioning** function.

As a result, their prototype glasses could only function in four corners of a computer screen with the head held still, which wasn't practical.

The team **reckoned** that with lots of experiments and calculations, a **pattern** of eye movement could be **traced** and programmed.

For 20 days they worked wearing a neck brace before they finally made a breakthrough with a head localization algorithm, which can accurately locate the target and **execute** commands.

"Many times when I took off the neck brace, I felt that it was hard to move my eyes and my neck was killing me," said Yang. "But it was worth the pain."

Xbox experts were excited to learn that Xight was even quicker than hand-waving **karate** moves when playing Fruit Ninja at a national competition **sponsored** by Microsoft. Mark Taylor, director of Development and **Platform Evangelism** Group, is amazed by the potential of Xight's work.

"This product not only **showcased** technical **brainpower** but also a **promising** market perspective," said Taylor.

Taylor is right.

In the US, software and digital glasses with a similar function cost $8,000. But Xight's can be much more competitive.

"Even if we **refine** the appearance of the glasses and the function in a more user-friendly way, it won't cost more than 500 yuan," said Yang.

Many **investors** have already **contacted** the team trying to put the invention into commercial production. But the team refused.

"At present, our focus is to improve Xight and make it an ideal application for disabled people. When we achieve this, we'll consider **commercializing** our innovation," said Yang, who has been busy preparing a **thesis** and materials for Xight's patent application.

Not surprisingly, the team won the top prize in the innovation competition.

The four are **racking** their brains to **incorporate** new elements like gesture control and voice control in Xight to **spice** up the human-machine **interface** concept.

"One day, when you return home, you will tell the computer to **dim** the light, use a hand gesture to turn on the TV and glance at the air **conditioner** to lower the temperature," said Yang.

译文

伟大的发明

在古希腊神话中，美杜莎的注视可以把看到她的人变成石头。而杨硕，武汉大学软件专业的大三学生，可以在玩《水果忍者》游戏时仅仅通过移动视线来切水果。最近，这位21岁的大学生和队友们共同研发了一个面具，可以通过眼部运动来操控电脑。

这项发明的目的是帮助身体残疾人士，而且有可能在计算机操控技术方面开创一个新的时代。他们的产品可以用来帮助那些肌无力患者或残疾用户操作电脑。

用户的眼球运动能够被安装在眼镜上的数码相机捕捉到，这样双眼就可以起到鼠标的作用。

杨硕是一支名为"Xight"的团队的队长，他说："我们希望研发一项技术，能够帮助到别人，同时也能够解决最困难的问题。"

21岁的李今也是武汉大学软件专业的大三学生。他于去年的一次校外活动中参观了重庆残疾人联合会，期间他发现了一个富有挑战性的问题。他注意到，残疾人士希望通过互联网与他人交流，但很多人因为身体条件的限制而无法实现这一愿望。

"让我们想想自己能做些什么。"杨硕这样说。

于是，用双眼来控制电脑的想法应运而生。"因为眼睛是人体最灵活的部位之一。"李今说。

然而，该团队发现眼球运动的速度过快，使得相机无法捕捉它的运动状况，继而无法实现精确定位的功能。

结果，他们最初制作的眼镜原型只能在头部保持不动的情况下控制电脑屏幕的四个角，这是不实用的。

经过思考，团队成员认为通过大量的实验和计算可以跟踪眼球运动的方式，并据此进行编程。

在戴着颈托工作了20天之后，他们终于取得了突破，完成了一个头部定位程序。这个程序可以精确地定位目标并执行指令。

杨硕说："有很多次，在摘下颈托后，我感觉眼睛几乎都动不了了，脖子也疼得要命，但这些痛苦都是值得的。"

在由微软公司赞助的一项全国性的比赛中，Xight团队玩《水果忍者》游戏时的动作甚至比空手道的挥手动作还要迅速。这一消息使微软Xbox游戏机的专家们感到很兴奋。微软公司开发及平台事业部的主管马克·泰勒也对Xight的作品中表现出来的潜力倍感惊奇。

泰勒说："这个产品不仅展现出了技术上的智能性，更展示出了一个很好的市场前景。"

泰勒是正确的。

在美国，具有相似功能的软件和数码眼镜的价格高达8000美元，与之相比，Xight的产品价格非常有竞争力。

杨硕说："即使我们进一步改善眼镜的外观和功能，使其更适合用户使用，其成本也不会超过500元人民币。"

许多投资商已经与Xight团队取得了联系，希望将这项发明投入到商业生产中去，但都遭到了拒绝。

杨硕说："我们目前的重点是改进Xight，使它成为一个适合残疾人士使用的理想的发明。在我们实现这一步之后，才会考虑将它商业化。"他正忙着准备论文及相关材料以便为Xight申请专利。

不出所料，Xight团队最终在该创新大赛中赢得了头等奖。

目前，四位成员正在绞尽脑汁地在Xight中融合一些新元素，比如手势控制和声音控制，从而让人机交互界面的理念更加有趣。

"会有这么一天，当你回到家后，可以通过声音告诉电脑调暗灯光，用手势打开电视，只要看一眼空调就能调低温度。"杨硕说。

mythology [mɪ'θɒlədʒi]
释 *n.* 神话；神话学

onlooker ['ɒnlʊkə(r)]
释 *n.* 观看者；旁观者

major ['meɪdʒə(r)]
释 *n.* 专业；(大学专业的)专修学生；少校
a. 主要的 *v.* 主修，专攻

pioneer [,paɪə'nɪə(r)]
释 *n.* 先驱者 *v.* 开拓，开创

capture ['kæptʃə(r)]
释 *v.* 捕捉；俘获；夺取 *n.* 战利品
例 The penalty for these *captured* aid workers could range from expulsion to a jail term, and death sentence. 这些被抓的外援工人可能面临着被驱逐出境、入狱甚至死刑的处罚。

federation [,fedə'reɪʃn]
释 *n.* 联合会；联邦；联盟

agile ['ædʒaɪl]
释 *a.* 灵活的；活泼的；机敏的

positioning [pə'zɪʃənɪŋ]
释 *n.* 定位

reckon ['rekən]
释 *v.* 认为；估计；测算，测量
用 reckon on 依靠，指望；reckon with 考虑；重视
例 The newly released album is *reckoned* as the best of the year. 这张新发行的专辑被认为是年度最佳专辑。

pattern ['pætn]
释 *n.* 模式；样式 *v.* 仿制

trace [treɪs]
释 *v.* 跟踪；查出；描摹 *n.* 痕迹；微量

execute ['eksɪkjuːt]
释 *v.* 执行，实行；使生效；处决

karate [kə'rɑːti]
释 *n.* 空手道

sponsor ['spɒnsə(r)]
释 *v.* 赞助；担保；倡议

platform ['plætfɔːm]
释 *n.* 平台；站台

evangelism [ɪ'vændʒɪlɪzəm]
释 *n.* 福音传道；宣传

showcase ['ʃəʊkeɪs]
释 *n.* 陈列橱 *v.* 显示

brainpower ['breɪnpaʊə(r)]
释 *n.* 智能；智囊团

promising ['prɒmɪsɪŋ]
释 *a.* 有希望的，有前途的

refine [rɪ'faɪn]
释 *v.* 净化；精炼；使完善；使有教养；推敲
用 refine on/upon 琢磨，改进；推敲，润色
例 Watching good movies helps to *refine* one's taste. 观看好的电影有助于提高一个人的品位。

investor [ɪn'vestə(r)]
释 *n.* 投资者

contact ['kɒntækt]
释 *n./v.* 联系；接触
用 contact lens 隐形眼镜
例 To obtain a visa of one country, we advise that you should visit or *contact* the nearest consular mission. 要想获得一个国家的签证，我们建议你拜访或联系一下离你最近的领事馆。

commercialize [kə'mɜːʃəlaɪz]
释 *v.* 使商业化

thesis ['θiːsɪs]
释 *n.* 论文；论题，论点

rack [ræk]

释 n. 挂架；搁架 v. 使痛苦

用 rack ones brains 绞尽脑汁，冥思苦想；on the rack (肉体或精神上)受极大折磨

incorporate [ɪnˈkɔːpəreɪt]

释 v. 将某事物包括进去，包含；组成公司 a. 合并的

spice [spaɪs]

释 n. 香料；趣味 v. 使增添趣味；加香料

interface [ˈɪntəfeɪs]

释 n. 界面；分界面；接口

例 You're likely to encounter only one type of *interface* on most PCs. 在大多数的个人电脑上，你可能只会遇到一种类型的界面。

dim [dɪm]

释 a. 昏暗的；愚笨的 v. (使)暗淡

conditioner [kənˈdɪʃənə(r)]

释 n. 调节装置；调节剂

💡 单词家族

科技实验

activate [ˈæktɪveɪt] v. 激活；使产生放射性

amorphous [əˈmɔːfəs] a. 无定形的

ascertain [ˌæsəˈteɪn] v. 查明；弄清

assortment [əˈsɔːtmənt] n. 混合物

atomic [əˈtɒmɪk] a. 原子(能)的

axis [ˈæksɪs] n. 轴；主线，中枢

bewilder [bɪˈwɪldə(r)] v. 使迷惑，难住

calibration [ˌkælɪˈbreɪʃn] n. 校准；刻度

collate [kəˈleɪt] v. 对照；核对

combustion [kəmˈbʌstʃən] n. 燃烧，氧化

condensation [ˌkɒndenˈseɪʃn] n. 浓缩；凝结

dimension [daɪˈmenʃn; dɪˈmenʃn] n. 尺寸；维(数)

echolocation [ˌekəʊləʊˈkeɪʃn] n. 回声定位法

equation [ɪˈkweɪʒn] n. 等式，方程式；相等

forerunner [ˈfɔːrʌnə(r)] n. 先驱(者)；预兆

friction [ˈfrɪkʃn] n. 摩擦；摩擦力

hazardous [ˈhæzədəs] a. 危险的；冒险的

horsepower [ˈhɔːspaʊə(r)] n. 马力

impurity [ɪmˈpjʊərəti] n. 不纯；杂质

inductive [ɪnˈdʌktɪv] a. 归纳的；电磁感应的

ingeniously [ɪnˈdʒiːniəsli] ad. 善于用新的或简单的方法解决复杂问题的；心灵手巧的

insoluble [ɪnˈsɒljəbl] a. 不能溶解的；不能解决的

metallurgy [məˈtælədʒi] n. 冶金学

modulate [ˈmɒdjuleɪt] v. 调整；(信号)调制

momentum [məˈmentəm] n. 动力，势头；动量

optical [ˈɒptɪkl] a. 视力的；光学的

particle [ˈpɑːtɪkl] n. 粒子，微粒；小品词

penetration [ˌpenəˈtreɪʃn] n. 渗透；突破，进入

perplex [pəˈpleks] v. 使困惑；使费解

plank [plæŋk] n. 厚木板；支架；政策或政纲的准则

precision [prɪˈsɪʒn] n. 精确，精确度

prerequisite [ˌpriːˈrekwəzɪt] n. 先决条件

propulsion [prə'pʌlʃn] n. 推进；推进力

radioactive [ˌreɪdiəʊ'æktɪv] a. 放射性的；有辐射的

resultant [rɪ'zʌltənt] a. 结果的；合成的 n. 合力；生成物

rotary ['rəʊtəri] a. 旋转的

rust [rʌst] n. 铁锈 v. (使)生锈；腐蚀

shred [ʃred] n. 碎片；少量剩余

solution [sə'luːʃn] n. 解决办法；溶解；溶液

solvent ['sɒlvənt] n. 溶剂；溶媒

spectrum ['spektrəm] n. 光谱，频谱；范围

static ['stætɪk] a. 静态的；静力的

subdivision [ˌsʌbdɪ'vɪʒn; 'sʌbdɪvɪʒn] n. 进一步细分

substantive [səb'stæntɪv; 'sʌbstəntɪv] a. 真实的；实际的

sulphide ['sʌlfaɪd] n. 硫化物

symmetry ['sɪmətri] n. 对称(性)；匀称，整齐

systematize ['sɪstəmətaɪz] v. 使系统化；将…分类

tentative ['tentətɪv] a. 试验性质的；试探性的

thermal ['θɜːml] a. 热的，热量的

vertical ['vɜːtɪkl] a. 垂直的 n. 垂线

worthwhile [ˌwɜːθ'waɪl] a. 值得(做)的

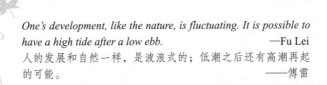

One's development, like the nature, is fluctuating. It is possible to have a high tide after a low ebb. —Fu Lei

人的发展和自然一样，是波浪式的；低潮之后还有高潮再起的可能。

——傅雷

Passage 29

Space Tourism

Make your reservations now. The space tourism industry is officially open for business, and tickets are going for a mere $20 million for a one-week stay in space. Despite reluctance from National Air and Space Administration (NASA), Russia made American businessman Dennis Tito the world's first space tourist. Tito flew into space aboard a Russian Soyuz rocket that arrived at the International Space Station (ISS) on April 30, 2001. The second space tourist, South African businessman Mark Shuttleworth, took off aboard the Russian Soyuz on April 25, 2002, also bound for the ISS.

Lance Bass of 'N Sync was supposed to be the third to make the $20 million trip, but he did not join the three-man crew as they blasted off on October 30, 2002, due to lack of payment. Probably the most incredible aspect of this proposed space tour was that NASA approved of it.

These trips are the beginning of what could be a profitable 21st century industry. There are already several space tourism companies planning to build suborbital vehicles and orbital cities within the next two decades. These companies have invested millions, believing that the space tourism industry is on the verge of taking off.

In 1997, NASA published a report concluding that selling trips into space to private citizens could be worth billions of dollars. A Japanese report supports these findings, and projects that space tourism could be a $10 billion per year industry within the next two decades. The only obstacles to opening up space to tourists are the space agencies, who are concerned with safety and the development of a reliable, reusable launch vehicle.

Russia's Mir space station was supposed to be the first destination for space tourists. But in March 2001, the Russian Aerospace Agency brought Mir down into the Pacific Ocean. As it turned out, bringing down Mir only temporarily delayed the first tourist trip into space.

The Mir crash did cancel plans for a new reality-based game show from NBC, which was going to be called *Destination Mir*. The *Survivor*-like TV show was scheduled to air in fall 2001. Participants on the show were to go through training at Russia's cosmonaut training center, Star City. Each week, one of the participants would be eliminated from the show, with the winner receiving a trip to the Mir space station. The Mir crash has ruled out NBC's space plans for now. NASA is against beginning space tourism until the International Space Station is completed in 2006.

Initially, space tourism will offer simple accommodations at best. For instance, if the International Space Station is used as a tourist attraction, guests won't find the **luxurious** surroundings of a hotel room on Earth. It has been designed for conducting research, not entertainment. However, the first generation of space hotels should offer tourists a much more comfortable experience.

Many companies believe that they have to offer an extremely enjoyable experience in order for passengers to pay thousands, if not millions, of dollars to ride into space. So will space create another separation between the haves and have-nots?

Will space be an **exotic retreat** reserved for only the wealthy? Or will middle-class folks have a chance to take their families to space? Make no mistake about it, going to space will be the most expensive vacation you ever take. Prices right now are in the tens of millions of dollars. Currently, the only vehicles that can take you into space are the space **shuttle** and the Russian Soyuz, both of which are terribly inefficient. Each spacecraft requires millions of pounds of fuel to take off into space, which makes them expensive to launch. One pound of **payload** costs about $10,000 to put into Earth's **orbit**.

NASA and Lockheed Martin are currently developing a single-stage-to-orbit launch space plane, called the VentureStar, that could be launched for about a tenth of what the space shuttle costs to launch. If the VentureStar takes off, the number of people who could afford to take a trip into space would move into the millions.

译文

太空旅行

现在就预订吧！太空旅游业已经正式开始运营，在太空停留一周的票价仅为2000万美元。尽管美国国家航空航天局很不情愿，俄罗斯还是让美国商人丹尼斯·蒂托成为了世界上第一位太空游客。蒂托乘坐俄罗斯的"联盟号"宇宙飞船飞入太空并于2001年4月30日抵达国际空间站。第二位太空游客是南非商人马克·沙特尔沃思，他于2002年4月25日登上俄罗斯的"联盟号"宇宙飞船，也前往了国际空间站。

超级男孩乐队成员兰斯·贝斯原本应该是第三位花费2000万美元进入外太空旅行的人，但是他因无法支付款项，而没有在2002年10月30日飞船发射当天与三位飞行员一起飞向太空。也许这次原计划的太空旅行最令人难以置信的一点是美国国家航空航天局竟然批准了。

这三次旅行标志着21世纪高利润行业的兴起。目前已经有几家太空旅行公司计划在未来20年内开发亚轨道运载工具和轨道城市。这些公司已经投入了数百万资金，他们坚信太空旅游业正蓄势待发。

1997年，美国国家航空航天局在发表的一篇报道中得出这样一个结论：经营面向普通民众的太空旅行的收益每年可能高达数十亿美元。日本的一篇报道也对此结论表示支持，并预测在未来20年内太空旅行业每年的收益应该在100亿美元。向游客开放太空唯一的障碍是航天局，他们关心安全问题以及可靠的且可重复使用的运载工具的开发问题。

俄罗斯的"和平号"空间站本应该是太空旅行者的第一个目的地，但是在2001年3月，俄罗斯航空航天局将其坠毁于太平洋中。结果证明，"和平号"的坠毁只是暂时推迟了第一位太空游客进入太空的时间。

"和平号"的坠毁使得美国国家广播公司的一档新出的纪实性游戏竞赛节目被迫取消，该节目原本计划叫作《目的地和平号》。这个类似于《幸存者》的电视节目原计划在2001年秋天开播。节目的所有参与者都将在俄罗斯宇航员训练中心星城接受培训。每周都会有一名参赛者被淘汰，最后胜出的那名选手将获得前往"和平号"空间站旅行的机会。"和平号"空间站的坠毁彻底毁掉了美国国家广播公司的太空秀计划。直到2006年国际空间站建成之后，美国国家航空航天局才开始不再反对开展太空旅游业。

最初，太空旅行最多会提供简单的住宿。例如，如果将国际空间站作为旅游景点，游客将看不到像地球上的酒店房间那样的豪华布置。空间站是用来进行研究的，而不是用于娱乐的。但是，第一代太空酒店应该会提供给游客一种舒适得多的住宿体验。

很多公司认为，为了吸引游客花费不是数百万美元就是数千万美元进入太空，他们不得不为游客提供极其愉快的太空体验。那么太空旅行会创造出另一种贫富差距吗？

太空会成为一个专为有钱人保留的异域休闲地吗？中产阶级有机会带家人去太空吗？毫无疑问，去太空旅行将是你生平度过的最昂贵的假期。现在进入太空的费用高达数千万美元。目前，只有航天飞机和俄国的"联盟号"宇宙飞船能载人进入太空，并且这两种运载工具的运行效率都非常低。两者都需要消耗几百万磅的燃料才能飞入太空，这使得发射变得非常昂贵。一磅的有效运载量需要向地球轨道投入一万美元。

美国国家航空航天局和洛克希德·马丁公司目前正在研发一个名为"冒险之星"的单极入轨发射的航天飞机，其发射所需的费用是太空飞船发射的十分之一。如果"冒险之星"可以成功起飞的话，那么可以负担起太空旅行的人将会上升到数百万。

reservation [ˌrezə'veɪʃn]

释 n. (住处、座位等的)预订；预定；保留

用 hotel reservation 预订酒店；make a reservation 预订

例 I have a *reservation* in the name of Tom Carter. 我以汤姆·卡特的名字预订的。

officially [ə'fɪʃəli]

释 ad. 正式地；公务地；官方地

crew [kruː]

释 n. (轮船、飞行器等上的)工作人员；一伙，一帮

blast [blɑːst]

释 n. 一阵(大风)；爆炸；冲击波 v. 发射；爆炸；枯萎

due [djuː]

释 a. 由于；预期的；应得的；应支付的，到期的

例 *Due* to staff shortage, our company was unable to offer the service. 由于人手不足，我们公司无法提供该项服务。

incredible [ɪn'kredəbl]

释 a. 难以置信的，不可思议的

例 It seemed *incredible* that he had worked for the company for ten years. 他在这家公司工作了十年，让人觉得有点不可思议。

proposed [prə'pəʊzd]

释 a. (正式)提议的，建议的

approve [ə'pruːv]

释 v. 赞成；批准

用 approve of 赞成

例 The group unanimously *approved* the project. 小组一致通过了这个项目。

suborbital [ˌsʌb'ɔːbɪtl]

释 a. 亚轨道的；不足一周的

verge [vɜːdʒ]

释 n. 边缘 v. 倾向；濒于

用 on the verge of 濒临于；接近于

例 Losing her pet, she was on the *verge* of tears. 失去了宠物，她快要哭出来了。

launch [lɔːntʃ]

释 v. 发射；推出(产品)；使(船)下水 n. 发射；(船)下水；(新产品)投产

temporarily ['temprərəli]

释 ad. 临时地，暂时地

cancel ['kænsl]

释 v. 取消；抵消；删去

schedule ['ʃedjuːl]

释 n. 日程安排表；清单 v. 安排，预定

用 on schedule 按照预定时间；ahead of schedule 提前

例 We get used to working to a tight *schedule*. 我们习惯了把工作排得很满。

air [eə(r)]

释 n. 空气；神态；态度 v. 晾干；使通风；播放

participant [pɑː'tɪsɪpənt]

释 n. 参与者

initially [ɪ'nɪʃəli]

释 ad. 最初，首先

luxurious [lʌg'ʒʊəriəs]

释 a. 奢侈的，豪华的；丰富的；放纵的

exotic [ɪg'zɒtɪk]

释 a. 非本地的；吸引人的

retreat [rɪ'triːt]

释 v. 退却；规避 n. 撤退；退缩；隐退处，静居处

例 Never surrender and never *retreat*. 决不投降，决不撤退。

shuttle ['ʃʌtl]

释 n. 航天飞机；梭子；短程穿梭运行的飞机、公共汽车等 v. 穿梭般来回

用 space shuttle 航天飞机；shuttle bus 班车

payload ['peɪləʊd]

释 n. (运输工具的)净载重量；工资负担

orbit ['ɔ:bɪt]

释 n. 轨道 v. (绕…)作轨道运行

💡 单词家族

天体宇宙

aerial ['eəriəl] a. 空中的

aloft [ə'lɒft] ad. 在高处；在空中

atmosphere ['ætməsfɪə(r)] n. 大气(层)，空气；气氛

aurora [ɔ:'rɔ:rə] n. 极光

aviation [ˌeɪvi'eɪʃn] n. 航空(学)

capsule ['kæpsju:l] n. 胶囊；太空舱

celestial [sə'lestiəl] a. 天空的

comet ['kɒmɪt] n. 彗星

cosmic ['kɒzmɪk] a. 宇宙的

eclipse [ɪ'klɪps] n. 日食；月食

geomagnetic [ˌdʒi:əʊmæg'netɪk] a. 地磁的

hemisphere ['hemɪsfɪə(r)] n. 地球或天体的半球

horizon [hə'raɪzn] n. 地平线；[常pl.] 眼界，视野

hydrosphere ['haɪdrəʊsfɪə(r)] n. 水圈，水界

interstellar [ˌɪntə'stelə(r)] a. 星际的

Jupiter ['dʒu:pɪtə(r)] n. 木星

landmass ['lændmæs] n. 地块；大片陆地

longitude ['lɒŋgɪtju:d; 'lɒndʒɪtju:d] n. 经度，经线

lunar ['lu:nə(r)] a. 月亮的；月球的

meridian [mə'rɪdiən] n. 子午线

meteor ['mi:tiə(r); 'mi:tiɔ:(r)] n. 流星

meteorite ['mi:tiəraɪt] n. 陨石

meteorology [ˌmi:tiə'rɒlədʒi] n. 气象学

orbital ['ɔ:bɪtl] a. 轨道的

rainfall ['reɪnfɔ:l] n. 降雨；降雨量

Saturn ['sætɜ:n; 'sætən] n. 土星

sunset ['sʌnset] n. 日落

telescope ['telɪskəʊp] n. 望远镜

vacuum ['vækjuəm] n. 真空

Passage 30

What Will the World
Be Like in Fifty Years?

This week some top scientists, including the Nobel Prize winners, gave their vision of how the world will look in 2056, from gas-powered cars to extraordinary health advances.

For those of us lucky enough to live that long, 2056 will be a world of almost perpetual youth, where obesity is a remote memory and robots become our companions.

We will be rubbing shoulders with aliens and colonizing outer space. Better still, our descendants might at last live in a world at peace with itself.

The prediction is that we will have found a source of inexhaustible, safe, green energy, and that science will have killed off religion. If they are right we will have removed two of the main causes of war—our dependence on oil and religious prejudice.

Will we really, as today's scientists claim, be able to live for ever or at least cheat the ageing process so that the average person lives to 150?

Of course, all these predictions come with a scientific health warning. Harvard professor Steven Pinker says, "This is an invitation to look foolish, as with the predictions of domed cities and nuclear-powered vacuum cleaners that were made 50 years ago."

Living Longer

Anthony Atala, director of the Wake Forest Institute in North Carolina, believes failing organs will be repaired by injecting cells into the body. They will naturally go straight to the injury and help heal it. A system of injections without needles could also slow the ageing process by using the same process to "tune" cells.

Richard Miller, a professor at the University of Michigan, thinks scientists could develop "authentic anti-ageing drugs" by working out how cells in larger animals such as whales and humans resist many forms of injuries. He says, "It's now routine, in laboratory mammals, to extend lifespan by about 40%. Turning on the same protective systems in people should, by 2056, create the first class of 100-year-olds who are as vigorous and productive as today's people in their 60s".

Aliens

Conlin Pillinger, professor of planetary sciences at the Open University, says, "I fancy that at least we will be able to show that life did start to evolve on Mars as well as Earth." Within 50 years he hopes scientists will prove that alien life came here in Martian meteorites.

Chris McKay, a planetary scientist at NASA's Ames Research Center, believes that in 50 years we may find evidence of alien life in ancient permanent frost of Mars or on other planets.

He adds, "There is even a chance we will find alien life forms here on Earth. It might be as different as English is to Chinese."

Obesity

Sydney Brenner, senior distinguished fellow of the Crick-Jacobs Center in California, won the 2002 Nobel Prize for Medicine and says that if there is a global disaster some humans will survive—and evolution will favour small people with bodies large enough to support the required amount of brain power. "Obesity," he says, "will have been solved."

Robots

Rodney Brooks, professor of robotics at MIT, says the problems of developing artificial intelligence for robots will be at least partly overcome. As a result, "the possibilities for robots working with people will open up immensely."

Energy

Bill Joy, green technology expert in California, says, "The most significant breakthrough would be to have an inexhaustible source of safe, green energy that is substantially cheaper than any existing energy source."

Ideally, such a source would be safe in that it could not be made into weapons and would not make hazardous or toxic waste or carbon dioxide, the main greenhouse gas blamed for global warming.

Society

Geoffrey Miller, evolutionary psychologist at the University of New Mexico, says, "The US will follow the UK in realizing that religion is not a prerequisite for ordinary human decency.

"Thus, science will kill religion—not by reason challenging faith but by offering a more practical, universal and rewarding moral framework for human interaction."

He also predicts that "absurdly wasteful" displays of wealth will become unfashionable while the importance of close-knit communities and families will become clearer.

These three changes, he says, will help make us all "brighter, wiser, happier and kinder".

50年后世界将是什么样的?

本周,包括诺贝尔奖得主在内的一些顶尖的科学家构想了他们心目中2056年世界的样子,包括从天然气动力汽车到健康方面的卓越进展。

对于我们当中有幸活到那时的人来说,2056年将会是一个青春永驻的世界,那时肥胖症将成为遥远的记忆,机器人将成为我们的同伴。

我们将会与外星人来往,还会移民到外太空。更好的是,我们的后代将终于可以生活在一个和平的世界里。

预言称我们将找到一种取之不尽的、安全的绿色能源,而且科学将会终止宗教信仰。如果这些预言是正确的,我们将会消除战争的两大诱因——对石油的依赖和宗教偏见。

真的可以像今天的科学家们所宣称的那样,可以长生不老或者至少可以摆脱衰老的过程从而使我们普通人都能活到150岁吗?

当然,所有的这些预测都是伴随着科学的健康警示一起产生的。哈佛大学教授史蒂文·平克说道:"这会让人们作出一些愚蠢的推论,正如50年前对圆顶城市和核能真空吸尘器的预测一样。"

活得更久

北卡罗来纳州唤醒森林研究所主任安东尼·阿塔拉认为,受损器官可以通过将细胞注入人体而得到修复。这些细胞将自然地直接进入受损区域,并帮助其愈合。一种无针注射系统也能通过同样的过程来"调节"细胞,从而减缓衰老进程。

密歇根大学教授理查德·米勒认为,科学家可以通过研究鲸鱼和人类等体型较大的动物体内的细胞如何抵抗多种形式的损伤研发出"真正的抗衰老药品"。他说:"一般情况下实验室内的哺乳动物的寿命能延长约40%。到2056年,在人体内开启同样的保护系统就会产生第一批跟现在60多岁的人一样的精力充沛且具有生产力的百岁老人。"

外星人

英国开放大学的行星科学教授科林·皮林格说:"我相信,我们将至少能够证明火星跟地球一样,曾有过生物的进化。"他希望50年内科学家们将能够证明外星生命曾通过火星陨石来过地球。

美国国家航空航天局埃姆斯研究中心的行星科学家克里斯·麦凯认为，50年内，我们可能会在火星或其他行星上的古老的永冻土中发现外星生命存在的证据。

他补充道："我们甚至有可能在地球上找到外星生命。也许他们和我们的差别正如英国人和中国人的差别一样大。"

肥胖

加利福尼亚克里克·雅各布斯中心的资深研究员悉尼·布伦纳是2002年诺贝尔医学奖的获得者。他表示，如果有全球性的大灾难的话，部分人类会幸存——进化过程会选择那些身高较低但拥有足够大的身体来提供所需脑力的人类。"肥胖问题也已经得到解决。"他说道。

机器人

麻省理工学院的机器人学教授罗德尼·布鲁克斯认为，科学家们至少会解决开发人工智能机器人的部分问题，因此"机器人和人一起工作的可能性将会大大增加"。

能源

加利福尼亚州的绿色技术专家比尔·乔伊说道："最有意义的突破是我们将拥有取之不尽的、安全的绿色能源，而且这种能源比今天的任何能源都要便宜很多。"

理想情况下，这种能源将会很安全，因为它既不能被用来制造武器，也不会产生有害或者有毒的废弃物，或者产生导致全球变暖的温室气体——二氧化碳。

社会

新墨西哥大学的进化心理学家杰弗里·米勒说道："继英国之后，美国也将意识到宗教并不是衡量普通人礼仪的前提。

"因此，科学将消灭宗教——不是通过理智来挑战信仰，而是为人们交往提供一个更加实际、通用且有益的道德准则。"

他还预测，用"荒谬浪费的"方式炫耀财富将会过时，而紧密联系的社区和家庭的重要性将越来越明显。

他表示，这三个改变将帮助我们所有人变得"更加乐观、智慧、幸福和善良"。

vision ['vɪʒn]
释 n. 视觉；幻想，想象

extraordinary [ɪk'strɔːdnri]
释 a. 不同寻常的，非凡的

advance [əd'vɑːns]
释 v. 前进；取得进展；促进；增加 n. 前进；进步，发展；增加；预付 a. 预先的；在前的
用 in advance 预先，提前
例 We made great *advances* in education. 我们在教育方面取得了重大进展。

perpetual [pə'petʃuəl]
释 a. 永久的；连续不断的

remote [rɪ'məʊt]
释 a. 遥远的；疏远的；偏僻的；远程的
用 remote control 遥控装置

alien ['eɪliən]
释 n. 外国人；外星人 a. 外国的；陌生的

descendant [dɪ'sendənt]
释 n. 后代，子孙

prediction [prɪ'dɪkʃn]
释 n. 预言，预测

prejudice ['predʒudɪs]
释 n. 偏见，成见；损害，伤害 v. 使产生偏见
用 racial prejudice 种族偏见
例 The decision is based on pride and *prejudice*. 这个决定是基于傲慢与偏见作出的。

organ ['ɔːgən]
释 n. 器官；风琴；机构

inject [ɪn'dʒekt]
释 v. 给…注射；注入；插进

heal [hiːl]
释 v. 治愈，(使)痊愈；康复；消除，和解

authentic [ɔː'θentɪk]
释 a. 真正的；可靠的

resist [rɪ'zɪst]
释 v. 抵抗，反抗；抵制，抗拒；抗(病等)

routine [ruː'tiːn]
释 n. 例行公事；惯例，常规 a. 常规的，通常的

extend [ɪk'stend]
释 v. 延长；延展；舒展(肢体)

lifespan ['laɪfspæn]
释 n. 寿命；预期生命期限
例 Some animals only have a *lifespan* of a few months. 有些动物的寿命只有几个月。

vigorous ['vɪgərəs]
释 a. 精力充沛的；有魄力的

productive [prə'dʌktɪv]
释 a. 有生产能力的，多产的；富有成效的

meteorite ['miːtiəraɪt]
释 n. 陨石

permanent ['pɜːmənənt]
释 a. 长久的，永久的；固定的
用 permanent resident 永久性居民

senior ['siːniə(r)]
释 a. 资格较老的；年长的；地位高的 n. 较年长者；(大学)四年级学生

distinguished [dɪ'stɪŋgwɪʃt]
释 a. 著名的，卓著的

survive [sə'vaɪv]
释 v. 幸存
例 The people have to *survive* by begging. 人们不得不靠乞讨度日。

evolution [ˌiːvə'luːʃn; ˌevə'luːʃn]
释 n. 演化，进化；进化论

breakthrough ['breɪkθruː]

释 n. 突破；成就，发明，突破性进展

用 make a breakthrough 取得重大突破

例 A major *breakthrough* in cancer research was made last year. 去年，癌症研究方面取得了重大突破。

inexhaustible [ˌɪnɪgˈzɔːstəbl]

释 a. 用不完的，取之不竭的

substantially [səbˈstænʃəli]

释 ad. 可观地，大量地；实质上

hazardous [ˈhæzədəs]

释 a. 危险的；冒险的

toxic [ˈtɒksɪk]

释 a. 有毒的；中毒的

blame [bleɪm]

释 v. 责备；归咎于 n. 过错；责备

用 be to blame 该受责备的，应承担责任的

例 You shouldn't *blame* anyone for your father's death. 关于你父亲的死，你不能指责任何人。

universal [ˌjuːnɪˈvɜːsl]

释 a. 普遍的；宇宙的；全体的；通用的

interaction [ˌɪntərˈækʃn]

释 n. 相互作用，相互影响；交流，交往

absurdly [əbˈsɜːdli]

释 ad. 荒谬地

unfashionable [ʌnˈfæʃnəbl]

释 a. 不流行的

💡 单词家族

医疗保健

acupuncture [ˈækjupʌŋktʃə(r)] n. 针刺疗法

acute [əˈkjuːt] a. 敏锐的；(疾病)急性的

antibiotic [ˌæntibaɪˈɒtɪk] n. 抗生素

chiropractor [ˈkaɪərəupræktə(r)] n. 按摩师

clinic [ˈklɪnɪk] n. 门诊部

dental [ˈdentl] a. 牙齿的；牙科的

detoxify [ˌdiːˈtɒksɪfaɪ] v. 解毒

diagnose [ˈdaɪəgnəuz] v. 诊断

disorder [dɪsˈɔːdə(r)] n. 混乱；失调

empirically [ɪmˈpɪrɪkli] ad. 以经验为主地

epidemic [ˌepɪˈdemɪk] a. 流行性的；传染的 n. 流行病

fracture [ˈfræktʃə(r)] n. 裂缝(痕)；骨折 v. (使)断裂；(使)折断

herb [hɜːb] n. 药草；草本植物

insomnia [ɪnˈsɒmniə] n. 失眠；失眠症

marrow [ˈmærəu] n. 骨髓；精华

overhaul [ˈəuvəhɔːl] v. 检查

panacea [ˌpænəˈsiːə] n. 万能药

pharmacy [ˈfɑːməsi] n. 药剂学；药店

radial [ˈreɪdiəl] a. 放射的；光线的

reagent [riˈeɪdʒənt] n. 试剂

recovery [rɪˈkʌvəri] n. 痊愈；恢复

robust [rəuˈbʌst] a. 健壮的

sane [seɪn] a. 心智健全的

scrutinize [ˈskruːtənaɪz] v. 详细检查

seclude [sɪˈkluːd] v. (使)隔离

sore [sɔː(r)] a. 疼痛的；痛心的

stethoscope [ˈsteθəskəup] n. 听诊器

sturdy [ˈstɜːdi] a. 强健的，结实的

susceptible [səˈseptəbl] a. 易受感染的；易受影响的

therapy [ˈθerəpi] n. 治疗；疗法

vaccine [ˈvæksiːn] n. 疫苗

wholesome [ˈhəulsəm] a. 有益健康的；有道德的

Passage 31

Bosses Say 'Yes' to Home Work

Rising costs of office space, time lost to stressful commuting, and a slow recognition that workers have lives beyond the office—all are strong arguments for letting staff work from home.

For the small business, there are additional benefits too—staff are more productive, and happier, enabling firms to keep their headcounts and their recruitment costs to a minimum. It can also provide a competitive advantage, especially when small businesses want to attract new staff but don't have the budget to offer huge salaries.

While company managers have known about the benefits for a long time, many have done little about it, sceptical of whether they could trust their employees to work to full capacity without supervision, or concerned about the additional expenses teleworking policies might incur as staff start charging their home phone bills to the business.

Yet this is now changing. When communications provider Inter-Tel researched the use of remote working solutions among small- and medium-sized UK businesses in April this year, it found that 28% more companies claimed to have introduced flexible working practices than a year ago.

Technology advances, including the widespread availability of broadband, are making the introduction of remote working a piece of cake.

For Wright Vigar, which has now equipped all of its fee-earners to be able to work at maximum productivity when away from the offices (whether that's from home, or while on the road), this strategy is not just about saving on commute time or cutting them loose from the office, but enabling them to work more flexible hours that fit around their home life.

O'Hern says, "Although most of our work is client-based and must fit around this, we can't see any reason why a parent can't be on hand to deal with something important at home, if they have the ability to complete a project later in the day."

Supporting this new way of working came with a price, though. Although the firm was updating its systems anyway, the company spent 10%–15% more per user to equip them with a laptop rather than a PC, and about the same to upgrade to a server that would enable remote staff to connect to the company's networks and access all their usual resources.

Although Wright Vigar hasn't yet quantified the business benefits, it claims that, in addition to being able to retain key staff with young families, it is able to save fee-earners a **substantial** amount of "dead" time in their working days.

That staff can do this without needing a fixed telephone line provides even more efficiency savings. "With Wi-Fi (fast, **wireless** Internet connections) **popping** up all over the place, even on trains, our fee-earners can be productive as they travel, and between meetings, instead of having to kill time at the shops," he adds.

The company will also be able to avoid the expense of having to **relocate** staff to temporary offices for several weeks when it begins **disruptive** office **renovations** soon.

It has enabled the company to **dispense** with its business **premises** altogether, following the realization that it just didn't need them any more. "The main **motivation** behind adopting home working was to increase my own productivity, as a single mum of an 11-year-old," says Hargreaves. "But I soon realized that, as most of our business is done on the phone, email and at off-site meetings, we didn't need our offices at all. We're now saving £16,000 a year on rent, **plus** the cost of utilities, not to mention what would have been spent on commuting."

译文

老板们同意在家办公

办公场所的费用不断增加，花在拥堵的交通上的时间太长，加上人们慢慢意识到员工的生活不应局限于办公室内——所有这些都成了支持员工在家办公的有力论据。

对小企业来说，这样做还有其他好处——员工生产效率更高，工作得更快乐，这样公司就可以把员工人数和招聘成本降到最低。在家办公还能提供一种竞争优势，尤其是在小型企业想招聘新员工却无法提供高薪的时候。

尽管公司经理们很久以前就知道这些好处，但大多数几乎没有付诸实践。他们或者怀疑是否可以信任员工在没有人监管的情况也能尽全力工作，或者担心远程办公政策带来的额外支出，因为员工可能会把自己家的电话费交由公司支付。

不过，目前这种情况正在改变。通信服务供应商Intel-Tel于4月份调查了英国中小型企业采用远程工作方案的情况，结果发现宣称采用弹性工作方法的公司比一年前增加了28%。

科技的进步，包括宽带的广泛利用，使远程办公的采用变得轻而易举。

赖特·瓦伊格公司目前已为其所有员工配备了设备，使大家不在办公室时也能以最高的效率工作（无论是在家里还是在路上）。对该公司来说，这样的策略不仅使员工节省了通勤时间，并摆脱了办公室的束缚，还能够让员工有更灵活的工作时间，从而兼顾到家庭生活。

奥赫恩说："虽然我们大部分的工作都是以客户为基础，而且必须以此为中心，但是如果一位父亲或母亲能够稍晚一点完成项目的话，我们找不到任何理由不让他们在家里处理一些重要的事情。"

然而，支持这种新的工作方式也需要付出代价。尽管公司无论如何都要更新它的系统，但在家办公的话公司要在每个员工身上多花10%—15%的钱来为其配备笔记本电脑，而非PC；并且还要再多花费10%—15%的钱来升级服务器，使远程工作的员工能与公司网络相连接，并能使用公司的常规资源。

尽管赖特·瓦伊格公司还没有将商业利益量化，但它声称，除了能留住刚结婚不久的骨干员工外，在家办公还能为员工从他们的工作日中省出一大把"无效"时间。

员工无须固定电话线就可以实现远程办公，这更加提高了效率。"随着Wi-Fi（快速的无线网络连接）的普及（甚至连火车上都有信号），我们的员工即使在旅途中或在会议的间隙也能高效工作，而不用在商店里消磨时间。"他补充道。

在将要开始翻新破旧的办公室时，公司将同样能够免去把员工安置到临时办公室工作几周的开销。

这让公司在意识到不再需要办公场所后彻底省去了这部分开销。"对于像我这样带着11岁小孩的单身妈妈来说，在家工作的主要动机是提高自己的工作效率。"哈格里夫斯说，"但我很快意识到，由于我们大部分的工作都是通过电话、邮件、非现场会议完成，我们根本就不需要办公室。现在我们每年就能省出16,000英镑的租金以及公共设施的开支，更不用说花在通勤上的费用了。"

💡 单词记事本

stressful ['stresfl]
释 *a.* 充满压力的，紧张的

recognition [,rekəg'nɪʃn]
释 *n.* 认识；认可，承认；赏识

headcount ['hedkaʊnt]
释 *n.* 总人数；点人头数

minimum ['mɪnɪməm]
释 *n.* 最小量；最低限度 *a.* 最小的

用 minimum wage 最低工资

budget ['bʌdʒɪt]
释 *n.* 预算；专用开支 *v.* 编入预算 *a.* 低廉的
用 financial budget 财务预算
例 The house is decorated on a tight *budget*. 装修房子的预算比较紧张。

sceptical ['skeptɪkl]
释 *a.* 怀疑的；不相信的

capacity [kə'pæsəti]
释 n. (生产、学习等的)能力；生产力；容量

supervision [ˌsuːpə'vɪʒn]
释 n. 监督；管理；指导

concern [kən'sɜːn]
释 n. 关切的事；关心；关系 v. 关系到；使担心

incur [ɪn'kɜː(r)]
释 v. 招致，引起；遭遇

introduce [ˌɪntrə'djuːs]
释 v. 引进；介绍；采用
用 introduce into 引进

flexible ['fleksəbl]
释 a. 易弯曲的；柔韧的；灵活的

widespread ['waɪdspred]
释 a. 分布(或散布)广的，普遍的

equip [ɪ'kwɪp]
释 v. 装备，配备；使具备；穿着
用 equip with 装备

maximum ['mæksɪməm]
释 a. 最高的，最大限度的 n. 最大量

update
释 [ˌʌp'deɪt] v. 更新，使现代化；为…提供最新信息
['ʌpdeɪt] n. 更新；最新报道
用 update information 更新信息
例 It's about time we *updated* our equipment. 是时候更新我们的设备了。

upgrade [ˌʌp'greɪd]
释 n. 向上的斜坡 v. 提高…的级别或等级

server ['sɜːvə(r)]
释 n. 服务者；(网球)发球人；服务器

access ['ækses]
释 n. 入口；进入；接近的机会；信息获取 v. 获取(计算机文件)
用 access to 接近；有权使用

例 The only *access* to the farm is across the bridge. 进入农场的唯一途径是跨过这座小桥。

substantial [səb'stænʃl]
释 a. 可观的，大量的；物质的；坚固的

wireless ['waɪələs]
释 a. 无线的

pop [pɒp]
释 v. (使)发出爆裂声；突然出现；向…开枪；典当 n. 爆裂声；流行音乐；起泡饮料，汽水 a. 流行的
用 pop away/off at 向…开枪；pop the question 求婚；pop across/down/out 迅速或突然地来去

relocate [ˌriːləʊ'keɪt]
释 v. 重新安置；改放

disruptive [dɪs'rʌptɪv]
释 a. 破坏的；制造混乱的；分裂性的

renovation [ˌrenə'veɪʃn]
释 n. 修复；革新；恢复活力

dispense [dɪ'spens]
释 v. 分配，分发；配(药)；实施，执行；施与恩惠；免除，豁免

premise ['premɪs]
释 n. [pl.]房屋，房产；前提，假设

motivation [ˌməʊtɪ'veɪʃn]
释 n. 动机；动力；刺激
用 motivation research 动机分析
例 What is the *motivation* behind the reform? 为什么要进行改革?

plus [plʌs]
释 prep. 加，加上；和 a. 比所示数量多的；零上的，正的 n. 加号，正号；正面因素，好处
例 All the children in the class are 12 *plus*. 这个班里所有的孩子都超过12岁。

职场生活

accountant [əˈkaʊntənt] n. 会计师

accreditation [əˌkredɪˈteɪʃn] n. 委派；鉴定合格

arduous [ˈɑːdjuəs] a. 费劲的；辛勤的

career [kəˈrɪə(r)] n. 生涯；职业

certificate [səˈtɪfɪkət] n. 证书，执照

coordinator [kəʊˈɔːdɪneɪtə(r)] n. 协调者；调度人

discredit [dɪsˈkredɪt] v. 怀疑；丧失信誉

dismiss [dɪsˈmɪs] v. 解雇；解散

drudgery [ˈdrʌdʒəri] n. 苦差事；苦工

employment [ɪmˈplɔɪmənt] n. 雇用，工作，职业

estimate [ˈestɪmeɪt] v. 估计；预算 [ˈestɪmət] n. 估计；估价；报价

executive [ɪgˈzekjətɪv] n. 执行者；主管人员

facsimile [fækˈsɪməli] n. 摹本；传真

headquarters [ˌhedˈkwɔːtəz] n. 总部；指挥部

induction [ɪnˈdʌkʃn] n. 就职；入会

inept [ɪˈnept] a. 不适当的；不称职的

layman [ˈleɪmən] n. 外行

leadership [ˈliːdəʃɪp] n. 领导(层)；领导能力

malpractice [ˌmælˈpræktɪs] n. 玩忽职守

managerial [ˌmænəˈdʒɪəriəl] a. 管理的；经理的

mastery [ˈmɑːstəri] n. 精通，熟练；控制

overwrought [ˌəʊvəˈrɔːt] a. 过度紧张的；过劳的

subsidy [ˈsʌbsədi] n. 津贴，补助金

treadmill [ˈtredmɪl] n. 乏味繁重的工作

underling [ˈʌndəlɪŋ] n. 职位低的人；下属

workaholic [ˌwɜːkəˈhɒlɪk] n. 工作狂

vocational [vəʊˈkeɪʃənl] a. 职业的

vacation [vəˈkeɪʃn; veɪˈkeɪʃn] n. 休假

vacancy [ˈveɪkənsi] n. 空职；空缺

Man is not made for defeat.

人不是生来就要被打败的。

—Ernest Hemingway

——欧内斯特·海明威

音频

Passage 32

Will There Be Another Einstein?

Will there ever be another Einstein? This is the undercurrent of conversation at Einstein **memorial** meetings throughout the year. A new Einstein will emerge, scientists say. But it may take a long time. After all, more than 200 years separated Einstein from his nearest rival, Isaac Newton.

Many physicists say the next Einstein hasn't been born yet, or is a baby now. That's because the **quest** for a **unified** theory that would account for all the forces of nature has pushed current mathematics to its **limits**. New math must be created before the problem can be solved.

But researchers say there are many other **factors** working against another Einstein emerging anytime soon.

For one thing, physics is a much different **field** today. In Einstein's day, there were only a few thousand physicists worldwide, and the theoreticians who could **intellectually** rival Einstein probably would fit into a streetcar with seats to **spare**.

Education is different, too. One **crucial aspect** of Einstein's training that is **overlooked** is the years of philosophy he read as a teenager—Kant, Schopenhauer and Spinoza, among others. It taught him how to think **independently** and **abstractly** about space and time, and it wasn't long before he became a philosopher himself.

"The independence created by philosophical **insight** is—in my opinion—the **mark** of **distinction** between a mere **artisan** or specialist and a real **seeker** after truth," Einstein wrote in 1944.

And he was an **accomplished** musician. The **interplay** between music and math is well known. Einstein would furiously play his violin as a way to think through a **knotty** physics problem.

Today, universities have produced millions of physicists. There aren't many jobs in science for them, so they go to Wall Street and Silicon Valley to apply their **analytical** skills to more practical—and rewarding—efforts.

"Maybe there is an Einstein out there today," said Columbia University physicist Brian Greene, "but it would be a lot harder for him to be heard."

Especially considering what Einstein was proposing.

"The actual **fabric** of space and time curving? My God, what an idea!" Greene said at a recent gathering at the Aspen Institute. "It takes a certain type of person who will bang his head against the wall because you believe you'll find the solution."

Perhaps the best examples are the five scientific papers Einstein wrote in his "miracle year" of 1905. These "thought experiments" were pages of **calculations** signed and **submitted** to the prestigious journal *Annalen der Physik* by a **virtual** unknown. There were no **footnotes** or citations.

What might happen to such a **submission** today?

"We all get papers like those in the mail," Greene said. "We put them in the junk file."

译 文

还会出现另一个爱因斯坦吗？

还会有另一个爱因斯坦出现吗？这是在今年的爱因斯坦纪念大会上大家谈论的潜在话题。科学家说会出现一位新的爱因斯坦，不过这可能需要很长时间。毕竟，爱因斯坦与离他最近的匹敌者艾萨克·牛顿还相差了200多年呢。

许多物理学家说下一个爱因斯坦还没有出生，或者现在还是个婴儿。因为对用于解释所有自然力的统一理论的探索已经将现在的数学推到了极限，所以在这个问题被解决之前，必须建立一种新的数学。

但是研究者说有许多其他的因素阻碍着另一个爱因斯坦在短期内出现。

首先，如今的物理学是一个相当不同的领域。在爱因斯坦时代，全世界只有几千位物理学家，在智力上能与爱因斯坦相匹敌的理论家可能连一辆有轨电车都坐不满。

今天的教育也有所不同。爱因斯坦所受教育的关键一环是他少年时期读哲学的岁月（这些哲学的代表人物主要包括康德、叔本华、斯宾诺莎等），而这一点被人们忽视了。哲学教会他如何独立、抽象地思考空间和时间，不久后他就成为了一名哲学家。

爱因斯坦于1944年写道："在我看来，由哲学的洞察力所产生的自主独立性是工匠或专家与一个真正追求真理的人之间不同的标志。"

另外，爱因斯坦还是一位造诣颇深的音乐家。音乐和数学的相互影响是众所周知的。爱因斯坦会把疯狂地拉小提琴作为思考复杂的物理难题的一个办法。

如今，大学培养了数百万的物理学家，但在科学领域却没有那么多的工作可以提供给他们。因此，他们去了华尔街和硅谷，把他们的分析能力应用到了更实际、回报更高的活动中去。

哥伦比亚大学的物理学家布赖恩·格林说："也许当今就有一个爱因斯坦，但是他要想为人所知会比以前困难得多。"

尤其是考虑到爱因斯坦所提出的理论。

"空间和时间的实际结构呈曲线形？天啊，多么奇怪的想法！如果你相信自己会找到谜底，这会让某些人用头撞墙的。"格林在阿斯彭研究院最近的一次聚会上这样说道。

也许最好的例子是爱因斯坦在他的"奇迹年"（1905年）所写的五篇科学论文。这些"思考实验"是一沓写满计算公式的纸，被一位实际上不为人知的人署名并提交给了知名期刊《物理学年鉴》。纸上没有任何脚注，也没有引语。

如今这样提交的论文会有何下场呢？

格林说："我们的邮箱中都会收到那样的论文。我们会把它们扔到垃圾文件夹里。"

💡 单词记事本

memorial [mə'mɔːriəl]
释 n. 纪念物，纪念碑；纪念仪式 a. 纪念的；悼念的
用 memorial service 追悼会
例 The painting is a *memorial* to a remarkable woman. 这幅画是为了纪念一位杰出的女性。

quest [kwest]
释 v./n. 寻求，探索
用 in quest of 试图找到，寻求

unified ['juːnɪfaɪd]
释 a. 统一的

limit ['lɪmɪt]
释 n. 极限；限制；[pl.] 范围 v. 限制

factor ['fæktə(r)]
释 n. 因素；【数】因数
例 The result depends on various *factors*. 许多因素造成了这一结果。

field [fiːld]
释 n. 田野；领域

intellectually [ˌɪntə'lektʃuəli]
释 ad. 智力上；理智地

spare [speə(r)]
释 a. 备用的；多余的 v. 省出；节约；剩下；饶恕；免去
用 spare tyre 备胎
例 I'm afraid I don't have any *spare* cash. 恐怕我没有多余的现金。

crucial ['kruːʃl]
释 a. 至关重要的，决定性的；严酷的

aspect ['æspekt]
释 n. 方面；方向；外貌

overlook [ˌəʊvə'lʊk]
释 v. 俯瞰；未注意到，忽略 n. 疏忽；俯瞰中的景色
例 She seems to have *overlooked* one important figure. 她似乎忽略了一个重要的数据。

independently [ˌɪndɪ'pendəntli]
释 ad. 独立地；自立地

abstractly ['æbstræktli]
释 ad. 抽象地

insight ['ɪnsaɪt]
释 n. 洞察力；领悟；顿悟

mark [maːk]
释 n. 痕迹；标记；(考试等的)分数；标志 v. 作记号于；给(试卷等)打分

distinction [dɪ'stɪŋkʃn]
释 n. 差别；区分；优秀；特性
用 without distinction 无差别
例 We should draw a *distinction* between the two products. 我们应该区别这两种产品。

artisan [ˌaːtɪ'zæn]
释 n. 工匠

seeker ['siːkə(r)]
释 n. 搜索者，探求者；自导导弹

accomplished [ə'kʌmplɪʃt]
释 a. 已完成的；有成就的；有技巧的，熟练的

interplay ['ɪntəpleɪ]
释 v./n. 相互作用，相互影响

例 There is an *interplay* between politics and the environment. 政治与环境间相互影响。

knotty ['nɒti]
释 a. 难解决的；棘手的；有节的

analytical [ˌænə'lɪtɪkl]
释 a. 分析的；解析的

fabric ['fæbrɪk]
释 n. 织物；构造，组织

calculation [ˌkælkju'leɪʃn]
释 n. 计算，计算出来的结果；考虑，分析；策划

submit [səb'mɪt]
释 v. 呈递；屈服
用 submit application 提交申请
例 He refused to *submit* to an unjust decision. 他拒绝服从不公正的决定。

virtual ['vɜːtʃuəl]
释 a. 事实上的，实际上的

footnote ['fʊtnəʊt]
释 n. 脚注

submission [səb'mɪʃn]
释 n. 提交，呈递；屈服

💡 单词家族

科技新知

accelerator [ək'seləreɪtə(r)] n. 加速器
achievement [ə'tʃiːvmənt] n. 成就；成绩
advanced [əd'vaːnst] a. 先进的，高级的；年老的
astronaut ['æstrənɔːt] n. 宇航员
automatic [ˌɔːtə'mætɪk] a. 自动的 n. 自动机械
concoct [kən'kɒkt] v. 调制，炮制

cylinder ['sɪlɪndə(r)] n. 圆柱体；气缸
decompression [ˌdiːkəm'preʃn] n. 减压；降压
deduce [dɪ'djuːs] v. 推论，演绎出
envision [ɪn'vɪʒn] v. 想象；预想
exploratory [ɪk'splɒrətri] a. 探测的；研究的
fallacy ['fæləsi] n. 谬误，谬论
foreseeable [fɔː'siːəbl] a. 可预知的

168

helix ['hi:lɪks] n. 螺旋(形)；螺旋结构

hypothesis [haɪ'pɒθəsɪs] n. 假设，假说；前提

ion ['aɪən; 'aɪɒn] n. 离子

materialistic [mə,tɪərɪə'lɪstɪk] a. 唯物主义(者)的

microbiology [,maɪkrəʊbaɪ'ɒlədʒi] n. 微生物学

microcosm ['maɪkrəʊkɒzəm] n. 微观世界；缩影

microprocessor [,maɪkrəʊ'prəʊsesə(r)] n. 微处理器

microscope ['maɪkrəskəʊp] n. 显微镜

missile ['mɪsaɪl] n. 发射物；导弹

parachute ['pærəʃu:t] n. 降落伞

patent ['pætnt; 'peɪtnt] n. 专利(权) v. 申请专利

probe [prəʊb] n. 探测器；探测飞船 v. 探查

prospect ['prɒspekt] n. 景色；前景 v. 寻找；勘探

radar ['reɪdɑ:(r)] n. 雷达

rectify ['rektɪfaɪ] v. 矫正，调整；净化，提纯；分馏，精馏

spacecraft ['speɪskrɑ:ft] n. 航天器

stability [stə'bɪləti] n. 稳定性；复原力；刚度，强度

supersonic [,su:pə'sɒnɪk; ,sju:pə'sɒnɪk] a. 超音速的

thermostat ['θɜ:məstæt] n. 恒温器；温度调节装置

transcendent [træn'sendənt] a. 超验的；超常的；卓越的

utilize ['ju:təlaɪz] v. 利用

valve [vælv] n. 阀；电子管

visible ['vɪzəbl] a. 可见的；有形的

vision ['vɪʒn] n. 想象力；视力，视野；幻象；美景

volatile ['vɒlətaɪl] a. 飞行的；挥发性的；易变的，短暂的

Weep no more, no sigh, nor groan. Sorrow calls no time that's gone.
—John Fletcher
别哭泣，别叹息，别呻吟。悲伤唤不回流逝的时光。
——约翰·弗莱彻

Passage 33

The Fridge of the Future Will Tell You What to Have for Dinner

A fridge of the future that tells you what to cook with your leftovers and automatically re-orders fresh food is being designed in the UK.

The self-cleaning "fridge of the future" will automatically place supermarket home delivery orders when required and move food near its use by date to the front of the shelves.

Researchers hope the fridge could clean itself, cut down on wasted food and offer up recipes—which could be tailored to different countries, cuisines and seasons depending on whether people want to whip up something Italian or fancy a curry.

With Brits putting in 36 million hours every year of free overtime—leaving little time for household chores—the fridge could help save precious time during hectic modern-day lives.

These new developments are in the pipeline thanks to collaborations between scientists at the University of Central Lancashire and online supermarket Ocado.

The planned new features include the ability for fridges to scan their shelves to see what is in stock and use this information to both plan meals and automatically place a supermarket food order—with Ocado saying they could be hooked up to their website making grocery requests even simpler.

The smart fridge will use "nano-articulated technology" shelf surfaces which, whilst smooth to the touch, will have millions of independently controlled micro-tiles which will manoeuvre products which soon need to be eaten to the front of the fridge.

The fridge will also monitor gases released by degrading foods and push these to the front of its shelves, according to the collaborators.

Ultrasound-scanning technology built into the door will allow the fridge to "swipe and capture" the food on a plate before and after mealtime, meaning it can assess what type and amount of food is wasted.

Similar technological advances in the kitchen bin, with its own management system, would allow it to be linked to the fridge giving a more accurate measure of how much and what kinds of food is thrown out rather than eaten.

The fridge of the future would then be able to cross **reference** and act on this data—reducing the **ingredients** used in future meal suggestions and helping to **minimize** food waste.

Dr. Simon Somerville, a future forecasting expert from the University of Central Lancashire, said that someone feeling lazy could use the proposed fridge to whip up a recipe for them.

He said, "Cookbooks are essentially **inventory** lists of food items. To this end the most available information that the refrigerator will have is a set of **permutations** that allow a set number of ingredients to produce a large number of quite different dishes.

"The key concept in the successful **implementation** of this process is accurate inventory tracking.

"Information contained within each menu, such as 'this dish is typical to the north of Italy', allows a menu selection based on geographical location—all the time the user choice is compared by the refrigerator to what it knows it holds.

"If the specific item for a recipe is not present, the refrigerator might suggest a delayed option, which allows time for delivery, or possibly attempt to find or propose a **passable** alternative for the missing ingredient."

 译文

未来冰箱帮你决定每餐吃什么

英国正在研制一种未来冰箱。它可以告诉你用剩菜能烹调什么，还能自动订购新鲜食物。

当家中需要食材时，这种可以自动清洁的"未来冰箱"会向超市自动下达送货上门的订单，还可以把快到保质期的食物移到冰箱内架的前端。

研究人员希望冰箱能自动清洁、减少食物浪费，还可以按照国家、菜系和季节的不同以及人们的需求提供食谱，比如临时想要做些意大利菜，或者来点儿咖喱。

英国人每年的无薪加班时间高达3600万小时，因此几乎没有时间做家务。而这款冰箱能帮助人们在繁忙的现代生活中节省宝贵的时间。

多亏了英国中央兰开夏大学的科学家与在线超市"奥克杜"的通力合作，这些新的功能的研发正在进行中。

按照计划，这款冰箱将具有扫描内架存货的新功能，并可以利用扫描的信息安排每顿饭的菜谱以及自动向超市下食物订单——在线超市"奥克杜"表示，如果冰箱可以与他们的网站绑定，那么提交食品需求订单将会更加简单。

这款智能冰箱的内架表面将采用"纳米合成技术"，这将使得内架不仅摸起来手感细腻平滑，而且可以通过自身数百万个独立控制的微型瓷砖，把需尽快食用的食物移至冰箱前端。

合作研制者们表示，冰箱还能监控变质食物释放的气体，并把那些食物也推至冰箱内架前端。

冰箱门内置的超声波扫描技术可使冰箱在餐前餐后"读取并记录"盘中的食物，这就意味着它可以分析被浪费食物的种类和数量。

类似的技术也将应用在厨房的垃圾桶上，使得垃圾桶通过内置的管理程序与冰箱连接，从而给出更为精确的统计：哪些食物没有被吃掉而是被丢弃了，以及丢弃的数量是多少。

然后，未来冰箱将参照并依据这些数据——在之后的菜谱建议中减少某些食材的使用，以帮助将食物浪费降至最低。

中央兰开夏大学的未来预测专家西蒙·萨默维尔博士说，懒得做饭的人可以按照这款冰箱的建议，为自己随便做点吃的。

他说："菜谱的本质就是食材的库存清单。为此，冰箱将对一定数量的食材进行最大限度的排列组合，以提供各式各样完全不同的饭菜。

"这个程序成功执行的关键在于对库存清单的精确跟踪。

"根据每份菜单里包含的信息，诸如'这是一道典型的意大利北方菜'，冰箱就可以按地理位置作出选择——它会随时将用户的选择和内置的食物做比较。

"在烹饪时，如果缺少菜谱中的某一种食材，冰箱可能会建议等到食材送到以后再做，或者可能会尝试寻找或建议使用其他可代替的食材。"

leftover ['leftəʊvə(r)]
释 n. 遗留物；剩余物；剩余的食物

tailor ['teɪlə(r)]
释 n. 裁缝 v. 剪裁；使适应(特定需要)
用 tailor sth. for/to sb./sth. (为某目的)做某事或适应某事物

cuisine [kwɪ'ziːn]
释 n. 烹饪法；(烹饪)风味

whip [wɪp]
释 n. 鞭子 v. 鞭打；搅打(鸡蛋、奶油等)使起泡；猛地移动；以尖锐语言攻击；纠集，集合；激起，鼓动；
用 whip up 赶出来(一顿饭)，迅速做(饭)；have a whip hand of 居领导地位；控制；whip into shape 进行强制改革；whip off 用鞭驱散；匆忙离去；突然拿走

fancy ['fænsi]
释 n. 想象力；幻想；迷恋；鉴赏力 a. 想象出来的；花式的；奇特的；特选的 v. 想象，幻想；希望得到，想要；喜欢，爱好
用 after one's fancy 合自己心意；have a fancy for 爱好；爱上，入迷；fancy oneself (as) 自以为是…，自命是…

curry ['kʌri]
释 n. 咖喱；用咖喱做的饭菜 v. 给…加咖喱；梳刷(马毛等)；讨好

overtime ['əʊvətaɪm]
释 a./ad. 超时的(地)；加班的(地) n. 加班时间

pipeline ['paɪplaɪn]
释 n. 管道；输油管；流水线；情报来源
用 in the pipeline 在筹备中；在进行中

articulate [ɑː'tɪkjuleɪt]
释 v. 形成关节，(用关节)连接；清楚明白地说 a. 关节相连的；明白的；发音清晰的

manoeuvre [mə'nuːvə(r)]
释 n. 调遣；部署；策略；花招 v. 演习；调动，部署；耍花招；巧妙地移动(转动)(尤指大而重的物件)

collaborator [kə'læbəreɪtə(r)]
释 n. 合作者；勾结者；通敌者

ultrasound ['ʌltrəsaʊnd]
释 n. 超声(波)

swipe [swaɪp]
释 n. 猛击；尖刻的话 v. 猛击；偷窃，抢走；刷(卡)

reference ['refrəns]
释 n. 参考，参照；参考书目；提到，涉及；推荐信(或人)
用 cross reference to 互相参看；give a reference to 提到，介绍；in/with reference to 关于，就…而论

ingredient [ɪn'griːdiənt]
释 n. (混合物的)组成部分；(构成)要素；原料
用 ingredients for soup 做汤的原料
例 Interviews with representatives of highly-ranked companies reveal the basic *ingredient* that marks a top employer. 对排名较高的公司代表的访谈向人们揭示了成为一名杰出的公司领导者所需要具备的基本要素。

minimize ['mɪnɪmaɪz]
释 v. (使)减少到最低限度；极力贬低

例 The adoption of clean energy will help *minimize* air pollution. 对清洁能源的采用将有助于把空气污染减少到最低限度。

inventory ['ɪnvəntri]
释 n. 详细目录；存货清单 v. 编制目录；开清单

permutation [ˌpɜːmju'teɪʃn]
释 n. 彻底改变；【数】排列(顺序)

implementation [ˌɪmplɪmen'teɪʃn]
释 n. 执行；安装启用
例 Some practical problems have prevented widespread *implementation* of the program. 一些实际性的问题阻止了该计划的大规模实施。

passable ['pɑːsəbl]
释 a. (指道路)可通行的；过得去的，尚可的

💡 单词家族

烹饪厨艺

additive ['ædətɪv] *n.* 添加剂
appetizer ['æpɪtaɪzə(r)] *n.* 开胃品；正餐前的开胃食物或饮料
beverage ['bevərɪdʒ] *n.* 饮料
brew [bruː] *v.* 酿造(啤酒)；冲泡(茶、咖啡等)
cloy [klɔɪ] *v.* (指甜食或美好的事物)因太多而生厌；吃腻；玩腻
dairy ['deəri] *n.* 牛奶场；奶制品
drool [druːl] *v.* 流口水
fowl [faʊl] *n.* 家禽；禽肉
goblet ['ɡɒblət] *n.* 高脚酒杯
grill [ɡrɪl] *n.* 烤架；烤肉
ketchup ['ketʃəp] *n.* 番茄酱

luncheon ['lʌntʃən] *n.* 午餐；午宴
mixer ['mɪksə(r)] *n.* 搅拌器
oyster ['ɔɪstə(r)] *n.* 牡蛎
pantry ['pæntri] *n.* 食品柜；餐具室
pickle ['pɪkl] *n.* 腌制食品；泡菜
rancid ['rænsɪd] *a.* 不新鲜的，变味的
roast [rəʊst] *v.* 烤，炙
sardine [ˌsɑː'diːn] *n.* 沙丁鱼
spaghetti [spə'ɡeti] *n.* 意大利面条
tender ['tendə(r)] *a.* 嫩的；容易嚼的；脆弱的
vinegar ['vɪnɪɡə(r)] *n.* 醋
yeast [jiːst] *n.* 酵母；发酵粉
yolk [jəʊk] *n.* 蛋黄

音频

Passage 34

What Space Smells Like

Meat, metal, raspberries, rum...

When astronauts return from space walks and remove their helmets, they are welcomed back with a peculiar smell. An odor that is distinct and weird: something, astronauts have described it, like "seared steak." And also: "hot metal." And also: "welding fumes."

Our extraterrestrial explorers are remarkably consistent in describing space scent in meaty-metallic terms. "Space", astronaut Tony Antonelli has said, "definitely has a smell that's different from anything else." "Space," three-time spacewalker Thomas Jones has put it, "carries a distinct odor of ozone, a faint acrid smell."

"Space," Jones elaborated, "smells a little like gunpowder. It is 'sulfurous'."

Add to all those anecdotal assessments the recent discovery, in a vast dust cloud at the center of our galaxy, of ethyl formate—and the fact that the ester is, among other things, the chemical responsible for the flavor of raspberries. Add to that the fact that ethyl formate itself smells like rum. Put all that together, and one thing becomes clear: The final frontier sort of stinks.

But...how does it stink, exactly? It turns out that we, and more specifically our atmosphere, are the ones who give space its special spice. According to one researcher, the aroma astronauts inhale as they move their mass from space to station is the result of "high-energy vibrations in particles brought back inside which mix with the air."

So NASA, now, is trying to reproduce that smell for training purposes—the better to help preemptively acclimate astronauts to the odors of the extra-atmospheric environment. And the better to help minimize the sensory surprises they'll encounter once they're there. The agency has hired the scent chemist Steve Pearce to recreate space stench, as much as possible, here on earth.

As for Pearce's NASA-commissioned eau de vacuum, he's working on the project in his spare time. And the wonderfully poetic descriptions provided by astronauts themselves are helping him as he goes along, such as this sweet-smelling stuff from wonder-astronaut Don Pettit:

"Each time, when I repressed the airlock, opened the hatch and welcomed two tired workers inside, a peculiar odor tickled my olfactory senses," Pettit recalled. "At first I couldn't quite place it. It must have come from the air ducts that repressed the compartment. Then I noticed that this smell was on their suit, helmet, gloves, and tools. It was more pronounced on fabrics than on metal or plastic surfaces."

He concluded:

"It is hard to describe this smell; it is definitely not the olfactory equivalent to describing the palette sensations of some new food as 'tastes like chicken.' The best description I can come up with is metallic, a rather pleasant sweet metallic sensation. It reminded me of my college summers where I labored for many hours with an arc welding torch repairing heavy equipment for a small logging outfit. It reminded me of pleasant sweet smelling welding fumes. That is the smell of space."

译文

太空的味道

肉、金属、树莓、朗姆酒……

当宇航员太空漫步归来、摘掉他们的面罩时，迎接他们的是一种奇特的味道，一种明显而怪异的味道。宇航员这样描述它："就像烤牛排，或者热金属，或者焊接产生的烟尘味。"

我们的外太空探索家们出奇一致地都用肉类和金属来描述太空的气味。宇航员托尼·安东内利说："太空肯定有一种与众不同的气味。"进行过三次太空漫步的托马斯·琼斯说："太空带着一种明显的臭氧味，有一种微弱的刺鼻的味道。"

琼斯又进一步仔细描述道："它闻起来有点像火药，并且是'含硫黄的'火药。"

除了这些有趣的看法外，最近发现在银河系中央的巨大尘埃云中存在着甲酸乙酯，而事实上，除了其他因素之外，酯是产生树莓气味的主因。而且事实上，甲酸乙酯本身闻起来就像朗姆酒。把所有这些发现归纳起来，这一点就变得明朗了，即太空闻起来有点臭。

但是……它具体是怎么个臭法？事实证明，是我们，或者更明确地说是我们的大气层赋予了太空一种特殊的气味。据一位研究者声称，在宇航员们从太空回到空间站期间，他们所闻到的气味是他们从外部带回的气体与空气混合后其粒子高能量振动的结果。

所以，为了训练宇航员，美国国家航空航天局正在尝试生成那种气味，以更好地帮助宇航员提前适应太空环境中的气味，同时更好地帮助他们缓解在外太空接触到这种气味时产生的感官上的冲击。航天局还雇用了气味化学家史蒂夫·皮尔斯，请他在地球上尽可能多地生成太空中的臭味气体。

至于美国国家航空航天局委托皮尔斯进行的真空香水项目，他正在业余时间里研究。在这个过程中，来自宇航员的富有诗意的精彩描述也为他提供了帮助。例如，太空漫游者唐·佩蒂特将那种气味描述成闻起来很甜的东西：

"每次当我按压气闸，打开密封舱，迎接两位疲惫的同事回来时，一股奇异的气味就刺激着我的嗅觉器官。起初我还弄不太明白，以为这种味道一定是来自隔舱的空气管道。随后，我才注意到这气味是从他们的衣服、面罩、手套和工具上散发出来的，当它附着在衣物纤维上时会比在金属或者塑料表面上味道更加明显。"佩蒂特回忆道。

他这样总结：

"很难去描述这种气味；我们在吃到一种从来没吃过的食物时，会对它的复杂感觉用'尝起来像鸡肉'之类的话语来描述，但这种气味对感官的刺激则完全不同。我能想到的最好的描述是像金属，一种让人感觉相当舒服的、甘甜的金属感。这让我回想起我的大学暑假，那时我为一个小型测井单位用弧焊喷枪做了数个小时的重型设备修理工作；也让我回想起了那宜人的、香甜的金属焊接气味。那就是太空的气味。"

💡 单词记事本

raspberry ['rɑːzbəri]
释 n. 树莓；嘘声

rum [rʌm]
释 n. 朗姆酒 a. 古怪的，奇特的
例 The old man is a *rum* character. 这个老人很古怪。

helmet ['helmɪt]
释 n. 头盔，钢盔；面罩
用 a football helmet 橄榄球头盔；crash helmet 头盔，安全帽；diving helmet 潜水帽

peculiar [pɪ'kjuːliə(r)]
释 a. 奇怪的；特有的，独特的

odor ['əudə(r)]
释 n. (香的或臭的)气味；名声
例 He is in rather bad *odor* with his boss at the moment. 现在他的老板对他很反感。

weird [wɪəd]
释 a. 古怪的

welding ['weldɪŋ]
释 n. 焊接，锻接

extraterrestrial [,ekstrətə'restriəl]
释 a. 地球或大气层外的；来自天外的

acrid ['ækrɪd]
释 a. 呛人的，刺激的；刻薄的

gunpowder ['gʌnpaudə(r)]
释 n. 火药

sulfurous ['sʌlfərəs]
释 a. 含有硫黄的

anecdotal [,ænɪk'dəutl]
释 a. 逸事的

assessment [ə'sesmənt]
释 n. 评价，看法；确定，评定；核定的付款额

177

galaxy ['gæləksi]
释 n. 星系；一群杰出的人；[the G-]银河系

ethyl ['eθɪl; 'iːθaɪl]
释 n. 乙烷基

formate ['fɔːmeɪt]
释 n. 甲酸盐

stink [stɪŋk]
释 v. 有臭味，发臭；遭人厌恶 n. 难闻的气体，臭味；麻烦，忙乱
用 stink out 把…熏出；使充满难闻的味道；like stink 拼命地，努力地；stink with 充满某种臭味；拥有大量某种财物
例 The whole business caused quite a *stink*. 整件事弄得乱七八糟。

aroma [ə'rəʊmə]
释 n. 芳香；气味

inhale [ɪn'heɪl]
释 v. 吸入；吸烟，抽烟

vibration [vaɪ'breɪʃn]
释 n. 振动，颤动；一次往复运动

preemptively [pri'emptɪvli]
释 ad. 先发制人地

acclimate ['ækləmeɪt]
释 v. 使适应(新的环境或习惯等)
例 The flowers and grasses have not yet *acclimated* to this climate. 这些花草还没有适应这种气候。

sensory ['sensəri]
释 a. (通常作定语)感觉官能的
用 sensory organs/nerves 感觉器官/神经；sensory deprivation 感觉丧失
例 You can get a *sensory* stimulus in seeing a horror movie. 看恐怖电影可以得到感官刺激。

airlock ['eəlɒk]
释 n. 气闸

olfactory [ɒl'fæktəri]
释 a. 嗅觉的

单词家族

太空探索

asteroid ['æstərɔɪd] n. 小行星

astrology [ə'strɒlədʒi] n. 占星学；占星术

astronomical [,æstrə'nɒmɪkl] a. 天文的，天文学的；极大的

comet ['kɒmɪt] n. 彗星

constellation [,kɒnstə'leɪʃn] n. 星座；相关的或相似的人群或事物

corona [kə'rəʊnə] n. 日冕，日华，月华；冠状物

elevation [,elɪ'veɪʃn] n. 高度，海拔；小山，高地；建筑物的立视图

gravitational [,grævɪ'teɪʃənl] a. 重力的；引力的

humidity [hjuː'mɪdəti] n. 湿气，湿度

intrude [ɪn'truːd] v. 侵入其他地层；侵入，闯入

magnetosphere [mæg'niːtəʊsfɪə(r)] n. 磁气圈

magnitude ['mægnɪtjuːd] n. 星等(表示星体亮度的等级)；巨大；量级

quasar ['kweɪzɑː(r)] n. 【天】类星体

snowflake ['snəʊfleɪk] n. 雪花

Passage 35

Smart House Feels Your Pain

Smart home applications can share all kinds of helpful info with homeowners, but a new housing platform can detect a strain on electricity—and a strain on the heart.

"There is a growing population of elderly people, and there are statistics to show that more and more of them are going to live alone in the home," said Johann Siau, a senior lecturer in digital communication systems at the University of Hertfordshire in the U.K., who is leading the InterHome project.

The system was originally designed to provide remote access to a house so owners could be more energy-efficient. In a small-scale prototype of the system, embedded controller devices connect securely to the Internet. The owner can then monitor them with a cell phone or computer. User feedback helps the system adapt to routines, saving on electricity.

While thinking about responding to user behavior and an increasingly elderly population, the researchers decided to add wristband technology that senses vitals such as body temperature and pulse, Siau said.

"In the event that someone were to fall, it would detect the fall and it would immediately trigger the monitor of the pulse to see if the person has gone into shock," he said. "It's an early warning system that can alert any parties registered to monitor the person."

The wristband communicates with the home system wirelessly. Data from the band can be securely piped to the home network and accessed by authorized users. A functioning prototype of the wristband technology exists, but it's still too bulky.

"We're working on trying to scale it down to a level where it could potentially be a wrist-sized product," Siau said.

The team is also looking at adding other services, including a geo-tagging coordinate system that could send an alert if someone with Alzheimer's were to get lost.

Siau said that the university received government funding, enabling the researchers to work with the independent research firm BRE Group in Watford on testing the platform in real houses.

Jim Gaston is director of the Smart Home program at Duke University, an interdisciplinary research initiative focusing on smart living. He called the InterHome system "a great idea" and added that Duke students worked on a similar idea using wearable radio frequency ID tags that could warn if the person wandered off or didn't move for a while.

But he cautioned that the technology presents new challenges.

"When you start instituting that on a larger scale, you have issues of privacy or security," he said.

Siau said the InterHome home system isn't intended to invade privacy. "We're thinking about the elderly people who are living alone with no one looking after them," he said. "Hopefully this will be able to alleviate some concerns and possibly save a few lives."

智能房屋与你"感同身受"

智能居家应用程序可以和房屋主人共享各种有用的信息，但目前出现了一个新型的房屋平台，不仅可以检测家庭用电的使用情况，而且还可以检测主人心脏压力的情况。

英国赫特福德大学数字通信系统专业的高级讲师约翰·肖是这个交互房屋项目的负责人，他说："目前老龄人口正在增长，有数据显示其中越来越多的人将开始独居生活。"

该系统的最初设计意图是通过提供一种远程访问房屋的途径，来使房主节约更多的能源。在该系统的小规模模型中，嵌入了可以与网络安全连接的控制设备。房主可以通过手机或电脑进行监控。用户反馈可以帮助系统适应房主的日常生活，从而节省用电量。

肖说，考虑到对用户行为的回应以及老龄人口数量的不断增加，研究者决定为该系统增加腕带技术。这项技术可以感知诸如体温、脉搏等重要指标。"

"在当事人快要跌倒的情况下，该系统可以探测到这种趋势，并立即启动脉搏监测，以判断跌倒者是否已经休克。"他说，"这是一个预警系统，任何经过注册登记来监控当事人的人都可以收到提醒。"

腕带与房屋系统通过无线方式进行通信。腕带得到的数据可以安全传输至房屋网络，被获得授权的用户自由访问。能够运作的腕带技术模型已经存在，但还不够小巧。

肖说："我们正在尝试把它缩小一些，让它能够成为一个与腕部粗细差不多的产品。"

　　设计团队也在尝试增加一些其他服务，比如地理坐标系统，这样当老年痴呆症患者要走失时就能发送警报。

　　肖说赫特福德大学得到了政府的资金支持，这样研究者们可以和位于沃特福德的独立研究公司BRE集团合作，在真正的房屋里测试这个平台。

　　吉姆·加斯顿是杜克大学智能居家项目的负责人，该项目主要关注智能生活的跨学科研究。他认为交互房屋系统是一个"伟大的想法"，并且表示杜克大学的学生也实践过一个类似的想法：让当事人使用一个可佩戴的能发出无线电频率的身份标志牌，如果佩戴人走失或长时间不动，它就会发出警报。

　　但是他警告说，这项技术面临着新的挑战。

　　"当开始在更大的范围内投入使用时，这会涉及隐私或者安全问题。"他说。

　　肖表示交互房屋系统并不会故意侵犯隐私，他说："我们考虑的是那些独居且无人照料的老年人。但愿这个系统能够帮助人们减少一些忧虑，并尽可能地挽救一些生命。"

💡 单词记事本

platform ['plætfɔːm]

释 n. 平台；讲台；站台；(政党的)纲领，宣言

detect [dɪ'tekt]

释 v. 发现，检测；查明，侦查

例 The machine has recorded the shrinking of ice sheets; it has also *detected* shifting ocean currents. 这个机器不仅记录了冰原的收缩，还探测到了迁移的洋流。

statistics [stə'tɪstɪks]

释 n. 数据，统计数字，统计资料；统计学

digital ['dɪdʒɪtl]

释 a. 数字的；手指的

例 The act of Googling oneself has become the *digital* age's premiere secret pleasure. 在谷歌网站上搜索自己已经成为这个数字时代人们首要的私密爱好。

energy ['enədʒi]

释 n. 精力，干劲；能量；能源

prototype ['prəʊtətaɪp]

释 n. 原型，蓝本

embed [ɪm'bed]

释 v. 栽种；埋入；使嵌入，使插入；使深留脑中

例 The idea became *embedded* in her mind. 这个想法深深地烙在了她的脑海里。

vital ['vaɪtl]

释 a. 维持生命所必需的；至关重要的；有活力的 n. [pl.](身体的)重要器官；(机器的)主要部件

用 vital statistics 生命统计，人口动态统计(人口数字或出生、婚姻、死亡的统计)

pulse [pʌls]

释 v. 搏动，跳动 n. 脉搏；脉冲

shock [ʃɒk]

释 n. 休克；震动；震惊；打击 v. (使)休克；(使)震动；(使)震惊；(使)受电击

用 shock therapy/treatment 电震疗法；休克疗法；culture shock 文化冲击

wirelessly ['waɪələsli]

释 ad. 无线地

authorized ['ɔːθə,raɪzd]

释 a. 经授权的

bulky ['bʌlki]

释 a. 庞大的，体积巨大的

interdisciplinary [,ɪntə'dɪsəplɪnəri]

释 a. 跨学科的

wearable ['weərəbl]

释 a. 可穿戴的，可佩戴的；适合穿戴的

institute ['ɪnstɪtjuːt]

释 n. 学会，学院，协会 v. 创立，建立；制定(规则、习俗等)；开始，着手

用 research institute 研究所，研究机构

例 Police have *instituted* inquiries into the matter. 警方已就此事展开调查。

privacy ['prɪvəsi]

释 n. 隐私；私密；隐居；隐居处

security [sɪ'kjʊərəti]

释 n. 安全；保障；抵押品；[pl.]证券

用 the Security Council (联合国)安全理事会；security risk (威胁国家安全的)危险人物；security guard 保安人员；护卫员

invade [ɪn'veɪd]

释 v. 侵犯；侵袭；侵略；涌入

alleviate [ə'liːvieɪt]

释 v. 减轻，缓解

例 A number of measures were taken by the government to *alleviate* the problem. 政府采取了大量的措施来缓解这个问题。

单词家族

科技发展

aeroplane ['eərəpleɪn] n. 飞机

anode ['ænəʊd] n. 阳极，正极

antenna [æn'tenə] n. (无线电或电视的)天线；触角

bakelite ['beɪkəlaɪt] n. 酚醛塑料；绝缘电木；胶木

ejection [i'dʒekʃn] n. 喷出；在紧急情况下将人从飞行器中弹出

industrialization [ɪn,dʌstriəlaɪ'zeɪʃn] n. 工业化；产业化

insulate ['ɪnsjuleɪt] v. 使绝缘；使隔热；隔离，使隔绝

lens [lenz] n. 透镜；镜片；镜头

panel ['pænl] n. 面板；仪表板；座谈小组；全体陪审员

pollinate ['pɒləneɪt] v. 给…授粉

propellant [prə'pelənt] n. 推进物；火箭燃料；发射火药 a. 推进的；起推动作用的

pump [pʌmp] n. 泵；抽水机 v. (用泵)抽(水)

ramification [,ræmɪfɪ'keɪʃn] n. 衍生物；分枝，分叉；支流

solar ['səʊlə(r)] a. 太阳的；(利用)太阳能的

steamer ['stiːmə(r)] *n.* 轮船；蒸汽机

sublimate ['sʌblɪmeɪt] *v.* (使)升华；净化

submarine [,sʌbmə'riːn] *n.* 潜水艇 *a.* 水下的；海底的

thermometer [θə'mɒmɪtə(r)] *n.* 温度计；寒暑表

Enterprising spirit, the intrinsic driving force, is the most miraculous and interesting thing in our lives. If you are not ambitious in your work, you are unlikely to make great achievement.

—George Wellman

进取心这种内在的推动力是我们生命中最神奇和最有趣的东西。如果你对工作缺乏野心，将很难成大事。

——乔治·韦尔曼

Passage 36

音频

Is Spam Causing Greenhouse Gas?

Is spam causing the environmental hazard of greenhouse gas emissions?

That's what McAfee says in its *Carbon Footprint of Spam* report released Wednesday, which states climate-change researchers from the firm ICF and McAfee's security staff calculated that the amount of energy needed to transmit, process and filter spam globally is equal to 33 billion kilowatt-hours each year. They say that can also be expressed as the equivalent to the electricity used in 2.4 million homes annually or the same green-house gas emissions from 3.1 million passenger cars using 2 billion gallons of gas.

"This has solid math and science behind it," says Dave Marcus, director of research and communications at McAfee. "This is the first type of research of its kind."

McAfee, which sells antispam filtering products, naturally wants organizations to invest in "state-of-the-art spam filtering technology," according to Jeff Green, senior vice president of product development, who thinks efficient spam filtering "will pay dividends to the planet by reducing carbon emissions as well."

While evoking greenhouse gases in the name of selling spam filtering is a novel approach, McAfee and ICF are dead earnest about the harmful effects of spam on the natural environment.

But the report also points out there's some environmental harm done by filtering spam, too.

According to the *Carbon Footprint of Spam* report, the average greenhouse gas emission with a single spam message is 0.3 grams of carbon dioxide (CO_2).

"That's like driving three feet (one meter)," the report states. "But when multiplied by the yearly volume of spam, it is equivalent to driving around the earth 1.6 million times."

Almost 80% of the energy use attributed to spam comes from users deleting spam and searching for legit e-mail. But spam filtering itself accounts for about 16% of spam-related energy use, according to the report.

So shutting down spam sources, such as the takedown of the notorious McColo spam machine, represents a huge energy savings to the environment, Marcus says.

When it comes to a country-by-country analysis of spam's harm to the environment, the United States and India are said to have proportionately higher emissions per e-mail than anywhere else. The United States, according to the report, "had emissions that were 38 times that of Spain."

While Canada, China, Brazil, India, the United States and the United Kingdom were deemed roughly equivalent in the spam study, Australia, Germany, France, Mexico and Spain came in 10% lower in environmental impact. Spain was the lowest, with the smallest amount of e-mail spam and energy use per e-mail user.

译文

垃圾邮件会引起温室气体排放吗？

垃圾邮件会排放温室气体从而对环境造成危害吗？

这是迈克菲公司在周三发布的名为《垃圾邮件的碳排放量》的报告中提到的。报告称，ICF公司气候变化研究员与迈克菲公司的信息安全员计算出，每年全球发送、处理和过滤垃圾邮件所需的能源相当于330亿千瓦时。他们表示，这个数量也可以通过以下对比进行说明：这些被消耗掉的能源相当于240万个家庭的年用电量，其排放的温室气体相当于310万辆客车消耗20亿加仑汽油所排放出的量。

迈克菲公司研究与通信部主管戴夫·马库斯说："这个结果有着可靠的数学和科学依据。它是该类型研究中的首例。"

迈克菲公司的业务之一就是销售垃圾邮件过滤产品，所以它自然希望各个组织能够投资"最先进的垃圾邮件过滤技术"。该公司产品开发部高级副总裁杰夫·格林认为，对垃圾邮件的有效过滤可以"通过减少碳排放量而造福地球"。

虽然通过出售垃圾邮件过滤产品来唤起人们对温室气体的关注是一种新颖的营销策略，但迈克菲和ICF对垃圾邮件危害自然环境的态度却相当认真。

然而，报告同时也指出，过滤垃圾邮件同样会对环境造成破坏。

根据《垃圾邮件的碳排放量》这篇报告，平均每封垃圾邮件所排放的温室气体是0.3克二氧化碳。

报告中这样说道："这相当于驾车行驶三英尺（也就是一米）所释放的气体。而把每年垃圾邮件的总排放量相加，其结果相当于驾车绕地球行驶160万次所排放的气体。"

根据这篇报告，垃圾邮件消耗的能源中有80%是在用户删除垃圾邮件和寻找有用邮件的过程中产生的，但是过滤垃圾邮件本身消耗的能源也占据垃圾邮件消耗能源总量的16%。

马库斯说，因此，清除垃圾邮件的根源，比如关闭臭名昭著的垃圾邮件制造者McColo，就会节省大量的能源。

谈及对不同国家中垃圾邮件对环境危害的比较，美国和印度的每封垃圾邮件所排放的温室气体所占比例高于其他国家。报告还指出，美国"垃圾邮件的温室气体排放量是西班牙的38倍"。

垃圾邮件的统计数字显示，加拿大、中国、巴西、印度、美国和英国的碳排量基本相当，而澳大利亚、德国、法国、墨西哥和西班牙对环境的危害要低10%。西班牙的碳排量最低，每个邮件用户收到的垃圾邮件数量和消耗的能源也相应最小。

💡 单词记事本

spam [spæm]
释 *n.* 垃圾邮件

emission [ɪ'mɪʃn]
释 *n.* (光、热等的)散发，发射，发出；散发物
用 air pollution emission 空气污染排放(物)；sponsored emission 广告节目

transmit [træns'mɪt; trænz'mɪt]
释 *v.* 发送；传播；发射；传输；传达；传染
例 The anxiety soon *transmitted* itself to all the members of the team. 这种焦虑的情绪很快感染了团队中的所有人。

kilowatt-hour ['kɪləwɒtaʊə(r)]
释 *n.* 千瓦时，一度电

solid ['sɒlɪd]
释 *a.* 固体的；稳固的；纯色的；可靠的 *n.* 固体

用 be in solid with sb. 受某人重视；与某人关系好；be/go solid against/for 全体一致反对/赞成

antispam ['æntispæm]
释 *n.* 反垃圾邮件

invest [ɪn'vest]
释 *v.* 投资；投入(时间、精力等)；授予，赋予
用 invest in 投资

efficient [ɪ'fɪʃnt]
释 *a.* 效率高的；能胜任的
用 an efficient government 高效的政府
例 They made more *efficient* use of petroleum-based fuel. 他们更加高效地利用了石油燃料。

dividend ['dɪvɪdend]
释 *n.* 股息，红利；利益，好处；被除数

用 an annual dividend 年度股息；pay dividends 产生效益；得到好处

例 I suggest you read more books, and sooner or later you'll find it pays *dividends*. 我建议你多看书，迟早你会发现很有好处。

evoke [ɪ'vəʊk]

释 v. 唤起，引起；博得

dead [ded]

释 a. 死的；呆板的 n. 死者 ad. 完全地

earnest ['ɜːnɪst]

释 a. 认真的；诚挚的；重要的

用 in dead/deadly/real earnest 有决心和精力；认真的(地)，诚挚的(地)

attribute [ə'trɪbjuːt]

释 n. 属性；特质 v. 把…归因于

用 attribute to 归因于，因为

例 Nancy *attributed* her weight loss to her mental disorder. 南希将自己体重下降的原因归结为精神失调。

legit [lɪ'dʒɪt]

释 a. 合法的，正当的

takedown ['teɪkdaʊn]

释 n. 拆卸

notorious [nəʊ'tɔːriəs]

释 a. 众所周知的；臭名昭著的

proportionately [prə'pɔːʃənətli]

释 ad. 相称地；成比例地

deem [diːm]

释 v. 认为；相信

例 This plan was *deemed* feasible. 大家认为这个计划行得通。

环境污染

aseptic [ˌeɪ'septɪk] a. 洁净的；无菌的

climatic [klaɪ'mætɪk] a. 气候(上)的

coal-mining ['kəʊl,maɪnɪŋ] a. 煤矿业的

contaminate [kən'tæmɪneɪt] v. 污染

debris ['debriː; 'deɪbriː] n. 废墟，残骸；垃圾；碎片

decimation [ˌdesɪ'meɪʃn] n. 大批杀害；大量毁坏

devastate ['devəsteɪt] v. 毁坏；摧毁；使震惊

erosion [ɪ'rəʊʒn] n. 腐蚀，侵蚀；磨损

glacier ['glæsiə(r)] n. 冰川；冰河

gulf [gʌlf] n. 海湾；深渊；漩涡；分歧

imperil [ɪm'perəl] v. (使)陷于危险中；危及

jeopardy ['dʒepədi] n. 危险

landfill ['lændfɪl] n. 垃圾堆；废渣埋填地

lithosphere ['lɪθəsfɪə(r)] n. 岩石圈

magma ['mægmə] n. 岩浆

marsh [maːʃ] n. 沼泽，湿地

noisome ['nɔɪsəm] a. 恶臭的；有害的

overrun [ˌəʊvə'rʌn] n. 泛滥成灾；超出限度 v. 泛滥；超过；蹂躏

polar ['pəʊlə(r)] a. 极地的；两极的

scant [skænt] a. 缺乏的，不足的

seep [siːp] v. 漏出，渗漏

seismic ['saɪzmɪk] a. 地震的；因地震而引起的

slag [slæg] n. 矿渣；炉渣；熔渣

sticky ['stɪki] a. 黏性的；(天气)湿热的

音 频

Passage 37

Oil in Your Coffee: A New
Source of Fuel Production

Running a diesel engine on a plant-based fuel is hardly a new idea. Indeed, one of the early demonstrations shown by Rudolph Diesel, the German engineer who invented the engines at the end of the 1800s, operated on pure peanut oil. Diesel fuel made from crude oil eventually won the day because it was easier to use and cheaper to produce. Now new forms of biodiesel are starting to change the picture again. And one of the latest sources comes from the remains of a drink enjoyed by the world over: coffee.

Biodiesels are becoming increasingly popular. In America, Minnesota has decreed that all diesel sold in the state has to contain 2% biodiesel (much of it from the crops grown by the state's soya farmers). Biodiesel can also be found blended into the fuel used by public and commercial vehicles and by trains in a number of countries. Aircraft-engine makers are also testing biofuel blends. Because biodiesels can be made from materials derived from plants, which use carbon dioxide to grow, they potentially have a much lower carbon footprint than petroleum-based fuels.

Coffee is also a plant product, but once the beans are ground and used they end up being thrown away or put on gardens as compost. Narasimha Rao Kondamudi, Susanta Mohapatra and Manoranjan Misra of the University of Nevada at Reno have found that coffee grounds can yield by weight 10%–15% of biodiesel relatively easily. Moreover, when run in an engine the fuel does not have an offensive smell—just a whiff of coffee. Some biodiesels made from used cooking-oil leave a car exhaust smelling like a fast-food joint. And after the diesel has been extracted, the coffee grounds can still be used for compost.

The researchers' work began two years ago when Dr. Misra, a heavy coffee drinker, left a cup unfinished and the next day noticed that the coffee was covered by a film of oil. Since he was investigating biofuels, Dr. Misra enlisted his colleagues to look at coffee's potential. The nearby Starbucks was happy to oblige by supplying grounds.

They found that coffee biodiesel is comparable to the best biodiesels on the market. But unlike soya- and other plant-based biodiesels, it does not use up plants or land that might otherwise be planted with food crops.

Unmodified oils from plants, like the peanut oil used by Diesel, have a high viscosity and require engine alterations. Diesel fuel is less thick and usually can be burned in an engine with little or no tinkering. The diesel-extraction for coffee grounds is similar to that used for other vegetable oils. It employs a process called transesterification, which reacts the grounds with an alcohol in the presence of a catalyst.

The researchers start off by drying their coffee grounds overnight and then pour in some common chemical solvents, such as hexane, ether and dichloromethane, to dissolve the oils. The grounds are then filtered out and the solvents separated (to be reused with the next batch of coffee grounds). The remaining oil is treated with an alkali to remove free fatty acids (which form a soap). Then transesterification takes place by heating the crude biodiesel to about 100 degrees Celsius to remove any water, and treating it with methanol and a catalyst. On cooling to room temperature and left to stand, the biodiesel floats up, leaving a layer of glycerine at the bottom. These layers are separated and the remaining biodiesel is cleaned to remove any residues.

Although some people try to brew their own diesel at home from leftovers and recycled cooking oils, coffee-based diesel seems better suited to larger-scale processes. Dr. Misra says that 1 litre of biodiesel requires 5–7kg of coffee grounds, depending on the oil content of the coffee used. In their laboratory his team has set up a one-gallon-a-day production facility, which uses between 19–26kg of coffee grounds. The biofuel should cost about $1 per gallon to make in a medium-sized installation, the researchers estimate.

Commercial production might be suitable for an operation that collects coffee grounds from big coffee chains and cafeterias. There is plenty available: a report by the United States Department of Agriculture says that annual world coffee demand consumes more than 7m tonnes of coffee, which the researchers estimate could produce some 340m gallons of biodiesel. Time, perhaps, for another cup before refilling the car.

咖啡也能做燃油

利用以植物为原料制成的燃料驱动柴油机已经不是什么新鲜事了。确实，德国人鲁道夫·狄塞尔发明柴油机是在19世纪末期，当时他就使用纯花生油作为燃料进行了早期的尝试。由于使用起来更加方便，生产成本也更低，原油逐渐成为了柴油机的主要燃料来源。而现在，一种新形式的生物柴油又将改变这一格局。最新的生物燃料之一源于咖啡这种风靡世界的饮料的残余物。

生物柴油现在正变得越来越普遍。在美国，明尼苏达州曾经颁布过一项法令：州内销售的所有柴油中必须含有2%的生物柴油（其中大部分来自该州农民种植的大豆作物)。在公共交通、商用车以及许多国家的火车所使用的汽油中也混有生物柴油。飞机引擎制造商也在测试使用混有生物燃料的燃油。由于生物柴油可以用植物原料制成，而植物依靠二氧化碳生长，因此使用生物柴油的碳排放量要比使用石油燃料小得多。

咖啡也是一种植物产品，但是当咖啡豆被研磨成粉之后，残渣往往会被扔掉或是扔在花园中作为堆肥。来自内华达大学里诺分校的纳拉辛哈·拉奥·孔达穆迪、苏桑塔·莫哈帕特拉和马诺拉杰·米斯拉发现，咖啡残渣能够相对容易地产生相当于自重10%—15%的生物柴油。除此之外，咖啡渣制成的燃料在引擎中燃烧时没有刺激性气味——只有阵阵咖啡香。而一些利用使用过的食用油制造的生物柴油在汽车的引擎中燃烧之后，汽车尾气则会有种类似快餐店的味道。而且当燃油被萃取出来之后，剩下的咖啡渣仍然可以用作肥料。

研究人员的工作两年前就开始进行了。那时，非常喜欢喝咖啡的米斯拉博士有一次把一杯没喝完的咖啡留到了第二天，结果发现咖啡表面覆盖着一层油状薄膜。由于他当时正在研究生物燃油，于是便号召同事一起研究将咖啡作为生物燃料的可行性。附近的星巴克咖啡店也很乐意提供咖啡残渣供他们研究。

研究发现，以咖啡渣作为原料生产的柴油可以和市场上最好的生物柴油媲美。不同于大豆或者其他植物燃料，以咖啡为原料的燃料不会用尽原本可以用作食物的植物，也不会占用用来种植粮食作物的土地。

未经处理的纯植物油具有很高的黏性，比如狄塞尔使用的花生油，而且使用这样的燃料需要对引擎进行一番改造。柴油黏性较低，通常只要很小的改动或者无须改动就可以在引擎中燃烧。从咖啡中萃取燃料与从其他植物油中萃取燃料类似，都需要经过一个叫作"酯基转移"的过程。这个过程就是在催化剂的作用下让咖啡渣与乙醇进行反应。

研究人员先将咖啡渣放置一夜进行干燥，然后在其中倒入一些常见的化学溶剂，例如正己烷、乙醚和二氯甲烷，以便将咖啡渣中的油脂溶解出来。然后，将咖啡渣过滤，将溶剂分离出来（这样溶剂就可以重复利用，继续溶解下一批咖啡渣）。然后将剩下的油用碱处理，将游离脂肪酸移除（这样就能制出肥皂）。然后将天然的生物柴油加热到100摄氏度左右，让它完全脱水，接着再用甲醇和催化剂对它进行处理，这时就会发生酯基转移反应。之后将其冷却至常温并静置，生物燃油就会浮在最上方，并在底部留下一层甘油。然后把这几层油分离，对剩余的生物燃料进行提纯，去掉其中的杂质。

　　尽管有人试着在家中利用食物残渣和重复使用过的烹饪用油自制柴油燃料，但以咖啡为原料制成的燃料似乎更适合大规模生产。米斯拉博士说，生产1升的生物燃料需要5—7公斤的咖啡残渣，而且因咖啡含油量的多少而有差别。在他们的实验室，他的团队制作了一个日产1加仑生物燃料的设备，该设备每天大约使用19—26公斤的咖啡渣。研究人员估计，如果用一个中型设备生产燃料，那么生产每加仑燃料的成本大约是1美元。

　　要进行商业化生产，最好的方法可能就是从大型咖啡连锁店和自助餐厅收集咖啡残渣。咖啡残渣是足够用的：美国农业部的一份报告显示，全世界每年要消耗超过700万吨的咖啡。据研究人员估计，这些咖啡的残渣可以生产3.4亿加仑的生物燃料。或许，以后给车加油之前应该先来一杯咖啡。

🔍 单词记事本

diesel ['diːzl]
释 *n.* 柴油机；柴油

crude [kruːd]
释 *a.* 天然的，未提炼的；粗糙的；粗俗的
用 crude materials 原料
例 Biofuels had reduced consumption of *crude* oil by millions of barrels a day. 生物燃料的使用使原油消耗量每天减少了无数桶。

biodiesel ['baɪəʊdiːzl]
释 *n.* 生物柴油

decree [dɪ'kriː]
释 *n.* 法令；判决 *v.* 判决；颁布法令
用 issue/sign a decree 颁布/签署法令

biofuel ['baɪəʊfjuːəl]
释 *n.* 生物燃料

derive [dɪ'raɪv]
释 *v.* 得到，获取；源自，源于
用 derive from 得自，衍生于
例 The enzyme is *derived* from human blood. 这种酶来自人体血液。

petroleum [pə'trəʊliəm]
释 *n.* 石油

compost ['kɒmpɒst]
释 *n.* 堆肥；混合物 *v.* 施堆肥

ground [graʊnd]
释 *n.* 地，地面；场地；范围；[*pl.*]渣滓，沉淀物 *v.* (指船)触海底，搁浅；(使)接触地面；停飞；打基础

用 gain ground 前进，改善；流行；get off the ground (使)取得进展；起飞；on the grounds of 因为，以…为理由

yield [jiːld]

释 v. 生产，产出；屈服，投降；让渡，放弃(权利、地位等)；承认，同意 n. 生产，产量；收益；回收率

用 yield to 屈服，让步；被代替或替换；yield to maturity 到期收益，有效利率

例 He would rather die than *yield*. 他宁死不投降。

offensive [əˈfensɪv]

释 a. 冒犯的；使人不快的；进攻的 n. 进攻，攻势

例 Because of the depression in recruiting, colleges and business schools are going on the *offensive*. 由于招聘形势低迷，大学与商学院都准备主动出击。

whiff [wɪf]

释 v. 吸；吹气 n. 吸气或吹气；一点点

extract

释 [ɪkˈstrækt] v. 提炼出，分离出；取出，拔出；推断出，引出；选取，摘录 [ˈekstrækt] n. 提炼出的东西，精华，汁；摘录，选集

enlist [ɪnˈlɪst]

释 v. 征募，(使)参军；争取，谋取，获得…的支持或帮助

例 Many men were forced to *enlist* in the army during the civil war. 内战期间，很多男性被迫参军。

comparable [ˈkɒmpərəbl]

释 a. 可比较的，比得上的；类似的；相对照的，相对等的

用 be comparable with/to 可与…相比的；与…类似的

unmodified [ˌʌnˈmɒdɪfaɪd]

释 a. 未更改的

viscosity [vɪˈskɒsəti]

释 n. 黏性，黏度

alteration [ˌɔːltəˈreɪʃn]

释 n. 改变，修改；变更

transesterification [ˌtrænsəsˌterəfɪˈkeɪʃn]

释 n. 【化】酯基转移

catalyst [ˈkætəlɪst]

释 n. 催化剂，触媒剂；促使事情发展的因素

dichloromethane [daɪklɔːrəˈmeθeɪn]

释 n. 【化】二氯甲烷

dissolve [dɪˈzɒlv]

释 v. (使)溶解；(使)分解，(使)分离；解散，结束；废除；(使)感动

用 dissolve away 溶解掉；dissolve in 溶解入；dissolve into 溶解到…中，溶化成

batch [bætʃ]

释 n. (面包等的)一炉；一次投料量，一次生产量；一组，一批

alkali [ˈælkəlaɪ]

释 n. 碱

methanol [ˈmeθənɒl]

释 n. 甲醇

residue [ˈrezɪdjuː]

释 n. 剩余物；残余；余款；【律】剩余遗产；木屑

用 for the residue 至于其余；说到其他

例 The *residue* contained traces of the amino acids that make up proteins. 该剩余物中含有构成蛋白质的氨基酸的痕迹。

植物生长

biodiversity [ˌbaɪəʊdaɪ'vɜːsəti] *n.* 生物多样性

blight [blaɪt] *n.* 植物枯萎病

burgeon ['bɜːdʒən] *v.* 萌芽；迅速成长

chrysanthemum [krɪ'sænθəməm; krɪ'zænθəməm] *n.* 菊花

coexist [ˌkəʊɪg'zɪst] *v.* 共存

coronary ['kɒrənri] *a.* 花冠的；冠状的

deciduous [dɪ'sɪdʒuəs; dɪ'sɪdjuəs] *a.* 每年落叶的

defoliate [ˌdiː'fəʊlieɪt] *v.* (使)落叶

desiccate ['desɪkeɪt] *v.* (使)完全干涸，脱水

entwine [ɪn'twaɪn] *v.* 缠住，盘绕

evergreen ['evəgriːn] *a.* 常绿的

exuberant [ɪg'zjuːbərənt] *a.* 繁茂的；充满活力的

flaggy ['flægi] *a.* 枯萎的；松软无力的

floral ['flɔːrəl] *a.* 花的；植物的

frond [frɒnd] *n.* 叶

fruition [fru'ɪʃn] *n.* 结果实；实现，完成

graft [grɑːft] *v.* 嫁接；移植；贪污

herbal ['hɜːbl] *a.* 草本植物的；草药的

insentient [ɪn'senʃɪənt] *a.* 无生命的；无知觉的

mahogany [mə'hɒɡəni] *n.* 桃花心木，红木

mildew ['mɪldjuː] *n.* 霉菌；(植物的)霉病

palmy ['pɑːmi] *a.* 棕榈的；繁荣的

pheromone ['ferəməʊn] *n.* 信息素，外激素

plantation [plɑːn'teɪʃn] *n.* 农场，种植园

pollination [ˌpɒlə'neɪʃn] *n.* 授粉

ramify ['ræmɪfaɪ] *v.* (使)分枝

redolent ['redələnt] *a.* 芬芳的，芳香的；有强烈气味的

rhubarb ['ruːbɑːb] *n.* (植物)大黄

sheath [ʃiːθ] *n.* 鞘，叶鞘；外壳

shrivel ['ʃrɪvl] *v.* (使)枯萎

sterile ['steraɪl] *a.* 贫瘠的；无菌的

stigma ['stɪgmə] *n.* (植物)柱头

verdant ['vɜːdnt] *a.* 青葱的，翠绿的

wither ['wɪðə(r)] *v.* (使)凋谢，(使)枯萎；消亡，破灭

Passage 38

音频

Google's Futuristic
Glasses Move Closer to Reality

Google helped create a world brimming with digital distractions for people spending more of their lives tethered to the Internet. It's a phenomenon that seems unlikely to change so Google is working on a way to search for information, read text messages, watch online video and post photos on social networks without having to fumble around with a hand-held device.

The breakthrough is a wearable computer—a pair of Internet-connected glasses that Google Inc. began secretly building more than two years ago. The technology progressed far enough for Google to announce "Project Glass" in April. Now the futuristic experiment is moving closer to becoming a mass-market product.

Google announced Wednesday that it's selling a prototype of the glasses to U.S. computer programmers attending a three-day conference that ends Friday. Developers willing to pay $1,500 for a pair of the glasses will receive them early next year.

The company is counting on the programmers to suggest improvements and build applications that will make the glasses even more useful.

"This is a new technology and we really want you to shape it," Google co-founder Sergey Brin told about 6,000 attendees. "We want to get it out into the hands of passionate people as soon as possible."

If it all goes well, a less expensive version of the glasses is expected to go on sale for consumers in early 2014. Without estimating a price for the consumer version, Brin made it clear the glasses will cost more than smartphones.

"We do view this as a premium sort of thing," Brin said during a question-and-answer session with reporters.

Brin acknowledged Google still needs to fix a variety of bugs in the glasses and figure out how to make the battery last longer so people can wear them all day.

Those challenges didn't deter Brin from providing conference attendees Wednesday with a tantalizing peek at how the glasses might change the way people interact with technology.

Google hired skydivers to jump out of a blimp hovering 7,000 feet above downtown San Francisco. They wore the Internet-connected glasses, which were equipped with a camera, to show how the product could unleash entirely new ways for people to share their most thrilling—or boring—moments. As the skydivers parachuted onto the roof of the building where the conference was held, the crowd inside was able to watch the descent through the skydivers' eyes as it happened.

"I think we are definitely pushing the limits," Brin told reporters after the demonstration. "That is our job: to push the edges of technology into the future."

The glasses have become the focal point of Brin's work since he stepped away from Google's day-to-day operations last year to join the engineers working on ambitious projects that might once have seemed like the stuff of science fiction. Besides the Internet-connected glass, the so-called Google X lab has also developed a fleet of driverless cars that cruise roads. The engineers there also dream of building elevators that could transport people into space.

While wearing Google's glasses, directions to a destination or a text message from a friend can appear literally before your eyes. You can converse with friends in a video chat, take a photo without taking out a camera or phone or even buy a few things online as you walk around.

The glasses will likely be seen by many critics as the latest innovation that shortens attention spans and makes it more difficult for people to fully appreciate what's happening around them. But Brin and the other engineers are hoping the glasses will make it easier for people to strike the proper balance between the virtual and physical worlds.

Isabelle Olsson, one of the engineers working on the project, said the glasses are meant to interact with people's senses, without blocking them. The display on the glasses' computer appears as a small rectangle on a rim above the right eye. During short test of the prototype glasses, a reporter for The Associated Press was able to watch a video of exploding fireworks on the tiny display screen while remaining engaged with the people around him.

The glasses seem likely to appeal to runners, bicyclists and other athletes who want to take pictures of their activities as they happen. Photos and videos can be programmed to be taken at automatic **intervals** during any activity.

Brin said he became excited about the project when he tossed his son in the air and a picture taken by the glasses captured the joyful moment, just the way he saw it.

"That was amazing," Brin said. "There was no way I could have that memory without this device."

译 文

谷歌的未来眼镜更加贴近现实

这个世界到处都是令人分心的数字化产品，使得人们把生活中越来越多的时间都花在了互联网上，而谷歌对于这种现象的形成起到了一定的促进作用。意识到这一现象似乎不太可能改变，谷歌正在研究一种无须使用手持设备就可以搜索信息、阅读短信、在线观看视频以及在社交网络上发布照片的方法。

其突破是一种可随身佩戴的计算机——一副可以上网的智能眼镜，这是谷歌公司于两年多以前就暗自开始的项目。这个技术进展得非常迅速，因此谷歌决定在4月份宣布这一"投影眼镜"的诞生。目前，这个超前的设备正在逐渐变成一款畅销产品。

周三，谷歌宣布将于当天至周五开办一场为期三天的销售会，届时将针对美国的电脑程序员销售这款智能眼镜的原型。愿意花费1500美元购买该眼镜的开发者将于来年年初收到产品。

谷歌公司还希望程序员能提出一些改进建议并开发出应用程序，以使该眼镜更为有用。

谷歌公司的联合创始人谢尔盖·布林对大约6000名与会者说："这是一项新技术，我们真心希望大家一起来完善它。我们希望能尽快将它送到对它充满热情的人们手中。"

如果一切顺利，这款眼镜的相对便宜的版本将在2014年初对消费者发售。虽然没有对消费者版本的零售价格作出预测，但布林明确表示这款眼镜将比智能手机的价格更高。

布林在记者问答环节时说："我们确实将其视为一款品质非常高的产品。"

布林承认，谷歌公司仍然需要对智能眼镜中存在的各种缺陷进行修复，并且找到能让电池持续更长时间的方法，这样人们就能一整天都戴着这种眼镜了。

虽然存在这些挑战，但这并没有阻止布林在周三的会议上向人们展示这款智能眼镜，展示其将如何改变人与科技的交互方式，这也极大地勾起了人们的好奇心。

谷歌聘请了跳伞运动员从位于旧金山市中心上方7000英尺（约2134米）的小飞艇上跳下。他们戴着连接到网络且配备了摄像头的谷歌智能眼镜，向人们展示这个产品如何提供一种全新的方式来让人们分享他们最激动人心的时刻，或者是最无聊的时刻。当跳伞运动员空降到此次会议所在大楼的屋顶上时，室内的与会者可以通过跳伞者的视角看到整个下降过程中发生的一切。

布林在展示结束后告诉记者："我认为我们确实挑战了极限。这就是我们的工作：将科技的极限推向未来。"

从前一年年初开始，布林不再负责谷歌的日常运营，而是加入到了那些专门研究野心勃勃的、或许只可能出现在科幻小说中的项目的工程师队伍中去，智能眼镜就成为了他的工作重点。除了可以联网的智能眼镜，名为"谷歌X"的实验室还研制了一队可以按路线行驶的无人驾驶汽车。工程师们还梦想着创造出可以将人运送到太空中的电梯。

当你戴着谷歌的智能眼镜时，前往某个目的地的路线或收到的一条来自朋友的短信都可以逐字显示在你眼前。当你在四处行走时，你可以和朋友视频聊天，可以无须拿出相机就能拍照，还可以打电话，甚至在网上购物。

许多批评家可能会认为智能眼镜这一最新的创新成果会减小人们的注意力范围，而且会让人们更难专心地感受周遭发生的事情。但布林和其他工程师却希望智能眼镜能帮助人们更容易找到虚拟世界和现实世界之间的平衡。

参与该项目的工程师伊莎贝尔·奥尔森表示，研发智能眼镜的本意是想让它与人的感官互动，而不是阻碍感官。眼镜的电脑显示器就是位于右眼上方的眼镜框上的一个长方形小方框。在对眼镜的原型进行短暂测试后，美联社的一名记者通过智能眼镜的小显示屏观看了一段燃放焰火的视频，发现仍然可以同时注意到周围的人。

智能眼镜似乎可能会吸引跑步者、骑自行车的人和其他想要拍摄活动过程照片的运动员们。通过设置，就可以在任何活动中以任意的间隔拍摄照片和视频。

布林说，当他把儿子抛到空中时，智能眼镜捕捉到了当时的快乐瞬间，与他所看到的景象完全一样，这让他对这个产品感到无比兴奋。

"那实在是太美妙了。"布林说，"如果没有这个设备，我不可能拥有那么美好的记忆瞬间。"

brim [brɪm]
释 n. (杯、碗等的)边，缘；(河、湖等的)边缘；帽檐 v. 盈满，充满
用 brim over (with) 充满，洋溢

distraction [dɪ'strækʃn]
释 n. 注意力分散；使人分心的事物；娱乐，消遣；心烦意乱
用 to distraction 几乎到疯狂的地步
例 You'll drive me to *distraction* with your silly questions! 你的那些傻问题简直要把我逼疯了!

tether ['teðə(r)]
释 v. 用绳或链拴住(牲畜)；限定，束缚 n. (拴牲畜的)绳或链；(知识、力量等的)限度，范围

breakthrough ['breɪkθruː]
释 n. 突破；突破性进展，重要的新发现；(价格等)猛涨；临界点
例 Pearson predicts a *breakthrough* in human-computer interaction. 皮尔逊预测人机交互方面将有突破性进展。

programmer ['prəʊɡræmə(r)]
释 n. 节目编排者；程序设计者；程序设计器

attendee [ˌæten'diː]
释 n. 出席者

smartphone ['smɑːtfəʊn]
释 n. 智能手机

premium ['priːmiəm]
释 n. 奖赏，奖金；保险金；额外的费用；酬金，佣金；高级，优质 a. 特佳的，特级的
用 at a premium (指公债和股票)超过正常或市面的价值，溢价；奇缺的；put/place a premium on 奖励，鼓励，重视

例 Many private insurance companies which present a variety of *premium* schemes to customers remain competitive in the auto industry. 许多向顾客提供多种保费方案的私人保险公司在汽车行业中很有竞争力。

bug [bʌɡ]
释 n. 虫子；窃听器；(机器等)故障，缺陷 v. 灭除(害虫)；窃听；烦扰

deter [dɪ'tɜː(r)]
释 v. 阻止，(使)断念

tantalizing ['tæntəlaɪzɪŋ]
释 a. 吸引人的，逗引性的

skydiver ['skaɪdaɪvə(r)]
释 n. 花样跳伞运动员

blimp [blɪmp]
释 n. 小型软式飞艇

hover ['hɒvə(r)]
释 v. (鸟等)翱翔，盘旋；彷徨，徘徊

thrilling ['θrɪlɪŋ]
释 a. 令人激动的；毛骨悚然的；刺骨的

descent [dɪ'sent]
释 n. 降落，落下；下坡；出身，血统，国籍；侵袭，袭击；出乎意料的或不合时宜的到访
例 There is a steep *descent* to the town below. 一条陡峭的坡道通往下面的小镇。

definitely ['defɪnətli]
释 ad. 明确地，清楚地；肯定地，确实地

demonstration [ˌdemən'streɪʃn]
释 n. 示范，展示；表示，表明；证明，论证；示威游行

fleet [fliːt]

释 *n.* 舰队；捕鱼船队；(同时运行的) 机群、车队等 *a.* 快速的；短暂的 *v.* 消磨；掠过

driverless ['draɪvə(r)ləs]

释 *a.* 无人驾驶的

cruise [kruːz]

释 *v.* 航游，巡航；(指机动车辆或飞行器)以中等速度行进 *n.* 海上航游；乘船游览

例 Please arrive 30 minutes prior to *cruise* departure. 请在巡游艇出发前30分钟到达港口。

converse

释 [kən'vɜːs] *v.* 谈话，交谈
['kɒnvɜːs] *n.* 相反的事物

例 He says she is satisfied, but I believe the *converse* to be true: she is very dissatisfied. 他说她已心满意足了，不过我认为实际情况相反：她很不满意。

rectangle ['rektæŋgl]

释 *n.* 长方形，矩形

rim [rɪm]

释 *n.* (圆形物体的)边 *v.* 形成…的边缘；给…镶边

interval ['ɪntəvl]

释 *n.* (时间的)间隔，间歇；(空间的)间隔，空隙；幕间(或工间)休息

搭 at intervals 不时，时时，每隔一段时间(或距离)

例 The *interval* between arrest and trial can be up to six months. 逮捕和审判之间的间隔最长可达六个月。

💡 单词家族

科技发展

automation [ˌɔːtə'meɪʃn] *n.* 自动化，自动操作

burrow ['bʌrəʊ] *v.* 钻研，查阅；挖掘 *n.* 地洞

diverse [daɪ'vɜːs] *a.* 不同的；变化的

duration [dju'reɪʃn] *n.* 波期；宽度；持续期间

facsimile [fæk'sɪməli] *n.* 摹本；传真本

inversion [ɪn'vɜːʃn] *n.* 倒置，颠倒；转化

multimedia [ˌmʌlti'miːdiə] *n.* 多媒体 *a.* 多媒体的

necessitate [nə'sesɪteɪt] *v.* 使成为必要

photocopy ['fəʊtəʊkɒpi] *v.* 影印，复印

projector [prə'dʒektə(r)] *n.* 放映机

stability [stə'bɪləti] *n.* 稳定性

telex ['teleks] *n.* 电报；电传收发机

Chapter 4

温馨情感

Passage 39

The Power of Kindness

A successful businessman, addressing the commercial club of his city, told a story in his after-dinner speech. It was the story of a boy named Jim, who was an orphan and the laughing stock of the whole town. He was twelve years old, slim and undersized. He never remembered having a kind word spoken to him in his whole life. He was accustomed to harsh words, suspicion, and rebuffs, and as a result became a shrinking, pitiful little figure, dodging people. And the more he dodged people, the more suspicious he became.

The only earthly possession of which Jim could boast was a dog that cringed and shrank almost as much as his master and was as much hated. Jim was not cruel to his dog except in words—and that is really the worst form of cruelty, even to a dog. A harsh, unkind word can cause more misery, heartache, and anguish than actual physical cruelty. A cruel, unkind tongue cuts like a sword.

One day as Jim walked down the street, he saw a bundle slip from the overloaded arms of a little lady just in front of him. As she stopped to pick it up, the others rolled down. Jim sprang to her assistance, gathering up the bundles and replacing them in her arms. "Thank you, dear. You are a nice little boy," she said kindly, and went on her way after giving him a bright smile.

Jim was amazed, a queer choky feeling passed over him. These were the first kind words he had ever heard in his whole twelve years of existence. He stood and stared after her. He knew that she was the busy little dressmaker who lived in a small cottage on the outskirts of town. He watched her until she was out of sight, then he whistled to Tige and made straight for the woods and a stream that wound around the town.

He sat down on the bank of the stream and did some thinking. "Thank you, dear. You are a nice little boy," he pondered.

"Come here, Tige," he commanded, and Tige slunk to his feet. Then Jim lowered his voice in imitation of the little faded lady and said, "You are a nice little dog." The effect on Tige was electrical. He pricked up his ears, and if a dog could stand at attention, Tige did. "Unum! Even a dog likes it," said Jim. "Well, Tige, I don't blame you. It is nice. I won't holler at you anymore." Tige wagged his tail joyously.

The boy continued to think, and the dog sat and watched him. Finally the boy pulled from the odds and ends in his pockets a piece of broken mirror and looked at himself. He saw nothing but **grime** and dirt, the **accumulation** of many days. He went down to the water's edge and **scrubbed** it off carefully, almost painfully. Then he looked again. He **scarcely** recognized himself. He was surprised. He stood **erect** and looked up instead of down for the first time since he could remember. He **distinctly** liked the **sensation**. A feeling of self-respect awoke him. **Ambition** sprang full-grown into life. At that moment the course of his life was changed, a determination to be worthy of the kind words spoken to him by the little dressmaker, and to pass them on, took possession of his soul.

After telling this story of Jim, the orphan boy, the speaker paused, and then he **electrified** the audience by saying, "Gentlemen, I was that boy. This city—your city, my city—was that little town of forty years ago. Our plant stands upon the spot where that gentle woman stood when she **implanted** in my life the first seed of kindness. She sleeps out **yonder** in what was then the **cemetery** of a country church. As a tribute to her memory I have told you this story."

Oh, all of us should learn the lesson: "Be kind to others." What transforming power it has!

友善的力量

一位成功的商人在他所在城市的商务俱乐部发表餐后演说时讲述了一则故事。故事的主人公是一个叫作吉姆的小男孩。吉姆是个孤儿，而且是全镇人取笑的对象。他12岁，又瘦又小。从小到大，他从不记得有谁对他说过一句友善的话，而且也早已习惯了别人的粗言秽语、无端猜疑和冷漠拒绝。这些最终导致他成为了一个畏首畏尾、见人就躲的可怜小家伙。可是他越是逃避人群就越显得形迹可疑。

吉姆在这个世界上唯一可以夸耀的所谓财产就是那条和它的主人一样畏畏缩缩、遭人唾弃的小狗。吉姆对他的狗除了在言语上比较残忍外还算友善——但即使对一条狗来说，这也是最残忍的方式。比起肉体上的折磨，一句刻薄无情的话可以带来更深的痛苦、心碎和痛楚。一句残酷、无情的话会像利剑一般伤人。

一天，吉姆沿着街道行走时看见一个包裹从前面一位娇小的女士手中滑落。这位女士怀中抱满了东西，当她蹲下去捡拾包裹时，其他的东西随之掉

203

落一地。吉姆迅速地跑过去，帮她捡回了掉落的包裹，并重新放到她的手中。她回报了他一个灿烂的微笑，然后亲切地说："谢谢你，亲爱的。你真是个好孩子。"然后便继续赶路了。

吉姆惊呆了，一种奇怪的令人窒息的感觉席卷了他。这是他在自己12年的人生当中第一次听到友善的话语。他站在那里，注视着她远去的背影。他知道她是一个忙碌的小裁缝，住在小镇远郊的一座小村舍里。他一直看着她，直到她消失在自己的视线，然后他向小狗蒂格吹了一声口哨，向围绕着镇子的树林和小溪跑去。

他在溪边坐了下来，反复思考着那句话："谢谢你，亲爱的。你真是个好孩子。"

"过来，蒂格！"他命令道。蒂格灰溜溜地跑到他的脚旁。然后吉姆压低声音，学着那位远去的女士的语气说道："你是一只好小狗。"这句话对蒂格产生了震撼的效果。它竖起了耳朵。如果狗能立正站好的话，蒂格现在的姿势就是那样。"嗯！连小狗都喜欢这样。"吉姆说道，"好的，蒂格，我不会再骂你了。这样很好。我再也不会对你大呼小叫了。"蒂格高兴地摇起了尾巴。

男孩继续想着，蒂格坐在旁边望着他。最后，男孩从他口袋里七零八碎的物品中掏出一面破碎的镜子。他看了看自己，却只看到了身上常年累积的污垢和尘土。他走到水边，仔细地擦掉所有的污迹，擦起来甚至有些痛。然后他又照了照镜子。这次他都快认不出自己了，这令他吃了一惊。他笔直地站着，没有再垂头丧气，而是昂起了头，这是他记事以来第一次这样做。显然，他喜欢这种感觉。一种自尊感唤醒了他。他的生命中充满了雄心壮志。就在这一瞬间，他的人生轨迹改变了，他的灵魂被一种要让小裁缝所说的话变得值得的决心、一种想把它们传递下去的勇气所占据。

讲完孤儿吉姆的故事，演讲者停顿了一会儿，接下来他说的话让听众大为震惊："先生们，我就是这个男孩！而这座城市——你我所在的城市——就是40年前的那个小镇。当年那位善良的女士在我生命中种下了第一颗善良的种子，而现在我们的工厂就矗立在她当年所站的地方之上。她长眠在当时的乡村教堂的公墓里。为了纪念她，我在此向你们讲述了这个故事。"

哦，这是我们所有人都应该学习的一课："善待他人"。它有着多么神奇的改造力量啊！

orphan ['ɔ:fn]
释 *n.* 孤儿

undersized [ˌʌndə'saɪzd]
释 *a.* (通常为贬义)较一般小的

accustomed [ə'kʌstəmd]
释 *a.* 习惯于…的；惯常的
例 I am not *accustomed* to high heels and only wear them on special occasions. 我不习惯穿高跟鞋，只在一些特殊场合才穿。

harsh [hɑ:ʃ]
释 *a.* 刻薄的；严厉的；刺耳的

suspicion [sə'spɪʃn]
释 *n.* 怀疑；涉嫌；少量

rebuff [rɪ'bʌf]
释 *n./v.* 轻蔑回绝；冷漠

dodge [dɒdʒ]
释 *v.* 躲开，躲避；施计避免做(某事) *n.* 躲闪；托辞

earthly ['ɜ:θli]
释 *a.* 现世的，尘世的；可能的

possession [pə'zeʃn]
释 *n.* 拥有；所有物，财产

boast [bəʊst]
释 *v./n.* 自夸，夸耀

misery ['mɪzəri]
释 *n.* 痛苦；悲惨的境遇

anguish ['æŋgwɪʃ]
释 *n.* 极度痛苦
例 People who are afflicted by depression always describe their mood as depressed, *anguished*, irritable or anxious. 患有抑郁症的人经常称自己情绪低落、极度痛苦、狂躁易怒或者焦虑不安。

sword [sɔ:d]
释 *n.* 剑；刀

bundle ['bʌndl]
释 *n.* 束、捆或包在一起的东西 *v.* 把某物捆成捆
用 bundle up 把…捆扎(或包)起来；使穿暖；bundle sth./sb. into 把某物扔到某处；把某人打发到某处

overloaded [ˌəʊvə'ləʊdɪd]
释 *a.* 超负荷的；超载的

spring [sprɪŋ]
释 *n.* 春天；泉水；跳跃 *v.* 跳跃；突然活动

assistance [ə'sɪstəns]
释 *n.* 帮助；辅助

queer [kwɪə(r)]
释 *a.* 奇怪的，异常的；不舒服的

choky ['tʃəʊki]
释 *a.* 令人窒息的

dressmaker ['dresmeɪkə(r)]
释 *n.* (制作女服或童装的)裁缝

outskirts ['aʊtskɜ:ts]
释 *n.* 郊区；外围地区

slink [slɪŋk]
释 *v.* 鬼鬼祟祟地移动；溜走

imitation [ˌɪmɪ'teɪʃn]
释 *n.* 模仿；仿制品
例 The student's latent capacity for *imitation* should be given the fullest scope and encouragement. 该学生具有模仿的潜能。学校应给予他充分的发展空间和鼓励。

fade [feɪd]
释 *v.* 褪色；凋谢；消失

prick [prɪk]

释 v. 刺；竖起 n. 刺；刺痛

用 prick up one's ears 竖起耳朵注意听

holler ['hɒlə(r)]

释 v. 叫喊；喊出

joyously ['dʒɔɪəsli]

释 ad. 快乐地，高兴地

grime [graɪm]

释 n. 污垢 v. 弄脏

accumulation [ə,kjuːmjə'leɪʃn]

释 n. 累积；堆积物

scrub [skrʌb]

释 v. 用力擦洗；取消(计划等) n. 擦洗；灌木丛

scarcely ['skeəsli]

释 ad. 几乎不；决不；才

用 scarcely ... when 一…就…，刚…便…

例 Radium was one of these *scarcely* understood new metals. 镭曾是那些几乎不被人了解的新金属中的一种。

erect [ɪ'rekt]

释 a. 竖立的；笔直的 v. 建造，设立；竖立，使直立

distinctly [dɪ'stɪŋktli]

释 ad. 清楚地；明显地；明白地

sensation [sen'seɪʃn]

释 n. 感觉；激动；轰动

ambition [æm'bɪʃn]

释 n. 雄心；野心；志气；抱负

例 I have to admit that *ambition* is a characteristic of all successful businessmen. 我必须承认，有野心是所有成功的商人的特点之一。

electrify [ɪ'lektrɪfaɪ]

释 v. 使充电；使震惊

implant [ɪm'plɑːnt]

释 v. 注入，灌输

yonder ['jɒndə(r)]

释 ad./a. 在那边(的)；远处(的)

cemetery ['semətri]

释 n. 公墓

💡 单词家族

情绪感受

acknowledge [ək'nɒlɪdʒ] v. 对…表示谢意；承认；认出

admirable ['ædmərəbl] a. 值得赞扬的；令人钦佩的

aggravating ['ægrəveɪtɪŋ] a. 激怒的，惹恼的

apathetic [,æpə'θetɪk] a. 缺乏兴趣的；无动于衷的

apologetic [ə,pɒlə'dʒetɪk] a. 道歉的；认错的

appall [ə'pɔːl] v. 使惊骇，使大吃一惊

begrudge [bɪ'grʌdʒ] v. 对…不满；嫉妒

complaint [kəm'pleɪnt] n. 抱怨，诉苦

consolation [,kɒnsə'leɪʃn] n. 安慰；慰问

conviviality [kən,vɪvɪ'æləti] n. 欢乐，高兴；交游

daunt [dɔːnt] v. 使胆怯，使气馁

desperate ['despərət] a. 极度渴望的；绝望的

discontented [,dɪskən'tentɪd] a. 不满的；不满足的；不满意的

disobedient [ˌdɪsə'biːdiənt] a. 不服从的

elated [i'leɪtɪd] a. 情绪高昂的；兴高采烈的

esteem [ɪ'stiːm] v./n. 尊重，尊敬

exaltation [ˌegzɔːl'teɪʃn] n. (成功带来的)兴奋；得意

extol [ɪk'stəʊl] v. 赞美，颂扬

falter ['fɔːltə(r)] v. 支吾地说；结巴地讲出；犹豫；蹒跚

favorable ['feɪvərəbl] a. 赞许的；有利的

flaunt [flɔːnt] n. 招摇；炫耀

furious ['fjʊəriəs] a. 狂怒的，暴怒的；强烈的

gratify ['grætɪfaɪ] v. 使满意，使高兴；纵容

grieve [griːv] v. 使伤心；感到悲痛；感到懊悔

homage ['hɒmɪdʒ] n. 深表敬意的言行；褒扬某人或某品德的事物

peevish ['piːvɪʃ] a. 坏脾气的，易怒的

reassure [ˌriːə'ʃʊə(r); ˌriːə'ʃɔː(r)] v. 使…安心；打消…的疑虑

sympathize ['sɪmpəθaɪz] v. 同情，怜悯；赞同

Ideal is the beacon. Without ideal, there is no secure direction; without direction, there is no life.
——Leo Tolstoy

理想是指路明灯。没有理想，就没有坚定的方向；没有方向，就没有生活。
——列夫·托尔斯泰

音频

Passage 40

Memory in a Photograph

"She was the prettiest I'd ever seen," **recalled** my grandfather.

My brother and I were sitting **cross-legged** on the living room's floor. Doug was watching a western movie on the television, and I was **idly** looking through one of my grandparents' photo albums. One of the photographs of my grandmother had caught Grandpa's attention. His usual **hearty**, **buoyant** laughter was gone, and his **demeanor** was quiet and reflective. Suddenly, Grandpa's story had brought our full attention.

In his earlier years, my grandfather had been a tall, big-framed and **muscular** man used to working outdoors. The man in front of us was still larger than life to me and my five-year-old brother, but now his shoulders were stooped and his hands **knotted** with arthritis. He sat on the edge of the couch and studied us both, as if he was trying to determine whether we were old enough to fully **appreciate** what he was going to tell us. His **gaze** then turned to our grandmother sitting a few feet away. His eyes softened as he related the story of how they met.

His first **glimpse** of his future bride happened while she was in the company of her father and two of her sisters. Her father was conducting business, and the girls were sitting nearby in the back of his old pickup. As he warmed up to his story, Grandma's hands became still, and her **crochet** lay in a colorful fold on her **lap**. She listened to the familiar old story, caught up in the tale that we were hearing for the first time. She smiled warmly back at him.

"While her Daddy was busy with some other gentlemen," he said, "I was busy watching her and her two sisters. They were sitting there in the back of that old pickup, feet **dangling** and swinging, **giggling** and whispering to each other. She had the reddest hair, and she was about the prettiest thing I'd ever seen. I just couldn't help myself... "

Grandma was **beaming** with pleasure by this time. It wasn't too often Grandpa was this romantic, and she was enjoying the compliments. "...and so I just ran right over there, and bit her on the hind leg."

A **thunderous frown** knitted my grandmother's forehead, and her **dainty** fine eyebrows drew close together. Her mouth rounded into a **horrified** "Oh" as her blue eyes flashed. "Merle, you did not! Mercy, how could you tell stories like that to these grandkids!" But the damage was done. My brother and I **clutched** our middles as we rolled backwards in the floor, unable to control our laughter. Her **tirade** continued, to no effect. Grandpa laughed as hard as the rest of us.

Appearing **miffed**, Grandma picked up her crochet and started threading the **yarn** through her fingers, but I saw the quick look she sent my grandfather, complete with a wink. It was the same expression captured in the photograph in front of me.

I was reminded again years later of that look. It was a few months after my grandmother's death. I was sitting in their living room once again, visiting with Grandpa. I picked up an old photo album and began flipping through the pages, and came across the same photograph of Grandma.

She must have been about eighteen in the picture. She had a little hat **perched** on her head, and was **tossing** a **saucy** look back over her shoulder. She was laughing, and I was **struck** by how beautiful she had been.

Then I noticed that Grandpa had become quiet. He was sitting next to me, leaning over to look at the photograph. He reached over and placed a **callused** finger on the page. He studied the image a few moments longer before saying softly, "That there...that there's the reason I fell in love with her." Then he turned to me and **grinned**, "Did I ever tell you about the first time I saw her? Prettiest I'd ever seen..."

照片中的回忆

"她是我见过的最美的姑娘。"祖父回忆道。

我和弟弟正盘腿坐在客厅的地板上。道格正在看电视里播放的西部影片，而我无聊地翻着祖父母的一本相册。其中一张祖母的照片引起了祖父的注意。他平时那种爽朗、欢快的笑声不见了，取而代之的是安静和沉思。忽然，他讲起了这张照片的故事，将我和弟弟的注意力完全吸引了过去。

祖父年轻的时候是个高大魁梧、强壮有力的男人，经常在户外干活。现在，虽然他的背已经弯曲，手指也因患有关节炎而肿大，但在我和五岁的弟弟心目中他仍然气宇轩昂。他坐在沙发边缘盯着我们俩，好像在判断我们是不是足够成熟，是否能够完全理解他要讲的故事。他又转头看了看坐在不远处的祖母，然后开始讲述他和祖母是如何相遇的，眼神也变得柔和起来。

祖父第一眼看到他未来的新娘时，她正和她的父亲还有两个姐姐在一起。她的父亲在谈生意，她们几个女孩就坐在他那辆停在附近的老式小卡车的后面。当祖父准备好讲故事的时候，祖母停下手里的活，把她那五颜六色的编织品堆在膝头。她听着这个对我们来说是第一次听到但对她来说已非常熟悉的老故事，沉浸其中，冲祖父暖暖地笑了一下。

"在她父亲忙着和其他几位先生交谈的时候，"祖父说，"我也忙着打量她和她的两个姐姐。她们坐在那辆老式小卡车后面，脚晃来晃去，咯咯地笑着，互相之间窃窃私语着。她长着我所见过的最红的头发，可以说她是我见过的最美丽的人。我忍不住就……"

这时的祖母神色愉悦。因为祖父平时很少这么浪漫，所以她很乐意听到祖父的赞美。"……所以我就朝她奔了过去，一口咬在她的腿肚子上。"

祖母猛地皱起了眉，秀美的眉毛拧在了一起。她的嘴巴张得圆圆的，蓝色的眼睛也忽闪着，惊叫道："哦！默尔，不准乱讲！拜托，你怎么可以这样给孙子们讲故事呢！"可是为时已晚。我和弟弟抱着肚子在地上打滚儿，笑得停不下来。祖母还在大声地谴责着，可是根本不起作用。祖父和我们一样大笑不已。

假装生气的祖母拿起她的编织物，继续飞针走线，但我捕捉到她快速地看了祖父一眼，并眨了眨眼。那个表情与我面前的照片上的一模一样。

很多年后我又回想起了那个眼神。那是在祖母去世几个月之后，我来看望祖父，再一次坐在他们的客厅里。我拿起一本旧相册，一页一页地翻，然后又看到了祖母的那张照片。

照片上的她应该是十八岁左右，头上戴了顶小小的帽子，正带着俏皮的神情回头看着什么。她笑着，是那样的美丽动人。我被震撼了。

这时我注意到祖父安静了下来。他坐在我的旁边，倾过身来看那张照片。他伸出手来，结满老茧的手指放在照片上。他盯那张照片看了很长时间，然后幽幽地说："这就是……这就是我爱上她的原因。"接着他转向我，笑眯眯地说："我给你讲过我第一次遇见她的故事吗？她是我见过的最美的姑娘……"

💡 单词记事本

recall [rɪˈkɔːl]
释 v. 回想起；召回 n. 回想；召回

cross-legged [ˌkrɒsˈlegd; ˌkrɔːsˈlegd]
释 ad. 盘着腿

idly [ˈaɪdli]
释 ad. 懒懒地

hearty [ˈhɑːti]
释 a. 快活的；亲切友好的；热诚的

buoyant ['bɔɪənt]
释 a. (物体)漂浮的；快乐的

demeanor [dɪ'miːnə(r)]
释 n. 举止；行为；风度

muscular ['mʌskjələ(r)]
释 a. 肌肉的；强健的

knot [nɒt]
释 n. (绳等的)结 v. (使)打结，缠结；形成硬结(或肿块等)

appreciate [ə'priːʃɪeɪt]
释 v. 理解；欣赏；体谅
例 We *appreciated* Teacher Li's devotion of time and money to the English learning plan. 我们感谢李老师为这个英语学习计划所花费的时间和金钱。

gaze [geɪz]
释 n./v. 凝视

glimpse [glɪmps]
释 n./v. 一瞥，一看

crochet ['krəʊʃeɪ]
释 n. 钩针编织 v. 用钩针编织

lap [læp]
释 n. 大腿上方，膝上；(跑道的)一圈 v. 包扎；重叠；舔；(波浪)拍打
用 lap up 舔食；欣然接受

dangle ['dæŋgl]
释 v. 悬荡；拿着某物使其摆动

giggle ['gɪgl]
释 v./n. 咯咯笑

beam [biːm]
释 n. (光线等的)束；笑容 v. 面露喜色；发送

thunderous ['θʌndərəs]
释 a. 雷鸣般的；面色阴沉的，怒气冲冲的

frown [fraʊn]
释 v./n. 皱眉

用 frown on/upon 不同意；不满
例 My teacher's brows were knitted in a permanent *frown* since his mother's death. 自从老师的母亲去世后，他的眉头就一直紧锁着。

dainty ['deɪnti]
释 a. 秀丽的；精致的；挑剔的；美味的

horrified ['hɒrɪfaɪd]
释 a. 惊骇的；带有恐怖感的

clutch [klʌtʃ]
释 v. 抓住；抱住 n. 抓；控制；离合器；一次孵的蛋；一窝小鸟
用 clutch at 企图抓住
例 Johnson stood in the doorway, with the invitation *clutched* tightly in his hand. 约翰逊站在门口，手中紧紧握着邀请函。

tirade [taɪ'reɪd]
释 n. 长篇的批评性或谴责性讲话

miffed [mɪft]
释 a. 稍微恼火的

yarn [jɑːn]
释 n. 纱，线，(尤指)毛线；故事，奇谈

perch [pɜːtʃ]
释 n. (鸟类的)栖息处；高处 v. 栖息；停留；坐着；置于

toss [tɒs]
释 v. 扔；猛然扭(头等)；将(食品)拌上调料等 n. 扔；抛；摇荡
用 toss up 掷钱币决定胜负
例 Sara had tangled up the sheets on the bed as she could not sleep last night and lay *tossing* and turning. 萨拉昨天晚上睡不着觉，躺在床上辗转反侧，把床单弄得一团糟。

saucy ['sɔːsi]
释 a. 俏皮的；漂亮的；无礼的

strike [straɪk]

释 v. 打；(使)产生印象；罢工；(钟等)敲响 n. 罢工；袭击

callused ['kæləst]

释 a. 有老茧的

grin [grɪn]

释 n./v. 露齿而笑

用 grin and bear it 毫无怨言地忍受痛苦、挫折等

 单词家族

情感记忆

adore [ə'dɔ:(r)] v. 敬爱，崇敬；喜欢，爱慕

affective [ə'fektɪv] a. 感情方面的；由感情引起的

agreement [ə'gri:mənt] n. (感情)融洽，和睦；(意见)相合，一致；协议，承诺

bashful ['bæʃfl] a. 害羞的；难为情的

beloved [bɪ'lʌvd] a. 深爱的；心爱的 n. 心爱的人

distraught [dɪ'strɔ:t] a. 心烦意乱的；忧心如焚的

emotional [ɪ'məʊʃənl] a. 感情(上)的；易动感情的

infatuation [ɪnˌfætʃu'eɪʃn] n. 迷恋

sympathize ['sɪmpəθaɪz] v. 同情；体谅；赞同

upsurge ['ʌpsɜ:dʒ] n. 激发；(尤指感情的)突发

yearn [jɜ:n] v. 渴望；怀念；盼望

Don't part with your illusions. When they are gone you may still exist, but you have ceased to live. —Mark Twain

不要放弃你的幻想。当幻想没有了以后，你还可以生存，但是虽生犹死。 ——马克·吐温

Passage 41

My Forever Valentine

The traditional holidays in our house when I was a child were spent timing elaborate meals around football games. My father tried to make pleasant chitchat and eat as much as he could during halftime. At Christmas he found time to have a cup or two of holiday beer and do his holly-shaped bow tie. But he didn't truly shine until Valentine's Day.

I don't know whether it was because work at the office slowed during February or because the football season was over. But Valentine's Day was the time my father chose to show his love for the special people in his life. Over the years I fondly thought of him as my "Valentine Man".

My first recollection of the magic he could bring to Valentine's Day came when I was six. For several days I had been cutting out valentines for my classmates. Each of us was to decorate a "mailbox" and put it on our desk for others to give us cards. That box and its contents ushered in a succession of bittersweet memories of my entrance into a world of popularity contests marked by the number of cards received, the teasing about boyfriends/girlfriends and the tender care I gave to the card from the cutest boy in class.

That morning at the breakfast table I found a card and a gift—wrapped package at my chair. The card was signed "Love, Dad", and the gift was a ring with a small piece of red glass to represent my birthstone, a ruby. There is little difference between red glass and rubies to a child of six, and I remember wearing that ring with a pride that all the cards in the world could not surpass.

As I grew older, the gifts gave way to heart-shaped boxes filled with my favorite chocolates and always included a special card signed "Love, Dad". In those years my "Thank You" became more of a perfunctory response. The cards seemed less important, and I took for granted the valentine that would always be there. Long past the days of having a "mailbox" on my desk, I had placed my hopes and dreams in receiving cards and gifts from "significant others", and "Love, Dad" just didn't seem quite enough.

If my father knew then that he had been replaced, he never let it show. If he sensed any disappointment over valentines that didn't arrive for me, he just tried that much harder to create a positive atmosphere, giving me an extra hug and doing what he could to make my day a little brighter.

My mailbox eventually had a **rural** address, and the job of hand-delivering candy and cards was **relegated** to the U.S. Postal Service. Never in ten years was my father's package late—nor was it on the Valentine's Day eight years ago when I reached into the mailbox to find a card addressed to me in my mother's **handwriting**.

It was the kind of card that comes in an inexpensive **assortment** box sold by a child going door-to-door to try to earn money for a school project. It was the kind of card that you used to get from a grandmother or an aging aunt or, in this case, a dying father. It was the kind of card that put a lump in your throat and tears in your eyes because you knew the person no longer was able to go out and buy a real valentine. It was a card that **signaled** this would be the last you receive from him.

The card had a photograph of **tulips** on the outside, and on the inside my mother had printed "Happy Valentine's Day". Beneath it, **scrawled** in barely **legible** handwriting, was "Love, Dad".

His final card remains on my **bulletin** board today. It's a **reminder** of how special father can be and how important it had been to me over the years to know that I had a father who continued a tradition of love with a **generosity** of spirit, simple acts of understanding and an ability to express happiness over the people in his life.

Those things never die, nor does the memory of a man who never stopped being my valentine.

译文

永远的情人节

在我小时候，我们家过传统节日时通常会将精心准备的节日大餐安排在橄榄球比赛的中间。中场休息时，父亲总是尽他所能地一边聊些愉快的事情，一边填饱肚子。圣诞节时他则会找时间为庆祝节日喝上一两杯啤酒，然后戴上他那冬青叶形状的领结。但情人节才是父亲真正大放光彩的日子。

我不知道这是因为在二月份他的工作节奏放缓还是因为橄榄球赛季已经结束，反正情人节这天是父亲选择来向他生命中最特别的人表达爱意的日子。多少年来，我都天真地把他看作我的"情人"。

他带给我的第一次关于情人节的美妙回忆是在我六岁那年。一连几天，我都忙着给我的同学制作情人节卡片。我们每个人都会装饰一个"信箱"，然后把它放在课桌上收取贺卡。这个"信箱"和里面的卡片总能唤起关于那时甜涩参半的一连串回忆，如以收到卡片数量作为衡量标准的魅力竞赛、那些关于男女朋友的玩笑以及对来自班里最受欢迎的男生的贺卡的精心呵护。

那天早上在餐桌旁，我在自己的椅子上发现了一张贺卡和一份包装好的礼物。卡片上写着"爱你的爸爸"，礼物是一枚嵌着一小块红玻璃的戒指，代表我的诞生石——红宝石。对于一个六岁的孩子来说，红玻璃和红宝石并没有什么不同。我还记得自己一脸骄傲地戴着它，觉得所有卡片都黯然失色的样子。

当我长大了一点，礼物变成了心形的盒子，里面装满了我最喜爱的巧克力，而且总有一张特别的贺卡，上面写着"爱你的爸爸"。那些年，我通常只是例行公事地说一声"谢谢"。贺卡似乎不再那么重要，而且我也想当然地认为情人节礼物总会在那儿。在课桌上放"信箱"的日子早已远去，我也已经把希望和梦想都寄托于收到"白马王子"的卡片和礼物上，因此"爱你的爸爸"似乎已经无法满足我了。

如果那时父亲知道自己已经被取代，他也会装作若无其事。如果他感觉到我因为没有属于自己的情人节而感到失望，他就会格外努力地营造一种欢快的氛围，会多拥抱我一下或是设法做一些能让我这一天过得开心一些的事。

后来我搬到乡下居住，糖果和贺卡也转由邮政局送达。连续十年，父亲给我寄的礼物从不会迟到——就像八年前的那个情人节父亲送给我的贺卡一样准时，只是那张贺卡上的地址是我母亲的笔迹。

这种贺卡就是勤工俭学的孩子装在低廉的储物盒里，挨家挨户推销的那种，就是那种你经常从祖母或年迈的姑妈那儿收到的贺卡，或者像这次一样，来自弥留的父亲。这种贺卡让你哽咽欲泣，然后潸然泪下，因为你知道那个人已经无法外出去购买一张真正的情人节贺卡了。这张贺卡传递的信息就是，这将是你最后一次从他那儿收到情人节礼物了。

卡片的封面是一张郁金香的照片，里面是母亲打印的"情人节快乐"的字样，下面则是父亲难以辨认的字迹"爱你的爸爸"。

父亲送我的这张贺卡如今仍保存在我的记事板上。它时刻让我想起父亲是多么与众不同，让我知道父亲终其一生都在通过宽容、理解和尽力向所有人传递幸福来传承着一种爱的传统，这些对于我来说都非常重要。

这些将永不消逝。父亲永远都是我的"情人"，这份记忆我也将永远铭记在心。

elaborate

释 [ɪ'læbərət] *a.* 精心制作的；复杂的
[ɪ'læbəreɪt] *v.* 详述；详细制定

chitchat ['tʃɪttʃæt]

释 *n.* 闲谈，聊天

valentine ['væləntaɪn]

释 *n.* 情人；情人节贺卡

recollection [ˌrekə'lekʃn]

释 *n.* 回忆；记忆力；回想起来的事物

decorate ['dekəreɪt]

释 *v.* 装饰；布置

usher ['ʌʃə(r)]

释 *n.* 领座员 *v.* 引领；陪同

bitter-sweet [ˌbɪtə(r)'swiːt]

释 *a.* 又苦又甜的，苦乐参半的

popularity [ˌpɒpju'lærəti]

释 *n.* 受欢迎；普及，流行

tease [tiːz]

释 *v.* 逗乐，戏弄；强求 *n.* 爱取笑他人的人

例 My classmates always *teased* me about my hair since primary school. 从小学开始，我的同学就总是嘲笑我的头发。

wrapped [ræpt]

释 *a.* 有包装的

birthstone ['bɜːθstəʊn]

释 *n.* 诞生石

ruby ['ruːbi]

释 *n.* 红宝石

surpass [sə'pɑːs]

释 *v.* 超越；超过…的界限

perfunctory [pə'fʌŋktəri]

释 *a.* 例行公事般的；敷衍的

grant [grɑːnt]

释 *v.* 同意，准许；让与

用 take sb./sth. for granted 认为…理所当然

例 The bank finally granted me a £500 loan. 银行终于同意给我贷款500英镑。

rural ['rʊərəl]

释 *a.* 乡村的，农村的；田园的

relegate ['relɪgeɪt]

释 *v.* 把…移交给；降级，降职

handwriting ['hændraɪtɪŋ]

释 *n.* 笔迹；书法

assortment [ə'sɔːtmənt]

释 *n.* 各色俱备之物；分类

signal ['sɪgnəl]

释 *n.* 信号 *v.* (向…)发信号；标志着 *a.* 显著的

tulip ['tjuːlɪp]

释 *n.* 郁金香

scrawl [skrɔːl]

释 *v.* 潦草地写；乱涂

legible ['ledʒəbl]

释 *a.* (印刷或字迹)清楚的；易读的

例 The translator translated the ancient Chinese works into *legible* English. 译者把这些中国古代著作译成了通俗易懂的英语。

bulletin ['bʊlətɪn]

释 *n.* 布告；公告；学报
用 bulletin board 布告牌

reminder [rɪ'maɪndə(r)]

释 *n.* 提醒的事物；暗示

generosity [ˌdʒenə'rɒsəti]

释 *n.* 慷慨或宽容的行为；慷慨，大方；宽容

家人之间

ancestry ['ænsestri] *n.* 家世；血统

authoritative [ɔː'θɒrətətɪv] *a.* 有权威的；可信的；专断的

babysitter ['beɪbisɪtə(r)] *n.* 代人照顾婴儿者；临时保姆

commitment [kə'mɪtmənt] *n.* 承诺，保证；承担的义务

contradictory [ˌkɒntrə'dɪktəri] *a.* 反对的；矛盾的

guardian ['gɑːdiən] *n.* 护卫者；监护人

kindergarten ['kɪndəgɑːtn] *n.* 幼儿园

obstruction [əb'strʌkʃn] *n.* 障碍；阻碍

partiality [ˌpɑːʃi'æləti] *n.* 偏袒，偏心

puckish ['pʌkɪʃ] *a.* 恶作剧的；胡闹的；淘气的

rational ['ræʃnəl] *a.* 理性的；合理的

rebuke [rɪ'bjuːk] *v./n.* 指责，训斥

repudiate [rɪ'pjuːdieɪt] *v.* 脱离关系；批判

trifle ['traɪfl] *n.* 少量；琐事

We must accept finite disappointment, but we must never lose infinite hope.　　　　　　—Martin Luther King

我们必须接受失望，因为它是有限的，但千万不可失去希望，因为它是无穷的。　　　　——马丁·路德·金

Passage 42

That "Other Woman" in My Life

After 22 years of marriage, I've discovered the secret to keep love and intimacy alive in my relationship with my wife, Peggy: I started dating another woman.

The "other woman" my wife was encouraging me to date is my mother, a 72-year-old widow who has lived alone since my father died 20 years ago. Right after his death, I moved 2,500 miles away to California and started my own family and career. When I moved back near my hometown six years ago, I promised myself that I would spend more time with Mom. But with the demands of my job and three kids, I never got around to seeing her much beyond family get-togethers and holidays.

She was surprised and suspicious, then, when I called and suggested the two of us go out to dinner and a movie. "What's wrong?" she asked. My mother thinks anything out of the ordinary signals bad news. "I thought it would be nice to spend some time with you," I said. "Just the two of us." "I'd like that a lot," she replied.

As I drove to her house, I actually had a case of jitters. What would we talk about? What if she didn't like the restaurant I chose?

When I pulled into her driveway, she was waiting by the door with her coat on. Her hair was curled, and she was smiling. "I told my lady friends I was going out with my son, and they were all impressed," she said as she got into my car. "They can't wait to hear about our evening."

We didn't go anywhere fancy, just a neighborhood place where we could talk. My mother clutched my arm, half out of affection and half to help her negotiate the restaurant steps. Since her eyes now see only large shapes and shadows, I had to read the menu for both of us. Halfway through reciting the menu, I glanced up and saw Mom looking at me, a wistful smile on her lips. "I used to be the menu reader when you were little," she said. I understood what she was saying. From caregiver to cared-for, from cared-for to caregiver, our relationship had come in full circle. "Then it's time for you to relax and let me return the favor," I said. We had a nice talk over dinner. Nothing worth-shattering, just catching up with each other's lives. We talked for so long that we missed the movie. "I'll go out with you again," my mother said as I dropped her off, "but only if you let me buy dinner next time." I agreed.

"How was your date?" my wife asked when I got home that evening. "Nice...nicer than I thought it would be," I said. She smiled her told-you-so smile.

Mom and I go out for dinner a couple of times a month. Sometimes we take in a movie, but mostly we talk. I tell her about my **trials** at work and **brag** about the kids and Peggy. Mom fills me in on family **gossip** and tells me about her past. Now I know what it was like for her to work in a factory during World War II. I know how she met my father there, and how they nurtured a **trolley**-car **courtship** through those difficult times. I can't get enough of these stories. They are important to me, a part of my history. We also talk about the future. Because of health problems, my mother worries about the days ahead. "I have so many things to do," she told me once. "I need to be there while my grandchildren grow up. I don't want to miss any of it."

I tend to fill my **calendar** to the brim as I struggle to fit family, career and friendships into my life. I often complain about how quickly time flies. Spending time with my mom has taught me the importance of slowing down.

译 文

我生命中的"另一个女人"

结婚22年后,我发现了同妻子佩吉保持爱火不熄、亲密无间的方法,那就是去和另一个女人约会。

我妻子鼓励我去与之约会的"另一个女人"就是我母亲。她是一位72岁的寡妇,自20年前我父亲去世后,就一直一个人住。父亲刚去世不久,我就搬到了离家2500英里(约762米)以外的加利福尼亚州成家立业。6年前我搬回离老家不远的地方,当时我就向自己保证要多花些时间陪妈妈。但由于工作繁忙,同时又要照顾3个孩子,所以除了家庭聚会和节假日外,我很少有时间去看望她。

因此当我打电话给她,约她单独和我出去吃饭、看电影时,她感到既惊讶又疑惑。"你这是怎么了?"她问。母亲会把任何与平常不一样的举动都看作是坏消息的信号。"我想如果能与您共度一段时光的话会很愉快。"我说,"就我们俩。"她回答说:"那太好了。"

当我驾车驶向母亲的住所时,实际上心里有些忐忑不安。我们该谈些什么呢?如果她不喜欢我选的餐厅怎么办?

当我驶进母亲家的车道时,她已经穿好外套等在门口了。她烫了头发,脸上带着笑容。"我告诉我的女性朋友们我要去和儿子约会,她们都很感动。"母亲边说边上了我的车,"她们急切地想知道我们今晚的情况。"

我们没有去高档的餐厅，只在附近找了一个方便聊天的地方。母亲紧紧地挽着我的胳膊，这既是因为想和我亲近一些，也是因为这样在上餐馆的台阶时会比较容易。由于她的眼睛现在只能看到东西的大概轮廓和影子，因此我得把菜单读出来方便我们点菜。当我念到一半时，抬头瞥见母亲正注视着我，嘴角泛着沉思的微笑。"在你小的时候我总是念菜单给你听。"她说。我理解母亲的意思。她已从关爱者变为受照顾者，而我则从受照顾者变成了关爱者，我们之间的角色互换了。"现在轮到你轻松一下了，让我来照顾你。"我说。我们边吃着饭边聊天，十分愉快。我们也没聊什么特别的事，只是谈谈彼此的生活状况。我们谈得太尽兴，连电影都错过了。当我送母亲回到家时，她说："下次我们再约会，但必须让我请客。"我同意了。

"你的约会怎么样？"那天晚上回到家时，妻子问我。"很好……比我想象得要好。"我说。她带着"我早就料到了"的神情笑了。

从此我和母亲每个月都要外出约会几次并共进晚餐。有时我们也会去看电影，但大部分时间都是聊天。我告诉她工作中的烦心事，也向她夸耀佩吉和孩子们。她对我讲了许多家长里短的事，也告诉了我一些她过去的经历。现在，我了解了二战期间她在一家工厂里做工的情况，也知道了她在那里如何与父亲相识，以及在那段艰苦的岁月里，他们如何在有轨电车上经营一段恋爱的故事。这些故事我怎么也听不够，因为它们对我来说很重要，是我个人经历的一部分。我们也会谈论未来。因为健康状况，母亲担心今后的日子。有一次她这样对我说："我还有好多事情要做呢。我要看着孙子孙女们长大。我不想错过任何事情。"

我总是忙着应对家庭、事业和朋友关系等各种事情，将自己的日程表排得满满的，并且还经常抱怨时光飞逝。而与母亲共度时光却让我明白了将生活节奏放慢的重要性。

单词记事本

intimacy   ['ɪntɪməsi]
释 *n.* 亲切，亲密；熟悉

date   [deɪt]
释 *n.* 日期；约会 *v.* 给…注明日期；追溯(到)；与…约会
用 out of date 过时的，不用的；to date 迄今为止；up to date 最新的；现代的

widow   ['wɪdəu]
释 *n.* 寡妇 *v.* 使成为寡妇

promise   ['prɒmɪs]
释 *v.* 允诺；有…可能 *n.* 承诺；可能性

jitters   ['dʒɪtəz]
释 *n.* 紧张不安

driveway   ['draɪvweɪ]
释 *n.* 车道

impress   [ɪm'pres]
释 *v.* 给…留下深刻印象，打动；使铭记；压印

用 impress on 使铭记；使印象深刻
例 I was deeply *impressed* by the hostess' hospitality and enjoyed the dinner party very much. 女主人的热情好客给我留下了深刻的印象；我十分享受这个晚宴。

fancy ['fænsi]
释 v. 想象；想要；喜爱 n. 想象力；渴望，喜爱 a. 悦目的，可口的；精选的，高档的
用 take a fancy to 喜欢上，爱上；fancy doing sth. 喜欢做某事

affection [ə'fekʃn]
释 n. 喜爱；钟爱；爱情

negotiate [nɪ'ɡəʊʃieɪt]
释 v. 商议，谈判；顺利通过

wistful ['wɪstfl]
释 a. 渴望的；沉思的；向往的

caregiver ['keəɡɪvə(r)]
释 n. 照料者；护理者

cared-for ['keədfɔː(r)]
释 n. 受关怀者

shatter ['ʃætə(r)]
释 v. (使)粉碎；(使)损坏；使震惊

trial ['traɪəl]
释 n. 审判；试用；烦恼的事情 a. 试验性的
用 by trial and error 反复试验，不断摸索
例 These drugs have hitherto been the most generally used in clinical *trials*. 迄今为止，这些药品是临床试验中最常用的。

brag [bræɡ]
释 v./n. 吹嘘，夸耀；自夸

gossip ['ɡɒsɪp]
释 n. 流言蜚语；闲话 v. 传播流言蜚语
例 Why do we need celebrities? In effect, the media create celebrities to satisfy our primitive need for *gossip*. 为什么我们需要名人？实际上，媒体创造名人是为了满足我们对说闲语的原始需求。

trolley ['trɒli]
释 n. 手推车；电车

courtship ['kɔːtʃɪp]
释 n. 求爱，恋爱；求爱期

calendar ['kælɪndə(r)]
释 n. 日历，月历；日程表
用 lunar calendar 阴历

💡 单词家族

亲子相处

content [kən'tent] a. 满意的 v. 使满意 ['kɒntent] n. 满意；[pl.]内容
delight [dɪ'laɪt] n. 高兴，喜悦 v. (使)高兴
indulgence [ɪn'dʌldʒəns] n. 放纵；纵容；嗜好
maternal [mə'tɜːnl] a. 母亲的；母性的

maternity [mə'tɜːnəti] n. 母性；母道
misgiving [ˌmɪs'ɡɪvɪŋ] n. 担忧，不安
parental [pə'rentl] a. 父的；母的；父母(般)的
reproach [rɪ'prəʊtʃ] v. 责备
scold [skəʊld] v. 责骂，斥责

Passage 43

Helicopter Moms vs. Free-Range Kids

Would you let your fourth-grader ride public transportation without an adult? Probably not. Still, when Lenore Skenazy, a columnist for *The New York Sun*, wrote about letting her son take the subway alone to get back to her Manhattan home from a department store on the Upper East Side, she didn't expect to get hit with a wave of criticism from readers.

"Long story short: My son got home, overjoyed with independence," Skenazy wrote on April 4 in *The New York Sun*. "Long story longer: Half the people I've told this episode to now want to turn me in for child abuse. As if keeping kids under lock and key and cell phone and careful watch is the right way to rear kids. It's not. It's debilitating—for us and for them."

Online message boards were soon full of people both applauding and condemning Skenazy's decision to let her son go it alone. She wound up defending herself on CNN (accompanied by her son) and on popular blogs like *The Huffington Post*, where her follow-up piece was ironically headlined "More From America's Worst Mom".

From the "she's an irresponsible mother" camp came: "Shame on you for being so careless about his safety," in Comments on *The Huffington Post*. And there was this from a mother of four: "How would you have felt if he didn't come home?" But Skenazy got a lot of support, too, with women and men writing in with stories about how they were allowed to take trips all by themselves at seven or eight. She also got heaps of praise for bucking the "helicopter parent" trend: "Good for this Mom," one commenter wrote on *The Huffington Post*. "This is a much-needed reality check."

Last week, encouraged by all the attention, Skenazy started her own blog—Free Range Kids—promoting the idea that modern children need some of the same independence that her generation had. In the good old days nine-year-old baby boomers rode their bikes to school, walked to the store, took buses—and even subways—all by themselves. Her blog, she says, is dedicated to sensible parenting. "At Free Range Kids, we believe in safe kids. We believe in car seats and safety belts. We do NOT believe that every time school-age children go outside, they need a security guard."

So why are some parents so nervous about letting their children out of their sight? Are cities and towns less safe and kids more vulnerable to crimes like child kidnap and sexual abuse than they were in previous generations?

Not exactly. New York City, for instance, is safer than it's ever been; it's ranked 136th in crime among all American cities. Nationwide, stranger kidnaps are extremely rare; there's a one-in-a-million chance a child will be taken by a stranger, according to the Justice Department. And 90 percent of sexual abuse cases are committed by someone the child knows. Mortality rates from all causes, including disease and accidents, for American children are lower now than they were 25 years ago.

Then there's the whole question of whether modern parents are more watchful and nervous about safety than previous generations. Yes, some are. Part of the problem is that with wall-to-wall Internet and cable news, every missing child case gets so much airtime that it's not surprising even normal parental anxiety can be amplified. And many middle-class parents have gotten used to managing their children's time and shuttling them to various enriching activities, so the idea of letting them out on their own can seem like a risk.

For those parents who wonder how and when they should start allowing their kids more freedom, there's no clear-cut answer. Child experts discourage a one-size-fits-all approach to parenting. What's right for Skenazy's nine-year-old could be inappropriate for another one. It all depends on developmental issues, maturity, and the psychological and emotional makeup of that child. Several factors must be taken into account, says Gallagher. "The ability to follow parent guidelines, the child's level of comfort in handling such situations, and a child's general judgment should be weighed."

Gallagher agrees with Skenazy that many nine-year-olds are ready for independence like taking public transportation alone. "At certain times of the day, on certain routes, the subways are generally safe for these children."

And for those who like the idea of free-range kids but still struggle with their inner helicopter parent, there may be a middle way. A new generation of GPS cell phones with tracking software make it easier than ever to follow a child's every movement via the Internet—without seeming to interfere or hover. Of course, when they go to college, they might start objecting to being monitored as they're on parole.

"直升机妈妈"与自由放养的孩子

你会让自己读四年级的孩子在没有大人陪同的情况下独自乘坐公共交通工具吗？你可能不会。尽管如此，当莉诺·斯肯纳兹——《纽约太阳报》的一位专栏作家，在文章中写道她让自己的儿子独自乘坐地铁从上东区的百货商店回到位于曼哈顿的家时，她没料到会受到读者如潮的批评。

斯肯纳兹在4月4日的《纽约太阳报》上写道："长话短说：我儿子到家后，为自己的独立感到非常高兴。长话长说：当我把这件事告诉人们之后，到现在为止有一半的人认为我虐待儿童而要把我告上法庭。就好像只有把孩子锁在屋里、给他配上手机、小心看护才是培养孩子的正确做法。然而并非如此。这只会使我们和孩子都变得脆弱。"

很快，网络留言板上就充斥着人们对斯肯纳兹让孩子独自外出这一决定褒贬不一的评论。斯肯纳兹最后在CNN（由儿子陪伴）和《赫芬顿邮报》等受欢迎的博客上为自己进行了辩护，而对她的后续报道却被讥讽地冠以"来自美国最糟糕妈妈的更多消息"的标题。

在《赫芬顿邮报》的评论中，有一条来自"她是个不负责任的母亲"阵营的评论："如此忽视孩子的安全，你应该感到羞耻。"还有一条来自有着四个孩子的母亲的评论："如果孩子没有回家，你会是什么样的感受？"但是斯肯纳兹也得到了很多支持。支持者们通过写故事的方式告诉人们他们的父母是如何允许他们在七八岁的时候独自出行的。她也因反对"直升机妈妈"趋势而广受赞誉。有一位评论者在《赫芬顿邮报》上写道："这位妈妈真棒，这是一种我们非常需要的对现实的审视。"

上周，在所有关注者的鼓励下，斯肯纳兹开始写她自己的博客——"放养孩子"来推广她的观点：这一代的孩子同样需要一些上一代人所拥有的独立。在过去那个美好的时代，婴儿潮时期出生的九岁大的孩子都是独自一人骑着自行车去学校，步行去商店，乘坐公交车甚至地铁。她说，她的博客专门用于推广明智的抚养方式。"在'放养孩子'这个博客中，我们相信孩子的安全。我们相信汽车座椅和安全带。我们不相信学龄孩子每次外出都需要一位安保人员。"

那么，为什么有的父母一让孩子离开自己的视线就如此紧张呢？是因为城镇不够安全，孩子比上几代人更易于受到像绑架孩童、性虐待这样的犯罪行为的伤害吗？

也不尽然。比如，纽约市现在就比以往更安全。在美国所有的城市中，纽约的犯罪率排在第136位。从全国来看，陌生人绑架儿童的案件极少发生。来自司法部门的信息显示，孩子被陌生人拐走的机会只有百万分之一。

而且90%的性虐待案件都是由孩子认识的人所犯的。对美国儿童来说，现在各种原因引起的死亡率，包括疾病、事故，都比25年前低。

现在总的问题是现代的父母是否比上几代人对孩子的安全更加小心、更加紧张。的确，有些人是这样的。部分问题在于，随着网络的广泛应用和有线电视新闻的频频出现，每一起儿童失踪案都得到非常充分的报道，因此正常的为人父母的焦虑被放大就不足为奇了。同时，许多中产阶级父母已经习惯管理自己孩子的时间，让他们在各种丰富的活动之间穿梭，所以让孩子单独出去的观点看起来似乎是一种冒险。

对于那些想知道从什么时候开始、怎样开始给孩子更多自由空间的家长来说，还没有明确的答案。儿童专家不赞成使用"一刀切"的方法来教育孩子。对斯肯纳兹的九岁孩子合适的方法不一定就适用于其他孩子。这完全取决于孩子自身的发育情况、成熟度和心理及情感状况。加拉格尔说，有几个因素必须考虑进去。"孩子听从父母教导的能力、孩子处理类似情况的舒适程度和孩子的一般判断力也需要权衡"。

加拉格尔赞成斯肯纳兹的观点，即许多九岁的孩子已经具备单独乘坐公共交通工具这样的独立能力。"在一天当中的某段时间和某些线路，地铁对于这些孩子来说通常是安全的。"

对于那些赞成自由放养孩子的观点而内心仍在挣扎是否做"直升机妈妈"的人来说，可能还有个折中的方法。新一代装有跟踪软件的GPS手机可以通过网络跟踪孩子的一举一动，这使得看管孩子变得更加容易——而且不会看起来像是干涉或者监督。当然，在孩子读大学后，他们可能会开始反对这种好似假释的监控。

💡 **单词记事本**

columnist ['kɒləmnɪst]
释 n. 专栏作家

abuse
释 [ə'bjuːz] v. 滥用；妄用；虐待；
[ə'bjuːs] n. 滥用；虐待；辱骂
用 abuse of power 滥用权力
例 What he did was an *abuse* of his position as a manager. 他滥用了他作为经理的职权。

debilitate [dɪ'bɪlɪteɪt]
释 v. 使衰弱，使虚弱

applaud [ə'plɔːd]
释 v. 给…鼓掌；称赞，赞成
用 applaud for 称赞
例 The audience rose to *applaud* the actors. 观众起立为演员鼓掌。

condemn [kən'dem]
释 v. 声讨，极力谴责；判刑

defend [dɪ'fend]
释 v. 保卫；为…辩护；(论文等)答辩
用 defend against 防卫

例 Troops have been sent to *defend* the people. 军队被派去保卫人民。

accompany ['ə'kʌmpəni]
释 v. 陪伴；伴随；为…伴奏

ironically [aɪ'rɒnɪkli]
释 ad. 具有讽刺意味地

headline ['hedlaɪn]
释 n. 标题；[pl.]新闻提要 v. 给…加标题
用 headline news 标题新闻

irresponsible [ˌɪrɪ'spɒnsəbl]
释 a. 不负责任的，没有责任感的

careless ['keələs]
释 a. 粗心的，大意的；由粗心引起的

praise [preɪz]
释 v. 赞扬，表扬 n. 赞美，赞扬；崇拜
用 in praise of 赞扬
例 We have nothing but *praise* for the way he handled the emergency. 我们唯有对他处理紧急情况的方式表示赞扬。

dedicate ['dedɪkeɪt]
释 v. 奉献，献身；题词；专门用于

sensible ['sensəbl]
释 a. 有感觉的；理智的，明智的

kidnap ['kɪdnæp]
释 n. 诱拐，绑架，劫持

previous ['priːviəs]
释 a. (时间或顺序上)先的，前的；过早的
用 previous page 上一页；上级菜单
例 No *previous* experience is necessary for the position of assistance. 助理职位不需要之前有工作经验。

rank [ræŋk]
释 n. 等级；军衔 v. 将…分等级；居某地位

watchful ['wɒtʃfl]
释 a. 留心的，注意的，警惕的

cable ['keɪbl]
释 n. 缆绳；电缆；(海底)电报 v. 给…发电报

amplify ['æmplɪfaɪ]
释 v. 放大，增强；详述

enrich [ɪn'rɪtʃ]
释 v. 使丰富；使富裕；使肥沃
用 enrich oneself 充实自我
例 The study of dance has *enriched* my life. 学习舞蹈丰富了我的生活。

guideline ['gaɪdlaɪn]
释 n. 指导方针，准则

comfort ['kʌmfət]
释 n. 舒适；安慰 v. 使舒适；安慰

weigh [weɪ]
释 v. 称重；认真考虑，衡量；被认为重要

route [ruːt]
释 n. 路线，路程

inner ['ɪnə(r)]
释 a. 内部的；内心的
用 inner peace 内心的平静
例 An *inner* voice told him to follow his dream. 内心的声音告诉他要追随自己的梦想。

track [træk]
释 n. 小路；跑道；(铁路)轨道；踪迹 v. 跟踪；循路而行；留下足迹

via ['vaɪə; 'viːə]
释 prep. 经由；通过

hover ['hɒvə(r)]
释 v. (鸟等)翱翔；留在近旁；徘徊；犹豫

object
释 ['ɒbdʒɪkt] n. 物体；对象；目标；宾语 [əb'dʒekt] v. 反对，不赞成
用 object to 反对
例 My sole *object* in life is to become a writer. 我唯一的人生目标是成为一名作家。

monitor ['mɒnɪtə(r)]

释 n. 监控器，监视屏；班长 v. 监控；检测

parole [pə'rəʊl]

释 n. 假释；(为获假释而作刑满前不逃跑或不犯罪的)誓言

💡 单词家族

家庭教育

bookcase ['bʊkkeɪs] n. 书架，书柜

caprice [kə'priːs] n. 反复无常，任性

disenchant [ˌdɪsɪn'tʃɑːnt] v. 使清醒

disport [dɪ'spɔːt] v. 玩耍，嬉戏

engross [ɪn'ɡrəʊs] v. 使全神贯注

excusable [ɪk'skjuːzəbl] a. 可原谅的；可容许的

grumpy ['ɡrʌmpi] a. 脾气暴躁的

halcyon ['hælsɪən] a. 平静的；愉快的

homily ['hɒməli] n. 令人讨厌的说教

impassioned [ɪm'pæʃnd] a. 充满激情的；热烈的

impudent ['ɪmpjədənt] a. 鲁莽的；无礼的，不尊重的

indoctrinate [ɪn'dɒktrɪneɪt] v. 教导；灌输思想

irk [ɜːk] v. 使苦恼，使厌烦

literacy ['lɪtərəsi] n. 读写能力；有教养

nonpareil [ˌnɒnpə'reɪl] a. 无可匹敌的

odious ['əʊdiəs] a. 可憎的，讨厌的

provident ['prɒvɪdənt] a. 深谋远虑的；节俭的

puberty ['pjuːbəti] n. 青春期

pusillanimous [ˌpjuːsɪ'lænɪməs] a. 胆小的，怯懦的

recalcitrant [rɪ'kælsɪtrənt] a. 不守纪律的；不服从的

rectitude ['rektɪtjuːd] n. 诚实，正直

reorient [ˌriː'ɔːrient] v. 再调整；(使)适应

rollicking ['rɒlɪkɪŋ] a. 欢闹的

stalwart ['stɔːlwət] a. 健壮的；坚定的

staunch [stɔːntʃ] a. 坚定的；忠诚的

tutelage ['tjuːtəlɪdʒ] n. 监护；指导

tutorial [tjuː'tɔːriəl] a. 家庭教师的；辅导的

unattended [ˌʌnə'tendɪd] a. 无人照管的；无人出席的

unrepentant [ˌʌnrɪ'pentənt] a. 不悔悟的

veracious [və'reɪʃəs] a. 诚实的；真实的

Passage 44

That's What Friends Do

Jack **tossed** the papers on my desk, his **eyebrows knitting** into a straight line as he glared at me.

"What's wrong?" I asked.

He **jabbed** a finger at the **proposal**. "Next time you want to change anything, ask me first," he said, turning on his heels and leaving me **stewing** in anger.

How he dare treat me like that, I thought. I had changed one long sentence, and corrected grammar—something I thought I was paid to do.

It's not that I hadn't been warned. The other women, who had served in my place before me, called him names I couldn't repeat. One co-worker took me aside the first day. "He's personally responsible for two different secretaries leaving the firm," she **whispered**.

As the weeks went by, I grew to **despise** Jack. It was against everything I believed in—turn the other cheek and love your enemies. But Jack quickly **slapped** a **verbal insult** on any cheek turned his way. I prayed about it, but to be honest, I wanted to put him in his place, not to love him.

One day, another of his **episodes** left me in tears. I stormed into his office, prepared to lose my job if needed, but not before I let the man know how I felt. I opened the door and Jack glanced up.

"What?" he said **abruptly**.

Suddenly I knew what I had to do. After all, he **deserved** it.

I sat across from him. "Jack, the way you've been treating me is wrong. I've never had anyone speak to me that way. As a professional, it's wrong, and it's wrong for me to allow it to continue," I said.

Jack **snickered** nervously and leaned back in his chair. I closed my eyes **briefly**. God help me, I prayed.

"I want to make you a promise. I will be a friend," I said. "I will treat you as you deserve to be treated, with respect and kindness. You deserve that," I said. "Everybody does." I slipped out of the chair and closed the door behind me.

Jack avoided me the rest of the week. Proposals, **specs** and letters appeared on my desk while I was at lunch, and the corrected versions were not seen again. I brought cookies to the office one day and left a batch on Jack's desk. Another day I left a note. "Hope your day is going great!" it read.

Over the next few weeks, Jack **reappeared**. He was **reserved**, but there were no other episodes. Co-workers **cornered** me in the break room.

"Guess you got to Jack," they said. "You must have told him off good." I shook my head.

"Jack and I are becoming friends," I said in faith. I refused to talk about him. Every time I saw Jack in the hall, I smiled at him.

After all, that's what friends do.

One year after our "talk", I discovered I had breast cancer. I was 32, the mother of three beautiful young children, and scared. The cancer had **metastasized** to my **lymph** nodes and the statistics were not great for long-term **survival**. After surgery, I was visited by friends and loved ones who tried to find the right words to say. No one knew what to say. Many said the wrong things. Others wept, and I tried to encourage them. I **clung** to hope.

The last day of my hospital stay, the door darkened and Jack stood **awkwardly** on the threshold. I waved him in with a smile and he walked over to my bed and, without a word, placed a **bundle** beside me. Inside laid several **bulbs**.

"Tulips," he said.

I smiled, not understanding.

He cleared his throat. "If you plant them when you get home, they'll come up next spring," he **shuffled** his feet. "I just wanted you to know that I think you'll be there to see them when they come up."

Tears clouded my eyes and I reached out my hand.

"Thank you," I whispered.

Jack grasped my hand and **gruffly** replied, "You're welcome. You can't see it now, but next spring you'll see the colors I picked out for you." He turned and left without a word.

I have seen those red and white **striped** tulips push through the soil every spring for over ten years now. In fact, this September the doctor will declare me **cured**. I've seen my children graduate from high school and enter college.

In a moment when I prayed for just the right word, a man with very few words said all the right things.

After all, that's what friends do.

 译文

这就是朋友所为

杰克把文件扔到我桌上，他的眉毛皱成了一条直线，眼睛瞪着我。

"怎么了？"我问他。

他用一根手指戳着提案说："下次你要改动什么，事先问我一声。"说完转身离去，留下我独自一人生闷气。

我在想他怎么能如此对待我。我改动了一个长句子，改正了其中的语法错误——我认为既然公司给我发薪水我就应该这么做。

曾经也有人提醒过我。在我之前担任此职的女士曾用很难听的话咒骂他。在我上班的第一天就有一位同事把我叫到一旁，悄悄告诉我："之前有两个秘书离开公司都是因为他。"

几周过去后，我也逐渐开始鄙视杰克。这有悖于我的人生信条——我一直坚信即使左脸被打，也要把右脸转过去，要爱你的敌人。但是杰克却对转向他的脸恶语相向。我为此祈祷，不过老实说，我只希望能让他有所收敛，而不是爱他。

一天，他又发作了一次，并且把我弄哭了。我气冲冲地冲进他的办公室，并作好了有可能丢掉工作的心理准备，不过在离开前我必须让这家伙知道我的感受。我推开门，杰克抬头瞥了一眼。

"怎么了？"他生硬地说。

突然，我知道了我应该怎么做。毕竟，这是他自找的。

我在他对面坐下，说道："杰克，你一直以来对待我的方式都是错误的。从来没有人那样跟我说过话。作为一名职场人士，这样做是不对的，而且我不会允许这样的事情再继续下去。"

杰克紧张地笑了一下，向后靠在椅背上。我飞快地闭了一下眼睛，祈祷道："上帝保佑。"

"我向你承诺，我会成为你的朋友。"我说，"我会尊重并善待你，因为你应该受到这样的对待。每个人都应该被这样对待。"然后我起身离开，随手带上了身后的屋门。

那一周的剩下几天里，杰克都躲着我。提案、说明书和信件统统都在我去吃午餐的时候放在了我的桌上，那些更改过的版本也没有再出现。一天，我带了曲奇饼干到办公室，放了几块在杰克的桌上。又有一天，我给他留了一张便条，上面写着："愿你今天一切顺利！"

又过了几周，杰克重新出现了。他话不多，不过再也没有什么不愉快的事情发生。在休息室里，同事们团团围住了我。

"想必你已经制服了杰克。"他们说，"你一定好好地教训了他一顿吧。"而我摇了摇头。

"我和杰克正在成为朋友。"我认真地说，拒绝谈论与他有关的事情。每次在大厅见到他，我都会对他微笑。

毕竟，朋友应当这样。

在我们那次"谈话"的一年之后，我发现自己患上了乳腺癌。当时我32岁，有3个年纪尚幼的漂亮孩子，因此我很害怕。癌症转移到了淋巴结，诊断显示我的日子所剩无几。手术过后，亲朋好友来看我。他们都试图找些话来安慰我，但又不知道该说什么才好。许多人说了不合适的话，有些人则只会哭泣，而我倒尽力安慰他们。我紧紧抓着最后一丝希望。

在我住院的最后一天，我感到病房门口的光线暗了下来，原来杰克正局促不安地站在门口。我笑着向他招手。他走到我的床边，一句话也没有说，而是将一束东西放在我身旁，里面包着的是几棵植物的球茎。

"这是郁金香。"他说。

我笑了笑，但不明白他是什么意思。

他清了清嗓子，说："你回家后把它们种起来，明年春天就会开花。"他挪了挪脚，接着说："我只是想让你知道，我觉得你能看到它们开花。"

泪水模糊了我的双眼，我伸出手来。

"谢谢你。"我低声说。

杰克抓住我的手，粗声粗气地说："不用谢。虽然现在还看不到，不过等到明年春天你就会看到我给你选了哪些颜色。"然后他转身离去，一句话也没说。

到如今已过去了十余年，每年春天我都会看到那些红白相间的郁金香破土而出的情景。事实上，今年九月医生就会宣布我的癌症已经痊愈，而我也亲眼看着我的孩子们高中毕业、升入了大学。

在我祈祷大家说些我需要的恰当的话语时，那位寡言少语的男士做到了。

毕竟，这就是朋友所为。

💡 单词记事本

toss [tɒs]
释 v. 扔；(使)摇摆，颠簸；辗转反侧
n. 扔，掷
用 win/lose the toss 猜中/猜错掷硬币的结果

eyebrow ['aɪbraʊ]
释 n. 眉毛

knit [nɪt]
释 v. 编结；皱(眉)

jab [dʒæb]
释 v. 戳；猛刺 n. 刺，戳

proposal [prə'pəʊzl]
释 n. 提案，建议；求婚

stew [stjuː]
释 v. 焖，炖；思考；担忧

whisper ['wɪspə(r)]
释 v. 低声说出，耳语；飒飒地响 n. 私语；耳语

despise [dɪ'spaɪz]

释 v. 鄙视，看不起

例 Practice is as important as theory, so it's wrong to value the latter and *despise* the former. 实践与理论一样重要，因此重理论而轻实践的做法是错误的。

slap [slæp]

释 v./n. 捆；拍击；侮辱

verbal ['vɜːbl]

释 a. 口头的；言语的；动词的

insult

释 [ɪn'sʌlt] v. 侮辱；无礼
['ɪnsʌlt] n. 侮辱；损害

episode ['epɪsəʊd]

释 n. 事件；插曲

abruptly [ə'brʌptli]

释 ad. 突然地；唐突地，生硬地

deserve [dɪ'zɜːv]

释 v. 应得，应受；值得

用 deserve well/ill of sb. 应受到某人好的/坏的待遇

snicker ['snɪkə(r)]

释 v./n. 窃笑，暗笑

briefly ['briːfli]

释 ad. 短时间地；简要地

spec [spek]

释 n. (=specification)说明书

reappear [ˌriːə'pɪə(r)]

释 v. 再出现；再发生

reserved [rɪ'zɜːvd]

释 a. 寡言的，含蓄的，内敛的

corner ['kɔːnə(r)]

释 n. 角落；困境 v. 将…围到角落；将…逼入困境

用 around/round the corner 临近；在附近；cut corners 走捷径；省钱(或人力、时间等)；turn the corner 转危为安

metastasize [mə'tæstəsaɪz]

释 v. 转移；迁徙

lymph [lɪmf]

释 n. 淋巴(液)；血清

survival [sə'vaɪvl]

释 n. 生存；幸存；幸存者，残存物

cling [klɪŋ]

释 v. 紧紧抓住；紧贴；墨守

awkwardly ['ɔːkwədli]

释 ad. 局促不安地；笨拙地

bundle ['bʌndl]

释 n. 捆，束，包；包袱，包裹；巨款 v. 捆，扎；胡乱塞进

bulb [bʌlb]

释 n. 球茎(植物的地下茎)；灯泡

shuffle ['ʃʌfl]

释 v./n. 拖着脚步走；洗牌；搅乱

例 The man *shuffles* through the contents of the drawer and brings out a small pile of photographs. 那个人胡乱翻着抽屉里面的东西，然后拿出了一小摞照片。

gruffly ['grʌfli]

释 ad. 粗暴地；生硬地

striped [straɪpt]

释 a. 有条纹的

cure [kjʊə(r)]

释 v. 治愈；纠正，矫正 n. 治愈；疗法

朋友之间

acquaintance [ə'kweɪntəns] *n.* 认识；了解

alienate ['eɪlɪəneɪt] *v.* 使疏远，离间；转让

antagonist [æn'tægənɪst] *n.* 敌手；对手

collaboration [kə,læbə'reɪʃn] *n.* 合作；勾结

confederacy [kən'fedərəsi] *n.* 联盟；同盟

conversational [,kɒnvə'seɪʃənl] *a.* 对话的；健谈的

egalitarian [i,gælɪ'teərɪən] *n./a.* 平等主义(的)

exemplary [ɪg'zempləri] *a.* 模范的

harmonious [hɑː'məʊnɪəs] *a.* 和谐的；悦耳的

immutable [ɪ'mjuːtəbl] *a.* 不变的

intrinsic [ɪn'trɪnsɪk] *a.* 本质的；固有的

mutual ['mjuːtʃuəl] *a.* 相互的；共同的

pal [pæl] *n.* 朋友，伙伴

slavish ['sleɪvɪʃ] *a.* 卑屈的；盲从的

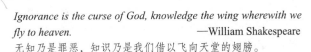

Ignorance is the curse of God, knowledge the wing wherewith we fly to heaven.
　　　　　　　　　　　　　—William Shakespeare

无知乃是罪恶，知识乃是我们借以飞向天堂的翅膀。
　　　　　　　　　　　　　——莎士比亚

Passage 45

Home

A freezing downpour washed the black **asphalt** street in front of the small town bar. I sat gazing into the **watery** darkness, alone as usual. Across the **rain-drenched** roadway was the town park: five acres of grass, giant **elm** trees and, tonight, an ankle-deep covering of cold water.

I had been in that **battered** old pub for half an hour, quietly **nursing** a drink, when my thoughtful stare finally focused on a medium-sized lump in a **grassy puddle** a hundred feet away. For another ten minutes, I looked out through the tear-streaked **windowpane** trying to decide if the lump was an animal or just a wet and **inanimate** something.

The night before, a German **shepherd** looking **mongrel** had come into the bar begging for potato chips. He was **mangy** and starving and just the size of the lump in question. "Why would a dog lie in a cold puddle in the freezing rain?" I asked myself. The answer was simple: either it wasn't a dog, or if it was, he was too weak to get up.

The **shrapnel** wound in my right shoulder ached all the way down to my fingers. I didn't want to go out in that storm. Hey, it wasn't my dog; it wasn't anybody's dog. It was just a **stray** on a cold night in the rain, a lonely drifter. So was I, I thought, as I tossed down what was left of my drink and headed out the door.

He was lying in three inches of water. When I touched him, he didn't move. I thought he was dead. I put my hands around his chest and hoisted him to his feet. He stood unsteadily in the puddle, his head hung like a weight at the end of his neck. Half his body was covered with mange. His **floppy** ears were just hairless pieces of flesh **dotted** with open sores.

"Come on," I said, hoping I wouldn't have to carry his **infected carcass** to shelter. His tail wagged once and he **plodded** weakly after me. I led him to an **alcove** next to the bar, where he lay on the cold **cement** and closed his eyes.

A block away I could see the lights of a late-night convenience store. It was still open. I bought three cans of Alpo and stuffed them into my leather coat. I was wet and ugly and the clerk looked **relieved** as I left. The race-type **exhausts** on my old Harley Davidson **rattled** the windows in the bar as I rode back to it.

The barmaid opened the cans for me and said the dog's name was Shep. She told me he was about a year old and that his owner had gone to Germany and left him on the street. He ate all three cans of dog food with an awe-inspiring singleness of purpose. I wanted to pet him, but he smelled like death and looked even worse. "Good luck," I said. Then I got on my bike and rode away.

The next day I got a job driving a dump truck for a small paving company. As I hauled a load of gravel through the center of town, I saw Shep standing on the sidewalk near the bar. I yelled to him and thought I saw his tail wag. His reaction made me feel good.

After work I bought three more cans of Alpo and a cheeseburger. My new friend and I ate dinner together on the sidewalk. He finished his first.

The next night, when I brought his food, he welcomed me with wild enthusiasm. Now and then, his malnourished legs buckled and he fell to the pavement. Other humans had deserted him and mistreated him, but now he had a friend and his appreciation was more than obvious.

I didn't see him the next day as I hauled load after load up the main street past the bar. I wondered if someone had taken him home.

After work I parked my black Harley on the street and walked down the sidewalk looking for him. I was afraid of what I would find. He was lying on his side in an alley nearby. His tongue hung out in the dirt and only the tip of his tail moved when he saw me.

The local veterinarian was still at his office, so I borrowed a pickup truck from my employer and loaded the limp mongrel into the cab. "Is this your dog?" the vet asked after checking the pitiful specimen that lay helplessly on his examining table.

"No," I said, "he's just a stray."

"He's got the beginnings of distemper," the vet said sadly. "If he doesn't have a home, the kindest thing we can do is put him out of his misery."

I put my hand on the dog's shoulder. His mangy tail thumped weakly against the stainless steel table. I sighed loudly. "He's got a home," I said.

For the next three nights and two days, the dog—I named him Shep—lay on his side in my apartment. My roommate and I spent hours putting water in his mouth and trying to get him to swallow a few scrambled eggs. He couldn't do it, but whenever I touched him, his tail wagged slightly at the very tip.

At about 10:00 a.m. on the third day, I went home to open the apartment for the telephone installer. As I stepped through the door, I was nearly flattened by a jumping, wiggling mass of euphoric mutt. Shep had recovered.

With time, the mangy starving dog that nearly died in my living room grew into an eighty-pound block of solid muscle, with a massive chest and a super thick coat of **shiny** black fur. Many times, when loneliness and depression have nearly gotten the best of me, Shep has returned my favor by showering me with his **unbridled** friendship until I have no choice but to smile and trade my **melancholy** for a fast game of fetch-the-stick.

When I look back, I can see that Shep and I met at the low point of both of our lives. But we aren't lonely drifters anymore. I'd say we've both come home.

译文

家

冰冷的大雨倾盆而下，冲刷着小城酒吧门前漆黑的柏油马路。我像往常一样独自一人坐在那里，凝视着这潮湿的黑夜。被雨水打湿的马路对面是小城的公园：它有着五英亩（约2公顷）的草地、巨大的榆树，在今夜还多了深至脚踝的冷雨。

我已经在那个破旧的酒吧里坐了半个小时，慢条斯理地自斟自饮。我若有所思的目光四处游移，最终锁定在了100英尺（约30米）外那个长满草的水坑里的一团不大不小的东西上。在接下来的10分钟里，我都在透过淌着雨珠的窗玻璃往外看，想分辨出那团东西到底是一只动物，还是只是一个被雨水淋湿的没有生命的东西。

前一天晚上，一条看上去血统不纯的德国牧羊犬跑到酒吧来讨土豆片吃。它又脏又饿，大小跟我心存疑虑的那团湿漉漉的东西差不多。我暗自琢磨：在这样寒冷的雨夜，这条狗为什么躺在冰冷的水坑里呢？答案很简单：要么那不是狗，要么是狗，但肯定虚弱得爬不起来。

我右肩的弹片伤隐隐作痛，疼痛一直传到了手指。我不想冒着暴风雨出去。再说，那既不是我的狗，也不是任何人的狗。那只是一条在寒冷的雨夜中迷路的、孤独的流浪狗。"正如我一样。"我这样想道，于是把剩下的酒一饮而尽，朝门外走去。

它躺在三英寸（约7.62厘米）深的水里。我碰了碰它，没有动静。我想它是冻僵了。我拦腰扶它站了起来。它在水坑里摇摇晃晃，脑袋垂着，仿佛那只是个挂在脖子上的重物。它的半个身子上长满了疥癣，耷拉的耳朵简直就是两片长满了烂疮的没毛的肉片。

"跟我来。"我对它说，希望可以不用抱着它那因感染而变得满目疮痍的躯体去寻找避雨的地方。它的尾巴摇动了一下，然后拖着虚弱的身体跟着我沉重地往前走。我把它带到了酒吧旁边一个凹进去的避雨处之后，它就躺在冰凉的水泥地上，闭上了眼睛。

在相隔一个街区的地方，我看到一家深夜仍在营业的便利店还亮着灯。我买了三罐"爱宝"狗罐头，并把它们塞进了皮衣的口袋。我浑身湿透，样子也很难看，所以当我离开便利店时，店员好像松了口气。当我骑着那辆哈雷·戴维森摩托车回到酒吧时，它那赛车专用的排气管把酒吧玻璃窗震得直响。

酒吧的女招待替我开了罐头，并告诉我这条狗的名字叫谢普，大概一岁。它的主人去了德国，就把它丢在了街上。这条狗很快把三罐罐头全吃光了，专注的程度令人惊叹。我想摸摸它，但它身上发出一股死狗的臭味，样子更是惨不忍睹。我说了句"祝你好运"，然后便跨上摩托车绝尘而去。

第二天，我得到了一份为一家小型筑路公司开自动倾卸卡车的工作。当我拉着一车石子穿过城中心时，看见谢普站在酒吧旁边的人行道上。我朝它大喊，觉得它好像摇了摇尾巴。这个反应让我感觉不错。

下班后，我又买了三罐"爱宝"罐头和一个芝士汉堡包。我和我的新朋友一起坐在人行道上吃起了晚餐。它先吃完了它的那份。

第三天晚上，当我带着食物来找它时，它极度热情地迎接了我。时不时地，它那因为营养不良而无法支撑身体的瘸腿使它跌倒在人行道上。别的人遗弃了它，虐待了它，而现在它有了朋友，因此它对我的感激显而易见。

第四天，当我拉着一车石子沿着主干道经过酒吧时，我没有看见那只狗。我想也许有人把它带回家了。

下班后，我把我那辆黑色哈雷摩托停在街边，沿着人行道找它。我害怕最后找到的结果。在附近的小巷里，我看到谢普侧身躺着。它的舌头耷拉到了泥土里，看见我时，它只是动了动尾巴尖。

当地的兽医还没有下班，于是我从雇主那儿借了辆小卡车，把这只瘸狗放进了驾驶室。当兽医检查完这只躺在桌子上不知所措、令人怜悯的狗以后，问道："这是你的狗吗？"

"不是。"我回答说，"这是条野狗。"

"它已经出现犬热病的前兆了。"兽医难过地说道，"要是它没有家的话，我们能做的最仁慈的做法就是结束它的生命，让它从痛苦中解脱。"

我把手放在它的肩上，它那长着疥癣的尾巴有气无力地摇着，拍打着不锈钢的检查桌。我深深地叹了口气说："它有家。"

随后的两天三夜，谢普（我也这么叫它）就侧卧在我公寓的地板上。我和我的室友花了几个小时给它喂水，试着喂它吃下一点儿炒鸡蛋。尽管它吃不下，但当我每次碰它时，它的尾巴尖都会轻轻地动一下。

到了，第三天上午10点左右，我回家给前来安装电话的人开门。我刚一进门，差点儿被那只欢快地蹦蹦跳跳、扭来扭去的狗扑倒在地。谢普康复了！

渐渐地，原来那只长满疥癣、饥肠辘辘、差点死在我房间里的狗长成了80磅重、有着满身紧实肌肉的家伙。它胸膛结实，长着一身厚实且有光泽的黑毛。有很多次，当孤独和沮丧几乎吞噬了我的整个身心时，谢普都以它那毫无保留的友情来报答我的恩情，直到我不得不将悲伤转为笑容，和它玩"丢棍捡棍"的游戏。

回首往事，我发现当谢普和我相遇时，我们都处在生活的低谷。但现在我们不再是孤单的流浪者了。我想说：我们俩都回家了。

💡 单词记事本

asphalt ['æsfælt]
释 *n.* 沥青，柏油 *v.* 以沥青铺(尤指道路)

watery ['wɔːtəri]
释 *a.* 水的；潮湿的；(指颜色)淡的

rain-drenched [reɪn'drentʃt]
释 *a.* 雨水浸泡的

elm [elm]
释 *n.* 榆树

battered ['bætəd]
释 *a.* 破旧的；磨损的；弄垮的

nurse [nɜːs]
释 *n.* 护士；保姆 *v.* 护理，照顾；慢慢地吃或喝

grassy ['grɑːsi]
释 *a.* 长满草的；草绿色的

puddle ['pʌdl]
释 *n.* 水坑，泥潭

windowpane ['wɪndəupeɪn]
释 *n.* 窗玻璃

inanimate [ɪn'ænɪmət]
释 *a.* 没有生命的；无生气的；单调的
例 In a fable, the *inanimate* objects can talk and think like humans. 在寓言里，没有生命的东西可以像人一样讲话和思考。

shepherd ['ʃepəd]
释 *n.* 牧民；牧羊人；牧羊犬 *v.* 带领；引导

mongrel ['mʌŋgrəl]
释 *n.* 杂种动物；混血儿

mangy ['meɪndʒi]
释 *a.* 患疥癣的；肮脏的；污秽的

shrapnel ['ʃræpnəl]
释 *n.* 弹片

stray [streɪ]
释 *n.* 走失的家畜 *v.* 走失；偏离 *a.* 迷路的；离群的
例 He gave the scraps of food to a *stray* dog. 他把剩饭喂给了流浪狗。

floppy ['flɒpi]
释 *a.* 松软的；下垂的；衰弱的；懒散的
用 floppy disk 软盘

dot [dɒt]
释 *n.* 点 *v.* 打点于；散布于，布满

infected [ɪn'fektɪd]
释 *a.* 受感染的

carcass ['kɑːkəs]
释 *n.* (动物的)尸体；身躯，躯壳；残骸

plod [plɒd]
释 *v.* 沉重缓慢地走；吃力地干

alcove ['ælkəʊv]

释 *n.* 凹室；壁橱

cement [sɪ'ment]

释 *n.* 水泥 *v.* 用水泥铺；巩固；使团结

relieved [rɪ'liːvd]

释 *a.* 宽慰的，放心的，解脱的

exhaust [ɪg'zɔːst]

释 *n.* 排气管；废气 *v.* (使)筋疲力尽；用尽

rattle ['rætl]

释 *v.* (使某物)颤动出声；使窘迫不安
n. 连续短促的尖利声

用 rattle on 喋喋不休；rattle off 飞快地说出

barmaid ['bɑːmeɪd]

释 *n.* 酒吧女招待

awe-inspiring ['ɔːɪnˌspaɪərɪŋ]

释 *a.* 令人惊叹的；令人敬畏的

haul [hɔːl]

释 *v.* (用力)拖；(用车等)运送 *n.* 拖；拖运

例 We are tidying up our living room and now trying to *haul* the sofa into my bedroom. 我们正在打扫客厅，现在想把沙发拖到我的卧室去。

enthusiasm [ɪn'θjuːziæzəm]

释 *n.* 热心；热情；热衷的事物

malnourished [ˌmæl'nʌrɪʃt]

释 *a.* 营养不良的

buckle ['bʌkl]

释 *n.* 皮带扣环 *v.* 扣紧；(使)弯曲；(使)变形

用 buckle down to sth. 决定做某事；buckle up 把…扣紧

pavement ['peɪvmənt]

释 *n.* 人行道

mistreat [ˌmɪs'triːt]

释 *v.* 虐待；糟蹋

alley ['æli]

释 *n.* 小巷；胡同

veterinarian [ˌvetərɪ'neəriən]

释 *n.* 兽医

specimen ['spesɪmən]

释 *n.* 范例；标本，样本

distemper [dɪ'stempə(r)]

释 *n.* 犬瘟热；不安，动乱

stainless ['steɪnləs]

释 *a.* 无污点的；不生锈的

scramble ['skræmbl]

释 *v.* 攀登；争夺；搅乱；炒(蛋) *n.* 攀登；争夺

例 The parents *scrambled* to inoculate their children. 父母们争相给他们的孩子打预防针。

wiggle ['wɪgl]

释 *v.* 扭动

euphoric [juː'fɒrɪk]

释 *a.* 心情愉快的；心满意足的

mutt [mʌt]

释 *n.* 杂种狗；笨蛋

massive ['mæsɪv]

释 *a.* 大量的；大块的；结实的

shiny ['ʃaɪni]

释 *a.* 有光泽的；闪耀的；晴朗的

unbridled [ʌn'braɪdld]

释 *a.* 不受控制的，不加约束的

melancholy ['melənkəli; 'melənkɒli]

释 *a.* 忧郁的 *n.* 忧郁

房屋住宿

bungalow ['bʌŋgələʊ] *n.* (带走廊的)平房；小屋

cellar ['selə(r)] *n.* 地窖，地下室

chamber ['tʃeɪmbə(r)] *n.* 房间；寝室；会议厅

closet ['klɒzɪt] *n.* 壁橱；小房间

colonnade [,kɒlə'neɪd] *n.* 柱廊

concrete ['kɒŋkri:t] *n.* 混凝土

decrepit [dɪ'krepɪt] *a.* 衰老的；破旧的

dilapidated [dɪ'læpɪdeɪtɪd] *a.* 残破的；失修的

evict [ɪ'vɪkt] *v.* 逐出(租户)

faucet ['fɔ:sɪt] *n.* 水龙头；插口

habitable ['hæbɪtəbl] *a.* 可居住的

indispensable [,ɪndɪ'spensəbl] *a.* 必不可少的，必需的

knob [nɒb] *n.* 门把，(球形)把手

landlord ['lændlɔ:d] *n.* 地主；房东

laundry ['lɔ:ndri] *n.* 洗衣房；待洗衣服

patio ['pætiəʊ] *n.* 天井；院子；露台

permanently ['pɜ:mənəntli] *ad.* 永久地

purlieus ['pɜ:lju:z] *n.* [*pl.*] 边缘部分；郊区

refurbishment [,ri:'fɜ:bɪʃmənt] *n.* 整修；翻新

requisite ['rekwɪzɪt] *a.* 需要的；必备的

residential [,rezɪ'denʃl] *a.* 居住的；住宅的

rustic ['rʌstɪk] *a.* 乡村的

shanty ['ʃænti] *n.* 简陋小屋，棚屋

steeple ['sti:pl] *n.* (教堂的)尖塔

tenant ['tenənt] *n.* 承租人；房客

traverse ['trævɜ:s] *n.* 横贯；(建筑物的)横梁

vacate [və'keɪt; veɪ'keɪt] *v.* 腾出，空出

ventilate ['ventɪleɪt] *v.* 使通风；给…装通风设备

You have to believe in yourself. That's the secret of success.

—Charles Chaplin

人必须相信自己，这是成功的秘密。

——查尔斯·卓别林

Passage 46

My Bosom Friend Arnold

I recently lost my best friend Arnold in an automobile accident while moving my family to our new home in Arizona. Arnold was an 8-month-old pot belly who taught me so much about love, devotion and companionship. I am devastated by his loss, but thank God daily for blessing me with the joy of having Arnold for his short life.

Anyone contemplating a pot belly as a pet should know that if you are a true pet lover and devote yourself to them, a pot belly will make the most wonderful friend. You will be assured of endless hours of fascination and entertainment as you both grow together in understanding the human/pot belly relationship. Words cannot describe this relationship and it can only be fully understood by experiencing it.

Arnold didn't know he was a pig—he thought he was just another member of our family—modeling his behavior through observing me, my wife, my two daughters and our beagles. He was convinced he was loved by all; and he was, even when he was ornery trying to just get our attention. He learned his name, how to sit and how to use the litter box all in the first week we had him (at 7 weeks old!).

He loved to sleep on your lap as you sat on the couch watching TV. He didn't care if he grew to weigh 45 pounds, and he still expected you to hoist him onto your lap at precisely 8:00 p.m. every evening where he would fall asleep within seconds after snuggling his wet nose between your neck and shoulder. If you didn't respond to his initial "honks" letting you know it was his nap time, he would bump your legs with his nose until you picked him up. With his weight as it was, you couldn't hold him all evening as he preferred, so you had to slide him off onto the couch next to you where he would sleep for hours with all four legs and his nose sticking straight up in the air. He would snore as long as he could feel you next to him but would immediately wake up if you tried to leave the couch. We had hours of fun balancing objects like a salt shaker on his flat nose while he slept soundly.

Arnold helped me in all my chores around our five acres in the country. Just being there at my feet, interested in what I was doing made even the most mundane tasks enjoyable. When he was out roaming and foraging and you called out his name, he would come running at top speed, honking the whole way until he got close to you where he would dodge you, zigzagging around with a few victory roles turning in circles before settling down and calmly walking up to you with his tail wagging as if to say (winking) "hah, got-cha".

He even helped me build a kit aircraft and a customized trailer to haul it around in. I was planning on taking him flying with me some day. He loved to play with my sockets and rolled them around on the shop floor. Just as I would struggle and get frustrated with some difficult task, Arnold would show up underneath the trailer, with his wet nose in my ear and honking—seeming to say, "Take a break and laugh with me for a while. That should make it all better." And it did, every time. God's marvelous creations minister to us in the most special ways if we can just stop for a few moments and observe them. God used Arnold to teach us this very important lesson in life which we will never forget.

My wife and two daughters began to say that Arnold and I were so close that he had become the son that I never had in our family. It seemed that we could no longer have any kind of conversation in our family or with our friends without Arnold being a main topic. The neighborhood kids would make appointments to visit Arnold and couldn't wait to come over and play with him.

Arnold went most everywhere with us—Pet's Mart, Wal-Mart, birthday parties, Christmas vacation to Grandma's. He loved riding in the car/shopping basket and was a big hit everywhere he went. Arnold had become such an important part of our life that when we found out that our family would have to move to another state, we insisted that the contract on our new house be contingent on the homeowners' association approval of Arnold in writing before we would agree to purchasing in our prestigious neighborhood.

On the day we left our old home town, we had a going away lunch with our friends from church. Everyone there just had to go out to the truck where Arnold and our other entire pet were and say goodbye. Arnold trusted me to take care of him and get him to his new home. Tragically, along the way, the wind blast from a semi knocked our trailers out of control and pushed our truck off a 40' bridge. We lost a big part of our family that day when our pets Arnold, Sweeti and Leanna were killed. I feel terrible for not being able to protect Arnold the way he trusted me to. However, I will be forever grateful for the fond memories of him which I will cherish forever.

我亲密的朋友阿诺德

最近，我们一家人在搬家前往亚利桑那州的途中发生了一起车祸，使我失去了我最好的朋友阿诺德。阿诺德是一只八个月大的宠物猪，他教给了我许多关于爱、奉献和友谊的事情。失去了他让我伤心欲绝，不过我仍然每天祈祷，感谢上帝让我拥有了那段与阿诺德相处的短暂而美好的时光。

任何计划养宠物猪的人都应该知道，如果你真心喜欢宠物并且全心全意地付出，小猪就会成为你最棒的朋友。你们一起成长，在体会到人与宠物猪的亲密关系的过程中，你一定会感到一种无时无刻不存在的欢娱并为之着迷。言语是无法形容这种关系的，只有在你亲身经历后才能完全体会。

阿诺德并不知道自己是只猪，他以为他就是我们家的一名成员——他会通过观察我、我妻子、我的两个女儿以及我们的小猎犬的举止，然后进行模仿。他坚信我们所有人都爱他，而事实确实如此，即使他有时会闹脾气来吸引注意。他来到我们家的一个星期之内（那时他才7周大！）就知道了自己的名字，学会了如何坐以及如何使用宠物厕所。

当你坐在沙发上看电视的时候，他喜欢睡在你的大腿上。他才不在乎自己是不是已经长到45磅重，仍然希望你每天晚上八点整准时把他抱到你的大腿上，在用自己湿乎乎的鼻子在你的脖子和肩膀周围依偎一阵之后，很快就会酣睡起来。如果你对他最开始提醒你睡觉时间到了的"哼哼"声无动于衷的话，他就会用鼻子撞你的腿，直到你把他抱起来为止。他体重那么重，你不可能像他希望的那样整晚都抱着他，所以不得不让他慢慢滑到旁边的沙发上。而他会在那里四仰八叉地睡上好几个小时。只要能感觉到你在他身边，他就会继续打着呼噜睡大觉；但是一旦你想离开沙发，他就会马上醒过来。在他熟睡的那几个小时，我们会乐此不疲地在他那扁鼻子上放一些盐罐子之类的小玩意，玩得很开心。

在我们乡下那五英亩（约2公顷）大小的地方，我做所有的家务事时阿诺德都会帮忙。他只要待在我的脚边，兴致勃勃地看着我所做的事情，就足以让最平淡无奇的杂务事变得充满乐趣。当他外出闲逛觅食时，只要你喊他的名字，他就会以最快的速度向你奔来，一路"哼哼"地叫着，跑到离你不远的地方时又会跟你玩起捉迷藏，左转右转地兜着圈跑，一副凯旋而归的模样，最后平静地走到你跟前，摇着尾巴，好像在眨着眼说："哈，找到你啦！"

他甚至帮我一起组装了一架小型飞机和一辆特制的运载飞机的拖车。我打算明天带他跟我一起在天空中翱翔。他喜欢玩插座，并在车间的地板上把它们翻来翻去。每当我因为困难的问题而伤透脑筋、感到灰心丧气时，阿诺德就会从拖车下面钻出来，把湿乎乎的鼻子凑到我耳边哼哼着，好像在说："休息一会儿，跟我一起笑一笑，这样一切都会好起来的。"而这每次都会奏效。上帝所创造的神奇万物总是以最特别的方式眷顾着我们，只要我们能稍微停下脚步来仔细观察，就会有所发现。上帝让阿诺德教会了我们这人生中的重要一课，我们将毕生难忘。

我们家没有儿子，我太太和两个女儿都说阿诺德跟我亲密得就像他是我儿子一样。我们在家里聊天或者和朋友交谈时，话题也总离不开阿诺德。邻居家的小孩也会约好时间来拜访阿诺德，迫不及待地想要过来和他玩耍。

阿诺德几乎与我们形影不离，无论是去宠物用品超市、沃尔玛超市、生日派对，还是去奶奶家过圣诞假期，他都跟我们在一起。他喜欢坐在购物车或者购物篮里，走到哪儿都备受瞩目。阿诺德已经成为我们生活中非常重要的一部分，所以当我们不得不搬到另一个州时，我们坚持新家的房屋合同要附有其他住户允许阿诺德与我们同住的联名同意书，只有这样我们才会同意在那个著名的社区购房。

在离开老家那一天，我们和教会的朋友们一起吃了饯行午餐。到场的每个人都走到货车旁跟阿诺德和我们其他的所有宠物告别。阿诺德是信任我的，他相信我会照顾他并把他带到新家去。不幸的是，在行驶途中，一辆呼啸而过的半挂车掀起的气流使我们的拖车失去了控制，继而坠落到了40英尺（约12米）的桥下。我们家损失了好几位成员——我们的宠物阿诺德、甜甜和莲娜都丧生了。我感到十分难过，因为我没能像阿诺德信任的那样保护他。但是，我将永远感激他带给我们的美好回忆，并永远珍惜这份记忆。

💡 单词记事本

bosom ['bʊzəm]
释 n. 胸部；乳房；对某事物的关怀和保护 a. 亲密的

devastated ['devəsteɪtɪd]
释 a. 悲痛欲绝的

contemplate ['kɒntəmpleɪt]
释 v. 考虑；盘算；思量；注视
例 There is no denying that some joint ventures have *contemplated* reducing the number of employees. 不可否认，一些合资企业已经在考虑裁员。

fascination [ˌfæsɪ'neɪʃn]
释 n. 入迷，迷恋

model ['mɒdl]
释 n. 模型；模范 v. 模拟；模仿，塑造 a. 模范的
用 model after/on/upon 模仿，仿造

beagle ['biːgl]
释 n. 小猎犬

convinced [kən'vɪnst]
释 a. 确信的，信服的

ornery ['ɔ:nəri]
释 a. 脾气坏的；低劣的

hoist [hɔɪst]
释 v. 举起；吊起 n. 起重机；举起

precisely [prɪ'saɪsli]
释 ad. 精确地；的确如此

snuggle ['snʌgl]
释 v. 挨近，依偎

honk [hɒŋk]
释 n. 鼻鼾声；汽车喇叭声

couch [kaʊtʃ]
释 n. 长沙发 v. 表达

snore [snɔ:(r)]
释 v. 打鼾 n. 鼾声

mundane [mʌn'deɪn]
释 a. 世界的；世俗的；平淡的

roam [rəʊm]
释 v. 漫无目的地走动，闲逛；漫游；漫谈 n. 漫步；徘徊
用 roam over sth. 漫谈某事
例 He used to *roam* the streets for several hours. 他过去常常沿着大街闲逛，一逛就是几个小时。

forage ['fɒrɪdʒ]
释 n. (牛马的)饲料 v. 搜寻；翻寻
例 She *foraged* about in the drawer, but couldn't find her favourite necklace. 她翻遍了抽屉，就是找不到她最喜欢的那条项链。

dodge [dɒdʒ]
释 v. 闪开，躲避；施计避免做某事 n. 躲闪，躲避；妙计，避免做某事的方法

zigzag ['zɪgzæg]
释 n. 之字形 a. 之字形的 v. 弯弯曲曲地行进

customize ['kʌstəmaɪz]
释 v. 定制，定做

frustrated [frʌ'streɪtɪd]
释 a. 令人灰心的；失意的，受挫的

underneath [ˌʌndə'ni:θ]
释 prep. 在…下面 ad. 在下面

marvelous ['mɑ:vələs]
释 a. 非凡的；不平常的

minister ['mɪnɪstə(r)]
释 n. [M-]部长，大臣；公使；牧师 v. 给予帮助；服侍

contingent [kən'tɪndʒənt]
释 a. 意外的；视情况而定的 n. 代表团；偶然的事情

purchase ['pɜ:tʃəs]
释 n./v. 购买

prestigious [pre'stɪdʒəs]
释 a. 有名望的；有影响力的

cherish ['tʃerɪʃ]
释 v. 珍爱；怀念

💡 单词家族

人物特征

activist ['æktɪvɪst] n. (政治活动的)积极分子

adamant ['ædəmənt] a. 坚强的；坚决的；倔强的

amiable ['eɪmiəbl] a. 和蔼可亲的；友好的

amicable ['æmɪkəbl] a. 友善的；无敌意的

arbitrary ['ɑːbɪtrəri] *a.* 专制的；武断的

bigoted ['bɪɡətɪd] *a.* 固执的；盲从的

considerate [kən'sɪdərət] *a.* 考虑周到的；体贴的

courteous ['kɜːtiəs] *a.* 彬彬有礼的；客气的

covetous ['kʌvətəs] *a.* 贪心的；贪求的

cursory ['kɜːsəri] *a.* 草率的；匆忙的

depraved [dɪ'preɪvd] *a.* 堕落的，腐化的；卑鄙的

despicable [dɪ'spɪkəbl] *a.* 可鄙的；卑劣的

diffident ['dɪfɪdənt] *a.* 缺乏自信的；谦虚谨慎的

dwarf [dwɔːf] *n.* 矮子，侏儒 *v.* (使)变矮小

elegant ['elɪɡənt] *a.* 优雅的；优美的

fatuous ['fætʃuəs] *a.* 愚昧的；昏庸的

haughty ['hɔːti] *a.* 傲慢的；不逊的

hypocritical [ˌhɪpə'krɪtɪkl] *a.* 虚伪的

impartially [ˌɪm'pɑːʃəli] *ad.* 公平地；无私地

imperturbable [ˌɪmpə'tɜːbəbl] *a.* 冷静的；沉着的

patriotic [ˌpeɪtri'ɒtɪk; ˌpætri'ɒtɪk] *a.* 爱国的；有爱国热情的

perfervid [pə'fɜːvɪd] *a.* 非常热心的

resolute ['rezəluːt] *a.* 坚决的；果断的

shrewd [ʃruːd] *a.* 机灵的；精明的

slick [slɪk] *a.* 圆滑的；口齿伶俐的

slippery ['slɪpəri] *a.* 狡猾的；不可靠的

slothful ['sləʊθfl] *a.* 迟钝的；懒惰的

sly [slaɪ] *a.* 狡猾的；会意的

stout [staʊt] *a.* 健壮的；有力的；勇敢的

stubborn ['stʌbən] *a.* 顽固的；倔强的

torpor ['tɔːpə(r)] *n.* 迟钝；不活泼

undaunted [ˌʌn'dɔːntɪd] *a.* 无畏的；勇敢的

valiantly ['væliəntli] *ad.* 勇猛地；英勇地

I tried to be a sponge, absorbing and questioning every good idea.
　　　　　　　　　　　　　　　　　　—Jack Welch
我把自己比作海绵，吸收并改进每一个好点子。
　　　　　　　　　　　　　　　　　——杰克·韦尔奇

Passage 47

音频

A Good Heart to Lean On

When I was growing up, I was embarrassed to be seen with my father. He was severely crippled and very short, and when we would walk together, his hand on my arm for balance, people would stare. I would inwardly squirm at the shy and unwanted attention. If he ever noticed or was bothered, he never let on.

It was difficult to coordinate our steps—his halting, mine impatient—and because of that, we didn't say much as we went along. But as we started out, he always said, "You set the pace. I will try to adjust to you." Our usual walk was to or from the subway, which was how he got to work. He went to work sick, and despite nasty weather. He almost never missed a day, and would make it to the office even if others could not. A matter of pride. When snow or ice was on the ground, it was impossible for him to walk, even with help. At such times my sisters or I would pull him through the streets of Brooklyn, NY, on a child's sleigh to the entrance of the subway. Once there, he would cling to the handrail until he reached the lower steps that the warmer tunnel air kept ice-free. In Manhattan the subway station was the basement of his office building, and he would not have to go outside again until we met him in Brooklyn on his way home.

When I think of it now, I marvel at how much courage it must have taken for a grown man to subject himself to such indignity and stress. And at how he did it—without bitterness or complaint. He never talked about himself as an object of pity, nor did he show any envy of the more fortunate or able. What he looked for in others was a "good heart", and if he found one, the owner was good enough for him. Now that I am older, I believe that is a proper standard by which to judge people, even though I still don't know precisely what a "good heart" is. But I know the times I don't have one myself.

Unable to engage in many activities, my father still tried to participate in some way. When a local sandlot baseball team found itself without a manager, he kept it going. He was a knowledgeable baseball fan and often took me to Ebbets Field to see the Brooklyn Dodgers play. He liked to go to dances and parties, where he could have a good time just sitting and watching. On one memorable occasion a fight broke out at a beach party, with everyone punching and shoving. He wasn't content to sit and watch, but he couldn't stand unaided on the soft sand.

In **frustration** he began to shout, "I'll fight anyone who will sit down with me!" Nobody did. But the next day people kidded him by saying it was the first time any fighter was **urged** to take a dive even before the **bout** began. I now know he participated in some things **vicariously** through me, his only son. When I played ball (poorly), he "played" too. When I joined the Navy, he "joined" too. And when I came home on leave, he saw to it that I visited his office. Introducing me, he was really saying, "This is my son, but it is also me, and I could have done this, too, if things had been different."

He has been gone many years now, but I think of him often. I wonder if he sensed my **reluctance** to be seen with him during our walks. If he did, I am sorry I never told him how sorry I was, how **unworthy** I was, and how I regretted it. I think of him when I complain about **trifles**, when I am **envious** of another's good fortune, and when I don't have a "good heart". At such times I put my hand on his arm to **regain** my balance, and say, "You set the pace. I will try to adjust to you."

译文

依靠一颗善良的心

在成长的过程中，我一直不愿被别人看见我和父亲在一起。父亲腿部严重残疾，而且身材矮小。我们一块儿走路时，他总是挽着我的胳膊来保持平衡，这时人们总会盯着我们看。我的羞怯和人们不必要的关注令我内心局促不安。如果父亲也注意到了这些或者因此感到困扰，他也绝不会表露出来。

走路时，我们的步伐很难协调一致——他步履蹒跚，而我步急促——因此，一路上我们都很少说话。但是每次出发前，他总是说："速度由你定。我尽量跟上你。"我们最常走的路就是在家和地铁站之间往返，因为他乘地铁上下班。无论生病还是在天气恶劣的情况下，他都会照常上班。值得骄傲的是他几乎从未误过一天工，即使其他人都去不了，他也会想办法按时到达。当冰封大地或满地积雪的时候，即使在别人的帮助下，他也寸步难行。每当这个时候，我或者我的姐妹们就用儿童雪橇拉着他走过纽约布鲁克林区的街道，一直把他送到地铁口。到了那里，他便紧紧抓住扶手，一直走到底部的台阶才松手。因为通道中的空气比较温暖，那里的地面不会结冰。在曼哈顿，地铁站就在他办公楼的地下，所以直到我们在布鲁克林接他下班回家之前，他都不用再走到户外。

现在每当想到这些，我都十分惊讶，一个成年男子需要多大的勇气才能经受住这种侮辱和压力。而他自己竟然能做到不痛苦、不抱怨。父亲从来没有把自己说成是需要同情的对象，也没有表现出一丁点对其他幸运之人或者四肢健全之人的嫉妒。他所关注的是别人的"善心"，只要他发现一点善心，那么那个人对他来说就是个好人。如今我已经长大成人，我相信"善心"是评价一个人的最恰当的标准，虽然我仍不太清楚它的确切含义，但我知道自己什么时候是缺乏善心的。

虽然有许多活动父亲都不能参加，但他仍然设法通过某种方式参与其中。当一个地方业余棒球队缺少一名经理时，他便担任了这个职位。他自己是个拥有丰富棒球知识的球迷，过去常带我去埃比茨棒球场观看布鲁克林道奇队的比赛。他喜欢参加舞会和聚会，仅仅是坐在一旁观看也能自得其乐。其中一次海边聚会的经历让我难以忘怀。当时有人打架，大家都动了手，推推搡搡。父亲不满足于坐在一旁观看，但又无法让自己从松软的沙滩上站起来。沮丧之下，他吼道："谁有本事坐下来和我打？"结果没人响应。但是第二天，人们都跟他开玩笑说，拳击比赛还没开始选手就被劝认输，这还是破天荒的第一次。我现在领悟了，父亲是通过我——他唯一的儿子来间接地参与一些事。当我打球时（尽管我打得很不好），他也在"打球"；当我加入海军时，他也"加入"了。当我休假回家时，他一定要让我去他的办公室看看。在介绍我时，他真真切切地说："这是我儿子，也是我自己。假如我自己不是这种情况的话，我也会像他那样去参军的。"

父亲已经去世很多年了，但我常常想起他。我想知道他是否察觉到了我不愿让人看到我和他走在一起。如果他知道这一切，我感到很抱歉，抱歉我从来没有告诉过他我是多么愧疚、多么不应该、多么懊悔。每当我因琐事而抱怨、因别人的好运而嫉妒时，每当我意识到自己缺乏"善心"时，我就会想起父亲。每当这样的时候，我都会挽着他的胳膊以重新获得平衡，并且说："速度由你定。我尽量跟上你。"

💡 单词记事本

embarrassed [ɪmˈbærəst]
释 a. 尴尬的；窘迫的

crippled [ˈkrɪpld]
释 a. 残废的

inwardly [ˈɪnwədli]
释 ad. 在内；在内心，思想上

squirm [skwɜːm]
释 v. 蠕动；扭动；难为情

coordinate
释 [kəʊˈɔːdɪnət] n. 坐标；[常pl.](女子的)配套衣物
[kəʊˈɔːdɪneɪt] v. (使各部分)协调
例 We should work in a *coordinated* effort to solve the problem of childhood obesity. 我们应齐心协力来解决儿童肥胖问题。

halting ['hɔːltɪŋ; 'hɒltɪŋ]

释 *a.* 蹒跚的；犹豫不决的

adjust [ə'dʒʌst]

释 *v.* 使适合，适应；整顿；安排；校准，校正

用 adjust to 适应于

nasty ['nɑːsti]

释 *a.* 令人讨厌的；卑鄙的；恶劣的

sleigh [sleɪ]

释 *n.* 雪橇

cling [klɪŋ]

释 *v.* 紧紧抓住，抱住；舍不得放弃，拒绝放弃；附着于；紧靠着

用 cling to sb. like a leech 纠缠某人不放；cling film 保鲜膜

handrail ['hændreɪl]

释 *n.* 栏杆；扶手

basement ['beɪsmənt]

释 *n.* 地下室

marvel ['mɑːvl]

释 *n.* 令人惊奇的事物 *v.* 对…感到惊异

用 marvel at 对…感到惊异

例 Martin grinned and accepted the invitation, *marveling* at his good luck. 马丁咧嘴笑着接受了这个邀请，惊异于自己的好运气。

indignity [ɪn'dɪgnəti]

释 *n.* 侮辱；轻蔑；侮辱性的言行

bitterness ['bɪtənəs]

释 *n.* 苦味；苦难；怨恨

sandlot ['sændlɒt]

释 *n.* (市郊)空地，沙地 *a.* 沙地的；(球队等)非正式的，业余的

memorable ['memərəbl]

释 *a.* 容易记住的，难忘的；值得纪念的

punch [pʌntʃ]

释 *v.* 穿孔；猛击 *n.* 冲床

例 My father gave me a *punching* bag, which I demolished a week later. 爸爸给了我一个拳击沙袋，一周后我就把它打烂了。

shove [ʃʌv]

释 *v.* 乱推；乱放 *n.* 猛推

用 shove off 乘船离开

unaided [ʌn'eɪdɪd]

释 *a.* 无助的；独立的

frustration [frʌ'streɪʃn]

释 *n.* 沮丧；不满

urge [ɜːdʒ]

释 *v.* 驱赶；催促，劝告 *n.* 强烈的欲望

bout [baʊt]

释 *n.* 拳击比赛；(疾病等)侵袭，发作

vicariously [vɪ'keəriəsli]

释 *ad.* 间接地感受到；代理地

reluctance [rɪ'lʌktəns]

释 *n.* 勉强；不情愿

例 I cannot understand your *reluctance* to talk to the press—it is a good chance for you. 我不理解你为何不愿同媒体交谈——这对你来说是一个好机会。

unworthy [ʌn'wɜːði]

释 *a.* 不值得的，不应得的；格格不入的；不能接受的

用 unworthy of 不值得

trifle ['traɪfl]

释 *n.* 无价值的事物，不重要的问题；少量的钱；松糕点心 *v.* 轻视，随便对待

用 a trifle 稍微，有点儿

envious ['enviəs]

释 *a.* 嫉妒的；羡慕的

regain [rɪ'geɪn]

释 *v.* 收回；恢复，重新夺得

爱心正义

adoptive [əˈdɒptɪv] *a.* 收养的；采用的

benefactor [ˈbenɪfæktə(r)] *n.* 恩人；捐助者

bounty [ˈbaʊnti] *n.* 慷慨；恩惠

charity [ˈtʃærəti] *n.* 慈善；慈善机构

cohesion [kəʊˈhiːʒn] *n.* 结合；凝聚力

compassionate [kəmˈpæʃənət] *a.* 有同情心的

cosmopolitan [ˌkɒzməˈpɒlɪtən] *a.* 无民族偏见的；四海为家的

endorse [ɪnˈdɔːs] *v.* 支持，赞同

endow [ɪnˈdaʊ] *v.* 捐赠

ethically [ˈeθɪkli] *ad.* 伦理上

humane [hjuːˈmeɪn] *a.* 仁慈的

justly [ˈdʒʌstli] *ad.* 公正地

notary [ˈnəʊtəri] *n.* 公证人

orphanage [ˈɔːfənɪdʒ] *n.* 孤儿院

succor [ˈsʌkə(r)] *v.* 救助，援助

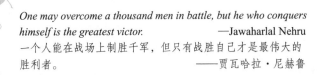

One may overcome a thousand men in battle, but he who conquers himself is the greatest victor.　　　　　　　—Jawaharlal Nehru

一个人能在战场上制胜千军，但只有战胜自己才是最伟大的胜利者。

——贾瓦哈拉·尼赫鲁

音频

Passage 48

Mother

When you were 1 year old, she fed you and bathed you. You thanked her by crying all night long.

When you were 2 years old, she taught you to walk. You thanked her by running away when she called.

When you were 3 years old, she made all your meals with love. You thanked her by tossing your plate on the floor.

When you were 4 years old, she gave you some crayons. You thanked her by coloring the dining room table.

When you were 5 years old, she dressed you for the holidays. You thanked her by plopping into the nearest mud-hole.

When you were 6 years old, she walked you to the school. You thanked her by screaming "I'm not going!"

When you were 7 years old, she bought you a baseball. You thanked her by throwing it through the next-door-neighbor's window.

When you were 8 years old, she handed you an ice cream. You thanked her by dripping it all over your lap.

When you were 9 years old, she paid for piano lessons. You thanked her by never even bothering to practice.

When you were 10 years old, she drove you all day, from soccer to gymnastics to one birthday party after another. You thanked her by jumping out of the car and never looking back.

When you were 11 years old, she took you and your friends to the movies. You thanked her by asking to sit in a different row.

When you were 12 years old, she warned you not to watch certain TV shows. You thanked her by waiting until she left the house.

When you were 13 years old, she suggested a haircut. You thanked her by telling her she had no taste.

When you were 14 years old, she paid for a month away at summer camp. You thanked her by forgetting to write a single letter.

When you were 15 years old, she came home from work, looking for a hug. You thanked her by having your bedroom door locked.

When you were 16 years old, she taught you how to drive her car. You thanked her by taking it every chance you could.

When you were 17 years old, she was expecting an important call. You thanked her by being on the phone all night.

When you were 18 years old, she cried at your high school graduation. You thanked her by staying out partying until dawn.

When you were 19 years old, she paid for your college tuition, drove you to campus, and carried your bags. You thanked her by saying good-bye outside the dorm so you wouldn't be embarrassed in front of your friends.

When you were 20 years old, she asked whether you were seeing anyone. You thanked her by saying, "It's none of your business."

When you were 21, she suggested certain careers for your future. You thanked her by saying, "I don't want to be like you."

When you were 22, she hugged you at your college graduation. You thanked her by asking whether she could pay for a trip to Europe.

When you were 23, she sent some furniture to your first apartment. You thanked her by telling your friends it was ugly.

When you were 24, she met your fiancé and asked about your plans for the future. You thanked her by glaring and growling, "Mother, please!"

When you were 25, she helped to pay for your wedding and she cried and told you how deeply she loved you. You thanked her by moving halfway across the country.

When you were 30, she called with some advice on the baby. You thanked her by telling her "Things are different now."

When you were 40, she called to remind you of a relative's birthday. You thanked her by saying you were "Really busy right now."

When you were 50, she fell ill and needed you to take care of her. You thanked her by talking about the burden parents become to the children.

And then, one day, she quietly died. And everything you never did came crashing down like thunder on YOUR HEART.

If your mom is still around, never forget to love her more than ever. And if she's not, remember her unconditional love and pass it on. Always remember to love your mother, because you only have one mother in your lifetime!

母亲

1岁时，她为你哺乳，给你洗澡。你回报她的是整夜的啼哭。

2岁时，她教你学会走路。你回报她的是在她呼唤你时远远跑开。

3岁时，她用满腔爱意为你准备三餐。你回报她的是把盘子摔到地上。

4岁时，她给你几支蜡笔。你回报她的是在餐桌上胡乱涂鸦。

5岁时，她为你穿上节日盛装。你回报她的是"扑通"一声摔进离你最近的泥坑。

6岁时，她步行送你去学校。你回报她的是大声叫喊"我不去！"

7岁时，她给你买了个棒球。你回报她的是用它砸破了邻居家的窗户。

8岁时，她递给你一个冰激凌。你回报她的是让冰激凌滴得满腿都是。

9岁时，她花钱让你学钢琴。你回报她的是从来都懒于练习。

10岁时，她整天开着车，把你从足球场送到体育馆，再送到一个又一个的生日聚会。你回报她的是跳下车后头也不回地就走开。

11岁时，她带着你和你的朋友们去看电影。你回报她的是不和她坐在同一排。

12岁时，她警告你不要看某些电视节目。你回报她的是等她不在家时再看。

13岁时，她建议你换个发型。你回报她的是说她没品位。

14岁时，她付钱让你参加一个月的夏令营。你回报她的是一封信都没写。

15岁时，她下班回到家，期待得到你的一个拥抱。你回报她的是将自己卧室的门锁上。

16岁时，她教你开她的车。你回报她的是一有机会就把她的车开走。

17岁时，她在等一个重要的电话。你回报她的是整晚煲着电话粥。

18岁时，她在你的高中毕业典礼上流泪。你回报她的是外出聚会彻夜不归。

19岁时，她为你交了大学学费，开车送你去报到，帮你拎着行李。你回报她的是在宿舍门外就跟她道别，免得自己在同学面前感到尴尬。

20岁时，她问你是否在和谁约会。你回报她的是对她说"这不关你的事"。

21岁时，她为你今后的职业提出建议。你回报她的是告诉她"我不想跟你一样"。

22岁时，她在你的大学毕业典礼上拥抱你。你回报她的是问她能否为你支付欧洲旅行的费用。

23岁时，她送了一些家具到你的第一个公寓。你回报她的是跟你的朋友们说它们很难看。

24岁时，她与你的未婚夫见面并询问你们将来的计划。你回报她的是怒目而视，咆哮着对她说："妈，拜托！"

25岁时，她花钱为你筹办婚礼，哭诉着她有多么爱你。你回报她的是在跨越大半个国家的地方安家。

30岁时，她打电话给你一些抚养宝宝的建议。你回报她的是告诉她"时代不同了"。

40岁时，她打电话提醒你一个亲戚的生日。你回报她的是说你"现在真的很忙"。

50岁时，她病了，需要你的照顾。你回报她的是念叨父母变成了孩子们的负担。

直到有一天，她安静地去世了。那些你从未做过的事仿佛霹雳一般，在心中轰然炸响。

如果你的母亲还健在，不要忘记比过去更爱她一些。如果她已经过世，要记住她那无条件的爱，并把这种爱传递下去。永远要记得爱你的母亲，因为在你的一生中，你只有这一个母亲！

💡 单词记事本

crayon ['kreɪən]
释 n. 蜡笔；炭笔 v. 用蜡笔画；勾轮廓

plop [plɒp]
释 v. 扑通落下 n. 扑通声

drip [drɪp]
释 v. 滴；漏下；洒下 n. 滴；滴水声；滴下的液体
例 Our progress was impeded by the tall wet grass and *dripping* boughs. 高高的湿草和湿漉漉的树枝阻碍了我们前进的道路。

gymnastics [dʒɪm'næstɪks]
释 n. 体操；体能训练

taste [teɪst]
释 n. 滋味；味觉；品位 v. 有…味道；品尝

dawn [dɔːn]
释 n. 破晓；开始，发端

tuition [tju'ɪʃn]
释 n. (某一学科的)教学；学费
用 tuition scholarship 学费助学金；tuition charges/fees 学费
例 With a summer holiday's hard work, he could cover *tuition* fees for the first year. 经过一个暑假的辛苦工作，他可以付得起第一年的学费了。

furniture ['fɜːnɪtʃə(r)]
释 n. 家具；设备

fiancé [fi'ɒnseɪ]
释 n. 未婚夫

glare [gleə(r)]
释 v. 怒目而视 n. 怒视；耀眼的光
用 glare at 怒目而视；in the full glare of publicity 在众目睽睽下；非常显眼

例 Although I had made some mistakes, no one complained or even *glared* at me. 尽管我犯了一些错误，但是没有人抱怨，甚至都没人瞪过我一眼。

growl [graʊl]
释 v. (动物)发出低沉的怒吼声；咆哮
n. 咆哮；怒吼声

remind [rɪ'maɪnd]
释 v. 提醒；使想起；使发生联想

relative ['relətɪv]
释 a. 相对的；有关的 n. 亲属，亲戚
用 be relative to 与…有关；涉及

crash [kræʃ]
释 v. 突然倒下；撞击发出声响；垮台 n. 碰撞；坠落；破裂声
例 Gigantic waves more than 12 meters high *crashed* against the boat. 超过12米高的巨浪拍打在小船上。

unconditional [ˌʌnkən'dɪʃənl]
释 a. 无条件的；绝对的

Ⓥ 单词家族

家庭成员

chap [tʃæp] n. 小伙子；家伙
descendant [dɪ'sendənt] n. 子孙，后代
fetus ['fiːtəs] n. 胎儿
genealogy [ˌdʒiːni'ælədʒi] n. 家谱
imp [ɪmp] n. 小鬼；顽童
intimate ['ɪntɪmət] a. 亲密的；密切的
juvenile ['dʒuːvənaɪl] n. 青少年；儿童
　　a. 青少年的；幼稚的
kin [kɪn] n. 家属；亲戚

marital ['mærɪtl] a. 婚姻的；夫妻的
offspring ['ɒfsprɪŋ] n. 子女；后代
paternity [pə'tɜːnəti] n. 父权；父子关系
patriarch ['peɪtriɑːk] n. 家长，族长
patriarchal [ˌpeɪtri'ɑːkl] a. 家长的；族长的
pedigree ['pedɪgriː] n. 家谱；血统
sibling ['sɪblɪŋ] n. 兄弟姊妹

Passage 49

Taking a Break
Helps with Your Relationship

There are times when a **relationship** reaches a **point** where one or both partners feel the need for some space and want a break from each other, believing that a break will do the relationship good. Can taking time apart from each other help with your relationship or is taking a break simply a way to **avoid** certain issues that will still be there waiting for you when you get back together?

Do not use breaks as a quick fix.

Every relationship **varies** and it is important that every couple understands that taking time apart is not a **substitute** for fixing or solving problems, because if you part when you are having problems, they will be waiting for you when you meet again—so it is essential that you talk about your issues first before you decide a break is needed and best for the relationship. Many get scared and **paranoid** when their partner asks for some time alone because they fear that their partner may not love them anymore or will not come back. Though it is always possible for your partner to change their mind during the break and decide not to continue with the relationship, there is no need to fear taking the break, because the two of you would **eventually** have broken up anyway, if your partner was already thinking of doing so before—so it is **inevitable**.

A break can help you re-discover your individual self.

Many times, one or both people in a relationship will lose themselves in some way or form and will begin to feel stress and **resentment** in the relationship, even though it may not be about their partner personally. In every relationship, couples will compromise their differences to keep things healthy and happy and in making these compromising and changes, you both have to let go of a part of yourselves. Sometimes this happens so often that one or both of you will feel like you have completely lost yourselves and will feel stressed and resentment towards each other, even though it has nothing to do with any of you in particular. Relationships can get so deep—and you both can connect as "one" so intensely that you neglect yourselves as individuals, and in order to re-discover yourselves, there will need to be some time apart from each other. Remember, you need to be whole as an individual first in order to be whole together as a couple, and time apart is best if one or both of you feel like you need to get back in touch with your individuality.

Slow down the pace to learn more about each other.

Some couples get so excited when they enter a relationship, that everything moves so fast, which can get stressful, pressuring and scary, in which a break is then a good idea as well. Taking time apart can help a relationship build a better bond because you will both replenish yourselves during the break and will then be able to give the relationship the efforts and attention needed to keep it healthy. If you are afraid that you will lose the relationship if you take a break, just remember that you would have broken up later anyway—not because of the break, but because you grew apart, had irreparable issues or maybe your partner (or you) just wanted to move on. So do not fear what is not in your control. Just stay calm and see what good a break can do for both of you and your relationship. Besides, you both owe it to yourselves to get back in touch with your individualities and learn more new things about yourselves, so that you will be able to teach your partner more about you—and the more you know about each other, the more you will understand your differences, and will be able to build the connection that works best for both of you.

译 文

短暂的分别有助于关系的发展

有时，当一段关系发展到一定的阶段，其中的一方或双方都会感觉需要一些个人空间，想要与对方分开一段时间，他们认为这样的分离会对两个人的关系发展有利。但短暂的分离真的能增进两人的关系吗？还是说这么做只是逃避某些问题的一种方式，而当他们再回到一起时，这些问题依然存在？

不要把"分开"当作快速修复工具

每段关系都是不同的。重要的是，每对恋人都应该理解，分开一段时间并不表示两人的关系不用修复或问题不用解决。因为如果分开时问题存在，那么复合时问题仍会再次出现。因此，在你们确定暂别一段时间是必要的而且对两人的关系是有好处的之前，先谈谈你们的问题，这是非常重要的。许多人在他们的伴侣提出需要独处一段时间时会感到紧张而多疑，因为他们害怕对方不再爱自己，或者不会再回来了。虽然这段时间内你的伴侣可能会改变主意，决定不再继续这段关系，但你也没有必要因此就害怕分开，因为如果你的伴侣早就打算结束，分开也就是早晚的事了，这是不可避免的。

分开一段时间能帮助你重新认识自我

很多时候，处于一段关系中的一方或双方会发现他们在某种程度或形式上迷失了自我，并开始背负压力、感到怨恨，即使这些情绪并不是针对伴侣的。在每段关系中，为了使一切得以健康、良好地发展，双方都会弱化自己身上的不同点。在作出妥协和改变的过程中，双方都必须放弃一部分自我。有时这种情况发生得太过频繁，其中一方或双方会发现自己完全失去了自我，感到心力交瘁、心怀怨恨，即使这与另一方并没有什么特别的关系。一段关系发展到很深入的程度，两个人会如胶似漆，亲密得仿佛"一个人"，所以你就会忽略了自己作为个人的需求。而想要重新发现自我，就需要彼此分开一段时间。要记住，要想让两个人的关系完整，首先你作为个人的自己必须是完整的。如果一方或双方都觉得自己需要找回自我，那么分开一段时间就是最好的选择。

放慢速度，充分了解彼此

有些恋人在开始一段关系时太过兴奋，使得一切都发展得过快，而这样会让人产生压力和恐慌。这时，分开一段时间也是个不错的主意。短暂的分离能加固两人之间的关系，因为双方在这段时间可以充实自我，继而能够努力、用心地维持这段关系，使其健康地发展。如果你担心分开一段时间会让你失去对方，那么你应该记住，你们无论如何都会分开的。并非暂时的分离让你们分开，而可能是你们俩合不来，你们之间存在无法解决的问题，或者是对方（或者你）想开始新的生活。因此，不要害怕那些你无法控制的事情。保持冷静，看看短暂的分离能给你和你们的关系带来什么好处。此外，你们彼此都需要回归自我，并去发现全新的自己，这样你才能让对方更加了解你。你们之间越了解，就越能理解彼此的不同，继而才能建立起能让双方都感到幸福的良好关系。

relationship [rɪ'leɪʃnʃɪp]
释 *n.* 关系；联系

point [pɔɪnt]
释 *n.* 观点；阶段，程度；尖端 *v.* 指向；表明
用 beside the point 离题的；不相关的；make a point of 特别注意；重视；on the point of 正要…之际；point out 指出；to the point 切题

avoid [ə'vɔɪd]
释 *v.* 避免，避开；预防
用 avoid doing sth. 避免做某事

fix [fɪks]
释 *v.* 修理；安装；安排 *n.* 困境；修复办法
用 fix on 确定；固定；使集中于；fix up 安排；修理；解决

vary ['veəri]
释 *v.* 变化；(使)不同

substitute ['sʌbstɪtjuːt]
释 *n.* 替代品；代理人；代用者 *v.* 代替
用 substitute for 代替
例 There is a hot debate about whether diet food can be a good *substitute* for ordinary food. 关于减肥食品能否代替普通食品的问题引起了一场激烈的争论。

paranoid ['pærənɔɪd]
释 *a.* 类偏执狂的；多疑的

eventually [ɪ'ventʃuəli]
释 *ad.* 最后；终于

inevitable [ɪn'evɪtəbl]
释 *a.* 不可避免的；必然(发生)的

例 Breaking a new shipping route is *inevitable* for the developing process of the world history. 开辟一条新航线是世界历史发展进程中的必然之举。

resentment [rɪ'zentmənt]
释 *n.* 愤恨，怨恨

intensely [ɪn'tensli]
释 *ad.* 强烈地，热烈地；剧烈地

neglect [nɪ'glekt]
释 *v./n.* 忽视；疏漏

pressure ['preʃə(r)]
释 *n.* 压(力)；压迫 *v.* 对…施加压力(或影响)；迫使
例 These days the excess weight kids are carrying the increasing risk of developing diabetes, heart disease, high blood *pressure*, cancer, and asthma. 如今，超重儿童患糖尿病、心脏病、高血压、癌症、哮喘的风险越来越大。

scary ['skeəri]
释 *a.* 引起恐慌的；胆小的

bond [bɒnd]
释 *n.* 联结；契约；债券 *v.* (使)黏合；(使)结合

replenish [rɪ'plenɪʃ]
释 *v.* 再装满；补充；充注精力

irreparable [ɪ'repərəbl]
释 *a.* 不能挽回的；不可弥补的

connection [kə'nekʃn]
释 *n.* 联系，关系；连接(部分)

男女相处

candidly ['kændɪdli] *ad.* 率直地；坦白地

cantankerous [kæn'tæŋkərəs] *a.* 脾气坏的；好争吵的

categorical [ˌkætə'gɒrɪkl] *a.* 无条件的；绝对的

clement ['klemənt] *a.* 仁慈的；温和的

debonair [ˌdebə'neə(r)] *a.* (通常指男人)愉快而自信的

despotic [dɪ'spɒtɪk] *a.* 专横的；暴虐的

disregard [ˌdɪsrɪ'gɑːd] *n./v.* 漠视；忽视

implicitly [ɪm'plɪsɪtli] *ad.* 含蓄地

infantile ['ɪnfəntaɪl] *a.* 幼稚的；孩子气的

keenly ['kiːnli] *ad.* 敏锐地

lachrymose ['lækrɪməʊs] *a.* 爱哭的

leniency ['liːniənsi] *n.* 温和；宽容

mushy ['mʌʃi] *a.* 软弱的；感伤多情的

nexus ['neksəs] *n.* 联系，关系

paroxysm ['pærəksɪzəm] *n.* (感情等)突发

perfidy ['pɜːfədi] *n.* 不忠；背叛

stagy ['steɪdʒi] *a.* 戏剧化的；做作的

testy ['testi] *a.* 性急的；暴躁的

unassuming [ˌʌnə'sjuːmɪŋ] *a.* 不爱表现自己的；谦逊的

unimpeachable [ˌʌnɪm'piːtʃəbl] *a.* 无可怀疑的；可靠的

untamed [ˌʌn'teɪmd] *a.* 难控制的

waspish ['wɒspɪʃ] *a.* 易怒的；尖刻的

Patience is bitter, but its fruit is sweet.

—Jean Jacques Rousseau

忍耐是痛苦的，但它的果实是甜蜜的。

——卢梭

Passage 50

Love's Strange Ways

It had been one of those days, hectic, offbeat and not very productive. Her job could at times be very much of a bore. She liked what she did well enough but it really graded on her nerves sometimes. It was no real surprise to her when she found out how glad she was to see quitting time come.

She left the office, made her way to the employee parking lot and retrieved her car. The traffic was as usual horrendous at that time of a day and it would be the middle of summer and the car's air conditioner was out of order. She rolled the window down and let the occasional, hot breathed breeze come her way.

What the heck to do about supper? She was in no mood to cook or for that matter to go out. Her husband was already at home so why not have him call out for a pizza! She picked up the cell phone and dialed her home number. It seemed to ring forever.

Finally, her husband answered but his voice was filled with agitation. It had become an all too familiar sound as of late. Such was life after so many years of marriage!

He reluctantly agreed to order the pizza if she would stop and get the beer. It meant a detour off the freeway but fair was fair—besides there was a convenience store on the way home.

Errands completed, she arrived at the small frame house and noticed none too happily that her flowers were wilting in the heat. What was wrong with the sprinkler system now?

She carried the bag of groceries in the house and found him sitting in the kitchen. He looked aggravated and upset. She did not have to ask why as the old truck he had seemed to be giving him problems all the time now. He did not want to go into the expense of buying a new one...but then, which was worse: constant repairs or monthly payments?

It seemed all too often a familiar routine with them both, constantly arguing and always at odds with each other. What had happened to the romance and the tenderness and the love?

They ate in silence and said little or nothing. For two people who had once had so much to say they were lost to have a civil conversation. He went back to work on the truck and she went out to water the garden after cleaning up the kitchen.

There is an **azalea** bush. No blooms this year and the leaves were falling off. She had tried everything but nothing seemed to work. Perhaps it would be best just to dig it up and **replant** a new one.

She continued the garden watering and then with a **resigned** sigh, she returned to the house as the last rays of a fading summer sun ended across the horizon.

The next day was the same as before, and on it went for another week or more. She kept working with the bush but nothing seemed to help. It was dying and that was that. She made an **offhanded** remark to him and he just looked at her quietly with a **veiled** look about his face.

The next day upon returning from work, she looked at her garden once more and noticed that something really seemed out of place. She was very surprised to find that the old azalea bush had been dug out and next to it was a brand new one, just planted.

She smiled softly to herself and said a silent thank you. Sometimes love does not always speak but shows up in the strangest of ways!

译文

爱情自有方式

这一天如同以往的日子一样，异常地忙碌却没有太大的收获。有时她的工作就是这样乏味。虽然她很喜欢自己所做的事情，但事实上这已经让她逐渐开始厌烦。所以当她发现每到快下班时自己就高兴极了的时候，她一点也不觉得奇怪。

她离开办公室，走到员工停车场找到自己的车。这个时候的交通跟往常一样糟糕至极。时值盛夏，车里的空调却坏了。于是她摇下车窗，让一阵阵温热的微风吹进车里。

晚饭该做些什么吃呢？她没有心情做饭，也没有心情外出就餐。她的丈夫已经到家了，那就让他打电话订个比萨饼吧！她拿起手机拨通了家里的号码，可电话响了很久也没人接。

最后她的丈夫终于接了电话，但是语气很不耐烦。这对她来说已经再熟悉不过了，这就是结婚多年后的生活！

他很不情愿地同意了订比萨饼，但要她顺道买些啤酒回来。这就意味着她得从高速路上下来绕道，不过还算公平——回家的路上还有一家便利店。

买完啤酒，她回到了他们的小木屋，可眼前的景象让她实在高兴不起来——她的花在酷暑下变得蔫头耷脑。是自动洒水装置出了什么问题吗？

她把买来的东西拿进屋里，发现丈夫正坐在厨房里，看起来烦躁不安、神情沮丧。她不必问就知道是什么原因：他那辆旧卡车好像总是给他带来麻烦。他不想花钱买一辆新车，可是无休无止地修理旧车和按月分期付款购买新车，哪种情况更糟呢？

对于他们来说，不断争吵、意见不合似乎已经成了家常便饭。浪漫去哪儿了？温柔与爱去哪儿了？

他们沉默地吃着饭，几乎不说一句话。曾经无话不说的两个人，如今却已无话可说。吃完饭，丈夫继续去修理卡车，而她把厨房收拾干净后，去给花园里的花浇水。

花园里有一丛杜鹃花。今年没有开花，叶子也已经开始凋零。她想尽一切办法都无济于事，也许最好的办法是把它挖掉，重新再种一些。

她继续浇灌着花园，然后长长地叹了一口气，走回了屋里。此时，夏日的夕阳带着最后一抹余晖消失在了地平线上。

第二天仍和以前一样，然后又这样过了一周或者更长的时间。她不断给花丛浇水，但似乎仍然于事无补。它也许真的要死了。她漫不经心地将这件事告诉丈夫，而他只是不动声色地静静看着她。

第二天下班后回到家，她再次走进她的花园，发现好像有些东西不一样了。她十分惊讶地看见，那丛枯萎的杜鹃花已被挖出，而在它旁边是一丛新栽上的杜鹃花。

她温柔地微笑着，默默地说了句"谢谢你"。有时候，爱并不总要说出口，它会以最不同寻常的方式表现出来！

💡 单词记事本

hectic ['hektɪk]
释 *a.* 繁忙的；兴奋的

offbeat [ˌɒf'biːt]
释 *n.* 弱拍 *a.* 反传统的；不平常的

bore [bɔː(r)]
释 *v.* 使厌烦；钻，挖 *n.* 令人讨厌的人（或事）

nerve [nɜːv]
释 *n.* 神经；勇气 *v.* 鼓起勇气

quit [kwɪt]
释 *v.* 停止；放弃；辞(职)

retrieve [rɪ'triːv]
释 *v.* 找回；检索；回忆
例 Much to people's surprise, most of the ransom was *retrieved* in the end. 令人大为吃惊的是，大多数赎金最终竟然都被追回了。

horrendous [hɒ'rendəs]
释 *a.* 可怕的；惊人的

occasional [ə'keɪʒənl]
释 *a.* 偶尔的；临时的

breeze [briːz]
释 *n.* 微风 *v.* 风吹动

mood [muːd]

释 n. 心情；语气；气氛

agitation [ˌædʒɪ'teɪʃn]

释 n. 烦乱；激烈辩论

reluctantly [rɪ'lʌktəntli]

释 ad. 不情愿地；嫌恶地

detour ['diːtʊə(r)]

释 n. 弯路，绕路 v. 迂回；绕道

例 We can't allow anything that *detours* us from the goal. 我们决不容许任何使我们偏离目标的事情发生。

errand ['erənd]

释 n. 差事

wilt [wɪlt]

释 v. (使)枯萎，凋谢，蔫；(使)萎靡
n. 枯萎

sprinkler ['sprɪŋklə(r)]

释 n. 洒水装置；洒水车；喷壶

grocery ['grəʊsəri]

释 n. 杂货；杂货店

aggravate ['æɡrəveɪt]

释 v. 使加重；惹恼，激怒

tenderness ['tendənəs]

释 n. 柔软，柔和；敏感

civil ['sɪvl]

释 a. 公民(间)的；国内的；民事的；文明的

azalea [ə'zeɪliə]

释 n. 杜鹃花

replant [ˌriː'plɑːnt]

释 v. 改种，移植；移居

resigned [rɪ'zaɪnd]

释 a. 逆来顺受的，顺从的

offhanded [ˌɒf'hændɪd]

释 a. 即席的；随便的

veiled [veɪld]

释 a. 以面罩遮掩的；不清楚的；含蓄的

夫妻相处

alluring [ə'lʊərɪŋ] a. 吸引人的；迷人的

bouquet [bu'keɪ] n. 花束；(酒的)芳香

gallant ['ɡælənt] a. (对女子)殷勤的；英勇的

jocund ['dʒɒkənd; 'dʒəʊkənd] a. 快乐的，高兴的

predilection [ˌpriːdɪ'lekʃn] n. 偏爱；爱好

soulful ['səʊlfl] a. 充满热情的；深情的

souvenir [ˌsuːvə'nɪə(r)] n. 纪念品，纪念物

tranquil ['træŋkwɪl] a. 平静的；稳定的

uxorious [ʌk'sɔːriəs] a. 宠爱妻子的

Passage 51

音频

A Gift of Love

The passengers on the bus watched sympathetically as the attractive young woman with the white cane made her way carefully up the steps. She paid the driver and, using her hands to feel the location of the seats, walked down the aisle and found the seat he'd told her was empty. Then she settled in, placed her briefcase on her lap and rested her cane against her leg.

It had been a year since Susan, 34, became blind. Due to a medical misdiagnosis she had been rendered sightless, and she was suddenly thrown into a world of darkness, anger, frustration and self-pity. And all she had to cling to was her husband, Mark.

Mark was an Air Force officer and he loved Susan with all his heart. When she first lost her sight, he watched her sink into despair and was determined to help his wife gain the strength and confidence she needed to become independent again.

Finally, Susan felt ready to return to her job, but how would she get there? She used to take the bus, but was now too frightened to get around the city by herself. Mark volunteered to drive her to work each day, even though they worked at opposite ends of the city. At first, this comforted Susan, and fulfilled Mark's need to protect his sightless wife who was so insecure about performing the slightest task.

Soon, however, Mark realized the arrangement wasn't working. Susan is going to have to start taking the bus again, he admitted to himself. But she was still so fragile, so angry—how would she react? Just as he predicted, Susan was horrified at the idea of taking the bus again.

"I'm blind!" she responded bitterly. "How am I supposed to know where I am going? I feel like you're abandoning me."

Mark's heart broke to hear these words, but he knew what had to be done. He promised Susan that each morning and evening he would ride the bus with her, for as long as it took, until she got the hang of it. And that is exactly what happened. For two solid weeks, Mark, military uniform and all, accompanied Susan to and from work each day.

He taught her how to rely on her other senses, specifically her hearing, to determine where she was and how to adapt to her new environment. He helped her befriend the bus drivers who could watch out for her, and save her a seat.

Finally, Susan decided that she was ready to try the trip on her own. Monday morning arrived, and before she left, she threw her arms around Mark, her **temporary** bus-riding **companion**, her husband, and her best friend. Her eyes filled with tears of gratitude for his loyalty, his patience, and his love. She said good-bye, and for the first time, they went their separate ways. Monday, Tuesday, Wednesday, Thursday... Each day on her own went perfectly, and Susan had never felt better. She was doing it! She was going to work all by herself.

On Friday morning, Susan took the bus to work as usual. As she was paying the **fare** to exit the bus, the driver said, "Boy, I sure do envy you." Susan wasn't sure if the driver was speaking to her or not. After all, who on earth would ever envy a blind woman who had struggled just to find the courage to live for the past year? Curious, she asked the driver, "Why do you say that you envy me?"

The driver responded, "It must feel good to be taken care of and protected like you are." Susan had no idea what the driver was talking about, and again asked, "What do you mean?"

The driver answered, "You know, every morning for the past week, a fine-looking gentleman in a military uniform has been standing across the corner watching you as you get off the bus. He makes sure you cross the street safely and he watches until you enter your office building. Then he blows you a kiss, gives you a little **salute** and walks away. You are one lucky lady."

Tears of happiness poured down Susan's cheeks. For although she couldn't physically see him, she had always felt Mark's presence. She was lucky, so lucky, for he had given her a gift more powerful than sight, a gift she didn't need to see to believe—the gift of love that can bring light where there is darkness.

 译文

爱的礼物

一位年轻漂亮的女子拄着白色手杖，小心翼翼地上了公交车。车里的乘客都同情地注视着她。她买了票，用手摸索着两边的座位，沿着过道往前走，找到了司机告诉她的那个空位。然后她坐了下来，把公事包放在膝上，拐杖则放在腿边。

苏珊是一年前失明的，那时她34岁。一次误诊导致她失去了视力。突然之间，她被抛进了一个充满着愤怒、挫折和自怜自艾的黑暗世界中。丈夫马克成了她的全部依靠。

马克是一位空军军官，他全心全意地爱着苏珊。当苏珊刚刚失明时，看着她渐渐坠入绝望的深渊，马克决定帮助她重新找回独立生活所需的力量和信心。

后来，苏珊终于觉得自己可以重新工作了，但她怎样去上班呢？过去，她常常乘坐公共汽车上下班，但现在她害怕一个人在城市中行走。于是马克每天主动开车送她去上班，尽管他们工作的地方位于城市不同的两端。一开始，这让苏珊感到很宽慰，同时也如马克所愿——他可以保护自己那连做点小事都非常不自信的失明的妻子。

但是，马克很快就意识到这样的安排不妥当。他认为，苏珊必须重新开始独自乘坐公交车。但她仍然那么脆弱，那么易怒——她会有何反应呢？正如他所料，听到要再次独自乘坐公交车时，苏珊害怕极了。

"我是个盲人！"她痛苦地回应道，"我怎么能知道自己在往哪里走啊？我觉得你想抛弃我。"

听到这些话，马克的心都碎了，但是他知道必须这么做。他向苏珊承诺每天早晚会同她一起乘车，直到她适应为止。他确实做到了，在接下来的连续两周内，马克每天都穿着一身军装，陪伴着苏珊上下班。

他教她怎样利用自己的其他感官，尤其是听觉，来确定自己的位置以及适应周围新的环境。他帮她同公交车司机交朋友，这样司机便会关照她，并给她留个座位。

最终，苏珊确定她已经准备好了独自一人上下班。周一早晨，在离家上班前，她伸出胳膊拥抱了马克：他是她的临时公交乘车伙伴，她的丈夫，也是她最好的朋友。她的眼中满含着感激的泪水，感谢他的忠诚、耐心和深情。她说了声再见，然后他们第一次分头去上班。周一，周二，周三，周四……每天她自己乘车都十分顺利，她从来没有感觉这么好过。她做到了！她可以一切都靠自己了。

周五的早上，苏珊如往常一样乘公交车去上班。正当她付了车费准备下车时，司机说："啊，我真羡慕你。"苏珊不确定司机是否是在跟她说话。毕竟，谁会羡慕一个失明的女人呢？在过去的一年里她都在挣扎寻找生活的勇气。出于好奇，她问了司机一句："您为什么羡慕我呢？"

司机回答说："如果能像你一样被人关心和保护，感觉一定很幸福。"苏珊不理解司机在说些什么，又问道："您是指什么呢？"

司机回答说："你知道吗，过去这周的每个早上，都有一位身穿军装的帅气先生站在对面的角落里，看着你下车、安全地穿过马路、走进办公大楼，然后给你一个飞吻，再敬一个军礼，最后才转身离开。你真是一个幸运的人啊。"

幸福的泪水沿着苏珊的面颊流了下来。尽管她看不到马克，但她一直能感觉到他在身旁。她是如此幸运，因为马克给予了她一件比光明更重要的礼物，一件无须亲眼看到也会相信的礼物——这就是能为黑暗带来光明的爱的礼物。

sympathetically [ˌsɪmpə'θetɪkli]
释 *ad.* 同情地；怜悯地

cane [keɪn]
释 *n.* (藤、竹等的)茎；手杖

settle ['setl]
释 *v.* 解决；定居；决定；坐下，安顿下来

misdiagnosis [ˌmɪsdaɪəg'nəʊsɪs]
释 *n.* 误诊

render ['rendə(r)]
释 *v.* 致使；提出，提供；报答
例 You can make good profits if you manage to *render* excellent service to every customer. 如果你能为每位顾客提供优质服务，你就能获得丰厚的利润。

sightless ['saɪtləs]
释 *a.* 失明的，看不见的

self-pity [ˌself'pɪti]
释 *n.* 自怜

cling [klɪŋ]
释 *v.* 紧紧抓住；依靠；附着；坚持
用 cling to 紧紧抓住(或抱住)；(感情上)依靠，依恋
例 U2, who have won three Grammy Awards, *cling* to their status as one of the biggest bands in the world. 获得三项格莱美大奖的U2乐队稳坐世界最著名乐队的宝座。

sink [sɪŋk]
释 *v.* (使)下沉；(使)消沉；挖掘 *n.* 水槽

frightened ['fraɪtnd]
释 *a.* 受惊吓的；害怕的

fulfill [fʊl'fɪl]
释 *v.* 履行，实现；满足

insecure [ˌɪnsɪ'kjʊə(r)]
释 *a.* 不安全的，不可靠的；缺乏安全感的

arrangement [ə'reɪndʒmənt]
释 *n.* 安排；准备工作；整理；布置

fragile ['frædʒaɪl]
释 *a.* 易碎的；脆弱的；不强健的

horrified ['hɒrɪfaɪd]
释 *a.* 非常震惊的

abandon [ə'bændən]
释 *v.* 离开，抛弃；完全放弃 *n.* 放纵，狂热
用 abandon oneself to 纵情于，沉溺于；with abandon 放纵地；纵情地
例 As you become more confident, you *abandon* worry, hesitation and, more importantly, you side-step fear. 随着自信的增加，你开始摒弃担忧、停止犹豫，更重要的是，你不再畏惧。

rely [rɪ'laɪ]
释 *v.* 依靠，依赖；信赖，信任

adapt [ə'dæpt]
释 *v.* (使)适应；改编，改写
用 adapt to 适应；adapt ... for ... 将…改编成…

befriend [bɪ'frend]
释 *v.* 与…交朋友；友好地对待；照顾

temporary ['temprəri]
释 *a.* 短暂的；暂时的；临时的

companion [kəm'pæniən]
释 *n.* 同伴；伴侣
例 Sam was helped by his *companions* when he was in trouble. 萨姆处于困境时得到了同伴们的帮助。

fare [feə(r)]
释 *n.* (车、船、飞机等的)票价；(付费的)乘客；食物 *v.* 进展

salute [sə'luːt]
释 *v.* 向…敬礼；赞扬 *n.* 敬礼；欢迎

幸福生活

compliment ['kɒmplɪmənt] *n.* 赞美

ecstatic [ɪk'stætɪk] *a.* 狂喜的，心花怒放的

exhilaration [ɪgˌzɪlə'reɪʃn] *n.* 高兴；兴奋

jubilation [ˌdʒuːbɪ'leɪʃn] *n.* 欢快；欢庆

laudable ['lɔːdəbl] *a.* 值得赞美的，值得称赞的

liberally ['lɪbərəli] *ad.* 随意地；不受限制地

mirth [mɜːθ] *n.* 欢乐；欢笑

perceptible [pə'septəbl] *a.* 可察觉的，可感知的

retrospect ['retrəspekt] *n.* 回顾；怀旧，追忆

sympathy ['sɪmpəθi] *n.* 同情；(思想感情上的)赞同

Do not, for one repulse, give up the purpose that you resolved to effect.
　　　　　　　　　　　　　　—William Shakespeare

不要只因一次失败，就放弃你原来决心想达到的目的。
　　　　　　　　　　　　　　　　　　——莎士比亚

Chapter ⑤

励志人生

Passage 52

Ask Yourself Five
Questions When Meeting Failure

As we go through life we have relationships that don't work out, jobs that just aren't right, exams that we **flunk**, **initiatives** that don't succeed. The more new things we try, the more failures we are likely to have. In fact, the only way to avoid failure is to do nothing new.

The important thing is how we deal with failure. It can be part of a downward **slide** in which lack of confidence reinforces feelings of **inadequacy** and **incompetence**. But experiencing failure can be a learning experience and an opportunity for a fresh start. A good way to begin this process is by asking yourself some tough questions.

1. What can I learn from this?

Take responsibility for what went wrong. OK, so it was not all your **fault**—but some of it was. Successful people don't make excuses or blame others. They take **ownership** of the issues. Be **critical** but **constructive**. Try to look at the experience **objectively**. Make a list of the key things that happened. Analyze the list step by step and look for the learning points.

2. What could I have done differently?

What other options did you have? What choices did you make? How could you have handled it differently? With the benefit of hindsight, what different steps would you have taken?

3. Do I need to acquire or improve some skills?

Did the problem **reveal** some lack of skill on your part? How could you learn or improve those skills? Perhaps there are books or courses or people you could turn to. Make a self-development plan to acquire the skills and experiences you need.

4. Who can I learn from?

Is there someone to whom you can turn for advice? Did a boss, colleague or a friend see what happened? If they are constructive and **supportive**, then ask them for some feedback and guidance. Most people do not ask for help because they believe it to be a sign of weakness rather than strength. It's not. It shows that you are ready to learn and change. Any good friend will be happy to help.

5. What will I do next?

Now draw up your action plan. Will you try something similar or something different? **Revisit** your goals and **objectives**. This **reversal** has been a **setback** on your journey but think of it as a **diversion** rather than a **halt**. You can now reset your sights on your destination and plan a new course.

If you read the life stories of successful people—especially inventors, explorers, scientists or **statesmen**—you will find that their early careers are **littered** with failures. Walt Disney, Thomas Edison and Henry Ford are typical examples. Abraham Lincoln suffered many **defeats** in his career in politics including losing the **nomination** for vice president in 1856 and his second run at being a U.S. **Senator** in 1858. Two years later he was **elected** president.

The important point is to use your setbacks as learning experiences and make them stepping stones to future success. There are always **positives** you can take from every episode in your life. Asking yourself these five questions can help find them.

译文

失败时问自己五个问题

在我们的一生中，总会遇到不好处理的人际关系、不太满意的工作、没有通过的考试，或者未能实现的计划。我们尝试的新事物越多，经历的失败就可能越多。事实上，除非不去尝试新的事物，否则难免会遭遇失败。

其实，最重要的是我们如何应对失败。失败有时就是一段下坡路，处于其中的人往往感到自卑，挫败感和无力感也随之增强。但经历失败也是一次学习和重新开始的机会。要想有一个好的开始，最好先问问自己以下五个问题。

1. 从失败中我学到了什么？

对所犯的错误承担责任。即便失败并非都是你的错，你也确实难辞其咎。成功的人从来不找借口或埋怨他人，而是坦然承担责任，提出建设性的批判，试着客观看待失败的经历，列出所发生的重要事情的清单，并逐条分析其中的问题，认真总结。

2. 如果当初换一种做法结果会有什么不同？

当初是否还有其他选择？你做了什么选择？你当时还能采取什么不同的方法来处理此事？现在回头看看，你会采取什么解决办法？

3. 我是否需要学习或提升一些技能?

这次的失败是不是也反映了你自身能力的一些不足? 你该如何学习或者提升这些能力? 也许, 你可以通过看书、上课或向人请教来提升。制订一个自我提升的计划来掌握所需的技巧、获得所需的经验吧。

4. 我可以向谁请教?

你周围是否有可以征求建议的人? 你的上司、同事或者朋友也见证了你所经历的这一切吗? 如果他们都支持你, 并能提出有建设性的建议, 可以请他们给予一些反馈和指导。很多人不愿意寻求帮助, 觉得求助是在示弱而非彰显能力。实则不然。向人求助表示你想要学习和改变, 朋友肯定会乐于伸出援手。

5. 接下来该怎么办?

制定出行动方案。你想一成不变还是作出改变? 重新审视自己的目标。这次失败是你人生旅程中的一次挫折, 但把它看作只是多走了一点弯路, 而非旅程的终止。现在, 你可以重新设定目标, 并为之制订一个新的计划。

如果你阅读成功人士的人生故事——尤其是发明家、探险家、科学家或政治家的, 你会发现他们在事业初期大都经历了重重失败。华特·迪士尼、托马斯·爱迪生以及亨利·福特都是典型的例子。亚伯拉罕·林肯在他的政治生涯中屡遭挫败, 包括1856年副总统提名落选以及1858年参议员连任失败。但是两年后, 他当选为总统。

所以说关键在于要把所经历过的失败看作是学习的机会, 使它们成为你今后成功的基石。生命中的每段历程都有你可以学习的积极的一面。多问问自己这五个问题, 你或许就会有所发现。

💡 单词记事本

flunk [flʌŋk]
释 v./n. 考试不及格; 失败

initiative [ɪ'nɪʃətɪv]
释 n. 主动的行动, 倡议; 主动权

slide [slaɪd]
释 v. 滑动; (使)悄悄地移动 n. 滑坡

inadequacy [ɪn'ædɪkwəsi]
释 n. 不充分; 无能, 无法胜任; 不足之处

incompetence [ɪn'kɒmpɪtəns]
释 n. 不胜任; 无能力

fault [fɔːlt]
释 n. 缺点; 过错; 【地质学】断层
用 at fault 有责任; 感到困惑; find fault with 抱怨, 找错

ownership ['əʊnəʃɪp]
释 n. 所有权; 物主身份

critical ['krɪtɪkl]

释 a. 批评的；关键的，危急的

例 Good understanding of team work is *critical* for one's career success. 对团队工作的良好理解对一个人的事业成功至关重要。

constructive [kən'strʌktɪv]

释 a. 建设性的，有助益的

objectively [əb'dʒektɪvli]

释 ad. 客观地

reveal [rɪ'viːl]

释 v. 揭露，揭示；展现，显示

supportive [sə'pɔːtɪv]

释 a. 支持的；赞助的

revisit [ˌriː'vɪzɪt]

释 v. 再访；重新审视；重游；回到 n. 重访；再次参观

objective [əb'dʒektɪv]

释 n. 目标，目的 a. 客观的

例 It's preferable to use subjective indicators as well as *objective* indicators. 最好是客观与主观两种衡量指标并用。

reversal [rɪ'vɜːsl]

释 n. 颠倒，反向；(位置、功能等的)转换；失败

setback ['setbæk]

释 n. 挫折；倒退

diversion [daɪ'vɜːʃn]

释 n. 偏离；转向；消遣

halt [hɔːlt; hɒlt]

释 n. 停顿；暂停 v. 止步，(使)停住，踌躇

statesman ['steɪtsmən]

释 n. 政治家

litter ['lɪtə(r)]

释 n. 垃圾，废弃物 v. 乱扔；使充满

defeat [dɪ'fiːt]

释 v. 击败；挫败 n. 战败；失败

例 I never realized an economic *defeat* could look so much like a military one. 我从来没想过一场经济打击居然能造成像军事打击一样的惨况。

nomination [ˌnɒmɪ'neɪʃn]

释 n. 提名；任命

senator ['senətə(r)]

释 n. 参议员

elect [ɪ'lekt]

释 v. 选举；选择

positive ['pɒzətɪv]

释 a. 积极的；确实的；完全的；正的 n. 正数，正量；积极的一面

💡单词家族

所思所想

ambidextrous [ˌæmbɪ'dekstrəs] a. 双手都很灵巧的；怀有二意的

astute [ə'stjuːt] a. 机敏的；精明的

credulous ['kredjələs] a. 轻信的

disabuse [ˌdɪsə'bjuːz] v. 打消(某人的)错误念头

envisage [ɪn'vɪzɪdʒ] v. 展望，想象

heed [hiːd] n. 注意；留意

implicit [ɪm'plɪsɪt] a. 含蓄的；不言明的；不明确的

incisive [ɪn'saɪsɪv] a. 深刻的；尖锐的

inkling ['ɪŋklɪŋ] n. 暗示

insidious [ɪn'sɪdɪəs] a. 阴险的；暗中为害的

instinct ['ɪnstɪŋkt] n. 本能，直觉

introspective [ˌɪntrə'spektɪv] a. 自省的，反省的

involuntary [ɪn'vɒləntri] a. 不知不觉的；无意识的

misperceive [ˌmɪspə'siːv] v. 误解；错误感觉

nostalgia [nɒ'stældʒə] n. 乡愁；怀旧

outlet ['aʊtlet] n. 发泄的方法；排遣

outwit [ˌaʊt'wɪt] v. 以智胜过；用计击败

penetrating ['penɪtreɪtɪŋ] a. (思想)敏锐的

pertinacious [ˌpɜːtɪ'neɪʃəs] a. 固执的；不妥协的

ponder ['pɒndə(r)] v. 沉思；考虑

preoccupied [pri'ɒkjupaɪd] a. 心事重重的；出神的

prophecy ['prɒfəsi] n. 预言；预言能力

relent [rɪ'lent] v. 发慈悲，变温和；减弱

subliminal [ˌsʌb'lɪmɪnl] a. 下意识的；潜意识的

uncanny [ʌn'kæni] a. 异乎寻常的；出乎意料的

Doubt is our traitor, often making us lose the possible victory for fear of trying.
——William Shakespeare

疑惑是叛徒，往往使我们因害怕尝试而输掉了可能会赢得的战果。
——莎士比亚

Passage 53

Leap of Faith

After ten years of working for a prestigious Wall Street bank and **slamming** into a glass ceiling, I **vehemently** said "Enough!"

If I was going to have an inspiring, **compelling** life and go beyond a clock-punching, nine-to-five job, I knew I had to make the decision to create it and shift **gears**.

I began looking. I'd never let my deafness **shortchange** my dreams. I wasn't about to start now.

After scanning local advertisements, I learned a financial giant was looking to hire more **stockbrokers**. I thought I can do that! With great excitement, I called a few people and made an appointment to see a branch **vice** president.

On the day of my appointment, I was terribly sick with a cold and a fever of 38.3 degrees Celsius that threatened to keep me in bed. Yet, I knew I couldn't let this golden opportunity slip away, so I reluctantly showed up for the interview.

We ended up talking for over three hours. It went so well that I was positive he would hire me on the **spot**. Instead, he told me to come back for 12 more interviews with his top **salespeople**!

Over the next five months, every one of them discouraged me from becoming a stockbroker.

"You're better off in a safe nine-to-five job," they **proclaimed**. "Eighty percent of newcomers fail within their first year," they added. "You have no investment experience."

"You won't make it."

The more they attacked my dream, the more my stomach **tightened**. I realized then that I would have to "make it."

The last interview with the vice president was scheduled on a cold, **blustery** January day. Five minutes into the meeting, it was obvious he didn't know what to do with me. He nervously played with a paper clip and pretended to read a report I had prepared on how I would build my business if I was hired.

It was now or never. With all the courage I could **muster**, I looked at him straight in the eye and captured his attention.

"Sir," I said, "if you don't hire me, you'll never know just how much I could have done for this firm." When I heard my own brazen words, I panicked. My God, I thought, what have I done? Can I really back that up?

I waited and waited. The seconds seemed like minutes and the minutes like hours.

He threw the paper clip in the wastebasket and finally spoke.

"Okay, you've got the job!" he announced.

I stood up triumphantly and was about to leave when he added, "On one condition."

I froze.

"First," he said, "you must first resign from your job, effective two weeks from today and enroll in our three-month training program. When you're done with that, you'll be required to take the Series 7 stockbroker exam. It's 250 questions long and you must pass it on the first try."

He then drove home his final point, "If you fail even by one point—you're out!"

My mouth went dry. I nearly choked at the prospect of taking a huge leap of faith into the unknown. I knew I stood to lose everything if I failed that test!

Then, captivated by this ultimate risk-taking opportunity and the courage I never knew I had, I swallowed hard and said, "I'll take it."

As instructed, I cut my lifeline to the bank and leapt into unproven waters.

After three months of training, I was ready to take the three-hour exam. The test site was a short distance from where I would be working, if I passed.

I remember taking the elevator to the seventh floor and registering. From the reception area, I could see the test room through the glass partition. It was full of computers, all deliberately spaced in several rows. The room was sparsely furnished with the barest of essentials: scrap paper, several sharpened pencils and uncomfortable-looking chairs.

The exam proctor cheerfully led me to my assigned computer. I thought, at least she wasn't taking the test!

Soon she gave me a signal to go ahead. I was very nervous but as the test progressed, I felt increasingly confident. Three hours passed quickly.

It was time for the final score—the computer would calculate it and flash it on the screen.

I sat there with my hands folded on my lap and stared at the computer that held the key to my future. I was positive someone could hear my heart thumping. The screen blinked on and off with the message, "Your scores are being tabulated by the computer, please wait."

I couldn't wait—I wanted it to be over with!

Finally, the scores were displayed.

I had passed! I let out an **audible** sigh of relief.

Since that day, I've never looked back. I **exceeded** not only my own expectations but also those of the manager who took a chance and hired me on that **fateful** day. Before being promoted upstairs, he was around long enough to **witness** my personal sales **soar** 1,700%, hand me several sales awards and see me interviewed on CNN.

That was in 1992. Four years later, I took another daring risk and left the **lucrative** securities industry to become an **inspirational** speaker and author.

My experiences confirmed the truth of Thoreau's words, "If one advances confidently in the direction of his dreams and endeavors to live the life which he has imagined, he will meet success unexpected in common hours."

译 文

信心的飞跃

在华尔街一家颇具知名度的银行里工作了十年后，我终于晋升到了高级管理层。这时我坚决地对自己说："这足够了！"

如果想要过一种令人振奋、引人注目的生活，脱离按时打卡、朝九晚五的工作模式的话，我知道我必须下决心来改变现状，为自己创造出这种生活。

我开始寻觅。我从不允许自身的盲目影响我对梦想的追逐。我只是暂时还没有开始行动。

在浏览了报纸上刊登的本地广告后，我得知一家金融巨头正在招聘更多的证券经纪人。我认为自己能够胜任！带着无比兴奋的心情，我打了几通电话，并与一个分行的副总裁约定了面谈时间。

到了约定的当天，我得了重感冒，高烧38.3℃，几乎起不了床。但我清楚自己不会让这个难得的机会就此溜走，于是我强撑着去参加了面试。

我们谈了三个多小时。面试进行得十分顺利，我甚至觉得他当场就会聘用我。然而，他却让我再与他的销售精英们进行另外12轮的面试！

在接下来的五个月里，这些对我进行面试的人都劝我不要当证券经纪人。

他们说："你最好还是从事朝九晚五的稳定工作。80%的新人在这行干不到一年就都走了。"然后又补充道，"况且你也没有投资经验。"

"你做不了的。"

他们越是打击我的梦想，我的决心就越坚定。也就是在那时我意识到我必须成功。

与副总裁的最后一次面试被安排在一月的一个寒风凛冽的日子。五分钟过去了，很显然他不知道该如何答复我。他紧张地摆弄着一个回形针，装作在看我的报告。在报告中，我陈述了如果被聘用，我将会如何开展业务。

这是最后的机会。我鼓足所有的勇气直视他的眼睛，以引起他的注意。

"先生，"我说，"如果您不录用我，您将永远不会知道我能为公司创造多少财富。"当听到自己所说的"大话"时，我都吓了一跳。天啊，我说了些什么？我真的能做到吗？

我等待着他作出回应，只觉得每一秒钟都那么漫长。

他把回形针扔到纸篓里，终于开口说话了。

"行，你被聘用了！"他宣布说。

我以成功者的姿态站了起来，然后准备离开，这时他又说道："但有一个条件。"

我僵住了。

"首先，"他说，"你必须先辞掉你现在的工作，从今天开始，在接下来的两星期里必须随叫随到，来参加我们为期三个月的培训。培训结束之后，你要参加证券经纪人系列7的测试。测试一共有250道问题，你必须一次性通过。"

接着，他说出了最后一点："即便你差一分，也将出局。"

我嘴唇发干。信心的飞跃将我带入到的这片未知的前景几乎令我窒息。我知道，如果通不过这个测试，我将一无所有。

然而，我被这个机会所带来的巨大风险和我自己前所未有的勇气深深吸引，咽了口唾沫，说道："我同意。"

按照要求，我辞去了银行的工作，迈进了未知的领域。

在三个月的培训后，我已经准备好参加那场三个小时的测试。考场离我将要工作的地方（如果我能通过测试的话）只有很短的一段距离。

我还记得当时乘电梯到七楼登记的场景。透过前台的玻璃挡板，可以看到进行测试的房间。里面满是电脑，被仔细地摆成几排。房间里只有一些必需品：草稿纸、几支削好的铅笔和一些看起来不太舒服的椅子。

考官高高兴兴地将我带到被分配的电脑前。我心想：反正她不用参加这次测试！

很快，她示意我可以开始答题了。我非常紧张，但随着测试往下进行，我越来越有自信。三个小时很快就过去了。

到了公布成绩的时候了——电脑会自动统计分数并显示在屏幕上。

我坐在那儿，双手紧握着放在腿上，紧盯着那台掌控我未来命运的电脑。我肯定一定有人能听到我怦怦的心跳声。屏幕上一直闪着："电脑正在将您的分数制成表格，请稍候。"

我等不下去了，只希望这一切赶快结束。

终于，成绩出来了！

我通过了！我长长地舒了一口气。

那天之后，我从未回首过去。我不仅超出了自己的期望，更超出了在那决定性的一天冒险雇用我的副总裁的期望。在他升职之前，他见证了我的个人销售额激增1700%的辉煌，并亲自给我颁发了几个销售奖，还看到了我在CNN上的专访。

那是1992年。四年后，我又抓住了另一个冒险的机会——离开利润丰厚的证券业，成为了一名励志宣讲人和作家。

我的经历证实了梭罗的话："如果一个人信心十足地朝着自己的梦想前进，为了自己设想的生活而奋力拼搏，他一定会在平凡的生命历程中获得意想不到的成功。"

💡 单词记事本

slam [slæm]
释 v. 砰地关上；猛烈抨击；奋力前进 n. 砰的一声

vehemently ['viːəməntli]
释 ad. 感情激烈地；热情地

compelling [kəm'pelɪŋ]
释 a. 引人注目的；令人佩服的；强制的

gear [gɪə(r)]
释 n. 齿轮；传动装置；排挡 v. 调节，使适应

shortchange [ˌʃɔːtˈtʃeɪndʒ]
释 v. (找钱时故意)少找零头；欺骗

stockbroker ['stɒkbrəʊkə(r)]
释 n. 股票(或证券)经纪人

vice [vaɪs]
释 n. 恶习；缺点 a. 副的

spot [spɒt]
释 n. 地点；斑点；少量 v. 认出；玷污；用点作记号

salespeople ['seɪlz,piːpl]
释 n. 推销员

proclaim [prə'kleɪm]
释 v. 宣告，公布；显示，表明

tighten ['taɪtn]
释 v. 变紧；变严格
例 Looming layoffs and *tightening* credit have crushed consumers' confidence. 潜在的解雇危机和紧缩的信贷打击了消费者的信心。

blustery ['blʌstəri]
释 a. 大风的；狂暴的

muster ['mʌstə(r)]
释 n. 召集；检阅；花名册 v. (人员)集合；鼓起(勇气等)

brazen ['breɪzn]
释 a. 厚颜无耻的；黄铜制的

panic ['pænɪk]
释 n./v. 恐慌

triumphantly [traɪˈʌmfəntli]
释 ad. 成功地；洋洋得意地

freeze [friːz]
释 v. 结冰；站住不动 n. 冻结；冰冻期

enroll [ɪnˈrəʊl]
释 v. 参加；登记

choke [tʃəʊk]
释 v. (使)窒息；堵塞 n. 窒息；(引擎)阻气门
用 choke back 忍住，抑制；choke up (因激动等)说不出话来

captivate [ˈkæptɪveɪt]
释 v. 迷住，迷惑；吸引

ultimate [ˈʌltɪmət]
释 a. 达到极限的；基本的 n. 最大的或最先进的事物

swallow [ˈswɒləʊ]
释 n. 燕子；一次吞咽的量 v. 吞，咽；忍受；吞没

leap [liːp]
释 v. 跳；急速行动 n. 跳；激增
用 by/in leaps and bounds 极其迅速地；leap at 迫不及待地接受
例 Coffee and orange juice prices made their biggest leaps on Friday. 咖啡和橙汁的价格在周五涨到最高。

unproven [ʌnˈpruːvn]
释 a. 未经证明的；未经检验的

partition [pɑːˈtɪʃn]
释 n. 分隔物；分割 v. 隔开；分割

deliberately [dɪˈlɪbərətli]
释 ad. 故意地；小心翼翼地，审慎地

sparsely [spɑːsli]
释 ad. 稀疏地；贫乏地

furnish [ˈfɜːnɪʃ]
释 v. 布置，配备家具；提供

proctor [ˈprɒktə(r)]
释 n. 学监；监考人

calculate [ˈkælkjuleɪt]
释 v. 计算；计划

thump [θʌmp]
释 v. 重击；(心)怦怦直跳 n. 重击(声)
例 The hunter aimed the deer and fired, and it fell with a thump. 猎人瞄准了那只鹿开枪，鹿砰的一声倒下了。

tabulate [ˈtæbjuleɪt]
释 v. 制成表格，列表；使成平面状

audible [ˈɔːdəbl]
释 a. 听得见的

exceed [ɪkˈsiːd]
释 v. 超过，超出；胜过

fateful [ˈfeɪtfl]
释 a. 重要的，决定性的

witness [ˈwɪtnəs]
释 n. 目击者；证据 v. 目睹；目击；为…作证

soar [sɔː(r)]
释 v. 猛增；(情绪、期望等)高涨；高耸

lucrative [ˈluːkrətɪv]
释 a. 赚钱的，可获利的

inspirational [ˌɪnspəˈreɪʃənl]
释 a. 有灵感的；鼓舞人心的

职业生涯

adequate ['ædɪkwət] *a.* 足够的；可以胜任的

allowance [ə'laʊəns] *n.* 津贴；补助

arrange [ə'reɪndʒ] *v.* 整理；安排；筹备

avail [ə'veɪl] *n.* 效用；利益

bonus ['bəʊnəs] *n.* 奖金；红利

candidate ['kændɪdət; 'kændɪdeɪt] *n.* 候选人；申请人

carpenter ['kɑːpəntə(r)] *n.* 木工，木匠

credentials [krə'denʃlz] *n.* 证明书；(学历等的)资格

dealer ['diːlə(r)] *n.* 商人，贩子

dedicate ['dedɪkeɪt] *v.* 奉献；把…用在

deduct [dɪ'dʌkt] *v.* 扣除(奖金等)

deputy ['depjuti] *n.* 代理人；代表

designate ['dezɪgneɪt] *v.* 指定；任命

dispatch [dɪ'spætʃ] *v.* 派遣；迅速处理 *n.* (公文)急件

displace [dɪs'pleɪs] *v.* 取代；移置

enterprise ['entəpraɪz] *n.* 事业；事业心

nominate ['nɒmɪneɪt] *v.* 提名；任命

obligation [ˌɒblɪ'geɪʃn] *n.* 义务，责任

partnership ['pɑːtnəʃɪp] *n.* 合伙(关系)；合伙经营(的企业)

plumber ['plʌmə(r)] *n.* 管子工；水暖工

predecessor ['priːdɪsesə(r)] *n.* 前任；(被取代的)原有事物

quarterly ['kwɔːtəli] *a.* 季度的 *ad.* 每季一次

questionnaire [ˌkwestʃə'neə(r)] *n.* (作统计或调查用的)问卷

succession [sək'seʃn] *n.* 连续；继任，继承

vacant ['veɪkənt] *a.* 未占用的；空的

vocation [vəʊ'keɪʃn] *n.* 职业，行业；使命感

welfare ['welfeə(r)] *n.* 福利；幸福

The most promising successor is not the talented, but those who are good at seizing every opportunity to explore. —Socrates

最有希望的成功者并不是才干出众的人，而是那些最善于利用每个时机去发掘开拓的人。 ——苏格拉底

Passage 54

Attitude Is Everything

Michael is the kind of guy you love to hate. He is always in a good mood and always has something positive to say. When someone would ask him how he was doing, he would reply, "If I were any better, I would be twins!" He was a natural motivator. If an employee was having a bad day, Michael was there telling the employee how to look on the positive side of the situation.

Seeing this style really made me curious, so one day I went up to Michael and asked him, "I don't get it! You can't be a positive person all of the time. How do you do it?" Michael replied, "Each morning I wake up and say to myself, 'Mike, you have two choices today.' You can choose to be in a good mood or you can choose to be in a bad mood. I choose to be in a good mood. Each time something bad happens, I can choose to be a victim or I can choose to learn from it. I choose to learn from it. Every time someone comes to me complaining, I can choose to accept their complaining or I can point out the positive side of life. I choose the positive side of life."

"Yeah, right, it's not that easy," I protested.

"Yes, it is," Michael said. "Life is all about choices. When you cut away all the junk, every situation is a choice. You choose how you react to situations. You choose how people will affect your mood. You choose to be in a good mood or bad mood. The bottom line: It's your choice how you live life."

I reflected on what Michael said. Soon thereafter, I left the Tower Industry to start my own business. We lost touch, but I often thought about him when I made a choice about life instead of reacting to it.

Several years later, I heard that Michael was involved in a serious accident, falling some 60 feet from a communications tower. After 18 hours of surgery and weeks of intensive care, Michael was released from the hospital with rods placed in his back. I saw Michael about six months after the accident. When I asked him how he was, he replied, "If I were any better, I'd be twins. Wanna see my scars?"

I declined to see his wounds, but did ask him what had gone through his mind as the accident took place. "The first thing that went through my mind was the well-being of my soon-to-be-born daughter," Michael replied. "Then, as I lay on the ground, I remembered that I had two choices: I could choose to live or I could choose to die. I chose to live."

"Weren't you scared? Did you lose **consciousness**?" I asked.

Michael continued, "The **paramedics** were great. They kept telling me I was going to be fine. But when they **wheeled** me into the ER and I saw the expressions on the faces of the doctors and nurses, I got really scared. In their eyes, I read 'he's a dead man.' I knew I needed to take action."

"What did you do?" I asked.

"Well, there was a big **burly** nurse shouting questions at me," said Michael. "She asked if I was **allergic** to anything. 'Yes,' I replied. The doctors and nurses stopped working as they waited for my reply. I took a deep breath and yelled, 'Gravity.' Over their laughter, I told them, 'I am choosing to live. **Operate** on me as if I am alive, not dead.'"

Michael lived, thanks to the skill of his doctors, but also because of his amazing **attitude**. I learned from him that every day we have the choice to live fully.

Attitude, after all, is everything.

译文

态度决定一切

迈克尔是那种让人又爱又恨的家伙。他总是心情很好，还总能说出一些积极向上的话来。每当有人问他近况如何时，他都会回答："好得不能再好了！"他天生善于激励别人。如果有哪个同事某天过得不太如意，迈克尔就会过去告诉他如何从积极的一面看待这件事情。

他的这种生活态度着实令我好奇，所以有一天我走上前去问他："我真搞不懂！你怎么能一直都这么积极乐观呢？你是怎么做到的？"迈克尔答道："每天早晨醒来，我都会对自己说：'迈克，你今天有两个选择，你可以选择有个好心情，也可以选择有个坏心情。'我选择有个好心情。每当有不好的事情发生时，我可以选择成为受害者，也可以选择从中吸取教训。我选择从中吸取教训。每当有人来找我抱怨时，我可以选择接受他们的抱怨，也可以为他们指出生活中的积极面。我选择为他们指出生活中的积极面。"

"是的，话虽如此，可做起来没那么容易吧。"我对此表示异议。

"其实我挺容易。"迈克尔说道，"生活就是由选择组成的。当你抛却那些无关紧要的细枝末节，你会发现生活中面对的每件事其实都是一次选择。你选择如何应对这些境遇。你选择让人们如何影响你的心情。你选择是开心还是沮丧。说到底就是，你选择怎样来过自己的生活。"

我仔细思考了迈克尔的话。不久后，我离开了托尔工业公司，开始自己创业。我们失去了联系，但每当我在生活中作出选择而非被动接受时，我总会想起他。

几年后，我听说迈克尔遭遇了一场严重的事故——他从一座大约60英尺（约18.3米）高的通讯塔上摔了下来。历经18个小时的手术和数周的精心特护后，迈克尔才出院。他的背部植入了金属棍。那场事故之后大约过了半年，我见到了迈克尔。当我问他过得如何时，他回答道："我好极了，没有谁能比我过得更好了。想看看我的伤疤吗？"

我没有看他的伤口，而是问他事故发生时，他在想些什么。迈克尔回答道："我首先想到的是我即将出生的女儿以后的幸福生活。然后我躺在地上，想着我有两个选择。我可以选择活下去，也可以选择死去。我选择了活下去。"

"你就不害怕吗？你有没有失去知觉？"我问道。

迈克尔继续说："那些救护人员棒极了。他们一直告诉我，我会没事的。然而，当他们将我推入急诊室的时候，我看到了医生和护士脸上的表情，我真的感到害怕了。从他们的眼睛中，我看到了'他不行了'这几个字。我知道我必须做些什么。"

"你是怎么做的？"我问道。

"是这样，有一位高大的护士大声地冲我提问。"迈克尔说道，"她问我是否对某些东西过敏。我回答说'是的'。医生和护士都停了下来，等着我继续说。我深吸了一口气，大声喊道：'万有引力。'他们都笑了，然后我告诉他们：'我选择活下去。请把我当成活人而不是死人来医治。'"

迈克尔活了下来，这归功于医生们的高明医术，但也和他那令人惊叹的生活态度分不开。从他身上，我学到了每天我们都可以选择充实地生活。

归根结底，态度决定一切。

💡 单词记事本

natural ['nætʃrəl]
释 a. 自然的；天生的；本能的

motivator ['məʊtɪveɪtə(r)]
释 n. 动力；激励因素；激励者

curious ['kjʊəriəs]
释 a. 好奇的；有求知欲的；奇特的

victim ['vɪktɪm]
释 n. 受害者；牺牲品

complain [kəm'pleɪn]
释 v. 抱怨，诉苦；投诉，控告
搭 complain of/about 抱怨；complain to 向…抱怨

例 After we *complained* to the family living upstairs, the noise was muffled considerably. 我们向楼上的住户投诉之后，噪音降低了很多。

protest
释 [prə'test] *v.* (公开)反对；抗议 ['prəʊtest] *n.* 抗议；反对

junk [dʒʌŋk]
释 *n.* 无用或无价值的东西；废旧物品 *v.* 丢弃，废弃

react [ri'ækt]
释 *v.* 作出反应，回应；反对；起化学反应；起作用
用 react against 反对；反抗；react with 起化学反应；react on/upon 对…有影响，起作用
例 Imagine being asked to spend twelve or so years of your life in a society which consisted only of members of your own sex. How would you *react*? 想象一下让你在一个同性社会里生活12年左右，你会有何反应？

reflect [rɪ'flekt]
释 *v.* 反射；反映；深思；反省
用 reflect on/upon 仔细考虑，反省；对…不利，使…名誉受影响

thereafter [ˌðeər'ɑːftə(r)]
释 *ad.* 之后，此后

surgery ['sɜːdʒəri]
释 *n.* 外科；外科手术；手术室

intensive [ɪn'tensɪv]
释 *a.* 加强的；集中的；精心的

release [rɪ'liːs]
释 *v./n.* 释放；解除，解放；准许离开；发表

用 release of bank account 银行存款解冻；day release 脱产学习

rod [rɒd]
释 *n.* 杆，棒

decline [dɪ'klaɪn]
释 *v.* 下降；衰落；拒绝，谢绝 *n.* 下降，衰落
用 fall/sink into a decline 开始衰落，体力衰退(尤指因患肺病而衰弱)；on the decline 走下坡路，在衰退中；the decline of life 晚年，暮年
例 As is showed in the pie chart, there is a slight *decline* in gross profit in the first quarter. 如饼状图所示，第一季度的毛利润略有下降。

consciousness ['kɒnʃəsnəs]
释 *n.* 知觉，意识；觉悟

paramedic [ˌpærə'medɪk]
释 *n.* 医务人员

wheel [wiːl]
释 *n.* 轮，车轮；旋转 *v.* 推；转动

burly ['bɜːli]
释 *a.* 强壮的；粗鲁的 *n.* 身材魁梧的人

allergic [ə'lɜːdʒɪk]
释 *a.* 过敏的；对…讨厌的
用 allergic to 厌恶

operate ['ɒpəreɪt]
释 *v.* 动手术；起作用；经营

attitude ['ætɪtjuːd]
释 *n.* 态度；看法；姿势
用 attitude toward(s) 对…的看法、态度
例 This genial *attitude* is a key reason why he won the election. 和蔼的态度是他在选举中获胜的一个关键原因。

人际交往

buoyancy ['bɔɪənsi] n. 轻快；欢乐

complacency [kəm'pleɪsnsi] n. 自满；自得

complimentary [ˌkɒmplɪ'mentri] a. 赞美的；恭维的

connive [kə'naɪv] v. 默许；纵容；共谋

contender [kən'tendə(r)] n. 竞争者；争夺者

deferential [ˌdefə'renʃl] a. 恭敬的，恭顺的

disparage [dɪ'spærɪdʒ] v. 蔑视，贬损

eclecticism [ɪ'klektɪsɪzəm] n. 折中主义

fatalist ['feɪtəlɪst] n. 宿命论者

gallantry ['gæləntri] n. 勇敢；殷勤

irritable ['ɪrɪtəbl] a. 急躁的；易怒的

namby-pamby [ˌnæmbi'pæmbi] a. 伤感的；矫饰的

overconfident [ˌəʊvə'kɒnfɪdənt] a. 过于自信的；自负的

patronizing ['pætrənaɪzɪŋ] a. 以恩人自居的

pique [piːk] v. 激怒；激起

sentimentalism [ˌsentɪ'mentəlɪzəm] n. 感情用事

shilly-shally ['ʃɪliʃæli] v. 犹豫不决

simmer ['sɪmə(r)] v. 内心充满(怒火等)；即将爆发

transient ['trænziənt] n. 短暂停留的人或物；过客

turbulent ['tɜːbjələnt] a. 混乱的；吵闹的

vapid ['væpɪd] a. 索然无味的

Love what you do, because success of any type requires passion.

—Carly Fiorina

爱你所做的事，成功是需要热情的。

——卡莉·菲奥里纳

Passage 55

Tips for Happiness in Daily Life

Daily life can be made happier. It is a matter of choice. It is our attitude that makes us feel happy or unhappy. It is true, we meet all kinds of situations during the day, and some of them may not be conductive to happiness. We can choose to keep thinking about the unhappy events, and we can choose to refuse to think about them, and instead, relish the happy moments. All of us constantly go through various situations and circumstances, but we do not have to let them influence our reactions and feelings. We can choose to be happy, and we can do a lot to add happiness to our lives.

What is happiness? It is a feeling of inner peace and satisfaction. It is usually experienced when there are no worries, fears or obsessing thoughts, and this usually happens when we do something we love to do or when we get, win, gain or achieve something that we value. It seems to be the outcome of positive events, but it actually comes from the inside, triggered by outer events.

For most people happiness seems fleeting, because they let changing outer circumstances affect it. One of the best ways to keep it, is to gain inner peace through daily meditation.

Here are a few tips for increasing happiness in daily life:

1) Endeavor to change the way you look at things. Always look at the bright side. The mind may drag you to think about negativity and difficulties. Don't let it. Look at the good and positive side of every situation.

2) Think of solutions, not problems.

3) Listen to relaxing, uplifting music.

4) Watch funny comedies that make you laugh.

5) Each day, devote some time to reading a few pages of an inspiring book or article.

6) Watch your thoughts. Whenever you catch yourself thinking negative thoughts, start thinking of pleasant things.

7) Each day do something good for yourself. It can be something small, such as buying a book, eating something you love, watching your favorite program on TV, going to a movie, or just having a stroll on the beach.

8) Each day do at least one act to make others happy. This can be a kind word, helping your colleagues, stopping your car at the crossroad to let people cross, giving your seat in a bus to someone else, or giving a small present to someone you love. The possibilities are infinite. When you make someone happy, you become happy, and then people try to make you happy.

9) Always expect happiness.

10) Do not envy people who are happy. On the contrary, be happy for their happiness.

11) Associate with happy people, and try to learn from them to be happy. Remember, happiness is contagious.

12) Do your best to stay detached, when things do not proceed as intended and desired. Detachment will help you stay calm and control your moods and reactions. Detachment is not indifference. It is the acceptance of the good and the bad and staying balanced. Detachment has much to do with inner peace, and inner peace is conductive to happiness.

13) Smile more often.

 译 文

如何才能幸福生活

我们每天的生活可以过得更开心一些。这只是一个选择的问题，是我们的态度决定了自己的快乐与否。的确，我们每天都会遇到各种各样的状况，其中一些状况可能会让我们不开心。我们可以选择深陷坏情绪之中不可自拔，也可以选择不去想这些，而是去回味那些幸福的时刻。每个人都会经常遭遇各种各样的境况，但我们没有必要让它们影响我们的看法和感受。我们可以选择保持快乐的心情，可以做许多事情使我们的生活更加幸福。

幸福是什么？幸福是一种内心的宁静与满足。没有担忧、恐惧或纷扰的思绪时，那就是幸福；做自己喜欢做的事情，得到、赢得、收获我们珍视的事物或取得辉煌的成就时，那也是幸福。幸福看起来似乎是积极事件的产物，但它其实来自于内心，只是受到了外界事物的激发而已。

对大多数人而言，幸福似乎是短暂的，这是因为他们让不断变化的外界环境影响了它。想要保持幸福，最佳的方法之一就是通过每天的冥想来获得内心的宁静。

以下是一些能让你在每天的生活中增加幸福感的建议：

1) 努力改变看待事物的方式。要经常看到事物的积极面。你的思绪也许会不由自主地强迫你去想那些消极面和困难。可别让它得逞。要看到每件事情美好而积极的一面。

2) 思考解决问题的方案，而非问题本身。

3) 听些能够使人放松、振奋的音乐。

4) 看些能让你开怀大笑的喜剧片。

5) 每天花点时间读几页励志的书或文章。

6) 时刻关注自己的想法。当发现自己在想消极的事情时，就赶紧开始想点开心事。

7) 每天做点对自己有益的事情。它可以很微小，比如买本书，吃点儿自己爱吃的东西，看看自己最喜爱的电视节目，看场电影或者在海滩漫步。

8) 每天至少做一件让他人开心的事情。它可以是说一句善意的话，帮同事一个小忙，在十字路口停车让行人先过，在公交车上给人让座或者送你爱的人一个小礼物。这种小事数不胜数。当你让别人开心时，你自己也会感到快乐，别人也才会努力让你开心。

9) 始终要憧憬幸福。

10) 不要嫉妒那些幸福的人，要为他们的幸福感到高兴。

11) 和那些总是很开心的人交往，努力向他们学习，让自己也变得开心起来。记住，开心是会相互感染的。

12) 当事情的进展不如预计或者期望中顺利时，要努力使自己保持超然的心态。超然会帮你保持冷静，从而控制你的情绪和言行。超然并不是漠不关心，而是接纳所有的好与不好，并保持平衡的心态。超然和内心的平静有很大的关系，而内心的平静则会带来幸福。

13) 要经常微笑。

💡 单词记事本

conductive   [kən'dʌktɪv]
释 a. 传导的，有传导力的

relish   ['relɪʃ]
释 n. (美食等的)享受；乐趣；吸引力
v. 享受；从…中获得乐趣

constantly   ['kɒnstəntli]
释 ad. 不断地；经常地

reaction   [ri'ækʃn]
释 n. 反应，回应；看法，意见

satisfaction   [ˌsætɪs'fækʃn]
释 n. 满足；赔偿(物)；乐事

obsessing   [əb'sesɪŋ]
释 a. 困扰的

outcome   ['aʊtkʌm]
释 n. 结果，结局；成果

trigger   ['trɪɡə(r)]
释 n. 扳机 v. 引发，导致

fleeting   ['fliːtɪŋ]
释 a. 短暂的，飞逝的

meditation   [ˌmedɪ'teɪʃn]
释 n. 沉思，冥想；默念

例 To manage creeping stress, you can take some basic relaxation measures like *meditation* or paced breathing. 为了设法减轻压力，你可以采取一些基本的放松措施，如冥想或有节奏的呼吸。

endeavor [ɪn'devə(r)]
v./n. 努力；尽力

negativity [ˌnegə'tɪvəti]
n. 否定性；消极性

uplifting [ˌʌp'lɪftɪŋ]
a. 令人振奋的

stroll [strəʊl]
v./n. 闲逛，漫步

infinite ['ɪnfɪnət]
a. 无限的；无边无际的

contrary ['kɒntrəri]
n. 相反；反面 *a.* 相反的；对抗的

on the contrary 正相反；to the contrary 与此相反(的)；be contrary to 与…相反的

例 The robot will go on with its routine work unless it gets the order to the *contrary*. 这个机器人会一直做它的日常工作，除非它得到了相反的命令。

contagious [kən'teɪdʒəs]
a. 传染性的；有感染力的

detached [dɪ'tætʃt]
a. 分开的；超然的

proceed [prə'siːd]
v. 进行；(沿特定路线)行进或前进
例 How do you *proceed* with your thesis proposal? 你的论文开题报告进行得怎么样了？

intend [ɪn'tend]
v. 想要，打算；企图

indifference [ɪn'dɪfrəns]
n. 冷漠，无兴趣

acceptance [ək'septəns]
n. 接受；赞同，承认

🔍 单词家族

身心状态

baffle ['bæfl] *v.* 使困惑；难住
befuddlement [bɪ'fʌdlmənt] *n.* 迷惑不解
blissful ['blɪsfl] *a.* 充满喜悦的
blithe [blaɪð] *a.* 快乐的；无忧的
bouncing ['baʊnsɪŋ] *a.* 跳跃的；活泼的
breadth [bredθ] *n.* 宽宏大度
careworn ['keəwɔːn] *a.* 忧心忡忡的
choleric ['kɒlərɪk] *a.* 易怒的；暴躁的
complacence [kəm'pleɪsns] *n.* 自满；满足
dishearten [dɪs'hɑːtn] *v.* 使…灰心

dismay [dɪs'meɪ] *n.* 惊愕；失望
effervesce [ˌefə'ves] *v.* 兴奋；愉快
exhilarating [ɪg'zɪləreɪtɪŋ] *a.* 令人高兴的；使人兴奋的
flaccid ['flæsɪd; 'flæksɪd] *a.* 软弱的
fortitude ['fɔːtɪtjuːd] *n.* 坚毅；坚忍不拔
frantic ['fræntɪk] *a.* 发疯的；发狂的
frenetic [frə'netɪk] *a.* 狂乱的；发狂的
guileless ['gaɪlləs] *a.* 厚道的，老实的
gumption ['gʌmpʃn] *n.* 进取心；魄力
incredulity [ˌɪnkrə'djuːləti] *n.* 怀疑；不相信

jaunty ['dʒɔːnti] *a.* 愉快的

jocular ['dʒɒkjələ(r)] *a.* 滑稽的；诙谐的

jubilant ['dʒuːbɪlənt] *a.* 欢腾的；欣喜的

languor ['læŋgə(r)] *n.* 身心疲惫；恬静

leisurely ['leʒəli] *a.* 从容的；悠闲的

obstinate ['ɒbstɪnət] *a.* 固执的；顽强的

offish ['ɒfɪʃ] *a.* 冷淡的

oleaginous [ˌəuli'ædʒɪnəs] *a.* 油嘴滑舌的；善于恭维的

oscillation [ˌɒsɪ'leɪʃn] *n.* 踌躇

rancor ['ræŋkə(r)] *n.* 怨恨；敌意

rile [raɪl] *v.* 使恼火，激怒

sedulous ['sedjuləs] *a.* 聚精会神的；勤勉的

sensitize ['sensətaɪz] *v.* 使敏感

suavity ['swɑːvəti] *n.* 温和；愉快

sullen ['sʌlən] *a.* 愠怒的；郁郁寡欢的

tact [tækt] *n.* 圆滑；机敏

ticklish ['tɪklɪʃ] *a.* 怕痒的；易怒的

vacuous ['vækjuəs] *a.* 精神空虚的

vengeful ['vendʒfl] *a.* 报复的；复仇的

vigilant ['vɪdʒɪlənt] *a.* 警惕的；警觉的

wroth [rəʊθ] *a.* 激怒的

zesty ['zesti] *a.* 热望的

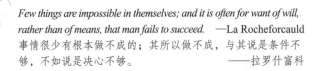

Few things are impossible in themselves; and it is often for want of will, rather than of means, that man fails to succeed. —La Rocheforcauld
事情很少有根本做不成的；其所以做不成，与其说是条件不够，不如说是决心不够。 ——拉罗什富科

Passage 56

Carrot, Egg, and Coffee Bean

A daughter complained to her father about her life and how things were so hard for her. She did not know how she was going to make it and wanted to give up. She was tired of fighting and struggling. It seemed that as one problem was solved, a new one arose.

Her father, a chef, took her to the kitchen. He filled three pots with water and placed each on a high fire. Soon, the pots came to a boil. In one, he placed carrots, in the second he placed eggs, and in the last, he placed ground coffee beans. He let them sit and boil, without saying a word.

The daughter sucked her teeth and impatiently waited, wondering what he was doing. In about twenty minutes, he turned off the burners. He fished the carrots out and placed them in a bowl. He pulled the eggs out and placed them in a bowl. Then he ladled the coffee out and placed it in a bowl. Turning to her he asked, "Darling, what do you see?"

"Carrots, eggs and coffee," she replied.

He brought her closer and asked her to feel the carrots. She did and noted that they were soft. He then asked her to take an egg and break it. After pulling off the shell, she observed the hard-boiled egg. Finally he asked her to sip the coffee. She smiled as she tasted its rich aroma. She humbly asked, "What does it mean, Father?"

He explained that each of them had faced the same adversity, boiling water, but each reacted differently. The carrot went in strong, hard and unrelenting, but after being subjected to the boiling water, it softened and became weak. The egg had been fragile. Its thin outer shell had protected its liquid interior, but after sitting through the boiling water, its inside became hardened.

But the ground coffee beans were unique. After they were in the boiling water, they had changed the water. "Which are you?" he asked his daughter. "When adversity knocks on your door, how do you respond? Are you a carrot, an egg or a coffee bean?"

How about you? Are you the carrot that seems hard, but with pain and adversity do you wilt and become soft and lose your strength?

Are you the egg, which starts off with a malleable heart? Were you a fluid spirit, but after a death, a breakup, a divorce, or a layoff, have you become hardened and **stiff**? Your shell looks the same, but are you **bitter** and **tough** with a stiff spirit and heart?

Or are you like the coffee bean? The bean changed the hot water, the thing that had brought the pain, to its **peak** flavor when it reached 100 degrees **Celsius**.

If you are like the bean, when things are at their worst, you get better and make things better around you.

No matter how bad and difficult it is during times of adversity, through **endurance** and **perseverance** we will see the light in the dark. As long as we do not **succumb** to pain and hardship, we will always **emerge** a better person.

译文

胡萝卜、鸡蛋和咖啡豆

一个女儿向父亲抱怨她对生活的不满，认为所有的事情都太艰难。她不知道自己该如何应付，甚至想要放弃。她厌倦了抵抗和奋斗，感觉似乎一个问题刚刚解决，新的问题就又出现了。

她的父亲是位厨师，听完她的话后把她带到了厨房。他往三个锅里倒满水，然后把它们分别放在大火上。不久，水就沸腾了。他在第一个锅里放了一些胡萝卜，在第二个锅里放了几个鸡蛋，在最后一个锅里放入了磨过的咖啡豆，然后把锅放到火上开始煮，一句话也不说。

女儿噘着嘴，等得有些不耐烦，不明白父亲到底要做什么。大约过了20分钟，父亲关掉了火。他把胡萝卜捞出来放入一个碗里，把鸡蛋捞出来放入另一个碗里，接着又把咖啡舀到第三个碗里，然后才转身问女儿："亲爱的，你看到了什么？"

"胡萝卜、鸡蛋，还有咖啡。"她回答。

父亲让她上前来摸一摸那些胡萝卜。她摸了之后，发现它们变软了。父亲又让她拿一只鸡蛋，把蛋壳敲碎。在剥掉蛋壳后，她看到煮熟的鸡蛋很硬。最后父亲让她喝一口咖啡。品尝到香味浓郁的咖啡，她笑了。然后她不明就里地问道："爸爸，这意味着什么呢？"

父亲解释说，这三样东西面临了同一个逆境——沸腾的水，但各自的反应却截然不同。胡萝卜在被放入沸水之前很强硬、毫不示弱，但被放入沸水后，它变得柔软而虚弱。鸡蛋原本是易碎的，内部的液体由薄薄的一层外壳保护着，但是被沸水煮过之后，它的内部变坚硬了。

而磨碎的咖啡豆则很特别，进入沸水之后，它们反过来改变了水。"哪个是你呢？"他问向女儿，"当逆境来临时，你会作何反应？你是胡萝卜、鸡蛋，还是咖啡豆？"

那么你呢？你是看似坚硬，但遇到痛苦和逆境就畏缩、软弱、失去力量的胡萝卜吗？

你是内心可塑的鸡蛋吗？原本性情不定，但经过死亡、分离、离异或失业后，你是否会变得坚强？外表虽看似从前，但你是否已经有了一个坚定的信念和一颗坚强的心，变得更加坚定不移、不屈不挠了呢？

或者，你是咖啡豆？豆子改变了带给它痛苦的沸水，使其在水温达到100℃时散发出了最佳醇香。

如果你和咖啡豆一样，那么无论环境多么恶劣，你就都能振作起来，并努力改变环境使它变得更加美好。

不管处于多么糟糕和艰难的逆境中，只要我们有持久的耐力和坚定不移的信念，就能在黑暗中找到光明；只要我们不向痛苦和困难屈服，历经风雨后我们必将更加完美。

💡 单词记事本

arise [ə'raɪz]
释 v. 产生；由…引起；起身
用 arise from 从…中产生，由…而引起

chef [ʃef]
释 n. 厨师

impatiently [ɪm'peɪʃntli]
释 ad. 不耐烦地；无耐性地

wonder ['wʌndə(r)]
释 v. 想知道；惊讶；怀疑 n. 惊奇；奇迹

burner ['bɜːnə(r)]
释 n. 炉子

ladle ['leɪdl]
释 n. 长柄勺 v. (用勺子)舀；给予，赠送

observe [əb'zɜːv]
释 v. 注意到；观察；评说；遵守

hard-boiled [,haːd'bɔɪld]
释 a. (鸡蛋)煮得老的；无情的；强硬的

sip [sɪp]
释 v. 啜饮；呷 n. 小口喝；一小口的量

aroma [ə'rəumə]
释 n. 芳香，香气

humbly ['hʌmbli]
ad. 谦逊地；卑贱地；低声下气地

adversity [əd'vɜːsəti]
释 n. 逆境；不幸，灾难

unrelenting [,ʌnrɪ'lentɪŋ]
释 a. 不屈不挠的；无情的，冷酷的

subject
释 [səb'dʒekt] v. 使服从；使遭受
['sʌbdʒɪkt] n. 主题；学科 a. 受…支配的；易遭…的
例 He claims to be an expert in astronomy, but in actual fact he is quite ignorant on the *subject*. 他声称自己是一名天文学专家，但事实上他对这门学科一无所知。

soften ['sɒfn]
释 v. (使)变柔软；(使)变柔和；减轻

296

interior [ɪn'tɪəriə(r)]

翼 *n.* 内部；内地 *a.* 内部的；内地的；国内的；本质的

unique [ju'niːk]

翼 *a.* 独特的；唯一的；突出的

malleable ['mæliəbl]

翼 *a.* (指金属)可锻造的，有延展性的；(指人)易受影响的，易变的

breakup ['breɪkʌp]

翼 *n.* 破裂，分离；崩溃

layoff ['leɪɒf]

翼 *n.* 解雇；关闭；停工期间

stiff [stɪf]

翼 *a.* 坚硬的；不灵活的；拘谨的 *ad.* 极其，非常

bitter ['bɪtə(r)]

翼 *a.* 使人痛苦的；严寒的；有苦味的；坚定不移的

tough [tʌf]

翼 *a.* 困难的；坚韧的

peak [piːk]

翼 *n.* 山峰；最高点 *a.* 到最高点的；极致的 *v.* 憔悴；达到顶点

Celsius ['selsiəs]

翼 *a.* 摄氏的

endurance [ɪn'djʊərəns]

翼 *n.* 忍耐力；持久(力)

例 The job called for both experience and *endurance* of hard physical labor. 这项工作要求既要有经验，又要对艰苦的体力劳动有忍耐力。

perseverance [ˌpɜːsɪ'vɪərəns]

翼 *n.* 坚持，不屈不挠

succumb [sə'kʌm]

翼 *v.* 屈服，屈从；不再抵抗，死亡

emerge [i'mɜːdʒ]

翼 *v.* (从水中)出来；现出，显露；(事实等)暴露；(自困境中)摆脱，脱颖而出

🔎 单词家族

外貌仪态

bald [bɔːld] *a.* 秃的，秃头的
beard [bɪəd] *n.* 胡须
blush [blʌʃ] *v.* 脸红；羞愧 *n.* 脸红
brow [braʊ] *n.* 额；[常*pl.*]眉(毛)
chin [tʃɪn] *n.* 下巴；颏
feminine ['femənɪn] *a.* 有女性特点的；娇柔的
lissome ['lɪsəm] *a.* 轻盈的；柔软的
prim [prɪm] *a.* 端庄的；一本正经的
radiant ['reɪdiənt] *a.* 容光焕发的；光芒四射的

shabby ['ʃæbi] *a.* 衣衫褴褛的；失修的；卑鄙的
slender ['slendə(r)] *a.* 修长的，苗条的；柔弱的
slim [slɪm] *a.* 苗条的；纤弱的
stoop [stuːp] *v.* 弯腰；(习惯性)弓背
tan [tæn] *n.* 晒黑的肤色 *v.* 晒黑
temperament ['tempərəmənt] *n.* 性情；气质

Passage 57

Passion Is Your Fuel

Passion is your fuel. It motivates you to press on. It propels you up the mountain of your dreams and goals. Have a passion for life, for people, for animals, for your causes and your convictions, and you will be nearly unstoppable. Be a champion for those who have great needs and can't do anything about it themselves. Speak with passion, teach with passion, lead with passion, love with passion, play with passion, and enjoy with passion. Someone who is passionate is intriguing to watch and to listen to. They are usually energizing to be around. They put great care into each and every detail of what they have passion for.

A passionate musician plays a piece over and over until it is perfection for him and the audience. Each sound is perfectly crafted and resonates purely, hauntingly, and brilliantly. Every song on the album may not be perfect, and sometimes it misses the mark, but we recognize the passion and are moved by the story told, how it was done and perhaps why it was done.

When you come to roadblocks in life, your passion is what brings you beyond each and every halt. When there is passion involved, you have a need to move forward, and reach beyond every expectation towards the fulfillment of dreams and goals. If you become stopped in life, and if you have passion for life or for an aspect of your work, dig deep within yourself to find what really motivates and captivates you, and create new paths with your passion and deep desires.

A person who does not have that passion can wallow in the low points of his life, and have great trouble finding the meaning of it. You must give meaning to your own life. You must discover the passions of your life and work. When you start to become passionate about something, then you want to spend as much of your time as you can by being in and around it. You want to learn everything about that aspect. You want to be with other people who have the same interests and passions. Their passion and love fuels your passion. Remember, small things can become big dreams if you are passionate about them. Take care of the small details with the same care and regard as if it were a great big event and you will move up the mountain with a steady sure foot.

Passionate leaders recognize passionate people, and they hire and promote passionate workers, and create openings for those people. You can be passionate about anything. And remember that anything becomes something to the right person. Small or large, if you are passionate about it, you can see huge results; your passion can take you to great places.

Anyway, your passion will open a new door. So have passion, take risks and step out in faith. Live a passionate life, and you will attract other passionate people, and you will fulfill your dreams. Tell yourself "I **embrace** the **fullness** of my life." Do it. You won't regret a minute of your life that way.

译 文

热情是生活的动力

热情是你生活的动力。它会激励你坚持向前，推动你攀上梦想和目标的高峰。对待生活、对待他人、对待动物、对待你的目标和信念时都要充满热情，这样你将锐不可当。支持并全力帮助那些有需要但无能为力的人。带着热情去交谈，带着热情去教导，带着热情去指引，带着热情去爱，带着热情去玩乐，带着热情去享受。充满热情的人总能吸引人们去注意和倾听。他们总是充满活力，对自己所热爱的一切乃至每一个细节都无比关心。

充满热情的音乐家会一遍遍地演奏一首乐曲，直到自己和观众都认为完美为止。每个音符都被完美地演绎，展现出演奏者的精湛技艺，从而使观众产生强烈的共鸣，难以忘怀。唱片中收录的每首乐曲或许都不那么完美，有时候甚至会走调，但我们却能感受到其中的热情，并被它所讲述的故事、它的演绎方式，甚至它的创作背景所打动。

当遭遇人生道路上的重重障碍时，你所具有的热情会帮助你跨越每一道关卡。只要有热情，你就有前进的动力，从而达到所有的期望直至实现你的梦想和目标。如果你在生活中停滞不前，但你对生活或工作的某个方面还充满热情，那么深入挖掘自己，去发现真正能激励你、吸引你的东西，用激情和深切的渴望去开创新的道路。

一个对生活没有热情的人会被人生的低谷所吞噬，很难找到生活的意义。你必须赋予生活意义，必须发掘对生活和工作的热情。当你开始对某件事充满热情时，你就会想尽办法为之多花点时间，并学习与它相关的所有事物。你会希望跟志趣相投并同样充满热情的人为伍。他们的激情会激发出你的热情。记住，只要你对一件事充满热情，即使它再小也会成为伟大的梦想。用同样的热情去关注小细节，把它们当作大事来对待，你将会迈着稳健的步伐一步步地攀上高峰。

充满热情的领导赏识充满热情的人，他们会聘用并提拔充满热情的员工并为他们创造机会。你可以对任何事情充满热情。记住，不同的事情在相应的人眼里都会变得举足轻重。不论事情是大是小，如果你对它充满热情，你就有希望看到伟大的成果，因为你的热情会带领你进入一个意想不到的美妙世界。

也就是说，热情会为你打开一扇新的门。所以，怀着热情，凭着信念，勇敢迈出这冒险的一步吧。过上一种充满热情的生活，你会吸引其他充满热情的人，你们也将实现各自的梦想。告诉自己"我拥抱美满充实的生活"，并付诸行动吧。这样，你就不会为生命中的每一分钟感到遗憾。

💡 单词记事本

passion ['pæʃn]
释 *n.* 激情，热情；酷爱，热爱

press [pres]
释 *n.* 新闻，出版社；压 *v.* 压；压迫；催促
例 press on 坚定地继续

conviction [kən'vɪkʃn]
释 *n.* 判罪；坚定的看法或信仰；可信性

unstoppable [ʌn'stɒpəbl]
释 *a.* 无法停止的；不可阻挡的

champion ['tʃæmpiən]
释 *n.* 冠军，获胜者；斗士，拥护者，捍卫者 *v.* 拥护；支持

passionate ['pæʃənət]
释 *a.* 充满激情的；热切的，强烈的

intriguing [ɪn'triːgɪŋ]
释 *a.* 引起兴趣的；迷人的

energize ['enədʒaɪz]
释 *v.* 给…精力或活力
例 Before your journey, *energize* yourself with a slice of pepperoni. 旅程开始之前，先吃一片辣味香肠给自己补充点能量。

craft [krɑːft]
释 *n.* 行业；手艺；工艺；船舶；飞行器；骗术 *v.* 精心制作，精心构思

resonate ['rezəneɪt]
释 *v.* (使)共鸣；(使)共振

hauntingly ['hɔːntɪŋli]
释 *ad.* 萦绕于心头地，难以忘怀地

brilliantly ['brɪliəntli]
释 *ad.* 辉煌地；技艺精湛地，才华横溢地；杰出地

roadblock ['rəʊdblɒk]
释 *n.* 路障；障碍，障碍物

fulfillment [fʊl'fɪlmənt]
释 *n.* 履行，实现

captivate ['kæptɪveɪt]
释 *v.* 吸引，迷住；迷惑

fuel ['fjuːəl]
释 *n.* 燃料；刺激因素 *v.* 给…加燃料；激起

promote [prə'məʊt]
释 *v.* 促进；提升；宣传
例 Many tourists complain that the travel agency's level of service should be *promoted*. 许多游客投诉说旅行社的服务水平有待提高。

embrace [ɪm'breɪs]
释 *v.* 拥抱；欣然接受；包括，包含 *n.* 拥抱

fullness ['fʊlnəs]
释 *n.* 满，充满；充实，丰富；成熟；丰满；(颜色等的)浓度

性格特点

ardent ['ɑːdnt] *a.* 热心的，热情的

arrogant ['ærəgənt] *a.* 傲慢的，自大的

aspiration [ˌæspə'reɪʃn] *n.* 志向，抱负

audacious [ɔː'deɪʃəs] *a.* 大胆的；有冒险精神的

autocrat ['ɔːtəkræt] *n.* 独裁者；专横霸道的人

avarice ['ævərɪs] *n.* 贪财；贪婪

benevolent [bə'nevələnt] *a.* 仁慈的；乐善好施的

boastful ['bəʊstfl] *a.* 吹嘘的；自负的

bombast ['bɒmbæst] *n.* 高调；夸大之辞

brash [bræʃ] *a.* 无礼的；自以为是的

cynical ['sɪnɪkl] *a.* 愤世嫉俗的

deviance ['diːvɪəns] *n.* 异常的行为(或特征)

dictatorial [ˌdɪktə'tɔːriəl] *a.* 傲慢的；蛮横的

docile ['dəʊsaɪl] *a.* 驯服的；听话的

dogged ['dɒgɪd] *a.* 顽固的；顽强的

eccentric [ɪk'sentrɪk] *a.* 古怪的

endearing [ɪn'dɪərɪŋ] *a.* 讨人喜欢的

extrovert ['ekstrəvɜːt] *n.* 性格外向的人

fickle ['fɪkl] *a.* 易变的；无常的

genial ['dʒiːniəl] *a.* 亲切的；和蔼的

hardy ['hɑːdi] *a.* 能吃苦的；坚强的

headstrong ['hedstrɒŋ] *a.* 刚愎自用的

hospitable [hɒ'spɪtəbl; 'hɒspɪtəbl] *a.* 好客的

hubris ['hjuːbrɪs] *n.* 傲慢

illiberal [ɪ'lɪbərəl] *a.* 气量狭窄的

insincerity [ˌɪnsɪn'serəti] *n.* 伪善；虚伪的言行

insolence ['ɪnsələns] *n.* 傲慢，无礼

introvert ['ɪntrəvɜːt] *n.* 性格内向的人

lenient ['liːniənt] *a.* 宽大的；仁慈的

lukewarm [ˌluːk'wɔːm] *a.* 冷淡的；不热烈的

parsimony ['pɑːsɪməni] *n.* 吝啬

peculiarity [pɪˌkjuːli'ærəti] *n.* 特性；怪癖

premature ['premətʃə(r)] *a.* 不成熟的

sleek [sliːk] *a.* 圆滑的；井然有序的

streak [striːk] *n.* 个性特征；癖性

tractability [ˌtræktə'bɪləti] *n.* 温顺

unpretentious [ˌʌnprɪ'tenʃəs] *a.* 不炫耀的；谦虚的

upfront [ˌʌp'frʌnt] *a.* 坦率的；正直的

Passage 58

音频

The Real Power of Affirmation

"I think, therefore I am." is a phrase affirming one's existence as a being. It may be a simple phrase, but it says everything about the being saying it. It indicates confidence not commonly found among other beings.

But why do people need affirmation? Why do beings need to be affirmed? Is existence relative to one's affirmation?

Affirmation is a very powerful technique to empower one's subconscious. Through affirmation, beings are empowered to do, to work, and to strive for more things. Affirmation allows people to believe in themselves and to put their thoughts into action.

Affirmation is a combination of verbal and visual techniques of a preferred state of mind of a person. Strong affirmations can be very powerful, and can be used by almost anyone to achieve his goals and fulfill his desires. However, the power of an affirmation depends on how strong or weak an affirmation is.

A strong affirmation should be stated in the present tense to be more effective. An affirmation of "I am now a happy being" is more effective than an affirmation saying, "I am going to become a happy being." Affirmation should always be in positive terms because it is supposed to work for you and not against you. Instead of saying, "I am not sad," why not make an affirmation saying, "I am happy."?

An affirmation should be made up of simple but concise words, and it should be short to be more effective. A very long affirmation can work the other way around, instead of creating a positive mindset for a person. A short affirmation can be easily spoken and repeated by a person. It can serve as a mantra that can be repeated over and over again.

To be effective, an affirmation must be repeated. Repetition works and influences the subconscious, which in turn motivates the person into acting out his affirmation. A person who creates the affirmation should be deeply involved with the words he will be using, so he will be able to actualize his affirmation. Writing words that one believes in can be very powerful, and this can be put to good use when creating an affirmation.

However, creating an affirmation alone and repeating them a million times would not make the affirmation a state of mind. The important thing is to live one's affirmation and to be open-minded enough to do the things that would help the affirmation become a **reality**. Feeling the affirmation and applying it in one's life will help in making the affirmation a reality.

While affirmation is generally used to make an individual better, it can also be used to **boost** or **confirm** another person's value. By affirming another person's existence, you are helping him improve his **self-worth**.

Affirmation is a very simple thing that can make a very big difference in a person's life. It can be a great motivator and can make things happen.

NOW is the time!

译 文

肯定的真实力量

"我思故我在"这一说法肯定了一个人作为生命体的存在。它或许只是一个简单的短语，却道出了所言者的一切。它表明了一种在其他生物中通常找不到的自信。

然而人为什么需要被肯定？人为什么需要被认可？人的存在是否与他人对自己的肯定有关？

肯定是一种唤醒个人潜意识的非常有力的方式。通过肯定，人们可以获得去做事情、工作以及努力争取更多东西的力量。肯定能使人们相信自己，并把自己的想法付诸行动。

肯定是语言技巧和视觉技巧的结合，它体现了一个人良好的精神状态。语气坚定的肯定话语具有强大的力量，它能使几乎所有人都从中获得激励，继而实现自己的目标和愿望。虽然如此，肯定的话语所具有的力量大小还是要取决于它的语气强弱程度。

强烈的肯定应该用一般现在时来表述，这样会更有效。"我是个快乐的人"要比"我要成为一个快乐的人"更加有说服力。肯定应该用积极的话语来表达，因为它的目的是给你带来正面的力量，而非从负面影响你。所以，当你想说"我不伤心"时，就说成肯定句"我很高兴"吧。

肯定的陈述应该由简洁的话语组成，力求简短而有效。冗长的肯定之词不会为一个人创造出积极乐观的心态，而会适得其反。简短的肯定话语便于表达和陈述。它可以像咒语一样被重复无数遍。

为了达到效果，肯定的话语必须重复多次。重复可以影响人的潜意识，这样反过来还能激励人们去将肯定之事付诸行动。说出肯定之语的人，应该谨慎地考虑自己的措辞，以便实现自己所肯定的事情。记下自己坚信的话语是很有用的，这在作出肯定时可以充分加以利用。

然而，仅仅说出肯定的话语并重复多次并不会成为一种精神状态。真正重要的是去践行自己的话语，开阔思路去做那些有助于将肯定之事变为现实的事情。感受肯定的力量，并将其运用到生活中，这将帮助你实现自己所肯定的事情。

肯定通常不仅可以完善一个人，还能用来提升并证实其他人的价值。通过肯定他人的存在，你还可以帮助他人提升自我价值。

肯定是一件极其简单的事情，但可以彻底改变一个人的一生。它可以成为一个强大的激励因素，推动梦想成为现实。

现在就行动起来吧！

💡 单词记事本

affirm [ə'fɜːm]
释 v. 肯定；断言，坚持声称

affirmation [ˌæfə'meɪʃn]
释 n. 肯定；断言

empower [ɪm'paʊə(r)]
释 v. 使能够；授予，准许

subconscious [ˌsʌb'kɒnʃəs]
释 n. 潜意识

strive [straɪv]
释 v. 奋斗，努力；反抗

combination [ˌkɒmbɪ'neɪʃn]
释 n. 结合(体)，联合(体)；化合

visual ['vɪʒuəl]
释 a. 视觉的；用于视觉的
用 visual impact 视觉冲击

tense [tens]
释 a. 紧张的；拉紧的；易怒的 v. (使)变得紧张 n. (动词的)时态

suppose [sə'pəʊz]
释 v. 猜想；假定；期望，要求
用 be supposed to 应该；被期望
例 The book is *supposed* to provoke the readers into thinking about their own life. 这本书旨在激发读者思考人生。

concise [kən'saɪs]
释 a. 简洁的；简明的

mindset ['maɪndset]
释 n. 精神状态，心态；思想倾向

mantra ['mæntrə]
释 n. 颂歌；符咒

repetition [ˌrepə'tɪʃn]
释 n. 重复；反复

actualize ['æktʃuəlaɪz]
释 v. 实施，实行；实现

open-minded [ˌəʊpən'maɪndɪd]
释 a. 愿接受新思想的；无偏见的

reality [ri'æləti]
释 n. 现实，实际；真实(性)
用 in reality 实际上，事实上

boost [buːst]
释 v. 增强，提高；鼓励；促进；提升；宣扬 n. 增加；鼓励
例 There is little evidence that efforts to *boost* financial know-how help students make better decisions outside the classroom. 几乎没有证据表明，努力帮助学生提升财政方面的技能能够使学生在课堂之外作出好的决策。

confirm [kən'fɜːm]	self-worth [,self'wɜːθ]
释 v. 证实，肯定；批准，使有效	释 n. 自我价值；自尊

💡 单词家族

肯定赞扬

acclaim [ə'kleɪm] v. 向…欢呼，为…喝彩 n. 称赞

adhere [əd'hɪə(r)] v. 黏附；坚持

advisable [əd'vaɪzəbl] a. 可取的；适当的

allege [ə'ledʒ] v. 断言，宣称

applaud [ə'plɔːd] v. 欢呼，鼓掌；称赞

approval [ə'pruːvl] n. 赞成，认可

approve [ə'pruːv] v. 赞成，同意；批准

assurance [ə'ʃuərəns; ə'ʃɔːrəns] n. 确保；保证

certainty ['sɜːtnti] n. 必然；确定的事

commend [kə'mend] v. 表扬；推荐；托付

consensus [kən'sensəs] n. (意见等)一致

consent [kən'sent] v./n. 同意；允许

incline [ɪn'klaɪn] v. (使)倾斜；赞同

permission [pə'mɪʃn] n. 允许；同意

permit [pə'mɪt] v. 许可，允许

plausible ['plɔːzəbl] a. 似乎合理的

pledge [pledʒ] v. 发誓；保证

recommend [,rekə'mend] v. 推荐；劝告；建议

Only those who have the patience to do simple things perfectly ever acquire the skill to do difficult things easily. —Friedrich Schiller
只有有耐心圆满完成简单工作的人，才能够轻而易举地完成困难的事。
——弗里德里希·席勒

Passage 59

Finding a New Spring

Once upon a time a certain tradesman was leading a caravan to another country to sell his goods. Along the way they came to the edge of a severe hot-sand desert. They asked about and found that during the daytime the sun heats up the fine sand until it's as hot as charcoal, so no one can walk on it—not even bullocks or camels! So the caravan leader hired a desert guide, one who could follow the stars, so that they could travel only at night when the sand cooled down. They began the dangerous nighttime journey across the desert.

A couple of nights later, after eating their evening meal, and waiting for the sand to cool, they started out again. Later that night the desert guide, who was driving the first cart, saw from the stars that they were getting close to the other side of the desert. He had also overeaten, so that when he relaxed, he dozed off to sleep. Then the bullocks who, of course, couldn't tell directions by reading the stars, gradually turned to the side and went in a big wide circle until they ended up at the same place they had started from!

By then it was morning, and the people realized they were back at the same spot they'd camped at the day before. They lost heart and began to cry about their condition. Since the desert crossing was supposed to be over by now, they had no more water and were afraid they would die of thirst. They even began to blame the caravan leader and the desert guide—"We can do nothing without water!" they complained.

Then the tradesman thought to himself, "If I lose courage now, in the middle of this disastrous situation, my leadership has no meaning. If I fall to weeping and regretting this misfortune, and do nothing, all these goods and bullocks and even the lives of the people, including myself, may be lost. I must be energetic and face the situation!" So he began walking back and forth, trying to think out a plan to save them all.

Remaining alert, out of the corner of his eye, he noticed a small clump of grass. He thought, "Without water, no plant could live in this desert." So he called over the most energetic of his fellow travellers and asked them to dig up the ground on that very spot. They dug and dug, and after a while they got down to a large stone. Seeing it they stopped, and began to blame the leader again, saying, "This effort is useless. We're just wasting our time!" But the tradesman replied, "No no, my friends, if we give up the effort we will all be ruined and our poor animals will die—let us be encouraged!"

As he said this, he got down into the hole, put his ear to the stone, and heard the sound of flowing water. Immediately, he called over a boy who had been digging and said, "If you give up, we will all **perish**—so take this heavy **hammer** and strike the rock."

The boy lifted the hammer over his head and hit the rock as hard as he could—and he himself was the most surprised when the rock split in two and a **mighty** flow of water **gushed** out from under it! Suddenly, all the people were **overjoyed**. They drank and bathed and washed the animals and cooked their food and ate.

Before they left, they raised a high **banner** so that other travellers could see it from afar and come to the new spring in the middle of the hot-sand desert. Then they continued on safely to the end of their journey.

译文

寻找一潭新泉水

从前，有一个商人带领商队去另外一个国家销售商品。途中，他们来到了一片异常炎热的沙漠。四处询问后他们得知，在白天细沙会被太阳炙烤得如同火炭一样炽热，没有人能够在上面行走，即使是牛和骆驼也不行。于是这个商人雇了一个沙漠向导，这个向导能够依靠星星来辨别方向，这样等到晚上沙子冷却下来后他们就能赶路了。于是，他们开始了夜间穿越沙漠的危险之旅。

就这样，他们在沙漠中穿行了几个晚上。这晚，吃过晚饭，等沙子冷却下来后，他们再次上路了。赶着第一辆车的向导通过星星推断出他们快要穿过沙漠了。由于晚饭吃多了，放松下来后他就打起盹来。但拉车的牛自然是不会通过星星辨别方向的，于是它们逐渐偏离了原来的方向，绕了一个很大的圈子又回到了出发的地方。

这时天已经亮了，人们发现又回到了前一天扎营的地方。他们灰心丧气，开始为自己的处境而痛哭。因为按照计划此时他们已经穿越了沙漠，所以他们的水已经喝光了。人们开始担忧自己会渴死，甚至开始责怪领队的商人和沙漠向导——"没有水，我们什么都做不了！"他们抱怨说。

商人心想："在此时这个危急关头，如果我也丢掉勇气的话，那么我的领导也就没有任何意义了；如果我也哭哭啼啼、抱怨命运不公，然后什么都不做的话，所有的商品和牲畜，甚至所有人的性命，包括我自己的，都有可能丢掉，所以我必须积极、勇敢地面对眼前的情况！"于是他开始来回踱步，努力思考能够拯救大家的办法。

他一直保持警觉，这时眼角的余光瞥见了一小丛杂草。他想："如果没有水，植物是不可能在沙漠里生长的。"于是他叫来商队中精力最充沛的人，让他们在那块长草的地方挖下去。他们挖啊挖，过了一会儿，挖到了一块大石头。看到石头，他们停了下来，又开始抱怨起领队来："这么做是没用的。我们只是在浪费时间！"但是这个商人回答道："不，不，朋友们，如果现在放弃，我们大家都会死掉，我们可怜的牲畜也难幸免——让我们一起振作起来吧！"

话音未落，他跳进坑里，将一只耳朵贴在石头上，听到了下方有流水的声音。于是他立刻叫来一个一直在挖掘的小伙子，说道："如果你放弃了，那么我们大家都会死，所以，拿起这柄大锤砸碎这块石头吧。"

小伙子将锤头举过头顶，用尽全身力气朝大石砸了下去——当石头一分为二时，小伙子无比惊讶地看到一股巨大的水流从中间喷涌而出！霎时，所有的人都欣喜若狂。他们尽情畅饮，尽情地洗澡，把拉车的牲畜也洗了个干干净净，然后就地做饭、进餐。

在离开之前，他们在泉水旁边立了一面高高的旗帜，以便其他旅人从很远的地方就能看到炎热沙漠中的这股新泉。随后他们继续前进，平安地结束了他们的沙漠之旅。

💡 单词记事本

tradesman ['treɪdzmən]
释 *n.* 商人；店主；零售商

caravan ['kærəvæn]
释 *n.* 旅行拖车，大篷车；(穿越沙漠地带的)旅行队，商队

edge [edʒ]
释 *n.* 边缘；刀刃；优势 *v.* 使锐利

severe [sɪ'vɪə(r)]
释 *a.* 严重的；严厉的；剧烈的，非常恶劣的；朴素的
例 A *severe* accident has disrupted the railway services into and out of the city. 一起严重的交通事故使这座城市的铁路交通陷入混乱之中。

charcoal ['tʃɑːkəʊl]
释 *n.* 炭，木炭；炭笔

bullock ['bʊlək]
释 *n.* 小公牛

overeat [,əʊvər'iːt]
释 *v.* 吃得过多

doze [dəʊz]
释 *v./n.* 小睡，打盹儿
用 doze off 打盹儿

disastrous [dɪ'zɑːstrəs]
释 *a.* 灾难性的；损失惨重的；悲惨的

weep [wiːp]
释 *v./n.* 哭泣，流泪；渗出液体

misfortune [,mɪs'fɔːtʃuːn]
释 *n.* 不幸；逆境；灾难

energetic [,enə'dʒetɪk]
释 *a.* 积极的；精力充沛的

例 The President is an *energetic* advocate for the cooperation on international issues. 这位总统积极提倡在国际事务上进行合作。

alert [əˈlɜːt]

释 *a.* 警惕的；活跃的 *n.* 警戒(期间)；警报 *v.* 使警戒；提醒

用 on the alert 警惕；提防

clump [klʌmp]

释 *n.* (树、灌木等的)丛；(密密的)一团；沉重的脚步声 *v.* 丛生；用沉重的脚步行走

perish [ˈperɪʃ]

释 *v.* 死亡，毁灭；(橡胶、皮革等)失去弹性

hammer [ˈhæmə(r)]

释 *n.* 锤，榔头 *v.* 锤击

用 hammer (away) at 努力做；hammer out 竭力想出(解决办法等)

mighty [ˈmaɪti]

释 *a.* 强有力的；强大的；伟大的

gush [gʌʃ]

释 *v.* (突然大量地)流出；滔滔不绝地说 *n.* 喷；迸发

例 The two mothers smiled and *gushed* over their babies. 两位母亲笑着，滔滔不绝地说着她们的孩子。

overjoyed [ˌəʊvəˈdʒɔɪd]

释 *a.* 狂喜的，极高兴的

banner [ˈbænə(r)]

释 *n.* 横幅；旗，旗帜

单词家族

乐观积极

consideration [kənˌsɪdəˈreɪʃn] *n.* 考虑；为别人着想

grateful [ˈgreɪtfl] *a.* 感激的；感谢的

gratitude [ˈgrætɪtjuːd] *n.* 感激；感谢

hopeful [ˈhəʊpfl] *a.* 怀有希望的；乐观的

jolly [ˈdʒɒli] *a.* 欢乐的，高兴的

keen [kiːn] *a.* 热心的；敏锐的

laughter [ˈlɑːftə(r)] *n.* 笑，笑声

persist [pəˈsɪst] *v.* 坚持；持续

propel [prəˈpel] *v.* 推进；激励

rejoice [rɪˈdʒɔɪs] *v.* 欢庆；高兴

sincere [sɪnˈsɪə(r)] *a.* 诚挚的；真实的

sociable [ˈsəʊʃəbl] *a.* 友善的；好交际的

sympathetic [ˌsɪmpəˈθetɪk] *a.* 和谐的；赞成的；同情的

zeal [ziːl] *n.* 热情，热忱

Passage 60

The Road to Success

It is well that young men should begin at the beginning and occupy the most subordinate positions. Many of the leading businessmen of Pittsburgh had a serious responsibility thrust upon them at the very threshold of their career. They were introduced to the broom, and spent the first hours of their business lives sweeping out the office. I notice we have janitors and janitresses now in offices, and our young men unfortunately miss that salutary branch of a business education. But if by chance the professional sweeper is absent any morning, the boy who has the genius for the future partner in him will not hesitate to try his hand at the broom. It does not hurt the newest comer to sweep out the office if necessary. I was one of those sweepers myself.

Assuming that you have all obtained employment and are fairly started, my advice to you is aim high. I would not give a fig for the young man who does not already see himself as the partner or the head of an important firm. Do not rest content for a moment in your thoughts as head clerk, or foreman, or general manager in any concern, no matter how extensive. Say to yourself, "my place is at the top." Be king in your dreams.

And here is the prime condition of success, the great secret: Concentrate your energy, thought and capital, exclusively upon the business in which you're engaged. Having begun in one line, resolve to fight it out on that line, to lead in it, adopt every improvement, have the best machinery, and know the most about it.

The concerns which fail are those which have scattered their capital, which means that they have scattered their brains also. They have investments in this, or that, or the other, here, there, and everywhere. "Don't put all your eggs in one basket is all wrong. I tell you to put all your eggs in one basket, and then watch that basket." Look round you and take notice: Men who do that not often fail. It is easy to watch and carry the one basket. It is trying to carry too many baskets that breaks most eggs in this country. He who carries three baskets must put one on his head, which is apt to tumble and trip him up. One fault of the American businessmen is lack of concentration.

To summarize what I have said: Aim for the highest, and never enter a bar room; do not touch liquor, or if at all, only at meals; never speculate; never endorse beyond your surplus cash fund; make the firm's interest yours; break orders always to save owners; concentrate; put all your eggs in one basket and watch that basket; **expenditure** always within **revenue**; lastly be not impatient, for, as Emerson says, "no one can cheat you out of ultimate success but yourselves."

成功之道

年轻人工作之初应该从最底层的职位做起，这是件好事。匹兹堡的许多商业巨头在事业初期都曾肩负过此"重任"。他们与扫帚为伴，在打扫办公室的过程中度过了自己职业生涯的最初时光。我发现如今的办公室都请了保洁员，这使年轻人不幸失去了商业教育中的这个有益的环节。不过，如果哪天早上专职的保洁员碰巧没来，那么，具有未来合伙人特质的某位青年就会毫不犹豫拿起扫帚开始清扫。在有必要时让新员工打扫一下办公室也无妨，我本人就曾经扫过地。

假如你已经被聘用，并具备了一个良好的开端，那我给你的忠告是"胸怀大志"。对那些不把自己看成是大公司未来合伙人或领导者的年轻人，我也会对他不屑一顾。不要仅仅满足于做一个总管、领班或是总经理，无论这些职位的发展空间有多大。要对自己说："我的位置在最高处。"要做自己梦想中的国王。

获得成功的首要条件和最大秘诀就是：将你的精力、想法和资本全部集中在你正在从事的事业上。一旦开始从事某一行，就要下定决心干出个名堂、闯出一片天地、接受每一点改进、采用最优良的设备，并且尽力通晓这一行。

一些企业之所以失败，就在于他们分散了资本，同时也意味着分散了精力。他们在这方面投资，在那方面投资，在各个方面都投资。"不要把所有的鸡蛋都放进一个篮子里"，这种说法大错特错。我要让你"把所有的鸡蛋都放进一个篮子，然后看好那个篮子"。注意观察你周围的人，你会发现那样做的人往往不会失败。看好并提好一个篮子会比较容易。在我们国家，想多提篮子的人打碎的鸡蛋也最多。提三个篮子的人就必须把一个顶在头上，而这个篮子很容易掉下来，而且会把自己绊倒。美国商人的一个通病就是不够专注。

我所说的话可以归纳如下：要胸怀大志，千万不要进酒吧；要滴酒不沾，即使必须喝，也只在用餐时喝一点儿；决不做投机买卖；决不签署盈余资金之外的票据；把公司的利益看作自己的利益；取消订单的目的永远在于挽救货主；要专心致志；要把所有的鸡蛋都放进一个篮子里并照看好它；要量入为出；最后，不要失去耐心。因为正如爱默生所言："除了你自己，谁也无法阻止你取得最终的成功。"

occupy ['ɒkjupaɪ]

释 v. 占用；(使)忙碌；(使)从事；把注意力集中于

subordinate

释 [sə'bɔːdɪnət] a. 下级的；次要的 n. 下级；部属

[sə'bɔːdɪneɪt] v. 使处于次要地位；使服从

用 subordinate to 次要的；从属的

例 My sister's personal life has been totally *subordinated* to her family. 我姐姐已经完全将家庭置于个人生活之上。

leading ['liːdɪŋ]

释 a. 最重要的，主要的；带头的，领衔的

threshold ['θreʃhəʊld]

释 n. 门槛，入口；开端，起始点

janitor ['dʒænɪtə(r)]

释 n. 房屋管理员；学校工友；看门人

janitress ['dʒænɪtrəs]

释 n. 女房屋管理员

salutary ['sæljətri]

释 a. 有益的；有益健康的

fig [fɪg]

释 n. 无花果

用 not give a fig 对…丝毫不在乎，完全不把…放在心上

foreman ['fɔːmən]

释 n. 领班；工头；首席陪审员

extensive [ɪk'stensɪv]

释 a. 广阔的；大量的，广泛的

用 extensive knowledge 广博的知识

prime [praɪm]

释 a. 首要的，主要的；最初的 n. 全盛时期 v. 使完成准备工作

concentrate ['kɒnsntreɪt]

释 v. 全神贯注，集中；浓缩 n. 浓缩物

用 concentrate on 集中，全神贯注于

例 I must *concentrate* all my efforts on finding the solution to this problem. 我必须集中所有精力寻找这个问题的解决办法。

capital ['kæpɪtl]

释 n. 资本；首都；大写字母 a. 首要的；大写的

exclusively [ɪk'skluːsɪvli]

释 ad. 唯一地；专有地；排外地

resolve [rɪ'zɒlv]

释 v. (使)下决心，决定；溶解 n. 决心；决定要做的事

machinery [mə'ʃiːnəri]

释 n. 机器，机械；机构；机制

用 diplomatic and political machinery 外交和政治机构

concern [kən'sɜːn]

释 n. 所关心的事；商行，企业；股份

scatter ['skætə(r)]

释 v. (使)散开，(使)分散；散布；散播

apt [æpt]

释 a. 有…倾向的；易于…的；适当的；灵敏的

用 be apt to 易于…的

tumble ['tʌmbl]

释 v. 跌倒；翻滚；(价格等)暴跌 n. 跌倒

用 tumble to (突然)明白，领悟

例 Uncle Sam *tumbled* down the stairs and badly hurt his wrist. 萨姆大叔从楼梯上摔了下来，严重摔伤了手腕。

summarize ['sʌməraɪz]

释 v. 概括，总结；摘要

speculate ['spekjuleɪt]

释 v. 深思；推测；投机

endorse [ɪn'dɔːs]

释 v. (在支票背面)签名，背书；签署；认可，赞同

expenditure [ɪk'spendɪtʃə(r)]

释 n. 花费，支出

例 Daily *expenditure* has been cut to an irreducible minimum. 日常开支已经被削减到了最低值。

revenue ['revənjuː]

释 n. (尤指大宗的)收入，收益；(政府的)税收；[*pl.*]各项的收入，总收入

单词家族

优秀特质

desirable [dɪ'zaɪərəbl] *a.* 称心的；值得要的

durable ['djʊərəbl] *a.* 持久的；耐久的

elastic [ɪ'læstɪk] *a.* 有弹性的；适应性强的

fluent ['fluːənt] *a.* 流利的，流畅的

lofty ['lɒfti] *a.* 崇高的；高傲的

perfection [pə'fekʃn] *n.* 尽善尽美；完美

predominant [prɪ'dɒmɪnənt] *a.* 卓越的；主要的

prior ['praɪə(r)] *a.* 优先的；较重要的

progressive [prə'gresɪv] *a.* 进步的；前进的

reasonable ['riːznəbl] *a.* 合理的；通情达理的

remarkable [rɪ'mɑːkəbl] *a.* 显著的；非凡的

satisfactory [ˌsætɪs'fæktəri] *a.* 令人满意的；符合要求的

spacious ['speɪʃəs] *a.* 知识广博的；宽裕的

subtle ['sʌtl] *a.* 精巧的；敏锐的

terrific [tə'rɪfɪk] *a.* 极好的；了不起的

Passage 61

Six Things We Can Learn
from *Alice in Wonderland*

It is easy to think that *Alice in Wonderland* is a dreamland fairy tale for children. On the surface it appears to be just that. However, if you look closer, you will realize that Alice's world translates into much more than a children's fairy tale.

The story has been studied and analyzed by psychoanalysts since the early 1900s and although it is filled with chaos there is lots to learn from its underlying messages.

1. Manage Your Personal Growth

The most important metaphor in the story is one of growth. We see Alice grow from tall to short and from big to small. Growing up is about changing body size, dealing with ups and downs, and feeling confident or insecure about oneself. When Alice eats, she grows; when she drinks, she shrinks. She soon learns to use the resources in her world to control her personal growth.

We spend our lives "growing up" in one way or another. What are you doing to manage your personal growth?

2. Be Specific about What You Want to Achieve

Alice learns about the importance of knowing what she wants. We can learn a great deal about the importance of goals from her conversation with the Cheshire Cat.

"Would you tell me, please, which way I ought to go from here?" said Alice.

"That depends a good deal on where you want to get to," said the Cat.

"I don't much care where," said Alice.

"Then it doesn't matter which way you go," said the Cat.

Think about what you will achieve over the next 90 days! Write it down together with steps that you will take to achieve that. Imagine specifically what you will see and hear as you achieve your goal. Think about it until you can run a mental movie of what you want over and over again. In particular, thinking about how to achieve your goal will make you feel and build the intensity of that emotion in your mind.

3. Develop Your Identity

The characters in wonderland continually ask Alice who she is. As a result, she questions her identity. When we have doubts about who we are and what we stand for, it affects our entire life. Consider the roles you have in your life, for example: a parent, a spouse, a son or a daughter, a colleague, a leader or a friend. Write out the qualities you believe you have in those roles, e.g. "I am a caring father" or "I am a creative business person". Remember that you will assume different behaviours in each role. As you learn more about yourself in each role, you will reinforce your self-belief and learn to develop your capabilities within each role.

4. Say What You Really Mean

Alice is continually told to say what she means. How often do you really say what you mean? When did you last have a really meaningful conversation? When you connect with people who share similar values, you will find that you share more meaningful thoughts, feelings and ideas.

5. Challenge Your Creativity

In the latest movie, Alice's father, a successful entrepreneur, tells her that he thinks of six impossible things before breakfast every day. Imagine if you just thought of one impossible thing per day. You could find ways to solve problems or create something that was never invented before. Get your creative juices flowing by thinking of one impossible thing every day.

6. Follow the Advice You Give Yourself

Alice generally gave herself good advice (though she very seldom followed it).

Do you give yourself good advice and do you follow it? Or are we better at giving others advice and expecting them to follow it?

Whether you enjoy this fairy tale for its entertainment value or search for the deeper meaning like I have, there is lots of value in it.

We spend all of our lives "growing up" in one way or another. The underlying messages in *Alice in Wonderland* are about personal growth and development. Growing up is about learning who we are, what we stand for, what we want to do, be and have. It is about dealing with difficulty, hurt and pain as well as love, laughter and fun. It is about overcoming fears, embracing new challenges and nurturing relationships. It is about using our talents and learning to be the best we can be.

This may be a children's story at heart, but we can learn a great deal from a young girl who acquires the confidence and courage to break free from rules to become that person she aspires to be.

《爱丽丝梦游仙境》告诉我们的六件事

人们很容易把《爱丽丝梦游仙境》当作儿童看的梦幻童话。表面上看也确实如此。然而，如果你观察得再仔细一点，就会发现爱丽丝的世界不仅仅可以解读成童话。

自20世纪初，一些心理分析学家就开始研究、分析这个故事，虽然仍然毫无头绪，但我们还是可以了解到许多潜在的信息。

1. 掌控你个人的成长

故事中最重要的隐喻就是个人的成长。我们看到爱丽丝从高变矮、从大变小。成长是身体尺寸变化的过程，是处理生活中的起起落落的过程，是感到自信或没有安全感的过程。爱丽丝吃东西时就长大，喝水时就变小。她很快就学会了利用自己世界里的资源来控制个人的成长。

在我们的生活中，我们自己也以这样或那样的方式成长着。你都做了什么来控制自身的成长呢？

2. 将你要达到的目标具体化

爱丽丝了解到明白自己的需求十分重要。我们可以从她与柴郡猫的对话中了解目标的重要性。

"请你告诉我，离开这里应该走哪条路，好吗？"爱丽丝说。

"这主要取决于你想去哪里。"猫说。

"去哪里，这我倒不太在乎。"爱丽丝说。

"那你要走哪条路也就无所谓喽。"猫说。

想一想三个月后你要达成什么目标！把目标及实现它的步骤一起写下来。具体想象一下当你达成目标时你将看到的和听到的。一直想，直到你想要的东西能在脑海里形成一部影片。尤其要思考如何达成目标才能令你感觉到自己心中那份强烈的情感，并将这份情感变为现实。

3. 自我定位

仙境里的各个角色一直问爱丽丝她是谁，结果就连她自己也开始质疑自己的身份。当我们开始对自己是谁、自己的立场是什么产生怀疑时，这将会影响我们的一生。细想一下你在自己的人生中所扮演的角色，例如：父母、配偶、子女、同事、领导或朋友。写下你认为自己身处这些角色时所具备的品质，例如："我是一个慈爱的父亲"或"我是一个富有创造力的商人"。

记住在每一个角色中，你都要有不同的行为。对你所扮演的每个角色了解得越多，你就会越自信，并将学着掌握每个角色所需要的能力。

4. 说出你真实的意思

爱丽丝不断地被告知要说清楚话中之意。你是否常能将你的意思真正地表达出来？你上次进行有意义的对话是在什么时候？当你接触到那些与你价值观相近的人时，你会发现你分享的思想、感觉和理念也变得更加有意义。

5. 挑战你的创造力

在最新拍成的电影中，爱丽丝的爸爸是一位成功的企业家。他告诉爱丽丝他每天早饭之前要思考六个不可能实现的问题。想象一下，就算每天只思考一件不可能的事情，你或许就能找到解决问题的办法，或者能创造出前所未有的一些东西。每天思考一件不可能的事情能让你的灵感有如泉涌。

6. 遵循你给自己的建议

爱丽丝总会给自己一些好的建议（虽然她很少遵从）。

你是否经常给自己提出建议并且严格执行？还是说我们更擅长给他人提建议，并期望他人能够遵循？

不论你是仅仅欣赏这篇童话的娱乐价值，还是像我一样思考它的深层含义，它都有很多值得我们借鉴的价值。

我们都以这样或那样的方式成长着。《爱丽丝梦游仙境》的深层含义是关于自我成长与发展的。成长就是了解我们是谁，我们的立场是什么，我们想做什么、想成为什么样的人、想拥有什么东西的过程；是对待爱、笑声、乐趣以及应对困难、伤害和痛苦的过程；是战胜恐惧、接受新挑战和培养人际关系的过程；是运用自己的天赋，学着成为最好的自己的过程。

这可能在本质上是一个儿童故事，但是我们可以从这个小女孩身上学到很多——她获得了自信和勇气去打破常规，成为了她所渴望成为的那个人。

💡 单词记事本

wonderland ['wʌndələnd]
释 n. (童话里的)仙境；奇妙的地方

dreamland ['driːmlænd]
释 n. 梦境

surface ['sɜːfɪs]
释 n. 表面；外表 v. 浮出水面；浮现
例 Those balls were rolling on the plane *surface*. 那几个球正在平面上滚动。

analyze ['ænəlaɪz]
释 v. 分析；解析，分解

psychoanalyst [ˌsaɪkəʊˈænəlɪst]
释 n. 心理分析学家

chaos ['keɪɒs]
释 n. 混乱，无秩序

underlying [ˌʌndəˈlaɪɪŋ]
释 a. 在下面的；潜在的
例 It did not solve the *underlying* problem.
这并没有解决潜在的问题。

metaphor ['metəfə(r); 'metəfɔː(r)]
释 n. 隐喻，暗喻

shrink [ʃrɪŋk]
释 v. (使)缩小，收缩；退缩，畏缩

Cheshire ['tʃeʃə(r)]
释 n. 柴郡(英国郡名)

intensity [ɪnˈtensəti]
释 n. 强烈，剧烈；热烈，热情；强度；密度

continually [kənˈtɪnjuəli]
释 ad. 不断地；频繁地

identity [aɪˈdentəti]
释 n. 身份；个性；同一性
例 Both sides reached an *identity* of view in terms of urban construction. 双方就城市建设问题达成了一致看法。

capability [ˌkeɪpəˈbɪləti]
释 n. 能力；潜质；容量

creativity [ˌkriːeɪˈtɪvəti]
释 n. 创造力，创造性

entrepreneur [ˌɒntrəprəˈnɜː(r)]
释 n. 企业家；承包人

entertainment [ˌentəˈteɪnmənt]
释 n. 娱乐，消遣；招待

overcome [ˌəʊvəˈkʌm]
释 v. 战胜，克服；(感情等)压倒

nurture ['nɜːtʃə(r)]
释 v. 培养，养育；给…营养物 n. 养育；营养物；照顾，支持；环境因素
例 We want to grow and *nurture* new talents.
我们想增加和培养新人才。

acquire [əˈkwaɪə(r)]
释 v. 取得，获得
用 an acquired taste 逐渐培养的爱好

aspire [əˈspaɪə(r)]
释 v. 渴望；追求；有志于
例 You said earlier you *aspired* to be the kind of person who had an adventurous spirit. 你早些时候说过你渴望成为有冒险精神的人。

正面评价

aggressive [əˈɡresɪv] a. 有进取心的
agreeable [əˈɡriːəbl] a. 易相处的
articulate [ɑːˈtɪkjələt] a. 善于表达的
brilliant ['brɪliənt] a. 光辉的；卓越的；有才华的

conscientious [ˌkɒnʃiˈenʃəs] a. 尽职尽责的
cordial ['kɔːdiəl] a. 诚恳的；热忱的
dignity ['dɪɡnəti] n. (举止、态度等的)庄重；高贵

diligent ['dɪlɪdʒənt] *a.* 勤奋的，用功的

discreet [dɪ'skriːt] *a.* 言行谨慎的

eloquent ['eləkwənt] *a.* 雄辩的；动人的

exquisite [ɪk'skwɪzɪt; 'ekskwɪzɪt] *a.* 优美的；高雅的

glamour ['glæmə(r)] *n.* 魅力，吸引力

independent [ˌɪndɪ'pendənt] *a.* 独立的，自主的

ingenious [ɪn'dʒiːniəs] *a.* 足智多谋的；心灵手巧的

mild [maɪld] *a.* 温柔的；温和的

modest ['mɒdɪst] *a.* 谦虚的；适度的

prudent ['pruːdnt] *a.* 谨慎的；深谋远虑的

sober ['səʊbə(r)] *a.* 清醒的；严肃的

straightforward [ˌstreɪt'fɔːwəd] *a.* 正直的；简单的

strenuous ['strenjuəs] *a.* 精力充沛的；积极的

swift [swɪft] *a.* 快速的；敏捷的

thorough ['θʌrə] *a.* 细心的；周到的

thoughtful ['θɔːtfl] *a.* 体贴的；深思的

vigorous ['vɪgərəs] *a.* 有魄力的；朝气蓬勃的

wisdom ['wɪzdəm] *n.* 智慧，才智；学识

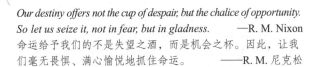

Our destiny offers not the cup of despair, but the chalice of opportunity.
So let us seize it, not in fear, but in gladness.   —R. M. Nixon
命运给予我们的不是失望之酒，而是机会之杯。因此，让我们毫无畏惧、满心愉悦地抓住命运。   ——R. M. 尼克松

Passage 62

Don't Work for Money

The world is filled with smart, talented, educated and gifted people. We meet them every day. A few days ago, my car was not running well. I pulled it into a garage, and the young mechanic had it fixed in just a few minutes. He knew what was wrong by simply listening to the engine. I was amazed. The sad truth is, great talent is not enough.

I am constantly shocked at how little talented people earn. I heard the other day that less than 5 percent of Americans earn more than $100,000 a year. A business consultant who specializes in the medical trade was telling me how many doctors, dentists and chiropractors struggle financially. All this time, I thought that when they graduated, the dollars would pour in. It was this business consultant who gave me the phrase, "They are one skill away from great wealth." What this phrase means is that most people need only to learn and master one more skill and their income would jump exponentially. I have mentioned before that financial intelligence is a synergy of accounting, investing, marketing and law. Combine those four technical skills and making money with money is easier. When it comes to money, the only skill most people know is to work hard.

When I graduated from the U.S. Merchant Marine Academy in 1969, my educated dad was happy. Standard Oil of California had hired me for its oil-tanker fleet. I had a great career ahead of me, yet I resigned after six months with the company and joined the Marine Corps to learn how to fly. My educated dad was devastated. Rich dad congratulated me.

Job security meant everything to my educated dad. Learning meant everything to my rich dad. Educated dad thought I went to school to learn to be a ship's officer. Rich dad knew that I went to school to study international trade. So as a student, I made cargo runs, navigating large freighters, oil tankers and passenger ships to the Far East and the South Pacific. While most of my classmates, including Mike, were partying at their fraternity houses, I was studying trade, people and cultures in Japan, Thailand, Singapore, Vietnam, South Korea and the Philippines. I also was partying, but it was not in any frat house. I grew up rapidly.

There is an old cliché that goes, "Job is an acronym for 'Just Over Broke.'" And unfortunately, I would say that the saying applies to millions of people.

Because school does not think financial **intelligence** is intelligence, most workers "live within their means." They work and they pay the bills. Instead I recommend to young people to seek work for what they will learn, more than what they will earn. Look down the road at what skills they want to acquire before choosing a specific profession and before getting trapped in the "Rat Race". Once people are trapped in the lifelong process of bill paying, they become like those little **hamsters** running around in those little metal wheels. Their little furry legs are spinning **furiously**, the wheel is turning furiously, but come tomorrow morning, they'll still be in the same cage: great job.

When I ask the classes I teach, "How many of you can cook a better hamburger than McDonald's?", almost all the students raise their hands. I then ask, "So if most of you can cook a better hamburger, how come McDonald's makes more money than you?" The answer is obvious: McDonald's is excellent at business systems. The reason why so many talented people are poor is that they focus on building a better hamburger and know little or nothing about business systems. The world is filled with talented poor people. All too often, they're poor or struggle financially or earn less than they are capable of, not because of what they know but because of what they do not know. They focus on **perfecting** their skills at building a better hamburger rather than the skills of selling and **delivering** the hamburger.

不要为钱而工作

世界上到处都是精明强干、才华横溢、知书达理以及颇具天赋之人。我们每天都会见到他们。前几天，我的汽车出了点问题，我用拖车把它拖进了维修厂。一位年轻的技师只花了几分钟就把它修好了。他仅仅听了听发动机的声音就知道是哪里出了问题，这让我惊奇不已。然而可悲的是，单凭非凡的才华是不够的。

有才华的人收入都很微薄，这一点常让我感到震惊。前几天我听人说，只有不到5％的美国人年收入在10万美元以上。一位专门研究药品行业的商务顾问曾告诉我，有许多医生、牙医和按摩师生活拮据。我过去一直以为他们一毕业就会财源广入。这位商务顾问还告诉了我这样一句话："想要获得财富，他们还缺少一项技能。"这句话的意思是说，大部分人需要多学一项技能并对此精通，这样他们的收入才能大幅增加。我曾提过，财商指的是财务、投资、市场营销和法律的综合能力。将这四种专业技能结合起来，以钱生钱就会更容易。说到钱，大部分人所知道的唯一技能就是拼命工作。

1969年，我从美国海运学院毕业。我那有学识的爸爸十分高兴。加州标准石油公司录用了我，让我加入他们的油轮船队。尽管我的职业前景十分美好，但我还是在六个月后选择从这家公司辞职，加入了海军陆战队学习飞行。对此我那有学识的爸爸极为震惊，而富有的爸爸则向我表示祝贺。

对于有学识的爸爸来说，稳定的工作就是一切；而对于富有的爸爸来说，学习才是一切。有学识的爸爸以为我上学是为了做一名船长，而富有的爸爸则知道我上学是为了学习国际贸易。因此，在还是学生时，我就跑过货运，驾驶过去远东及南太平洋的大型货轮、油轮和客轮。当我的大部分同班同学，包括迈克在内，正在联谊会会堂举办派对的时候，我在日本、泰国、新加坡、越南、韩国和菲律宾等国学习贸易、风土人情和文化背景。当然我也参加聚会，但不去任何联谊会。这样，我迅速地成长了起来。

常言道："工作（job）就是'比破产强一点（Just Over Broke）'的首字母缩写。"然而不幸的是，这句话确实适用于大多数人。因为学校没有把财商看作一种才智，所以大部分劳动者都过着节衣缩食的生活。他们工作挣钱，然后支付账单。相反，我建议年轻人在寻找工作时首先要看看能从中学到什么，而不是能挣到多少。在选择一种特定的职业和陷入激烈的竞争之前，要先好好想想自己到底想要获得什么技能。一旦人们为了生计而整天疲于奔命，就和那些在小铁圈里不停奔跑、转圈的小仓鼠一样了。仓鼠的小毛腿跑得飞快，小铁圈也转得飞快，可到了第二天早上，它们依然被困在那个笼里：真是"伟大的工作"啊。

当我在自己所教的班上问"你们当中有多少人能做出比麦当劳更美味的汉堡包？"时，几乎所有的学生都举起了手。接着我问："那么，如果你们当中的大部分人都能做出比麦当劳更好吃的汉堡包，为什么麦当劳比你们更能赚钱？"答案很明显：麦当劳有着卓越的商业体系。许多才华横溢之人之所以贫穷，就是因为他们专注于做出更好的汉堡包，而对商业体系几乎一无所知。世界上到处都是有才华的穷人。在很多情况下，他们之所以贫穷、生活拮据或者收入与其能力不相符，不在于他们所了解的东西而在于他们所不了解的东西。他们只将注意力集中在提高和完善做汉堡包的技术上，而忽视了提高销售和配送汉堡包的技能。

---

talented	['tæləntɪd]
释 a. 有才能的，有才干的	

amazed	[ə'meɪzd]
释 a. 十分惊奇的，惊愕的	

mechanic	[mə'kænɪk]
释 n. 技工，机修工 a. 手工的；机械的	

consultant	[kən'sʌltənt]
释 n. 顾问；会诊医师，顾问医师	

specialize ['speʃəlaɪz]

释 v. 专门研究，专攻；专注于

用 specialize in 专攻，专门研究

例 The consulting company *specializes* in making practical development plan for the local enterprise. 这家咨询公司专为地方企业制订实用的发展计划。

chiropractor ['kaɪərəupræktə(r)]

释 n. (脊椎)按摩师

exponentially [ˌekspə'nenʃəli]

释 ad. 以指数方式地，迅速增长地

synergy ['sɪnədʒi]

释 n. 协同作用，增效作用；协同，配合

resign [rɪ'zaɪn]

释 v. 辞去，辞职；使顺从

devastated ['devəsteɪtɪd]

释 a. 极为震惊的

cargo ['kɑːgəu]

释 n. (船、飞机等装载的)货物

navigate ['nævɪgeɪt]

释 v. 测定路线；导航；驾驶(船、飞机等)

例 The early explorers needed to design a special kind of boat in order to *navigate* the sea at a long distance. 早期的探险家为了在海上进行远距离的航行，需要设计一种特别的船只。

freighter ['freɪtə(r)]

释 n. 货船；运输机

fraternity [frə'tɜːnəti]

释 n. 手足之情；大学生联谊会

cliché ['kliːʃeɪ]

释 n. 老生常谈；陈腐的思想

acronym ['ækrənɪm]

释 n. 首字母缩略词

intelligence [ɪn'telɪdʒəns]

释 n. 智力；理解力；情报

例 A second aspect of the Web is that it is the first medium that honors the notion of multiple *intelligences*. 网络的第二个方面就是它是第一种实现多重智能概念的媒介。

hamster ['hæmstə(r)]

释 n. 仓鼠

furiously ['fjuəriəsli]

释 ad. 飞快地；猛烈地；狂怒地

perfect

释 ['pɜːfɪkt] a. 完美的；完全的；精通的
[pə'fekt] v. 使完善，使改善

deliver [dɪ'lɪvə(r)]

释 v. 递送，运送；支付；发表；接生；给予(打击等)

💡 单词家族

日常工作

adept [ə'dept] a. 内行的，擅长的；熟练的 n. 行家

administration [ədˌmɪnɪ'streɪʃn] n. 经营，管理；行政

administrative [əd'mɪnɪstrətɪv] a. 管理的；行政的

agenda [ə'dʒendə] n. 日程

allocate ['æləkeɪt] v. 分配

appoint [ə'pɔɪnt] v. 任命，选派

asset ['æset] n. 有价值的技能或人；[pl.] 财产，资产；优势

collaborate [kə'læbəreɪt] v. 协作，合作

colleague ['kɒliːg] n. 同事；同僚

competing [kəm'piːtɪŋ] a. 竞争性的；互相矛盾的

coordination [kəʊˌɔːdɪ'neɪʃn] n. 协调，协同

deadlock ['dedlɒk] n. 僵局

deft [deft] a. 灵巧的，熟练的

delegate ['delɪgət] n. 代表

dilemma [dɪ'lemə; daɪ'lemə] n. 进退两难的局面

effectiveness [ɪ'fektɪvnəs] n. 效率；效能

elite [eɪ'liːt; ɪ'liːt] n. 精英

freshness ['freʃnəs] n. 新鲜；活力

hasten ['heɪsn] v. 加速；催促

nominee [ˌnɒmɪ'niː] n. 被提名的候选人；被任命者

overdue [ˌəʊvə'djuː] a. 迟到的；逾期的

oversee [ˌəʊvə'siː] v. 监督，管理

overtire [ˌəʊvə'taɪə(r)] v. (使)过度疲劳

painstaking ['peɪnzteɪkɪŋ] a. 辛苦的；勤勉的

personnel [ˌpɜːsə'nel] n. 全体人员，员工

professional [prə'feʃənl] a. 职业的 n. 专业人员

qualification [ˌkwɒlɪfɪ'keɪʃn] n. 资格；技能；证书，执照

subsidiary [səb'sɪdiəri] n. 支流；子公司

The people who get on in this world are the people who get up and look for circumstances they want, and if they cannot find them, make them.
　　　　　　　　　　　　　　　　　　　—George Bernard Shaw
在这个世界上，取得成功的人是那些努力寻找他们想要的机会的人；如果找不到，他们就自己创造机会。——萧伯纳

Passage 63

Six Secrets of High-Energy People

There's an energy crisis in America, and it has nothing to do with fossil fuels. Millions of us get up each morning already weary over the day holds. But it's not physical energy that most of us lack. Sure, we could all use extra sleep and a better diet. But in truth, people are healthier today than at any time in history. I can almost guarantee that if you long for more energy, the problem is not with your body.

What you're seeking is not physical energy. It's emotional energy. Unlike physical energy, which is finite and diminishes with age, emotional energy is unlimited and has nothing to do with genes or upbringing. So how do you get it? You can't simply tell yourself to be positive. You must take action. Here are six practical strategies that work.

1. Do something new.

Very little that's new occurs in our lives. The impact of this sameness on our emotional energy is gradual, but huge: It's like a tire with a slow leak. You don't notice it at first, but eventually you'll get a flat. It's up to you to plug the leak—even though there are always a dozen reasons to stay stuck in your dull routines of life.

Here's a challenge: If it's something you wouldn't ordinarily do, do it. Try a dish you've never eaten. Listen to music you'd ordinarily tune out. You'll discover these small things add to your emotional energy.

2. Reclaim life's meaning.

So many of my patients tell me that their lives used to have meaning, but that somewhere along the line things went stale. The first step in solving this meaning shortage is to figure out what you really care about, and then do something about it.

3. Put yourself in the fun zone.

Most of us grown-ups are seriously fun-deprived. High-energy people have the same day-to-day work as the rest of us, but they manage to find something enjoyable in every situation. We all define fun differently, of course, but I can guarantee this: If you put just a bit of it into your day, your energy will increase quickly.

4. Bid farewell to guilt and regret.

Everyone's past is filled with regrets that still cause pain. But from an emotional energy point of view, they are dead weights that keep us from moving forward. While they can't **merely** be willed away, I do **recommend** you remind yourself that whatever happened is in the past, and nothing can change that. Holding on to the memory only allows the damage to continue into the present.

5. Make up your mind.

Say you've been thinking about cutting your hair short. Will it look stylish—or too **extreme**?

You **endlessly** think it over. Having the decision hanging over your head is a huge energy **drain**.

Every time you can't decide, you **burden** yourself with alternatives. Quit thinking that you have to make the right decision; instead, make a choice and don't look back.

6. Give to get.

Emotional energy has a kind of **magical** quality: the more you give, the more you get back. This is the difference between emotional and physical energy. With the latter, you have to get it to be able to give it. With the former, however, you get it by giving it.

Start by asking everyone you meet, "How are you?" as if you really want to know, and then listen to the **reply**. Be the one who hears. Most of us also need to smile more often. If you don't smile at the person you love first thing in the morning, you're sucking energy out of your relationship. Finally, help another person—and make the help real, **concrete**.

After all, if it's true that what goes around comes around, why not make sure that what's **circulating** around you is the good stuff?

🔅 译 文

精力充沛人士的六个秘密

美国出现了一种"能量危机",它与矿物燃料全然无关。我们中数以万计的人清晨起床时就已经厌倦了这新的一天,而大部分人并不缺乏体力。当然,我们都可以稍微多睡一会儿,吃得好点。但事实上,现在的人比历史上任何时候都健康。我几乎可以保证,如果你渴望获得更多的精力,问题肯定不在于你的身体状况。

你需要的不是体力,而是情感能量。跟有限的且会随年龄渐逝的体力不一样,情感能量是无穷的,且与基因或教养无关。那么我们怎样才能获得它呢?你不能简单地告诉自己要变得积极。你必须采取行动。下面是六个切实可行的策略。

1. 做些新鲜事

生活中鲜有新鲜事。这种千篇一律的重复对我们情感能量的影响虽然缓慢，但是巨大。它就如同轮胎上有一个小洞在慢慢漏气，开始时你并不会注意，但最后气会全部漏光。是否堵住漏洞取决于你——即使总有许多理由让你继续困在沉闷的日程中。

试试这个挑战：如果有些事情是你平常不做的，那就去做吧。尝试一道从未吃过的菜，听一些你通常不听的音乐，你会发现这些微小的事情会增强你的情感能量。

2. 重拾生命的意义

我的很多病人都告诉我，他们的生命曾经很有意义，但是从人生的某个时刻开始，一切都变得索然无味。要从这种缺乏意义的生活中解脱出来，第一步就是要明白你真正关心的是什么，然后再朝那个方向努力。

3. 置身乐区

我们绝大部分成年人的生活都严重缺乏乐趣。与其他人一样，精力充沛的人也要日复一日地工作，但是他们在任何场合都能找到能让自己快乐的东西。当然，我们对快乐都有着自己不同的定义，但我可以保证：如果你能在每天的生活中都增加一点点快乐，你的精力将迅速增加。

4. 挥别内疚与遗憾

每个人的过去都充满着遗憾，让人回想起来仍感到痛苦不已。但从情感能量的角度来看，这些都是影响我们前行的包袱。尽管我们难以将其抛弃，但我建议你提醒自己无论以前发生了什么，那都已经过去，我们无法对之作出改变。紧抓着回忆不放只能令伤害蔓延至今。

5. 下定决心

比如说，你一直想把头发剪短。它看起来会时髦吗，还是太极端？

你不断地思前想后。而一直在脑子里反复思考某个决定会极大地消耗你的精力。

每当你无法作出决定时，你就使自己背负着可供选择的其他事物。停止你必须作出正确的决定这一想法，而是作出一个选择，并且不再回头。

6. 有舍才有得

情感能量有一种神奇的特质：你给得越多，获得的就越多。这恰恰就是情感能量和体力的区别。对于后者，你必须先有体力才能够付出。而对于前者，通过付出，你才能得到它。

从向你遇见的每个人问好开始吧，问一句"你好吗？"，就像你真的很想知道答案一样，然后等待对方回应。做一个懂得聆听的人。我们中的大多数都需要更经常地微笑。如果你早晨的第一件事不是对你爱的人微笑，那你正在从你们的关系中吸走能量。最后，帮助别人，并且让你的帮助真实而具体。

毕竟，如果真的是"善有善报，恶有恶报"，那么为什么不让围绕在你周围的都是美好的事物呢？

💡单词记事本

fossil ['fɒsl]
释 *n.* 化石；老顽固
用 fossil fuel 化石燃料

weary ['wɪəri]
释 *a.* 疲惫的；无兴趣或热情的，厌倦的；令人厌倦的 *v.* 厌倦，不满

lack [læk]
释 *v./n.* 缺乏，缺少；不足；没有
例 There was no *lack* of volunteers in seniors' home. 养老院不缺少志愿者。

diet ['daɪət]
释 *n.* 日常饮食；节食 *v.* 节食
用 balanced diet 均衡饮食
例 Could you give me some advice on *diet*? 你能给我一些关于饮食的建议吗？

finite ['faɪnaɪt]
释 *a.* 有限的；限定的

diminish [dɪ'mɪnɪʃ]
释 *v.* 变小，减少；降低；贬低
例 With the passage of time, the book's influence has *diminished*. 随着时间的流逝，这本书的影响逐渐变小了。

unlimited [ʌn'lɪmɪtɪd]
释 *a.* 无限的；极大的

upbringing ['ʌpbrɪŋɪŋ]
释 *n.* 养育，教育，培养

occur [ə'kɜː(r)]
释 *v.* 发生；存在；想到
用 occur as 以…的形式出现
例 It didn't *occur* to her that her husband was caught in trouble. 她没想到她老公会陷入困境。

tire ['taɪə(r)]
释 *n.* 轮胎 *v.* (使)疲劳；(使)厌倦

leak [liːk]
释 *v.* (使)漏；泄露；泄密 *n.* 泄漏；漏洞；(消息等的)走漏

flat [flæt]
释 *a.* 平坦的；单调的；扁平的 *n.* 一套公寓；平面部分；平地；漏了气的轮胎 *ad.* 平直地；直截了当地

plug [plʌg]
释 *n.* 插头；塞子 *v.* 把…塞住

ordinarily ['ɔːdnrəli]
释 *ad.* 平常地，通常地

reclaim [rɪ'kleɪm]
释 *v.* 重新找回；回收再利用；改造；开垦(土地)

stale [steɪl]
释 *a.* 变质的；陈旧的，乏味的

shortage ['ʃɔːtɪdʒ]
释 *n.* 不足，缺少

搭 shortage of 缺少

例 There is no *shortage* of water in the village. 这个村子不缺水。

figure ['fɪgə(r)]
释 n. 数字；人物；图形；体态 v. 想；计算；描绘

define [dɪ'faɪn]
释 v. 下定义；规定；使明确

guilt [gɪlt]
释 n. 内疚；有罪，责任

merely ['mɪəli]
释 ad. 仅仅，只不过

recommend [ˌrekə'mend]
释 v. 推荐，举荐；劝告，建议

extreme [ɪk'striːm]
释 n. 极端；最大程度 a. 极度的；极端的，偏激的

endlessly ['endləsli]
释 ad. 不断地，无穷尽地

drain [dreɪn]
释 n. 排水；下水道；消耗 v. 排水；耗尽

burden ['bɜːdn]
释 n. 重担；精神负担；船的载重量 v. 使负担；烦扰；负重

搭 financial burden 经济负担

例 I become a *burden* to my children when I'm sick. 当我生病的时候，我就变成了孩子们的负担。

magical ['mædʒɪkl]
释 a. (像)魔法的；不可思议的

reply [rɪ'plaɪ]
释 v./n. 回答，答复；以…作答

搭 reply to 答复

例 I can't figure out why he has never *replied* to any of my letters. 我不明白他为什么从不回我的信。

concrete ['kɒnkriːt]
释 a. 具体的；有形的 n. 混凝土

circulate ['sɜːkjəleɪt]
释 v. (使)循环；(使)流通；(使)流传

💡 单词家族

身体症状

aggravate ['ægrəveɪt] v. 恶化；加剧

ailing ['eɪlɪŋ] a. 生病的；不舒服的

airsickness ['eəsɪknəs] n. 晕机

asphyxia [æs'fɪksiə; əs'fɪksiə] n. 窒息；昏厥

blotch [blɒtʃ] n. (皮肤上的)斑点；疙瘩

callous ['kæləs] a. 结硬块的；起老茧的

congenital [kən'dʒenɪtl] a. 先天的，天生的

corporeal [kɔː'pɔːriəl] a. 肉体的，身体的

counteract [ˌkaʊntər'ækt] v. 对…起反作用；抵消

debility [dɪ'bɪləti] n. 衰弱；虚弱

degenerate [dɪ'dʒenəreɪt] v. 恶化；衰退；堕落

dislocate ['dɪsləkeɪt] v. 使脱臼；把…弄乱

distention [dɪ'stenʃn] n. 膨胀；肿胀

dizziness ['dɪzinəs] n. 头昏眼花，眩晕

dysfunctional [dɪs'fʌŋkʃənl] a. 功能失调的

excrete [ɪk'skriːt] v. 排泄；分泌

frail [freɪl] a. 身体虚弱的

gastritis [gæ'straɪtɪs] n. 胃炎

hamstring ['hæmstrɪŋ] v. 使不能正常工作

inflamed [ɪn'fleɪmd] a. 发炎的

intoxication [ɪnˌtɒksɪ'keɪʃn] n. 醉酒；中毒

lacerate ['læsəreɪt] v. 撕裂；深深伤害

measly ['miːzli] a. 患麻疹的；小得可怜的

nauseate ['nɔːzieɪt; 'nɔːsieɪt] v. (使)作呕；(使)厌恶

ossify ['ɒsɪfaɪ] v. 硬化；骨化

pestilential [ˌpestɪ'lenʃl] a. 引起瘟疫的

prognosis [prɒg'nəʊsɪs] n. 对疾病症状的预断

protuberance [prə'tjuːbərəns] n. 凸出，隆起；结节，瘤

rend [rend] v. 撕裂；猛拉

rheum [ruːm] n. 感冒；发炎性分泌物

sprain [spreɪn] v. 扭伤

ulcer ['ʌlsə(r)] n. 溃疡；腐烂物

ulcerate ['ʌlsəreɪt] v. 溃烂；腐败

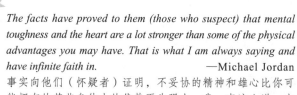

The facts have proved to them (those who suspect) that mental toughness and the heart are a lot stronger than some of the physical advantages you may have. That is what I am always saying and have infinite faith in.
—Michael Jordan

事实向他们（怀疑者）证明，不妥协的精神和雄心比你可能拥有的某些身体上的优势更为强大。我一直这么说，也一直对此坚信不疑。

——迈克尔·乔丹

Passage 64

Why Integrity Matters

What Is Integrity?

The key to integrity is **consistency**—not only setting high personal standards for oneself (honesty, responsibility, respect for others, **fairness**) but also living up to those standards each and every day. One who has integrity is bound by and follows moral and ethical standards even when making life's hard choices, choices which may be clouded by **stress**, pressure to succeed, or **temptation**.

What happens if we lie, **cheat**, steal, or **violate** other **ethical** standards? We feel disappointed in ourselves and ashamed. But a **lapse** of integrity also affects our relationships with others. Trust is essential in any important relationship, whether personal or professional. Who can trust someone who is **dishonest** or unfair? Thus, integrity must be one of our most important goals.

Risky Business

We are each responsible for our own decisions, even if the decision-making process has been **undermined** by stress or peer pressure. The real test of character is whether we can learn from our mistake, by understanding why we acted as we did and then exploring ways to avoid similar problems in the future.

Making ethical decisions is a critical part of avoiding future problems. We must learn to recognize risks because if we can't see the risks we're taking, we can't make responsible choices. To identify risks, we need to know the rules and be aware of the facts. For example, one who doesn't know the rules about **plagiarism** may accidentally use words or ideas without giving proper credit, or one who fails to keep careful research notes may **unintentionally** fail to quote and **cite** sources as required. But the fact that such a violation is "unintentional" does not excuse the misconduct. **Ignorance** is not a defense.

Getting Away with It—or Not

Those who don't get caught pay an even higher price. A **cheater** doesn't learn from the test, which deprives him of an education. Cheating undermines confidence and independence; the cheater is a fraud, and knows that without **dishonesty**, he would have failed. Cheating destroys self-respect and integrity, leaving the cheater ashamed, guilty, and afraid of getting caught. Worst of all, a cheater who doesn't get caught the first time usually cheats again, not only because he is farther behind, but also because it seems "easier". This slippery **slope** of **eroding** ethics and bigger risks leads only to **disaster**. Eventually, the cheater gets caught, and the later he gets caught, the worse the consequences.

Cheating Hurts Others, Too

Cheaters often feel **invisible**, as if their actions "don't **count**" and don't really hurt anyone. But individual choices have an **intense cumulative** effect. Cheating can spread like a disease. Recent statistics suggest 30% or more of college students cheat. If a class is graded on a **curve**, cheating hurts others' grades. Even if there is no curve, cheating "poisons" the classroom, and others may feel pressured to join in. ("If I don't cheat, I can't compete with those who do.") Cheating also has a destructive impact on teachers. The real reward of good teaching is seeing students learn, but a cheater says, "I'm not interested in what you're trying to teach; all I care about is stealing a grade, regardless of the effect on others." The end result is a destructive attack on the quality of your education. Finally, cheating can hurt the reputation of the university and harm those who worked hard for their degree.

Why Integrity Matters

If cheating becomes the **norm**, then we are in big trouble. We must rely on the honesty and good **faith** of others. If not, we couldn't put money in the bank, buy food, clothing or medicine from others, drive across a bridge, get on a plane, go to the dentist—the list is endless. There are many examples of the vast harm that is caused when individuals forget or ignore the effect their dishonesty can have. The savings and loan **scandal**, the stock market and junk bond swindles, and, of course, Watergate, have undermined the faith of many Americans in the integrity of political and economic leaders and society as a whole. Such incidents take a **tremendous toll** on our nation's economy and our individual **well-being**. For example, but for the savings and loan **debacle**, there might be **funds** available to reduce the national debt and pay for education.

In sum, we all have a common **stake** in our school, our community, and our society. Our actions do matter. It is essential that we act with integrity in order to build the kind of world in which we want to live.

 译 文

诚实为何重要?

什么是诚实

诚实的关键在于一致性——不仅要给自己制定较高的个人标准（诚实、有责任心、尊重他人、公正），还要每天坚持遵守这些准则。即使在面对人生中可能混杂着紧张压抑、获得成功的压力或外界的诱惑的艰难抉择时，一个具有诚实品格的人也会受道德和伦理标准的约束，并遵守这些标准。

如果我们撒谎、作弊、偷盗或者违反了其他道德准则会怎样呢？我们会对自己感到失望和羞愧。但是不诚实也会影响我们与他人的关系。在任何重要的人际关系中，无论是私人的还是工作方面的，信任都是最为重要的。谁会相信不诚实的或不公正的人呢？因此，诚实必须是我们最重要的目标之一。

有风险的事情

我们每个人都要对自己的决定负责，即使做决定的过程因为内心的压力或来自同伴的压力而遭到了破坏。对于品格的真正考验在于我们是否能从错误中学习，明白我们之前为什么要那么做，然后找到方法来避免在将来出现类似的问题。

作出合乎道德的决定是避免未来犯错误的重要部分。我们必须要学会识别风险，因为如果我们不能意识到我们正在冒险，我们就不能作出负责任的抉择。为了识别风险，我们需要了解规则和实际情况。例如，如果一个人不知道关于剽窃的规则，他就可能不经意地未经允许而引用别人的词句或观点，或者如果一个人没有认真做调研笔记，他可能就会在无意间没有按要求标注引用来源。但事实上，"无意"违反规定不是做错事的借口。无知不是挡箭牌。

侥幸逃脱——或当场现形

那些没有被发现的人付出的代价更高。作弊的人没有从考试中学到知识，这就剥夺了他受教育的机会。作弊破坏了作弊者的自信心和独立性；作弊者是个骗子，他知道如果他不作弊就会不及格。作弊还破坏了作弊者的自尊和诚实，使其感到惭愧、内疚并害怕被抓到。最糟糕的是，第一次作弊没有被抓到的作弊者通常会再次作弊，不仅是因为他落后得太多，还因为作弊似乎"更简单"。这种遭到腐蚀的道德的急剧下滑和更大的风险只会导致灾难。最终，作弊者会被抓到。他被抓到得越晚，后果就越严重。

作弊也伤害他人

作弊者经常觉得他们不会被发现，就好像他们的行为"不算数"，没有真正地伤害到任何人。但是个人的选择会产生强烈的累积效果。作弊会像疾病一样四处蔓延。最近的统计数据表明，有30%或者更多的大学生作弊。如果用曲线来表示班级成绩的话，作弊就伤害到了其他人的成绩。即使没有曲线图表，作弊也会"毒害"到整个班级，其他人可能也会被迫去作弊（他们会认为："如果我不作弊，我就竞争不过那些作弊的人。"）。作弊对老师也有破坏性的影响。好的教学的真正奖励是看到学生们学有所获，而一位作弊者说："我对你要教的东西不感兴趣；我所关心的是偷到一个学分，不管对其他人会有什么影响。"最终的结果是对教师的教学质量造成了严重打击。最后，作弊可能会损害到大学的声誉，伤害到那些努力学习想获得学位的人。

为什么诚实很重要

如果作弊成了一种习惯，那我们就有大麻烦了。我们必须依靠他人的诚实和诚信。否则的话，我们就不会把钱存到银行，不会从别人那里买食物、衣服或者药物，不敢开车过桥，不敢坐飞机或去看牙医——可以没完没了地罗列下去。有很多例子都是关于一些人忘记或者忽视了他们的不诚实所造成的影响而带来重大伤害的。储蓄和贷款丑闻事件、股票市场和垃圾债券欺诈事件，当然还有水门事件，已经削弱了许多美国人对政治和经济领袖的诚实度以及整个社会的信任。这样的事件严重地损害了美国的经济和我们个人的幸福。例如，要不是因为储蓄和贷款丑闻事件，可能还有资金可以用于减少国债和资助教育。

总之，在学校、社区和社会里我们都有着共同的利益。我们的行为很重要。为了建立我们想要的良好的生活环境，我们都要诚信做事，这一点非常必要。

💡 单词记事本

integrity [ɪn'tegrəti]
释 *n.* 正直，诚实；整体

consistency [kən'sɪstənsi]
释 *n.* 一致性，一贯性；强度，硬度，浓度

fairness ['feənəs]
释 *n.* 公平，正直；美好；清晰

stress [stres]
释 *n.* 压力，紧张；强调；重音 *v.* 加压力于，使紧张；强调；重读
用 stress on 强调
例 *Stress* is a factor in the development of sickness. 压力是疾病形成的一个因素。

temptation [temp'teɪʃn]
释 *n.* 诱惑，引诱；诱惑物

cheat [tʃiːt]
释 *v.* 欺骗；作弊 *n.* 欺骗；作弊；骗子

violate ['vaɪəleɪt]
释 *v.* 违反，违背；亵渎；侵犯，干扰
用 violate the contract 违反合同
例 She accused the press of *violating* her privacy. 她控诉媒体侵犯了她的隐私。

ethical ['eθɪkl]
释 *a.* 道德的，伦理的；凭处方出售的

lapse [læps]
释 *n.* 错误，疏忽；行为失检；(时间的)流逝 *v.* 陷入；丧失，失效；终止

dishonest [dɪs'ɒnɪst]
释 *a.* 不诚实的

risky ['rɪski]
释 *a.* 危险的，有风险的；冒险的

undermine [ˌʌndə'maɪn]
释 v. 削弱，暗中破坏；在…下挖地道

plagiarism ['pleɪdʒərɪzəm]
释 n. (文章、学说等的)剽窃，抄袭；剽窃物

unintentionally [ˌʌnɪn'tenʃənəli]
释 ad. 非故意地，无意地

cite [saɪt]
释 v. 引用；传唤；想起

ignorance ['ɪɡnərəns]
释 n. 无知，愚昧
例 Everyone hates to admit the *ignorance*. 每个人都不愿意承认自己的无知。

cheater ['tʃiːtə(r)]
释 n. 骗子；作弊者；背叛者

dishonesty [dɪs'ɒnɪsti]
释 n. 不诚实

slope [sləʊp]
释 n. 斜坡；倾斜 v. (使)倾斜

erode [ɪ'rəʊd]
释 v. 侵蚀，腐蚀

disaster [dɪ'zɑːstə(r)]
释 n. 灾难；彻底失败的人或事物
用 natural disaster 自然灾害
例 Thousands of people died in the *disaster*. 成千上万的人在灾难中丧生了。

invisible [ɪn'vɪzəbl]
释 a. 看不见的；无形的

count [kaʊnt]
释 v. 点…的数目；把…算入；认为；有意义 n. 计数；计算

intense [ɪn'tens]
释 a. 强烈的；紧张的；非常的；热切的
用 intense competition 激烈的竞争
例 The marketing manager is under *intense* pressure to resign. 市场部经理迫于巨大的压力将要辞职。

cumulative ['kjuːmjələtɪv]
释 a. 累积的，渐增的

curve [kɜːv]
释 n. 曲线；弯曲；曲线图表 v. 弄弯；成曲形

norm [nɔːm]
释 n. 规范，标准；定额

faith [feɪθ]
释 n. 信任；信仰；宗教信仰
用 keep faith 守信；忠于信仰
例 I've lost *faith* in your promise. 我不再相信你的承诺了。

scandal ['skændl]
释 n. 丑闻；恶意诽谤；流言飞语

tremendous [trə'mendəs]
释 a. 惊人的，巨大的
用 tremendous accident 重大事故
例 People vary *tremendously* in their characters. 人们的性格差别很大。

toll [təʊl]
释 n. 通行费；伤亡人数；对某物造成的毁坏或损失 v. 征收；敲(钟)

well-being ['welbiːɪŋ]
释 n. 幸福，康乐

debacle [deɪ'bɑːkl; dɪ'bɑːkl]
释 n. 崩溃，彻底失败；大灾难；解冻

fund [fʌnd]
释 n. 基金，专款；资金，现款 v. 为…提供资金
用 investment fund 投资基金
例 The company is short of *funds* at the moment. 公司目前资金不足。

stake [steɪk]
释 n. 桩，棍子；利害关系；股份；赌注 v. 系在桩上；资助，支持；打赌

生活方式

austere [ɒ'stɪə(r); ɔː'stɪə(r)] *a.* 朴素的；严峻的；无装饰的

chipper ['tʃɪpə(r)] *a.* 精力充沛的；愉快的

constrained [kən'streɪnd] *a.* 约束的，节制的

hackneyed ['hæknid] *a.* 陈腐的；平庸的

livelihood ['laɪvlihʊd] *n.* 生活；生计

nontraditional [ˌnɒntrə'dɪʃənl] *a.* 不符合传统的

penury ['penjəri] *n.* 贫困，贫穷

picky ['pɪki] *a.* 挑剔的；过分讲究的

prodigal ['prɒdɪgl] *a.* 浪费的，挥霍的

seclusion [sɪ'kluːʒn] *n.* 隔离；隐居

sequester [sɪ'kwestə(r)] *v.* 使退隐；使隔绝

sparing ['speərɪŋ] *a.* 节俭的；保守的

subsist [səb'sɪst] *v.* 存活；供养

subsistence [səb'sɪstəns] *n.* 生存；生活

sybarite ['sɪbəraɪt] *n.* 爱奢侈享乐的人

teetotal [ˌtiː'təʊtl] *a.* 滴酒不沾的

timeworn ['taɪmwɔːn] *a.* 陈旧的；老朽的

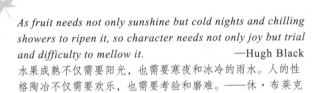

As fruit needs not only sunshine but cold nights and chilling showers to ripen it, so character needs not only joy but trial and difficulty to mellow it.
　　　　　　　　　　　　　　　　—Hugh Black
水果成熟不仅需要阳光，也需要寒夜和冰冷的雨水。人的性格陶冶不仅需要欢乐，也需要考验和磨难。——休·布莱克

附录：音标体系

单元音和双元音

音标	例词	音标	例词	音标	例词
iː	see	u	actual	eɪ	say
ɪ	bit	ɑː	father	aɪ	my
e	ten	ɔː	saw	ɔɪ	boy
æ	cat	uː	moon	əʊ	go
ɒ	got	ɜː	bird	aʊ	now
ʌ	cup	ʊ	put	ɪə	real
ə	about			eə	hair
i	family			ʊə	sure
				iə	peculiar

辅　音

音标	例词	音标	例词	音标	例词
p	pen	f	fall	h	hat
b	bad	v	view	m	map
t	tea	θ	think	n	no
d	day	ð	this	ŋ	sing
k	keep	s	so	l	leg
g	give	z	zip	r	red
tʃ	chain	ʃ	shoe	j	yes
dʒ	jam	ʒ	measure	w	wet
tr	treasure				
dr	drive				
ts	shirts				
dz	hands				

终极英语单词系列：

《终极英语单词12000—变身口语达人3000词》
《终极英语单词12000—成为英语学霸3000词》
《终极英语单词12000—畅读英文报刊3000词》
《终极英语单词12000—英语母语水平3000词》
（免费下载图书相关音频文件）

（日）ALC Press Inc. 著

"终极英语单词12000系列"由新东方从日本ALC集团引进，从40年累积的各类英文语料中精选而出，并根据英美人的使用频率，由浅入深分为四册。该系列已经在日本持续热销10年，深受好评。

《200个一定要学的英文词根词缀》
（免费下载图书相关音频文件）

新东方词汇研究中心 编著

◎ 共收录100个常用词根、50个常用前缀和50个常用后缀
◎ 深度剖析词根、词缀的起源及含义，拆解例词，给出精妙例句
◎ 所选词汇均为四六级难度，刚需实用
◎ 配有拓展词汇和阶段检测题

定价: 28元 开本: 32开 页码: 352页

《超实用15000词分类速记》
（免费下载图书相关音频文件）
俞敏洪 编著

◎ 20个主题，452个细分场景
◎ 7000余个搭配，2150余个实用句子
◎ 在真实语境中演练完美口语
◎ 单词分场景归纳记忆，打破A到Z传统形式
◎ 词条按认知顺序编排，提供搭配、句式
◎ 地道口语搭配，举一反三，现学现用
◎ 趣味讲解口语小词汇及其大用途
◎ 纯正英式外教朗读，扫码即听

定价: 55元 开本: 16开 页码: 540页

剑桥标准商务英语教程学生用书系列（第2版）：

《剑桥标准商务英语教程:初级学生用书(第2版)》
《剑桥标准商务英语教程:中级学生用书(第2版)》
《剑桥标准商务英语教程:高级学生用书(第2版)》
（免费下载图书相关音频文件）

（英）Norman Whitby, Guy Brook-Hart 编著

◎ 剑桥BEC官方备考资料，商务英语学习理想之选
◎ 话题源于职场生活，涵盖时新商业用语和商业报道
◎ 听力录音包含不同口音，还原真实商务语言交流情境
◎ 写作练习包含多种写作类型的模拟练习和写作范例
◎ 书后各附有1套真题，帮助考生熟悉考试题型
◎ 附赠自学手册，一课一练，同步提升词汇、语法、阅读和写作技能

读美国中小学课本学各科词汇系列：(1-6册、全6册套装)
（免费下载图书相关音频文件）
M. A. Putlack/e-Creative Contents 编著

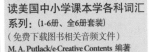

◎ 掌握美国中小学各科词汇，读懂英文课本很轻松
◎ 读过这套书，用英文学习数学、物理、化学、历史、地理，一点都不难
◎ 读美国课本，和美国学生同步学习，像学母语一样学英文
◎ 体验美国课堂，不必远赴重洋

《英语词缀词典》/《英语词根词典》

（韩）金正基 编著

◎ 适合中国学生使用的词汇学习书
◎ TOEFL、GRE、SAT、IELTS词汇，一本搞定
◎ 两本书为相辅相成的姊妹篇，共收录了33,000多个单词和词语，不但词汇量大，而且收词科学、实用

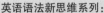

英语语法新思维系列：

《英语语法新思维初级教程：走近语法（第 2 版）》
《英语语法新思维中级教程：通悟语法（第 2 版）》
《英语语法新思维高级教程：驾驭语法（第 2 版）》
《英语语法新思维：语法体系及底层逻辑全解密》
《英语语法新思维—名词从句超精解》
《英语语法新思维—名词从句超精解（练习册）》
《英语语法新思维—定语从句超精解》
《英语语法新思维—定语从句超精解（练习册）》
《英语语法新思维—句子成分超精解》
《英语语法新思维—语法难点妙解》

张满胜 著

◎ 张满胜老师多年教学实践经验和深入研究的成果
◎ 从全新的思维角度讲解和剖析各类语法知识点，帮你轻松攻克语法学习难关
◎ 探求语法规则背后深层本质，助你把语法规则内化成英语思维

《英文语法有规则：151 个一学就会的语法规则》
《英文语法有规则：151 个一学就会的语法规则（练习册）》

（日）石黑昭博 著

◎ 口碑保障：特别为亚洲英语学习者编排，在英语学习大国日本热销多年
◎ 定位明确：适合初中生、高中生和一般基础语法学习者
◎ 版式编排：简明图片阐释语法内容，直观而易于理解
◎ 有学有练：配套练习册，先简述每一章的语法要点，再设置练习，方便巩固和检测

《16 天英语入门》

（免费下载图书相关音频文件）

张隽 卓佳 编著

◎ 专为英语零起点的成人学习者编写
◎ 将字母、音标、句型、单词、对话、语法点等入门知识划分为 16 天的课程
◎ 提供 26 个英文字母笔顺图，帮助读者掌握正确书写笔顺
◎ 细致讲解发音，提供 48 个国际音标真人口形图，将语音学习具体化
◎ 字母、语音、单词、句子和语法课课练，巩固知识
◎ 文字、图形、音频、练习相结合，带来立体化学习体验，高效学习

定价：32元 开本：32开 页码：168页

《美语发音秘诀》

（美）Ann Cook 著

◎ 用直观的图片助你理解语言现象的指导书
◎ 与现实中的语言行为一致的方法指南
◎ 蕴含绘声绘色的录音内容的发音书
◎ 讲练结合适合自学的辅导书
◎ 包含详细指导教学方法，可作为教材使用

定价：58元 开本：16开 页码：248页

《美音纠音、透析与突破》

（免费下载图书相关音频文件）

邱政政 编著

针对中国人在美式发音上的难点和误区，本着"语音"和"语调、节奏"双过关的宗旨，兼顾特色音变现象，简洁有效地列举出适合学习的美音规律和技巧。同时运用"模仿—自觉—自然"的学习规律，着重培养英语学习者的语感和听觉形象。

定价：28元 开本：16开 页码：192页

《彩图实境英语口语》

（免费下载图书相关音频文件）

（英）劳拉·费尔普斯 寂天语言工作室 著

本书分为社交生活、国外日常生活和职场生活三大情境，包括认识新朋友、畅聊电视节目与电影、租房、外出用餐、找工作等26个主题。每个主题从图解单词入手，逐步延伸至基本会话和生活实用句，举一反三，循序渐进，让读者真正做到身临其境，掌握实用且地道的生活口语。

定价：52元 开本：16开 页码：348页

《说出正确的口语——美音达人的语法书》

（美）Ann Cook 著

◎ 如果你语音语调正确，一张口却都是语法错误
◎ 如果你熟知语法规则，却无法将其应用到日常交流中
◎ 如果你想要一本既讲语法规则，又教授发音技巧的书
那么，这本书是你的理想选择！

定价：49元 开本：16开 页码：356页

剑桥实境英语系列：

（1-4级，每级含听说、阅读、写作分册）

（听说、写作各配有音频）

（英）Miles Craven 等 编著

本丛书实用性强、覆盖面广、题材丰富、图文并茂，可帮助英语学习者丰富英语知识，积累语言素材，培养良好的语言感觉，训练正确的思维方式，适合学生自学或课堂教学。

剑桥标准英语教程系列：

1-6级共18册，各级别包含学生用书（分为A、B两册）和教师用书，均配有音频并提供网站支持。

（英）Michael McCarthy等 编著

"剑桥标准英语教程"是一套针对青少年和成人英语学习者编写的，具有革新意义的综合英语教程。新版扩展为6个级别，新引入了符合中高级语言学习者需求的第5级和第6级（Viewpoint），并对第1-4级（Touchstone）进行升级改进，涵盖了英语初级到高级难度的内容。课程设置前后呼应，教学方式简单明晰，帮助英语学习者提高语言交流能力和英语综合技能。

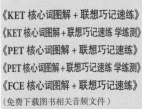

《KET 核心词图解 + 联想巧记速练》

《KET 核心词图解+联想巧记速练 学练测》

《PET 核心词图解 + 联想巧记速练》

《PET 核心词图解+联想巧记速练 学练测》

《FCE 核心词图解 + 联想巧记速练》

（免费下载图书相关音频文件）

俞敏洪 编著

◎ 以官方真题为蓝本，精选考试核心词与拓展词

◎ 提供联想记忆、图像记忆、比较记忆等多种适合小学生的单词记忆方法

◎ 精析单词，提供例句、搭配用法、词汇练习题，即学即练

◎ 纯正英美外教朗读单词、搭配、拓展词以及例句

◎ 附赠50组话题分类词汇和"词根词缀小课堂"

◎ 前两册兼具点读功能，与新东方点读笔搭配使用，效果更佳

剑桥综合教程系列：

《剑桥KET综合教程》

《剑桥PET综合教程》

《剑桥FCE综合教程》

（免费下载图书相关音频文件）

（英）Guy Brook-Hart 等 编著

◎ 剑桥通用英语考试官方备考资料

◎ 针对新版剑桥考试，提供考试信息和技能指导与训练

◎ 涵盖贴近青少年的话题单元和词汇、语法复习单元，练习册同步设置练习单元

◎ 依据剑桥学习者语料库编写练习，帮助考生有效规避常犯错误

剑桥官方模考题精讲精练系列：

《剑桥 KET 官方模考题精讲精练1》

《剑桥 PET 官方模考题精讲精练1》

《剑桥 FCE 官方模考题精讲精练2》

（英）Karen Saxby 等 著

◎ 剑桥通用英语考试官方备考资料，专业题源与讲解

◎ 科学仿真的6套官方模拟试题与透彻详尽的考试相关信息

◎ 补充技能训练与答题指导和建议

◎ 提供MP3听力练习音频和听力原文

剑桥常见错误精讲精练系列：

《剑桥KET常见错误精讲精练》

《剑桥PET常见错误精讲精练》

《剑桥FCE常见错误精讲精练》

（免费下载图书相关音频文件）

（英）Liz Driscoll, Susanne Tayfoor 编著

◎ 剑桥官方备考资料，解析常犯错误，助你轻松迎考

◎ 依据剑桥语料库编写而成，完全符合考试题型与难度

◎ 列举考生常犯错误，辨析错误原因，给出有效的纠正方法

◎ 人手一本的备考图书，获无数考生一致好评

图书在版编目（CIP）数据

英语词汇速记大全 . 4，语境记忆法 / 俞敏洪编著 . — 北京：世界图书出版有限公司北京分公司，2023.2
ISBN 978-7-5192-7693-5

Ⅰ . ①英… Ⅱ . ①俞… Ⅲ . ①英语 – 词汇 – 记忆术 Ⅳ . ① H313.1

中国版本图书馆 CIP 数据核字 (2022) 第 192300 号

书　　名	英语词汇速记大全 4——语境记忆法
	YINGYU CIHUI SUJI DAQUAN 4
编　　著	俞敏洪
责任编辑	梁沁宁
封面设计	理　海
版式设计	大愚设计

出版发行	世界图书出版有限公司北京分公司
地　　址	北京市东城区朝内大街 137 号
邮　　编	100010
电　　话	010-64038355（发行）　64033507（总编室）
网　　址	http://www.wpcbj.com.cn
邮　　箱	wpcbjst@vip.163.com
销　　售	新华书店
印　　刷	天津盛辉印刷有限公司
开　　本	880mm×1230mm　1/16
印　　张	11
字　　数	260 千字
版　　次	2023 年 2 月第 1 版
印　　次	2023 年 2 月第 1 次印刷
国际书号	ISBN 978-7-5192-7693-5
定　　价	40.00 元